START 4TH APRIL

J.RENNY.

HAMISH'S MOUNTAIN WALK

HAMISH'S MOUNTAIN WALK

The First Traverse of all the Scottish Munros in One Journey

by

HAMISH M. BROWN

LONDON
VICTOR GOLLANCZ LTD
1978

ISBN 0 575 02362 7

Unacknowledged poetry quotations that have been printed
without quotation marks are by the author

Printed in Great Britain by
The Camelot Press Ltd, Southampton

All men are free under the stars
Yet we bolt our doors and creep to bed,
All men are kings upon the earth
But some have sold their thrones, despaired and fled;
All men, in Adam, walked with God,
Now God, and walking, both are odd.

We were dreamers, dreaming greatly, in the man-stifled town:
We yearned beyond the sky-line where the strange roads go down

KIPLING

That is the difference between age and youth. Boys do things for no reason. I wonder do we get old because we do things by reason instead of instinct . . . ? A married man looks comfortable and settled: he looks finished if you understand me, and a bachelor looks unsettled and funny and he always wants to be running round seeing things

JAMES STEPHENS The Crock of Gold

CONTENTS

By Way of Introduction   13
The Historical Setting   17

     Genesis   29
1   Mull, Etive and Glencoe   33
2   Lyon and Lochay   62
3   Furthest South   78
4   Trans Tay and Tummel   97
5   The Southern Cairngorms   113
6   The Monadh Ruadh   133
7   Lochaber and Back   154
8   Laggan   178
9   West to Knoydart   191
10   Quoich—Glenelg   218
11   Skye   227
12   The Big Glens: Shiel, Affric, Farrar   245
13   Torridons   281
14   Fada—Fannich   291
15   The Deargs and the North   315
     Aftermath—or Reasons Why   333

    Appendices
I   Equipment   339
II   Food   342
III   The Questionnaires   344
IV   Statistics   345
V   Mountaineering Gaelic   347

A Short Bibliography and Useful Addresses   351
Index   355

ACKNOWLEDGEMENTS

The maps for this book were drawn by Jim Renny, to whom I am most grateful. Beryl Luke, Mrs Brown of Glasgow and Osborne House in Kirkcaldy valiantly typed my scribbled notes into something legible. The photographs are my own, except the historical ones which came largely from Scottish Mountaineering Club sources and I was also allowed to quote freely from its journal. Thanks also to Mr Lovat Dickson for permission to quote from Richard Hillary's *The Last Enemy*. Robin Campbell, Tom Weir, Jim Donaldson, John Hinde, Sandy Cousins and Tom Waghorn all provided material, and without the support of family and friends there would be no book. The Walk was much easier than the writing of the book! To all who appear in it I am indebted. I used a Rollei 35 camera which gave good results. Kodak film was used—also for the cover illustration enlarged from a Kodachrome 25 transparency.

H. M. B.

LIST OF ILLUSTRATIONS

Following page 128

Sir Hugh Munro

The first ever Scottish Mountaineering Club Meet, Dalmally, 1891

Sir Hugh Munro and other Scottish Mountaineering Club members at an early Meet of the Club

Sir Hugh Munro and friends "on the hill"

Rev. A. E. Robertson

John Hinde

Sandy Cousins at Cape Wrath

Brian Ripley

Hamish on Ben More, Mull; the start of the Long Walk

Glen Etive: Marina and Kenneth with support camp established

The Cruachan-Chochuill groups seen from the east

Blackrock Cottage, the L.S.C.C. climbing hut with the Buachaille Etive Mor behind

The early support team: brother David and his wife Marina

Beinn an Lochain from Ardkinglass in Argyll

"Grampian" type scenery near the Cairnwell road

A view from the top of Lochnagar

Cairngorms: Cairn Toul seen across the Lairig Ghru

The Corrour Bothy

A' Choinneach and the Saddle beyond Loch Avon

Hamish looking down the cliffs of Ben Alder

Gleouraich-Spidean Mialach seen from Sgurr na Ciche

Knoydart—over Garbh Chioch Mhor from Sgurr na Ciche to the saddle of Gulvain

Following page 224

Hamish with the Challis tent and folding Raleigh

The pass between Knoydart and Glen Dessary

"Kitchy"—Hamish's dog

Lorna's van by Loch Quoich

Red deer calf

The training schooner *Captain Scott* in Loch Linnhe

Inverie, the only village in remote Knoydart

Tea outside the tent near Loch Hourn

Knoydart—Luinne Bheinn seen from the boathouse at the Dubh Lochain

Ben Sgriol from the prehistoric hill fort of Torr Beag

Skye—a view along the ridge from Sgurr Alasdair

The pinnacles of Sgurr nan Gillean from Garbh-bheinn (Blaven)

Glenelg and the Glen Shiel hills

The Five Sisters of Kintail across Loch Duich

Loch Duich and far Ben Sgriol from the Gates of Affric

Following page 288

Sgurr nan Ceathreamhnan from Bienn Fhionnlaidh

Sgurr na Lapaich group from the Strathfarrar hills

Lurg Mhor, east of Achnashellach

Added since this walk as a Munro, Sgurr nan Ceannaichean

The peaks of Coire Lair above Achnashellach

Maol Chean-dearg from Beinn Damh

Ben Alligin, Torridon

Slioch from Grudie Bridge

From Shenavall Bothy looking to Beinn Dearg Beag

A' Mhaighdean and Ben Lair

Looking down into Loch Toll an Lochain of An Teallach

Seana Bhraigh

A waterfall spraying up straight into the air

The end—Ben Hope summit

LIST OF MAPS

	page
Etive—Glencoe	41
Lyon—Lochay	64
Trans-Tay—Tummel	64
Loch Fyne—Loch Tay	81
Southern Cairngorms	116
Cairngorms	135
Monadh Liaths	156
The A9 Munros	156
Loch Laggan—Mamores	165
Loch Lochy—Loch Hourn	192
Cuillin of Skye	229
Shiel—Affric	248
Strathfarrar—Strathcarron	269
Strathcarron to Torridon	282
Loch Maree, Loch Fannich and the Deargs	295

KEY TO MAP SYMBOLS

▲	Principal Summits (Munros).
●	Other Summits.
(loch)	Lochs.
➤	Lochans.
+++++	Railways.
=	Roads.
～	Rivers.
◇	Camp Site.
⊕	Hut, Bothy or Hotel.
△	Youth Hostel.
12/4	Date (12th April).
--➤-	Route and direction taken.

BY WAY OF INTRODUCTION

IT WAS A hot, stuffy day in the office: no ventilation, no windows, and monotonous work. After having spent twelve happy years in the field, pioneering outdoor education at Braehead School in Fife (only leaving when the school itself closed), I was now County Adviser on Mountain Activities. Every fibre rebelled at the incarceration. For the first time in my varied life I felt as caged as a poor lion in a den of Daniels. What was I doing tied to a desk with no view of sky and hill, no sound of bird or sea?

My eye fell on a map of Scotland. I spread it out on the floor and knelt over it. Immediately I received a wallop on the backside as a colleague banged through the door bearing one vital aspect of bureaucracy—the tea.

I sat sipping the tea (they never can drum-up properly) and gazed at the map on the floor. "God, how I love this land," I thought. With three rounds of the Munros done, and some of the summits ascended scores of times over decades of wandering in the highlands and islands, it needed little to set the memories dancing like heat-shimmers on the hill. Oh, to be tramping a far hill right then!

What could be new? different? demanding?

What about all the Munros? Those 279 summits over 3,000 feet?

But!

But I did no more work that afternoon. The seed was sown and no farmer eyed his unbroken ground more keenly than I the map at my feet. When I eventually folded it up I really folded up my job as well—burning my boots so to speak. I could hear the objections. Why risk security? You are forty now. What will you do afterwards? How can you afford it? It would be far too difficult to organise. Someone else might do it meantime.

So I said nothing—and worked the happier knowing the day appointed. The French have a saying: "The young aren't on to it, and the old aren't up to it." As far as I was concerned it was just the right time. The silence was also a necessity; it *is* a competitive world, and being second is not as good as being first. There are few enough things where I, Mr Average, might find the priority.

Of course there would be sacrifices: comfort and companionship, the ease of "normal" work and the indulgence of normal enjoyments. Unlike a condemned man, my privations were self-inflicted, so there could really be no complaint and no self pity. You need to be a bit older to realise the implications, old enough to know better in fact— and then to ignore them all and go for the joy of it. We are given only one life. Surely its days are to be spent rather than hoarded, and given rather than spent? Everything should go to grasp what is best while it can be meaningful. What use is "security" twenty years hence if that is *all* those years give? Life should be lived greatly from day to day.

At this period I had been doing a great deal of reading about sea voyages. I had had voyages as an instructor on the schooner, *Captain Scott*. The lure of sea is very similar to that of hills. Strange, though, that solitary sailors are hailed as heroes whereas the safer solo land-lubber is condemned.

One of the reasons we climb is the challenge—which can be as varied as the sizes and shapes and psyches of *homo sapiens*. My own interests are many: I am happy bird-watching, or merely Munro-bagging, canoeing, ski-ing, or on the sea, climbing, taking pictures; too many interests to excel at any. On rock the spirit is not what it used to be, but any walking challenge had to be as great. Rob Collister, in telling of a ski traverse from Zermatt to Verbier (in one day), puts it clearly: "If mountain travel is to be as enjoyable as mountain climbing, it must, in its own way, be equally demanding." So you make it so.

The idea had long been there but the shock was suddenly seeing oneself stepping forward to try it. Thus must a four-year-old feel when thrust out in public to compete in his first egg-and-spoon race.

This book has been written twice. Following all the interests my logs swelled into a mighty tome which would be beyond reason these days of economy. So it had to be hacked down like an unruly garden. It is still a patchwork; but that is what the Walk was—a thing of shreds and patches. It is not a guide book, yet you will really need the maps to follow it and it gives away quite a bit to the discerning reader. It is given largely from a walker's point of view. Some favoured spots are passed over quickly for elitist reasoning and the best and rarest of the wildlife is not described: osprey eyrie or snow bunting nest are more precious to me with the eggs left untouched!

Equipment and food notes are added at the back, for a trip like this is a logistical exercise—a part of the game which can keep participants talking till all hours. Planning is crucial: a message perhaps most needed to be learnt by the young, though the whole reason of the game must never be lost: we go because it is fun—and not just in retrospect!

Recently a group of teenage girls came to me asking if I would take them hill-walking and what did they need to begin? Resisting an easy, "Yes, I'll take you" (they were not unattractive), I said, "You can take yourselves, and all you need is a bus ticket to the Lomonds." I still believe that is how we should start—wanting enough to go, regardless. The beginner needs little else. That this trip took as much planning as any to the Andes or Himalayas was for the reason it was not a beginner's one.

Sandy Cousins, who did a Munro trip from Cape Wrath to Glasgow, was telling me how he had had requests from walkers from England who wanted all the details so they could do the same, often on their first trip north. Sandy's answers were not encouraging! You cannot become an instant mountaineer, no matter how firm a belief in a platter-existence you have. It does not come on a plate. Long Walks like this, or Sandy's, or John Hinde's, were the outcome of decades of knocking about in the highlands. We sinned with our eyes open!

Certainly dream dreams, that is the birthright of youth, but you cannot grow vegetables without digging the soil. *My* preparation was almost two thousand Munros long.

Do not funk the Gaelic names; they can become quite a fascination in time, giving all sorts of information—or puzzles—which enrich experience. Some help is given at the back of this book, though as a non-expert, I do not claim great accuracy. The experts only argue anyway.

I have a great many people to thank, obviously: all the family and members of my club, the Braes o' Fife, who assisted in so many ways—it is their story as much as mine. Robert Louis Stevenson wrote, "Every book is, in an intimate sense, a circular letter to the friends of him who writes it." This is particularly so with this tale.

It is, of necessity, much in the first person singular. It is a very personal narrative, yet I hope shows something of this great land of ours. The trip gave a marvellous intimacy with that land, such as cannot be found just on weekends and holidays. I feel somewhere along the line, man has gone astray. Perhaps the break came when we stopped leading sheep and began to drive them, when we turned from the hand loom to the machine, from foot and field and home to vehicles and railways and factory. We have rushed off after the good life—and have overshot the mark. This was a return to rock-reality, the womb-comfort, the joy of untrammelled simplicity. It is really the walking of years with the kernel of the three months of the Long Walk.

Both the Walk and this book were done, using the One Inch map with its individuality, spellings and heights. We had all grown so accustomed to its face—yet by the time this book is published we will be accepting the metrication of our mountains (force-feeding for some!) and future books will be in the new idiom. Eventually at least we can have really definitive Tables—of heights over 914 metres. The Munro game goes merrily on, however. I have tried to note some of the changes sprung upon us. What would Munro think of it all?

THE HISTORICAL SETTING

WE TEND TO regard hard walking as a modern phenomenon but the opposite is probably correct; we have largely forgotten how to walk.

The drovers who brought beasts from the Hebrides to the Falkirk Tryst, or those who took them on to Smithfield, knew what walking was; *any* Highlander did, and so did any one not gentry enough to own a horse. We even read of the regular tramping done by academics between London and Oxford or Cambridge.

There were next to no Highland roads before Wade and Caulfield built theirs during the eighteenth century. William Taylor's book, *The Military Roads in Scotland* (David and Charles), tells their story. Next time you take a day off from climbing in Glencoe and go bombing off up to Fort William, remember that the road was built as recently as 1786.

The aftermath of the 1745 Jacobite rising brought great social changes; people were more tied down locally, urban life was spreading—and at once we have the "escapist" reaction, which continues to this day. The end of the eighteenth century began a great period of "Tours" in the Highlands. Several of these are described in Maurice Lindsay's books, for which we should be grateful as the originals are often great tomes. Though most of these tourists made maximum use of ponies some great things were done on foot. The poet Keats for instance, hardly an athletic type, along with a friend, Brown, walked the 642 miles from Lancaster to Inverness in 42 days.

Some travellers seemed to revel in the roughness but it took a long time for mountains to be enjoyed simply for themselves. In 1767 an Edinburgh botanist, James Robertson, had quite happily wandered over Klibreck, Wyvis, and other hills in the north, taking river-crossings, snow storms and hill-cloud very much for granted. In 1771 he had a real Munro-bagging spree: Clova, Lochnagar, Ben Avon, Cairngorm, the Sgoran Dubhs, Nevis, the Killin hills, Rannoch ridges and the Monadh Liath. The acceptance was complete, even if under the banner of science.

Professor Forbes, "the discoverer of the Alps", was an important figure both in climbing and geographical terms yet, strangely, left little mark on Scotland. He covered vast distances on foot: in 1836 he included the first ascent of Sgurr nan Gillean, and in 1845 began six successive summers in the Highlands. A Michel de Bernhoff (who tramped from St Petersburg to Paris) considered thirty miles a day a fair average.

We should not overlook the early work of the surveyors: the Ordnance Survey did much on foot from necessity. Thomas Colby, the Director General from 1820 to 1846, cheerfully covered 513 miles in 22 days, had one day off, then did another 22 days over 586 miles. That was primarily exploratory rambling, the hard grind of carrying heavy camps and equipment was the main work, when several months might be spent on one mountain alone. The whole story would be quite a saga and one about which I wish the O.S. would give us a popular account.

In that pre-train, pre-car period the Highlands and Islands were incredibly remote of access and difficult to move about in, and they had seen a drastic fall in population. Today we are apt to question the deer forests as the sacred preserve of the rich, forgetting that these estates were carved out of a wilderness already created by the Clearances and the sheep. The Highland economy had collapsed. Deer for sport created jobs, as remote corners were opened up, roads constructed and houses built.

The general ignorance of the hills was remarkable. If we did not quite have the Alpine idea of dragons and demons (these we put in the lochs) the high summits were regarded as not worth visiting. We can hardly blame the O.S. for the cursory nature of some of its surveying of the more remote areas in this impossible terrain. Mountaineering had not been invented.

As a sport it was a nineteenth-century creation. The Highlanders, as ever, lived in and tramped over the hills, already perhaps as the servants of landed gentry up for the stalking. They had no real influence on mountaineering as we know it now, though for a while they did form a loose body of "guides" for tourists who desired Ben Lomond or Lochnagar or other "fabulous adventures". There were the odd scientists who were also out with the main flow—men such as the hectic Dr John Macculloch, who, in his geological wanderings which began in 1811, covered vast distances on foot, on pony, and by boat and could justly, for his day, claim to have ascended "almost every principal summit".

It was really the professional, middle class—lawyers, clerics, professors (including scientists)—who, bursting out of their urban strait-jackets, created the sport of recreational mountaineering. The Alpine Club was founded during the winter of 1857–58. Its members often enjoyed activities in the hills of Wales and Lakeland, and, to a lesser extent, Scotland. When the Scottish Mountaineering Club was formed in 1889, its membership included, or contributed, many members of the Alpine Club.

Between the dates of formation of the two clubs quite a few other small clubs or bodies had come into being, often local, which included the hills in their activities. Some people today have expressed surprise that no lead came from north of the Highland boundary, but in those regions practical experience of the hills was just a fact of life— mountaineering is basically a flight from urban pressures, escapism again, which becomes the more frantic and global, as the burden of civilisation grows heavier year by year. You do not find many keepers or shepherds indulging in recreational hill days, though probably the earliest British rock-climbers were the wildfowlers of St Kilda and the Hebrides, who climbed not only to obtain food but for pleasure.

Before Sir Hugh Munro brought out his *Tables of Heights over 3000 feet* (1891), it was generally believed only some thirty hills were of that height. A few of these were popular expeditions even in the eighteenth century, but suddenly to be given a tenfold inheritance was almost overwhelming. The formation of the Scottish Mountaineering Club played an important role in consolidating and expanding the trend. It began a systematic covering of the Scottish hills, soon discovering in them a playground as satisfying as the Alps and not just a poor substitute. The first journal appeared in 1890. Its preface starts with the curious quote: "Let thy words be few". (That was thirty volumes ago.) It then gave away the riches in store: there were possibly three hundred mountains over 3,000 feet, "some perhaps never ascended". What more natural than to list these? What more natural than to try and climb them? The list duly appeared in the second volume of the Journal and in a few years the "Munros" were an established game.

Munro's Tables are today a separate volume, periodically revised, published by the Scottish Mountaineering Trust and full of photographs, maps, references—and now, metric equivalents. Little did Sir Hugh know what he began. He was in the process of revising his list when he died, so we will never know if he intended a fuller definition of a "Munro". Of his list of tops some were elevated to the peerage of "separate mountains" and these took on the name of "Munros", the others remained "Tops", or "subsidiary summits"; which is all we have to go on. His reason for this classification has always been a fruitful source of debate.

A stricter definition was given to another series of hills more recently listed by J. R. Corbett, and named after him, the "Corbetts": hills over 2,500 feet, with a re-ascent all round of 500 feet (which is often erroneously thought to apply to Munros).

A brief look at Munro, the man, shows a warm personality and an enthusiast with many interests. He was an original member of the Scottish Mountaineering Club and its third President (1894–1897).

Hugh Thomas Munro was born in London in 1856, eldest of nine children, and much of his life was spent there or in the family's native Scotland, where he first managed and then inherited the estate of Lindertis near Kirriemuir. He was a great collector as a child: fossils, shells, eggs, butterflies; even as a young man, after a spell in South Africa, he returned with a collection of Basuto curios, antelope heads, a black boy, and a monkey.

He came to the mountains when a student in Stuttgart in his late teens. Travel could almost be regarded as a collecting activity with Munro, a game played all through his life, both professionally and for pleasure. He had a business training in London, but was also known as a good musician and dancer, and he had a flow of "capital talk". (When he and another great talker had a day on the hills together they both returned complaining they had been silent all day as each was unable to get a word in edgeways.)

Several years of this good life of business, travel and pleasure ended with pleurisy and in 1880 he went as Private Secretary to join Sir George Colley, Governor of Natal. During the Basuto War he served with an irregular cavalry corps and saw exciting times. Once back in Britain he spent more time at Lindertis, and the hills came to play an important part in his life. In 1885 he stood as parliamentary candidate for Kirkcaldy Burghs in Fife, as forlorn a Tory hope then as now, but nobody else would come forward to do battle. He never stood for his local Forfar seat, though active behind the scenes.

When his children were old enough they were dragged off to Germany, Greece, Morocco, the States, Japan, Ceylon and other lands near and far. Munro in Yosemite is a nice thought. He was a natural choice for a King's Messenger—an official courier bearing documents about the world. It is a pity that photography was still in the frozen pose state in those days, for we have few pictures of the man as he must have been; he was certainly no bog-bound laird but a man of wide experience, talents and knowledge, and he enlivened any company. He would travel back from the ends of the earth for an S.M.C. Meet and the Journal published over eighty of his articles and notes.

In 1914 he was past military age but went out to Malta to work, and in 1918 he organised a canteen in the castle town of Tarascon. The following spring a chill developed into pneumonia and he died, at the age of sixty-three.

This is the man who gave us the Tables which we gave back as "Munros" (he disliked eponymous mountain names), to make surely one of the oddest of best-selling books.

Munro loved nothing better than to undertake long through-routes, often in winter, often alone, and clad in uniform of cape, knickerbockers (or kilt), and Balmoral bunnet, with a long ice axe. He was a skilled all-rounder but was less enthusiastic about rock-climbing. Aneroid and notebook ensured the Journal was peppered with observations and corrections to the map. He was a Survey in himself, and a deal more accurate, and this before railways or motor cars. When these new modes of travel appeared, he actually wrote articles to show how they could open up new approaches to the hills. Nobody used the new-fangled machinery to better advantage.

I mention one or two of his trips later, but just one example here. In 1891 he crossed from Blair Atholl to near Kirkmichael, "heavy walking all day in soft snow. . . . At Diranean they had to scrape me down with a knife to get the frozen snow off." On Beinn a' Ghlo the snow was blowing "in spiral columns several hundred feet high, penetrating everything, filling pockets and drifting between waistcoat and shirt, where it melted and then froze into a solid wedge of ice. . . . I never suffered so severely from the cold."

Munro never completed the ascent of the Munros and Tops he had listed. He had kept for last the easy Carn Clioch Mhuillin above the Dee as it was near home and would make a good celebratory summit— ponies carrying up the champagne—and then there was the Inaccessible Pinnacle, the end to many Munroist hopes. He was driven out of Skye by atrocious weather in 1895; in 1897 a Yachting Meet could not even anchor safely; in 1905 arrangements with Harold Raeburn (the

MacInnes of his day) fell through. He was there as late as 1915, but without success.

In 1901 the Rev. A. E. Robertson was the first man to complete the Munros, and it was twenty-two years before the second round was made—by another Reverend. "A. E. R." was a colourful personality, too, and also President of the Scottish Mountaineering Club (1930–1932). He was more of a climber than Sir Hugh, a trait marked on his first, solo, ascent, Goatfell on Arran, when he chose to scramble the last thousand feet to the summit. He was then twelve or so. One of the surprises following my own trip was to be introduced to his spry widow, sadly now no longer with us. He married twice (Munro, on the other hand, was a widower most of his life) and died in 1958, aged 88.

Archibald Eneas Robertson's parish was at Rannoch, an appropriate hill setting. In two successive years he thought nothing of knocking off 72 or 75 Munros in three-month holiday blitzes. What he called "a desultory campaign of about ten years" saw the task accomplished. Pony-trap and boat helped, and above all a push bike, for he was a great cyclist. For the rest he walked, and found accommodation in the wilds, usually with shepherds or keepers for, speaking their language as he did, and with so many common interests, he was always a welcome guest—even when he appeared with no warning. He stayed with the McCooks at Ben Alder on many occasions after dropping in there for the first time in 1893. The Aonach Eagach, with his wife and his oldest friend, Alexander (later Lord) Moncrieff, gave A. E. R. his final Munro. He kissed both the cairn and his wife—in that order.

Good gear and meticulous planning was part of his success. He often carried a whole-plate camera into the wilds and produced some superb pictures, and he was also a historian of note, an interest shown in an article on "coffin" roads and tracks in the North West, which appeared in the S.M.C. Journal in 1941. There are extracts from his diaries in the Journals of 1948 and 1949. In connection with this interest he rose to high position in both the Scottish Rights of Way Society and the Royal Scottish Geographical Society. A bridge over the Elchaig below the Falls of Glomach was built as a memorial to Robertson. He was a skilled man with his hands, making a table for the C.I.C. Hut for instance.

The Rev. A. R. G. Burn not only repeated the Munros in 1923, but added the subsidiary Tops. J. A. Parker, Munroist number three in 1929, added the "Furth of Scotland"—the resonant term for the

3,000ers of England, Wales and Ireland. The first "grand slam" of Munros, Tops and Furth fell to W. Docherty in 1949, a surprisingly late date. Munroist number four was Corbett, of that ilk, in 1930. In 1947 Mrs John Hirst completed the first female round, and also a husband-wife combination. The Macdonalds in 1958 saw a father-and-son Munro effort, and in 1974 a father-and-son Munro and Tops success went to the Lawsons. The "grand slam" was made by Anne Littlejohn in 1960. There are fifteen females in a 1977 list of 143 Munroists which now grows at an annual average rate of five people.

In 1964 Philip Tranter did them all again and in 1966 Eric Maxwell repeated not just the Munros but Tops as well. George Smith and I repeated in 1969 and I did a third round while with Braehead School. The School was after a "school's round" before it closed down and was demolished. The pupils succeeded—and so did Kitchy, my dog, in 1971. The trip recorded in this book gave a round in a single expedition, and not so long after it a fifth personal round slipped in. Basically I am not a Munro-bagger, at least no more than anyone else; as I ski, climb, canoe, go abroad a great deal, my proportion of Munro-days to others could well be less than that of most people. I just happen to have had a vast number of happy days in the hills.

Doing the Munros has become an immensely popular activity. And why not? Metrication will soon give the list a certain archaic charm, but a new substitute list of 1,000 metre summits is not likely to take over as there would be too few to make a worthwhile challenge. The Munros are a perfect target. Even allowing for the Great War it seems surprising that only eight people had done the Munros before the Second War. Our new ease of travel, and longer holidays and affluence, has changed things dramatically. The S.M.C. Journal keeps the list up to date and at present those within (or is it without?) the pale number 143. Only fifteen have done the "grand slam", perhaps showing a tendency to be content with minimal standards. A high proportion of English Munroists are in the list and though many are claimed by the S.M.C., they are basically Rucksackers or Fell and Rockers. The Grampian Club has provided a large number too. Perhaps a score of modest(?) walkers have kept their success private; a pity, as it leaves records incomplete. A name in a list means little enough and anyway the whole game is played by a small and suspect section of the population. The S.M.C. Journal briefly notes new additions to the list each year and welcomes information.

I was not really conscious of Munros until I went to Braehead School, but my post there, the first to organise outdoor pursuits in a state school in Scotland, soon led to the discovery. Kids are competitive and when we formed a club, an entry qualification of ten Munros was a safeguard: each member would have been away several times by then—and was usually hooked. I kept a careful log from that time onwards, a habit maintained on this Walk. From its notes has come this book.

Two developments made the Walk a goal to aim for after Braehead closed down. In the sixties the R.A.F. Rescue teams made several north–south and east–west expeditions over numerous Munros. I met John Hinde, who was involved and whose accounts had stirred up readers; he was not the first in either direction, but has done both and led the biggest expedition in 1968. He stresses it is not a competitive game, any cutting corners leads to lack of safety. These R.A.F. trips were very much team-work and part of training. Few civilians had the time or the organisational support to try it and the statistics were frightening. Pete McGowan (Valley Team leader) ran up 100,000 feet of ascent in 19 days, 350 miles for 58 Munros. Here is the development of the traverses in the sixties:

Nov. 1962	East–West	(K. Shaw, McKerron, Ballantyne)	11 Munros
Summer 1964	North–South	(Armstrong, Golton, Raven)	37 Munros
Summer 1966	North–South	(Ward, Morrison, Bradshaw)	32 Munros
Summer 1966	West–East	(Hinde, R. Shaw)	30 Munros
Summer 1967	South–North	(Gilligan, Ward, Wagg)	26 Munros
Nov. 1968	North–South	(McGowan, Tomlinson, Hinde, Blyth)	58, 49, 48, 45 Munros

John Hinde said he lost weight but gained fitness on this last trek. Ben Humble, a veteran S.M.C. member who met the party on Ben Lomond, thought John looked older with the strain, but then their last days had been continuously wild and wet. Another civilian who was in at the end was a younger Munro enthusiast Sandy Cousins who, three years later, in 1971, was to make a big trek, north–south, from Cape Wrath home to Glasgow, over 47 Munros, 370 miles and 90,000 feet of ascent. A full account of this journey can be found in the 1972 S.M.C. Journal.

I followed these trips with interest, and dreamed dreams, but the other development, even more daring, came in 1967 when Brian and Alan Ripley made an attempt on all the Munros in a single walk. They were Karabiner Mountaineering Club members with little Scottish tradition, so their effort of 230 Munros, 1,325 miles and 337,850 feet was phenomenal. I read Tom Waghorn's article in *The Climber and Rambler* at the time and marvelled.

The Ripley brothers did not succeed on account of several factors, many of which stemmed from not really knowing beforehand just what they were in for: the midges in August and September, wet and wind and snow later, the persistent strain of clashing with stalking interests, worries about food (their base being in Manchester), packs weighing fifty pounds or more at times, difficult rivers, blisters and sores, ever-shortening hours of daylight. Brian's log reads like a graph: ups and downs but each down just that bit lower than the last as the burden grew heavier. The environment was hostile yet often they were bored and had to bully themselves on. Few can appreciate what these young lads went through. Their youth was against them I suppose; powerful all-round hillmen as they were, Scotland was not known to them as it was to, say, John, Sandy or me—who were all a score of years older— on our trips. The August start alone was a vital mistake.

The starting date was dictated largely by other engagements, and Brian was off to the Himalayas the following summer. He was a strong mountaineer with such ascents as the Bonatti Pillar on the Dru, for instance, to his name. He was tragically killed by stonefall on Malubiting, 25,451 feet. This trip of mine could so easily have been his, or Philip Tranter's, a powerful Scottish all-rounder, who died in a car crash on the way back from climbing in Turkey, much more worthy lads.

Sandy's Walk was much more in mind when I was planning mine, but two things were remembered from the Ripleys' attempt: first, they had had dietary troubles and secondly, they took lifts. The former gave me some concern but I could not make too many enquiries for fear of giving the game away; the latter I felt was unaesthetic, the only "rule" I made was that the journey should be all self-propelled. I loathe walking on tarred roads so decided I could, morally, use a push bike— especially for the long hauls to and from the island Munros on Skye and

Mull and also round the A9. I toyed with the idea of canoeing to and from these islands but reluctantly decided it was too chancy and too much of an imposition on others. An island became the starting point to save one diversion. Off-duty travel would be legitimate, I thought, but in practice was a rare indulgence. And I knew I had to finish by the start of the stalking season.

Reading the Ripleys' log I feel they first bent and then broke the idea of self-propulsion; the odd bus or car, the runs on Skye, and then to and from Mull from Glencoe—and another factor consciously or unconsciously was added to the mental burden. Time and finance were problems, perhaps undermining body as well as soul. You can only take so much. Brian's log is brief and often cryptic; it reads like a thriller. They began on August 13th, and ended on November 10th on Beinn Dorain, when they were beaten off by the worst weather of all. Alan's ankles were swelling badly at the end and Brian had slit the back of his boots to make them bearable. A doctor said Alan was suffering from iron deficiencies. David Summerfield, another Karabiner Mountaineering Club member, was with them for about half of the trip but had to drop out. The early days saw an agony of sore feet, sore shoulders and a communal collection of 25 blisters.

They had great days, of course, and even some of the poor weather days did not deter from fine things—such as a traverse of the Cuillin Ridge. Ironically they had a succession of fine days in the Blackmount just before the end.

These, then, were my influences. They were all from the mountaineering tradition. It was only after the Walk I read books or articles by Hillaby, Merrill or Snow, and they rather frightened me with their disciplined, clockwork routine. I prefer Eric Newby—or Shipton and Tilman who are perhaps my oldest mentors. They are in line with the most traditional means of travel. Adam and Eve walked. Amazingly, despite all man has done to himself, he still can walk. The greatest feats are all unrecorded, lost in anonymous treks of Boers or Americans, of Bushmen or Asians, of Aborigines or Russians. Our self-conscious efforts are mere self-indulgence, irrational and unnecessary. I have no guilty feeling, however, for if we did not, "whiles, dance, we would aye greet."

HAMISH'S MOUNTAIN WALK

GENESIS

GENESIS IS GOOD for you! The decision to do this trip certainly was refreshing and though it was a snap decision in some ways I had no illusions about what was involved. So much of my reading at this time was of others *doing* things yet I was desk-bound and frustrated, kept from action even at my job.

It was around Hallowe'en 1972 that I spread the map on the office floor—and knew just what I would do in 1974. The period between *was* the Walk in some ways, the toil was there, not in the actual walking. Right from the start I knew it would be a largely solo trip. It would simplify a whole host of problems—not even a committee of two to delay things and, God knows, I'd had my fill of committees. Tentage, the doubling of every bit of food, finding a second cycle or canoe, the difficulty of back-up and above all finding the right person—all these problems just did not happen. Close proximity with anyone over a long period, especially under stress, can be unhappy if not worse. Simplicity is the forgotten virtue.

I cannot recall when the actual timings were decided but obviously not immediately, as 1974 and not 1973 was chosen. I had some obligations to my job! That first winter, though, I doodled maps endlessly as I tried to link up the best line between the 277 summits. They even grew to 279 before I set off, as the O.S. caught up on their inadequate surveying of our North West. A mapboard faced desk/bed at home but of course much of it could be done in my head anyway. This gave me a pre-occupied air which some took for avid concentration on work in hand. One obvious joy would be to do endless days activating what an old friend Willie Docherty called "the creed of the long traverse".

The route clarified in general, though it was never static and in points altered even in the course of doing the trip. Sanely, not racing, how long would it take? I tackled this in various ways and the answer always seemed to be $3\frac{1}{2}$–4 months. May and June are usually the best months. There was the Stalking after July. That would suggest a start in early April; in fact the first of April seemed the obvious choice.

I went south–north both for romantic and practical reasons. I hoped

for the better weather in the north and west. By starting on Mull I cut
out one long arm. Bothies and huts in the north would help once into
the midgy months, when the enjoyment of camping is apt to wear thin.
All previous trips had been done north–south so perhaps there was an
element of cussedness too.

The costing was approached from various angles and gave £400.

The route eventually was worked out on ½-inch maps which went to
my brother so that he could follow my doings, and then the 1-inch
which I used. I needed 22 maps in all. Both Dollar and I would have
identical route-books with the day-to-day plans and a list of places
where I would phone, a safety factor. I began to accumulate gear for the
trip, selecting and testing—breaking in three new pairs of boots till I
knew they were comfortable—over Christmas–New Year doing two
weeks' non-stop to see how the unfit body would take it. In January I
began bringing in S.M.C. and B.F.M.C. friends who could act as
weekend support and, when David (my brother) and his wife, Marina,
agreed to act as "base" and even come as field support for the first part,
I really felt a surge of faith that it would "go". Later Mike Keates
agreed to come out for the last two weeks in the north. David lived at
Dollar in Clackmannanshire, Mike at Inverness, so this really covered
the land.

I thought of sponsorship but as I had saved enough, it was not a
desperate essential. If the Walk succeeded I could cash in a bit afterwards; but I wanted to enjoy it as my journey, untrammelled, and not
as a public stunt. There was also the lure of the priority. This was not
just my dream. Being first has its place, transient though it be; someone
can always do it faster or shorter, cleaner or bolder, backwards or on
their heads. The vital thing is to enjoy the doing of it.

As a keen canoeist I thought of canoeing to and from the islands
(Mull and Skye) but this would be too great a risk of precious time.
Later I did bring in the canoe for Loch Lomond. A cycle too could be
used on the long, dull, tarred roads which could not easily be avoided.
So long as it was *all* self-propelled it was valid.

I started using lunch breaks for wee jobs: mosaic-ing the maps to
suit, trimming candles, preparing labels, making lists; at weekends in
the north I would note the sites of telephone boxes and nibble away at
the weight problem, endlessly trying variations of gear. I could not
afford to buy much new stuff, so expediency played its part. My major
worry was a tent. I had a good Vango featherweight but it had so

many guys and bits and pieces—and it was nylon which meant condensation problems. This became almost an obsession, but when Dave Challis heard he offered me a tent, also nylon, $3\frac{1}{2}$ lb weight, with, he said, no problem. I was sceptical!

He brought it to a conference later and pitched it on display. It was not even new. It was all mine. A few filthy weekends persuaded me he had been correct. There was condensation, but it did not matter; by the simple method of keeping the tray-shaped groundsheet away from the walls with elastic the condensation just ran into the ground.

Various courses and a season in the Alps gave a pause in the summer, and once back I handed in my notice so was free to *do* again: a Hebridean trip in November, a month on the schooner *Captain Scott*, then the usual holiday courses in the North West. Time suddenly was running out.

Back home it was already mid-January 1974. The stockpile came down from the loft, a last big shopping to the Alliance Cash and Carry (could I eat all that?), and from Hughes, our local grocer. The dates of a proposed visit to the Polish Tatras eventually became known and put the starting date back a few days.

On the fourth of February we had an unusual wine and cheese party. We looked at slides of the Alps and various odd club doings but the main activity, saving me a 100 man-hours, was breaking down bulk food into one-man size pokes. Chaos: Ian and Mary in a bedroom dealing with a seven-pound bag of curry (one beer for every pound, it took), John and Penny in the kitchen with a sack of raisins (busy adding wisecrack comments on slips of paper), Val, Ian Mitchell and Patrick were in the front room and Bob and Liz Wallace, George and Beryl slaved in the hall, with peas, carrots, beans, coffee, tea, cocoa and so on. John Dunnett and Mike Duncan came in later and wondered what was going on—not being in the secret. Mother had wisely gone out to visit friends.

Not all even then knew the whole truth, which was disguised simply as a "marathon walk through the Highlands and Islands". It says something for the dream that quite a few people at once suggested the truth. I even had two telephone calls from people thinking about such a project and wanting advice. As they hoped it would take two or three weeks of a summer holiday, a few statistics ended their hopes.

Many food parcels were going to be required along the way. I had worked out three motor itineraries to lay these caches, entailing a thousand miles of motoring. The physical work of parcelling was immense. Cards were prepared for each parcel, for no two were the same, and these were scattered throughout the house. A sample card might look like this:

The translation: "Loch Duich cache site, food for four days plus reserves to see me to Affric Lodge. Map 18 to go into this parcel and it was to go to Mike Keates who would deliver it." There were 42 of these labels. Each type of food, plus things like candles, matches, toilet paper, film, books had to be taken round, in turn, from label to label and the right estimate left. This game was played by mother and I; you can imagine what the house looked like at the end of it.

The worst job of all came next—doing it all up. Again, no standardisation was possible, some were going to be actually buried in the hills, others would be safe indoors, most were going to destinations as yet unknown. We used 2,000 polybags from tiny to sack-size. Friends had been hoarding cartons and string for a year. A parcel took a good half-hour usually; each was double-checked against a "standard" list, and only a packet of Vitawheat was missed, all through. I reckon there are few mothers (never mind being an O.A.P. grannie too) who would take to grovelling on the floor for days playing this mad Father Christmas game.

The three car trips were made. It shows the highlander at his normal best that only once did the first person asked refuse to take in a parcel, and their jobs varied from forester to doctor to railway linesman to hotelier, roadman to policeman.

Caches contained a mixture of tinned food, for immediate use, and dehydrated for carrying on the way. As a supplement I would eat in hotels, buy fresh stuff, and at weekends various friends came up via Dollar, where Marina produced weekly treats of fresh meat, fruit, home baking and so on.

My Dormobile was finally packed as a mobile base store with reserves of all kinds and delivered to Dollar.

It was time for a holiday—the Tatras.

I

MULL, ETIVE AND GLENCOE

"I lived for the day when I could get out with my ship, and stay
away."

ALAN VILLIERS

———————————

Wednesday 3 April THE ROAD TO MOOLA

We left Dollar in fog—which began to thin only near Lix Toll—
steaming off the fields and holding to the line of the river. The whooper
swans were dabbling at their reflections in Loch Dochart. Ben More
thrust through like Fuji Yama: a snowy cone reaching up from
bountiful spring. The gift of such anticyclonic conditions was a blessing
indeed for the start of the venture.

Oban was urbane and peaceful in pre-season quietude. We drove on
to the ferry *Columba*. Every craft in the harbour had its inverted twin
until our wake washed them all away as we steamed off for Mull. The
bar had only one customer; everyone else sprawled on deck in the sun.
Duart Castle welcomed to the island; lying dark in the eye of the sun it
translated itself for us, the *black height*. It is the clan Maclean seat and
goes back to the thirteenth century, now the home of Sir Charles
Maclean, 27th chief, and also recently Chief Scout.

We stopped to change nephew Kenneth's nappies by Lochdonhead,
then ran up the slicing Glen More. The hills were hazy with the sweet
reek of burning and when we passed the source of the scent, by Loch
Scridain, it was replaced by the tang of the sea. There had been curlews
and wheatears in the glen, here oystercatchers and redshank added
their calls. It was full spring. The rushed days in Kinghorn and Dollar
had only been stations on the way back from Poland; suddenly this
felt home—where sun and sea and mountains meet, westwards where
all dreams lie.

I should have been "psyched-up" no doubt but found myself calm.
There was nothing to do—except savour the scene. Just the walking to
do now, and that was not in my control. I had planned and prepared.

B

I could do no more. So Mull was consciously savoured, its perfection an intoxicating joy.

Kenneth spent hours throwing stones, and himself, into the water. A gentlemanly heron watched from a boulder beyond, a perch he maintained while the tide turned and flowed and the sun dipped to halo his shape in gold. Sheep came and "scarted" themselves on the Dormobile and their lambs tripped over the guy lines of my tent. It was a bare feet and bare torsos day, doing nothing and then resting afterwards. I lay reading *Travels with a Donkey*—which might have been significant.

I had, actually, been re-reading much of Stevenson, a sadly-neglected author. Few have captured our landscape so well. In *Kidnapped* for instance, the shipwreck on Mull, the crossing of Rannoch Moor, the Ben Alder days at Cluny's Cage—these are gems of description. Every word of Stevenson is precise and right, truly a man who knew how to live.

We had established ourselves a diplomatic Kenneth-distance away from the tents of our B.F.M.C. friends, Lorna and Carol, Bob and Ian, who rolled in later, brosy with sun and good doings.

I was banned from cooking even, so sat by the shore, after removing a dead polecat. Kenneth was sent, protesting, to his Dormobile bed. The smoke of burning still veiled the hills at the head of the loch. The waters were purply bright. The ponderous heron and two struggling cormorants flew across, the eiders dodged among the weeds, commenting "Oh! Oh!" Curlews called on the hill, a pheasant honked in the wood, a buzzard mewed overhead. Lambs bleated. Two miles across the loch came children's laughter. These are the magic sounds of silence, the magic colours of content.

After supper we piled wreaths of seaweed on the bonfire so it belched out a great column of smoke and rattled away like musketry. A seal edged in to eavesdrop on our talk. Some deer crossed the road, white caudal patches showing in the moonlight. A big moon seemed to swell gradually, and spent its hours blowing stars across the chill sky. The dew fell. The burn talked in its sleep. . . .

And on the morrow the Long Walk would begin.

It might have been otherwise if David had not seen us gaily distributing "Napisan" instead of milk powder for the fireside brew.

Thursday 4 April THE BEN MORE GATHERING

Mull is one of the two islands which have Munros, but whereas Skye has a whole extravagant ridge of them, Ben More in Mull is the only other. The whole of Mull is worth exploring, the longer you spend on it after all, the less sore you will feel at the penal ferry cost of reaching it. It has a fascinating coast and the attached islands are all interesting: Iona, Ulva, Gometra, the Treshnish, Staffa of Fingal's Cave fame. . . .

Not far from the camp, round the Gribun, the sea cliffs tower over the road, and the houses fit tight in between road and sea, spaced regularly along, except, in one place there is no house but a big boulder. There was a cottage originally but the boulder crashed on to it, killing a newly wed couple within. The wedding guests were dancing in the barn and did not even know.

Along the Gribun is MacKinnon's Cave, one of the biggest in the country, over two hundred yards long; along again lie the miles of the Wilderness, a devastated area of boulders and 1,000-foot basalt cliffs. There is a 40-foot fossil tree.

Ben More queens it over all as the *big hill* should: a grey, saddle-backed peak, which can be seen from all directions on land or at sea. It radiates ridges in several directions from the summit which can cause confusion in the mist for the top is highly magnetic and the compass can be 180° out—which is always off-putting to those who have been taught always to trust the compass.

The finest approaches all converge on A'Choich first. This 2,730-foot top then allows a fine connecting ridge to the Munro. The best route is the most direct. We reached it up the Allt a' Ghlinne Dhuibhe—hugging shade and needing little excuse to stop. White hares and deer were more easily watched from a sitting position—and we could always take another picture of the girls in their bikinis. Bob gave us a cheerful dissertation on sheep's liver flukes.

In turn I told of Alex, an ex-pupil of mine who was reprimanded in the Cairngorms, on a course, for drinking the water straight. Did he not know of this hazard? "It is what all the old shepherds die of," came the dire warning. "You must boil it for twenty minutes." Alex took the line that as long as it was *old* shepherds dying of it, he was prepared to take the risk!

Romping back down to camp Bob managed to set some boulders bouncing down on top of me. I was a hundred yards ahead. I stopped one on my rucksack and another took the legs from under me. This was the most serious "accident" of the trip. Had I been facing uphill and got it on the front instead of the back of the knee there would have been a different tale. As it was I had grand itchy scabs to crinkle at every step for the next week.

The family were off to Iona in the Dormobile so I joined Lorna and Carol for tea. They were very touchy. Lay a finger on them and they leapt. Bikinis were a mistake. They were now in the pink—literally. Even a swim in the sea did not help. I wore my pyjamas (last time for three months) as protection against the sun. It was a long day of ease really. The traces had been freed.

Friday 5 April   BY THE SWEAT OF YOUR BROW

"Only 357,000 feet to go," I had joked on top of Ben More, little knowing this was 90,000 feet short of the reality, but such figures are meaningless anyway; in fifteen Everests, what's a Munro here and there? I underestimated the mileage too—but it had only been guessed at (1,200 miles) by using a piece of string on a small scale map. The detail that did matter was the daily "staging" which had been carefully worked out. The original 112-day estimate came out at 112 days. The strategy, if you like, was clear, the tactics were often decided on the spot.

Previous, extensive knowledge of the ground made this much easier. I could envisage the ground, a great asset, though not fully realised till looking back. John Hinde and his R.A.F. gangs, Sandy Cousins, all owed a lot to this too; in contrast, many of the failures on such efforts were younger, inexperienced lads. (The Ripley brothers were an exception. I did not consider myself in their class, so their failure was both a warning and a spur to which I paid great heed.)

The sheer scale and loneliness of the Scottish hills can prove a mental as well as a physical barrier. At Aultguish Inn I was told of one "Walk" which ended simply from the demoralising effect of rain. Flooded rivers had not been expected and the route and meeting points all went haywire. It became a nightmare of impracticability—and all the time the rain and wind pummelled and battered till the world became one great wetness and despair. It took only a few days to break the spirit.

Experience would have dealt with that, but experience takes time I suppose. Sandy and John had had years of soaking—maturing—and so, I suppose, had I. It all relates not only to a scheme like this, but also on the prickly topic of "Leadership". I find it horrifying for instance that people are leaving school intending to become mountain instructors. What can they know about it at that age? Experience is a key factor for success, though failure can be rewarding, giving as it does the most emphatic of all experience. So long as mistakes are not fatal, they are useful! "We are all, in a sense, survivors" as I once heard; but again, listening to a radio panel discussing climbing, the chairman drew it all together with the profound remark that "climbing is not for the beginner".

Today's circuitous route gave not even one Munro though I sweated as I have seldom done in Scotland—or elsewhere. It began gently.

I was off at 6.30 on a dewy morning when the only stir was the wild-life. I left the Broons sleeping, and Lorna and Carol breakfasting, for we were all catching the early ferry. I was using a Raleigh "Stowaway" cycle, as I would for several longer reaches of unavoidable tarred road. Walking hard roads is not my idea of fun. Legally, a bike is "an aid to pedestrianism" and not a vehicle or machine, and it kept my basic rule of self-propulsion. If you object, the solution is obvious! (But then you would have to swim to and from the islands, or go barefoot, or without food. You can soon reduce it to absurdity. The prime aim was enjoyment, after all.)

Six sorry sheep had marooned themselves on an islet at the head of the loch and a lamb in the black burnt area was bleating its woe at being born in such surroundings. Push bike was an apt description for the haul up Glen More. The girls bombed past on the pass. A redwing flew along with me for a while. At Ishriff I raced through a party of red deer (frightening) and at Loch Don a roe buck watched me pass. I suddenly realised it was still some way to Craignure and the boat left in thirteen minutes: intriguing possibilities, as the car had my rucksack with everything, including money, in it.

You cannot hurry cows, or heavy bikes. When I clattered on to the *Columba* with three minutes to spare I was quivering with the effort. Half an hour later she sailed.

We had a second breakfast while my clammy shirt dried, then prowled the deck, too aware of action ahead to play the placid tourist. Lorna and Carol were off for Glendessary which I would only reach in June.

Oban again, the bay full of eiders and reflections, the pier all bustle and calling voices. I made an inauspicious start by going over the handlebars. The pier planks are carefully laid with cycle-wheel-size gaps between!

There was a long brae out of town but I had stocked up, and on top of the hills found a nook among the primroses and celandine and consumed milk and hot-cross-buns. This was about the richest landscape I would ever see—which is why it is so full of the earliest marks of Scottish history.

I have never trained, as such; life is too hectic otherwise, even if the physical laziness could be overcome. Since much of my time is spent on the hill, I suppose some fitness carries over. The climbing and long ski trip in Poland had removed any surplus weight. I did not lose any more on the Walk.

Glen Lonan was pleasant going but lacked water, so at Taynuilt, on the main road again, I bought ice cream and peaches. Wayside indulgence became a principle in the months ahead. It was interesting to see what was chosen when faced with all the wealth of a grocery shop. I did not develop a chocolate craving as others seemed to have done but sweet, juicy things were top desires.

Taynuilt has a monument to Lord Nelson erected in 1805 by the Lorn furnacemen—thirty-seven years before the one in Trafalgar Square. The main road through the jaws of the Pass of Brander was quiet. Road, rail and river squeeze through here in promiscuous ribbons. The small dam on the river has an electric lift instead of a fish ladder. Brander is famed for fights by both Wallace and Bruce, the latter here clashing with the MacDougalls in 1308, a fray from which the Campbells gained. The main Campbell castle was on Innis Chonnail, down Loch Awe. Kilchurn was also theirs and inspired Wordsworth and others to versify. The clan only moved south to Inveraray in the late fifteenth century. Their motto is still "Cruachan" and the phrase, "It's a far cry to Lochow" (Loch Awe) has much of history in it beyond the pages of Neil Munro.

Neil Munro is another of the superb painters of the highland scene. His book, *The New Road,* is one of the best. He is probably better known as the creator of *Para Handy,* which he wrote under the name of Hugh Foulis.

For years Hydro and road works had been active along Loch Awe but now one can speed by—at twice the speed of seeing anything. A new tourist attraction is to take a minibus tour into the heart of the mountain to see the power station which is part of the second-largest pumped storage scheme in the world. The reservoir is 1,200 feet above the turbines, held in a corrie of Cruachan, whence I was bound after leaving the bike and collecting a parcel from Mrs Moyes at one of the Hydro houses. I also had a look at St Conan's.

This church is an odd hotch-pot architecturally but its setting by the loch makes it worth seeing. Plain glass windows sweep round the front of the church—nature giving a view no stained glass could match. A rib of Robert the Bruce is preserved here, the rest of him being home in Fife at Dunfermline Abbey.

Cruachan is really an array of summits, eight in all. Sir Hugh gave it two Munros and one of the anomalies of his Tables is that the Taynuilt Peak, 3,611 feet, a subsidiary summit of the Main Munro, 3,689 feet, is higher than the other Munro, Stob Diamh, 3,272 feet.

The toil up on to Cruachan was memorable for the intolerable heat. Every trickle of water was pounced on. Collapsing on the second day with heatstroke would be an odd ending to the Walk! There was a view down Loch Awe as far as New York. It is the longest loch in Scotland, though Loch Ness and Loch Lomond are bigger.

I passed the shapely dam and contoured round into the burn behind Beinn a' Bhuiridh. Glorious shade! I splashed in a pool with the gusto of a dipper, then followed beside or in the burn to pitch the tent near the col above—at about 2,300 feet. After a brew I went up Beinn a' Bhuiridh, 2,941 feet, a summit which was all lumps and bumps and pools of melt-water. This is a "Corbett", a mountain of over 2,500 feet, having a drop all round of 500 feet. A list made by their eponymous creator is now printed in with Munro's Tables. People often think the 500-foot clearance also applies to Munros, but this is not so. Corbetts are much better disciplined, and often much more satisfying besides being better viewpoints. Quinag, Beinn Dearg Mhor, Allival and Askival, The Cobbler—these are all Corbetts. Stac Polly or Suilven do not even reach that height; all of which shows what a daft game this is.

Sunset seemed quick: the burnished loch went out leaving a dull, raw world. A lone bird cried. It was gloriously lonely.

Saturday 6 April   SMITTEN BY THE SUN AND ADDICTED

Beira, Queen of Winter in Scottish mythology, who built the hills with her magic hammer, once forgot to cover a well on Cruachan, and overnight it flowed down to fill the valley below—hence Loch Awe. Now her well's overflow has a dam, and other powerful hammers have hollowed out her mountain. The reservoir for the power station has done little damage to the surroundings; so often in the months ahead I was to see others with disfiguring shorelines—like dirty bath rims.

As the weather still looked good I set off early to make use of the cool hours. Having the whole day and no base to return to gave a great freedom. I could hurry or dawdle as I saw fit. I averaged about a mile an hour this first hard day of carrying a pack; but the real enemy was the sun which gave a physical battering. At the end of the day it was interesting to see how the pace shot up—uphill—simply because there was shade again. I was quite sorry to leave my "nest among the stars" (Obadiah), and one outcome of the Walk has been a taste for high camping, even at weekends. The rewards make the effort worth while. You cannot know a mountain till you have slept on it.

A long ridge, snow edged, led to Stob Diamh (Stob Daff) from which I made the longer traverse to the Main Summit and back. Drochaid Glas had crags which looked like the Inca altar at Ollantaytambo. Litter today included such diverse objects as an egg-cosy, a U.S. coin, a watch glass and a usable biro. Good winter climbing is to be had in the northern corries but the only account I have read is in J. H. B. Bell's *A Progress in Mountaineering*. There was a lot of snow still. Stob Dearg is better known as the "Taynuilt Peak", and it was the poet W. P. Ker who whimsically, aptly, referred to the Nordend of Monte Rosa as its Taynuilt Peak.

I did not linger on Cruachan Beann, the *mountain of peaks*, but retraced with hopeful, but fruitless, diversions in search of water. I had to go past the last horn of Sron an Isean, the *nose of the imps*, before it was safe to drop down. With an ice axe there could have been a good glissade. The Lairig Noe was a lonely col but by traversing up and across I reached a good burn. The bliss of a hill brew! The purple saxifrages were wilting in the heat and deer let you pass twenty yards off as they were too done to move.

I followed up the burn which gave a noisy rush of coolness. The summit of Beinn a' Chochuill was pleasantly draughty. I left a questionnaire on the cairn—which was found the following weekend. This was a brief series of questions, which could give some idea of the usage Munros received, and I left them only on what were relatively remote summits. The results are given in an appendix. An Oban couple were on top and we met several times on the dip and rise to Beinn Eunaich.

I ETIVE–GLENCOE

Its snow rim was littered with thousands of small olive beetles. These summits translate as *peak of the hood* and *fowling hill*.

I had done two days' walking in one, and now dropped down the far side of these groups into Glen Kinglass, a glen many look down on, but few visit. The Starav hills beyond were the morrow's effort and I wanted to sleep high on them. First I dropped down to 200 feet, quite a brutal descent with the ground more complex than the map indicates. The glen was a heat-trap and though I had stripped to just underpants and boots, the sweat poured down. The potentially difficult river was a highway of blazing granite cobbles. I lay under the alders, actually in the water, while I brewed again. I could almost see the bracken fronds unrolling. An eagle spiralled in the sun till it mewed into a buzzard. It was an effort to go on again.

The Allt Hallater was a succession of granite slabs and blue pools—resisted till I pitched camp after a thousand feet had been gained, suddenly easy going as the sun was sinking and there was shade. It was another fine site with a view back to the Kinglass Rubicon. If the day had been almost grim at times I was not going to complain and tempt fate. I was happy to be smitten by the sun and addicted.

Sunday 7 April HALLELUJAH, I'M A BUM

The words of this song kept in my head all day; but at the end of it there was a certain twist to them. I was waddling like a jockey, trying not to rub my cheeks—Marina's cheery, "Ah, yes, nappy rash!" was all too accurate. Days of salt sweat streaming down my back and soaking my pants were the cause, an unusual one for Scotland.

I was a bit stiff and slow off the mark. Eating rice crispies with a knife was a frustrating game. Memo: remember a spoon next time!

Beinn nan Aighenan was just above but I went up to the col linking it to the Starav range so I could dump the sack a while and enjoy the rocky scramble. If you play it right you need hardly touch grass, or snow as it was today. It is one of many granite peaks hereabouts which just fail to produce anything for climbing. No more secret Etive Slabs. I reached the summit climbing up the shady side of everything. The fangs of Cruachan rising through the gentle haze tones were very Alpine. There was no sign of man's handiwork at all and hills simply ranged off in all directions. In some ways I was taking a chance, beginning the trip among these fairly hefty and demanding hills that range from Glencoe down to Loch Awe. They could have been in winter condition, instead of sun-beaten. Aighenan is *peak of the hinds* but I saw none. Starav is unhappily the *stout* (or *strong*) *hill* and Glas Bheinn Mhor just the *big grey lump*.

Back on the col I found the area teeming with frogs, something I had seen before. There were scores of them; a great moving and croaking. My steps set them leaping for the pools but as these had skimmed over with the night's frost the result was quite a pantomime as they skidded across the ice or went splintering through it.

Starav is king of the Etive hills, a bold shape with a tent-shaped summit. It rises straight from sea-level and makes you feel its 3,541 feet. It is a good winter peak with narrow ridges and deep corries. My east ridge of today is knife-edged in places and leads to a top which is often taken for the summit if it is cloudy. The highest point is round the rim to the north. It has a summit to linger on. I wandered about looking down the various sides. It has a commanding view down Loch Etive, a real fiord of a Loch. I thought of the words of Deirdre's "Farewell to Alban":

> "O Loch Etive, where the brothers
> Built our Doune for me, a bride;
> Joy to rise and there behold
> My fold of sunbeams—Etiveside."

Deirdre of the Sorrows was a first century Pictish princess who was married to a King of Ulster; there are several legends about her connected with Etive.

Glas Bheinn Mhor was a bit of a plod after Starav. Stob Coir' an Albanaich, the *peak of the Scotsman's corrie*, has a big cairn on top of which a smaller one had sprouted. The Ceitlein Glen is the best of those up Etive. One branch leads to a considerable gorge and there are areas of granite which will give some climbing. One pinnacle has the following guide-book description:

Patey's Old Man. 70ft. Unclassifiable. I.Rowe, W.Sproul May 1967. Protrudes from left wall of gorge. Lasso the top and climb the rope. Treat gently.

I had pulled on waterproof trousers to enjoy a good bum-slide from Albanaich, when its north-east corrie rumbled down an avalanche of rock and snow. Meall Tarsuinn beyond, was an annoying whaleback, which, like many Tarsuinns (the name means *transverse* or *cross peak*), lies between desired Munros. Almost always they should be traversed, not flanked. The col before the wet, grassy dome of Meall nan Eun, *hill of the birds*, is an unusual slot. The Ceitlein approach can be made up granite slabs unless the burn is in spate. This fifth Munro for the day was saturated with melting snow. It is a contender for the prize for the dullest Munro, so I left a questionnaire in the cairn. An Edinburgh lad found it next day.

Instead of going down the Ceitlein to Glen Etive and then up the Glen, I kept to the hill, cutting through behind Stob Dubh, 2,897 feet, to descend direct to camp. This summit dominates the Glen and is as fine as anything which happens just to be 103 feet higher. Very red deer were milling about in the pass, a mile of level-going. I took off my pants (all I'd had on all day again) in the hope that the rubbing would ease. I hoped the deer would not mind. There were a surprising number of dead ones, some recent and some just smell and bones. Scots pine, holly and so on grew in the gorge where grazing was not possible by the deer. It is sad to reflect that trees once covered the land from here to Deeside and north to Loch Maree. Man has made a right mess of his earth.

Stob Dubh's shadow was reaching out across my bows but I beat it to the first of the big pools in the river and, having only boots to remove, was soon splashing in the gasping cold of its melted snow water. My rolled-up shirt which had been stuffed up my back to let air in under the rucksack was as wet as if I'd thrown it in the pool, yet during the time taken by a few dives and lengths, it dried completely. I hung myself up, like a cormorant, to drip dry too.

The path led into shade—and there, ahead, was the Broon establishment: Dormobile and tents. I paddled straight over and joined Kenneth for Ribena. They were very pink Browns by now. Marina produced a tin of pears—and a spoon.

Monday 8 April   B. AND B. AND B.
Which stands for Buachaille, Buachaille and Bidean: a day of nearly 8,000 feet. Marina had slipped the late night forecast into the tent after I was asleep. It said "dry, but cooler"—so we had an even hotter day. I did not see them in the morning as their holiday hours and my early rising times were very different.

I went down to Dalness and up to the top of the Lairig Gartain, which is a text book example of a U-shaped glaciated pass. Its flanks were smooth grass, and twice sheep above sent stones bouncing past. The col was 1,600 feet, and rather than lose height I fought along a poor traverse on the Buachaille Etive Mor. This was not a good line and in the end I only climbed on to the crest after cutting steps up a snow slope—using an improvised porphyritic ice-axe. I discarded most of my clothes again to walk along to the Munro, Stob Dearg, the *red top*, at the far end. Not a soul was in sight on this most popular of hills. Rannoch Moor lay spread like a map over the notch of the Crowberry Tower, vanishing into haze, out of which Schiehallion rose in familiar conical shape.

I can still remember clearly the thrill of seeing the Buachaille with climber's eyes for the first time as we came over the Moor. I had walked and cycled in view of it often enough but I was out of my teens before really taking up rock climbing "properly"—with ropes and all the junk.

I was a missionary assistant in a Paisley parish (Martyrs' Memorial) at the time. It took the Asian 'flu epidemic to procure a rope. That virus was particularly lethal to old people; and when many of the ministers went down with it, I found myself having to conduct a number of funerals at the crematorium. You actually received a fee for that, so after a couple of weeks I was able to cycle off to Glasgow and purchase one of the new-fangled nylon, hawser-laid ropes. A hundred feet of it cost under £5. The next weekend it was used on the Buachaille, climbing Agag's Groove, the Rannoch Wall test-piece, before going on over the Tower to the top. It was a day just like today.

Often, though, you may have to queue for Agag's. Last time on it we found a notice affixed, which read: "Road narrows, no overtaking"! We have come a long way from the outlook of an English traveller in 1792 who called the Buachaille "the carcass of a mountain, peeled, sore and hideously disgustful".

I retreated back along the long crest and down to the glare and heat of the pass. The Buachaille Etive Beag's *black top*, Stob Dubh, is happily immediately above the col. It was still a sweaty pull up. The deer were much too weary to move; heads simply swivelled to watch and I half wondered what the result would be if I walked right round them a few times. . . .

The wee Buachaille once gave us the coldest cold I have ever met on the hills. We were traversing the crest in a spell of clear, winter weather which was most enjoyable. Suddenly, with nothing visibly different, we walked into a block of air that was super-cooled. It left us gasping. It was as easily left, and we went back and forth several times into it from sheer fascination before going on. One of the party had wet boots which froze at once, and he ended with frostbite.

Back down at the rucksack I was hot, tired and dusty. I took all the sweaty clothes, and boots, off to let them dry out. The Meta stove managed to set the grass alight and in seconds flames were darting among my scattered gear. By the time I had dealt with that I was even hotter and dirtier. I went across to the next pass to where there were pools and plunged into the freezing water. Bliss! The Lairig Eilde is also about 1,600 feet and cuts off the Bidean massif from the Buachailles. A creeping line of shadow drove me on upwards eventually. The broken crags above were covered in hard snow and no outflanking was possible, so a pole section from the tent this time had to do the work of an ice-axe.

I was soon up into the golden glow again and thankfully the slopes along and up to Stob Coire Sgreamhach were mossy and full of melt-runnels. There was a great temptation to camp. I drank again and again and went on for Bidean, outflanking a bit on a line I had picked out yesterday. Bidean was quite a thank-God summit, at 3,766 feet it is the highest in Argyll, and the highest of the trip to date.

The only other time I had done the combination of these three Munros was with the unlikely mixture of Marlborough, Eton, and Braehead schoolboys. It was unintentional, as we had only gone up to see Ossian's Cave, but one thing led to another. We were not provisioned for a long day, though, and were a bit weary by the Lairig Gartain. I discovered a mush of old raisins in a pocket and just a few of these each soon produced the zoom needed to do the last slope.

Bidean nam Bian's summit is hidden away behind an array of satellite peaks and corries and ridges. The Three Sisters which dominate Glencoe are merely the ends of spoke-like ridges which eventually lead to the top. The name means the *spiky summits of the skins or hides*; an old S.M.C. Journal suggests this is because of the quantity of epidermis lost on the rocks by generations of climbers.

I set off west over a subsidiary top we have always known as Ossian's Seat, then turned to drop down to one of the "Windows of Etive", a col separating Gleann Fhaolain leading to Etive, and the Fionn Ghleann leading to the Coe. The slope seemed to be made of loose boulders set on the vertical. They had a nasty feeling of impermanence.

The sun was dipping again, and I hurried to find a good site before it became too dark for a photograph. The procedure was becoming established: stove on while tent up, then while tea "mashed", a quick photo, then fill the gallon container and crawl in if need be till the next day. I could seal myself in, safe from rain or midges. These days it was the cold that drove indoors. I would linger outside till the sun went, then would escape the freezing shadows into the warm sleeping bag, the joy of simple, good food—and endless brews.

Tuesday 9 April NAKED BEFORE THE MOUNTAIN

Yesterday the actual glen of the Coe had hardly been noticed. All the days so far had been dominated by the glen and loch of Etive, which is how it was in the past when the sea approaches were the vital ones. South of a line from Etive to Iona the influence of Ireland long remained, while north and west of that the Norse influence was the main one.

I rose at five simply to relish the breathless cool and quiet. I have had several spells like this, even in Glencoe, which has the reputation of first filtering Scotland's weather before distributing it elsewhere. It can be worse on Rhum or in the Skye Cuillin, where the rocky landscape can make a shimmering oven which is overbearing. Not that you risk complaining about heat in Scotland. That would be tempting fate. Wordsworth wrote some lines about Glen Etive and its "playful waterfalls". He must have had it in its normal state.

I began the day with a descent, flanking under cliffs to reach the Bealach Fhionnghaill. Red rock changed to schisty grey and later in the day was to change again to golden granite. This bealach (*pass*) must have seen the flight of fugitives from the 1692 Massacre—of which more later. We once fled over it to avoid being devoured by the Etive midges, packing up a camp at dawn and heading for the safety and sanity of Ingrid's hostel. In the dark we had rubbed on stinking repellant and only daylight revealed the jaundiced result. We had used the wrong stuff—iodine. We had also fled this glen when a lad in our party complained of pains in his side. Appendicitis was our suspicion and was verified at the hospital, but he had had it out only about ten days before. The culprit was most indignant when he discovered we had hustled him to the local maternity hospital.

I did not recognise the col.

The *Peak of the Treasure*, Sgòr na h-Ulaidh, lay a couple of miles on along a ridge past it and gave some scrambling up "wee wa's" and lots of deer stumbling through the snow patches. The pools were full of frogs again. From the notched summit the Ben stood out in clear morning light.

I slid off down on the rims of snow.

Gaelic names are often far from straightforward. Cairnwell for instance should be An Carn Bhlag, the *hill of blisters*, A'Chralaig is Garbh-leac, Lawers is from labhar (the sound of rushing waters). Beinn Achaladair is corrupted from Beinn Achadh-Fhaladair—the aspirants simply dropped. Ben Vorlich is Ard Mhur'laig, *height of the sea bag*. An appendix is given at the end of this book to try to help a little.

Ulaidh is not often visited, being four miles from any road; but it has good ridge walking, good winter climbing and a commanding view. The glaciated pass between it and Beinn Fhionnlaidh (pronounced "Ula") has a strangely lost-world feeling. Plantings on both sides make it difficult to reach with its moraine humps and bumps. The north-east end of Fhionnlaidh has some intimidating, virgin, cliffs.

I took a slow-rising traverse line across its north flank, hugging the shade. The trig point lies a bit to the west on the flattish top. I baled off the quartz crest on the south side already knowing I had lost the race against the heat. *Finlay's mountain* was not mine.

The grilling below was the worst of the whole trip—and it was an odd repetition. Tom Izatt, my dog Kitchy, and I had done Sgulaird (where I was heading now) and Fhionnlaidh from Etiveside—an approach I would recommend only to my enemies. "The appearance is that of matter, incapable of form or usefulness, dismissed by Nature from her care, disinherited of her favours, left in its original elemental state, or quickened only with one sullen power of useless vegetation" (Dr Johnson). It was a close, hot, midgy day and the vegetatious descent to Etive almost reduced us to tears of vexation. Memorable of course.

Today it was simply sizzling hot. To prevent another dose of nappy rash I stripped off completely and wedged a sponge in the small of my back. Every ten minutes I had to wring it out. My rucksack soaked right through.

Pathetic dollops of dry spawn lay on the cracked, dried peatholes. A deer skull protruded from the dusty heather. The air smelt stale. In contrast, the lochans felt icy cold and I just could not bear to swim, I was too weary with the heat. At the lochan at the head of Glen Ure it was tempting just to camp. There was a delectable site. Tomorrow I could go on. However a drum-up restored initiative enough and on I went for the ridge of Beinn Sgulaird, the *mountain of yelping*. By the time I flopped on the summit I thought it well named. The Ripley brothers had commented too on the seeming length of this approach.

This is subjective of course: Sgulaird is a fine double-humped camel of a hill, looking over Appin and the West, built of sturdy granite with some slabs on the north flank. The east ridge is an endless succession of bumps which nearly drove me to distraction this day, adding to the toil and time. It was a dour ascent. I traversed into the east corrie and found it perversely wet. The summit proved not to be the summit— there was another beyond. It was one of those days. I descended gingerly to the rucksack and had yet another brew. The descent to sea-level down Glen Ure looked tough but a stalker's path simply led down into its sweltering depths. Buzzards were swooping and calling along the crags—far too like bloody vultures for comfort, I thought.

Glenure House at the foot was white and tidy looking but there was no sign of life. At Elleric across the valley I received a cheery wave from the occupants of deck chairs who sprawled with iced drinks in their hands. It was tempting to wave back, differently.

I turned up the glen, instead of down to Loch Creran, and a couple of miles of forestry track was enough. I was blown. A burn, and a litter of dry oak leaves to bed on, gave a fine site for the night. The Meta stove, which I used at some parts of the trip instead of Gaz, had to be perched on a stone for safety. Seldom can fire risk have been greater than during these few days past.

The site was noisy with wrens, tits and chaffinches. Long-tailed tits passed through. The blackthorn was out. It was good after all. I drank and drank and ate and drank and drank again. "Fresh food tomorrow" my log noted in expectation.

I quote it direct: "Survival today, not fun. A bit stiff, all over. Tendons tender; lighter boots take less effort but the feet have a harder hammering if there is a pack carried—bruising, not blisters. Both these days a bit too much, but able to force the body on. Still enjoyed. Nice to stop! Bare feet bliss. Primroses out. Sgulaird through a frieze of branches. About 6,000 feet today. 13 hours. Who wrote of the sun their undoing? Or being naked before the mountain?"

Wednesday 10 April   THE VAIR PAIR

Today, I reckon, ended the breaking-in period and, out of the heat and effort of the days so far, a fit body now crawled forth—rather like a dragonfly from its old shell. We pay for civilisation so called, with body as much as with soul. I am a bit scornful about the hardship aspect. Who is facing it in fact? Experiments with rats showed you could overwork them, starve them, freeze them, in general make life hell for them—and they thrived; but give them endless food and luxury, crowd them together in urban opulence—and they went mad.

The birds were still in full song when I woke. A yaffle was loudly calling nearby. Just a touch of rain was needed to set full spring racing through the lacework of branches. The oak wood ran out soon after I set off, and the miles of path above Salachail rose through dull plantations of fir, though still young enough to see over. An odd incident happened. I was deep in daydreams, thinking about youthful African days, when suddenly there was a coughing bark which made the hair on my neck stand upright. A lion! Of course it was nothing of the sort; just a wee roe deer which continued to roar away until I was out of hearing. Marvellous sound, all wild challenge.

This path is a marked forest trail over to Ballachulish village, and worth doing before the trees grow higher. The col is 1,400 ft. An old S.M.C. Journal tells of a crossing in 1913 when a party left Taynuilt for Glencoe, crossing Loch Etive, up the glen here and over direct: 22 miles, in nonstop rain. The Salachail stream nearly turned them back as the bridge had disintegrated into a length of rotting fir covered in nails "business end uppermost". The young bachelor of the party was made to straddle across first! At Glencoe they were told it had been raining for 72 hours. At the Clachaig they admitted "we did not despise a change and some warm food".

From the stile on the pass the Bheithir pair looked very dull; the circuit from the north is much better, and all of it from Beinn Bhan to Creag Ghorm should be done, the western arm is not boggy as the map might imply, the pools are due to the strata. I angled down to the forest that crept over the watershed from Glen Dura and lit the stove. A sheep made a wild dash from inside the forest and I winced as it reached the fence—but it simply broke through as though the wires did not exist. Even more amazing are stags, with full antlers, who wiggle themselves through such fences if the wires are not tight or close—or the fence simply low enough to jump over. They will clear a fence as high as a man can reach.

My earliest wanderings in hills were in South Africa, where we had landed as War refugees from Singapore. Hence my daydreams earlier. The Valley of the Thousand Hills is as beautiful as it sounds. The opening of Alan Paton's novel, *Cry the Beloved Country*, has the feel of it: "There is a lovely road that runs from Ixopo into the hills. These hills are grass-covered and rolling, and they are lovely beyond any singing of it. . . . About you there is grass and bracken and you may hear the forlorn crying of the birds of the veld. Below you is the valley of the Umzimkulu on its way from the Drakensberg to the sea; and beyond and behind the river, great hill after great hill . . ." Among those blue *kloofs* and *bergs*, in the eternal sun of youth, I had a passion for following streams, ever upwards, to the source if possible. Not having grown up, the habit persists—and was applied on Sgorr Dearg now.

The burn gave good scrambling on rock which resembled compressed raisins. Young, climbing on magical Brandon, aptly described climbing on fingers and toes what he held together with elbows and knees—it was that sort of fun. Little valour and much discretion drove me out from one pitch and I sat puffing and eating damp sandwiches for a while. A windcuffer hovered overhead. The gut ended with a tunnel under a wedge of old snow; scree led to the ridge above. East of Dearg, in winter, lies one of the most graceful arcs of snow-rim you will ever see, the perfect curve. Today it was an edge merely with a necklace of steps up it. These led to the stark, beckoning trig point.

I romped and glissaded down to the gale-battered fence on the col to Sgorr Dhonuill, the next Munro. It is a fine hill with a sweeping coastal view—and a long northern ridge with a prow pointing down to the new Ballachulish Bridge. The racket of its construction, even individual voices, came up with remarkable clarity. The cairn was stuffed with tins; full, they would have made a meal: orange juice, sardines, pork and beans, strawberries or pears, beer or coke. Wishful thinking! It is *Donald's peak* for reasons unknown.

I returned to the col, cut down steeply to the edge of the wood, picked up the sack and went singing off for civilisation accompanied by a bucking, bounding herd of cows.

I had dithered for the shops to open after lunch, but found it was half day. Ballachulish, being the ugliest village in Scotland, was soon left.

It reminds of some parts of Wales with its derelict quarries and abandoned station. Slate began to be quarried there in 1697.

On the footpath to the forest camp-site I met the Dollar Broons. Kenneth must have been puzzled by his vanishing and appearing uncle, a right peripatetic Jack-in-the-box. At the Dormobile I slowly unwound: washed clothes and self, ate and drank treats (fresh rolls and Kenneth's Ribena), did some more logistics . . . even the relaxing was quite hard work!

Thursday 11 April   GLENCOE REST DAY

I lay in bed till nine o'clock, aware that the wind had risen and the weather had turned cold and raw. It had to happen, I suppose. David, Marina and Kenneth went off to be tourists in the Dormobile. I wandered down to the Hotel at the crossroads and used it as an office. Quite a stack of mail to deal with as ever. I ordered some lightweight waterproofs from Tiso. The banter of a cheery waitress rounded off a pleasant lunch.

I had covered 112 miles and 38,000 feet, so my estimates were already out. The body was all right but needed to be treated gently a bit. The sore tendons were the only niggle, a common complaint of hard carrying. Miles and feet were obviously going to be a perpetual erratic equation.

After lunch I did a circuit of the valley which held so many happy memories. I wonder how many remember Ingrid at the Youth Hostel?

Ingrid and Jim Feeney were the wardens there for years and created a unique climbers' hostel. She was "aunty Ingrid" to all our Braehead kids, who loved her. One of them described her as "six foot—in every direction". It was marvellous to come off the hill to find tea ready and something cooking away for us in the oven, or to gather in the Clachaig, singing the evening out. They don't seem to make wardens like that any more, nor hostels. Names echo down the years: Mike McMullen, a young army officer, who was taken round the Ben Vair pair one winter by Mike Smith, one of my fourteen-year-olds. Later McMullen was to become an internationally famous yachtsman, then, tragically lost his wife—and then himself in a solo Atlantic race. Pete Thomas, now the old man of Skye, was a youngster then, foot-loose and Scotland free. Ian Clough was there often with R.A.F. gangs and Hamish MacInnes and Terry Sullivan ran their courses from Ingrid's. It was a smaller world then.

Last time I saw Ingrid was in Fort William in the height of the tourist season. From eighty yards away she spied me, and a great screech of "Hamish" had a hundred eyes turning. Faced with this, I too turned to look along the street. Heads were probably turning at Ballachulish. I was seized in a bear hug from behind. . . .

On up to the Clachaig Hotel. In the woody grounds before it, there used to be a fine little pond which acted as a reflecting pool to the walls of Bidean.

> I desire the high place,
> The place of sun-touched night,
> Of the veil of mist arising
> And eagled wings of light;
> Of red crags of Bidean,
> The blackness of the ridge,
> And a late splash in the river
> Below the bridge.

Years ago, some unimaginative person drained this pond. Today you would hardly know its site, a dream covered over with scrub and willow herb. . . .

One afternoon we were coming out of the Clachaig when Ingrid twisted her ankle on a pebble. We had been having afternoon tea. It took hours to return to the hostel, and the next day we took Ingrid to the old Belford Hospital in Fort William. Ingrid was well known there, as she often delivered injured climbers, so when we staggered in at the door together, the staff rushed up and grabbed me, leaving Ingrid perched on one leg crying, "It's me! it's me!"

By the Green a plaque commemorates the Massacre of Glencoe. In 1691 William of Orange proclaimed a pardon for all rebel clans provided they took an oath of allegiance before the year ran out. Many of the chiefs, loyal to the Stuarts, sought their exiled monarch's permission before acting. MacIan had procrastinated and obtained clearance only near the end of the year; the same day he reported to Colonel Hill, the Governor, at Fort William, to tender his submission.

As the oath had to be administered before the Sheriff of Argyll, Colonel Hill gave MacIan a covering letter and sent him south to Inveraray. Delays, unavoidable, meant the oath was not administered till January 6th. As a matter of routine, the documents were sent on to Edinburgh; but already plans were afoot to harry the clan, and doubtless to the bureaucratic bosses the letter of the law was an added convenience.

It was perhaps unfortunate that the Secretary of State, the ill-remembered Master of Stair, was in London, as were the two great Campbell earls: Argyll and Breadalbane. A month before the amnesty offer lapsed, Breadalbane and Stair were planning the massacre. (The former's lands had suffered at MacIan's hands, so there was no love lost.)

Stair wrote to Livingstone, the officer commanding the army in Scotland: "I hope the soldiers will not trouble the government with prisoners," and later, "I believe you will be satisfied it were a great advantage to the nation that thieving tribe were rooted out and cut off. It must be quietly done. . . ."

So the plans were laid. Colonel Hill was regarded as too sympathetic, and the second in command at Fort William took over.

On February 1st, 120 men were billeted on the people of the glen, a move not unusual when the garrison of Fort William was overbig. The MacDonalds were given promises of safety.

Campbell of Glenlyon was uncle to the wife of Alexander MacDonald, MacIan's second son, and blatant socialising continued even on the eve of betrayal, when they sat playing cards together.

It was a nasty business and, where officers were present, a barbarous one. MacIan was shot in the back as he rose from bed, his wife died after being stripped and mauled; babes and old men of eighty were butchered, while semi-naked wives and children fled into the howling blizzard. The soldiers obviously had no liking for their orders, and to this day the tradition is kind to them. Certainly only 40 corpses were produced from a population of 150, though the like number probably died of exposure. All the hamlets were pillaged and destroyed, the remnant left in desperate straits.

It was this aspect of "murder under trust" which horrified the high-lander. This was actually a crime, in Scots law, second only to treason. In the resulting furore, a commission of enquiry was appointed—of course. In the end it did little and the instigators suffered little, or not at all. The name Campbell, however, had taken on an eternal tarnish.

The remnant resettled in the glen, coming "out" in the 1715 and 1745 Stuart risings, growing and multiplying in the years that followed, until the glen, like much of the highlands, was overpopulated. Then came the sheep and the clearances: the people were evicted, the clachans destroyed, the fields reverted to grass.

Dorothy Wordsworth noted the dereliction in her diary in 1803, and not many years later, another traveller noted: "The sheep-farming system has done the work of extirpation more effectually than the Secretary's massacre."

Various books tell the story in great detail. For those wanting to know more of highland history from the seventeenth to nineteenth centuries, John Prebble's three books—*The Massacre of Glencoe*, *Culloden*, and *The Clearances*—are easily found (Penguin paperbacks), and though slightly journalistic, they quote sources and give facts. "An' facts are chiels that winna ding."

Friday 12 April   AONACH EAGACH

This famous tongue-twister probably gives the finest ridge to be found outwith the Cuillin of Skye. The name applies now to the three miles or so of wall enclosing Glencoe on the north. There are two Munros involved: Meall Dearg and Sgor nam Fiannaidh—the *peak of the Fianns* (Fingalians).

Running up the latter, the western end of the ridge, is the Clachaig Gully. It would have been a superb day for climbing what is reckoned as one of the really great gully routes. I have never seen it so dry, the rainfall here is, after all, ninety inches. Coming out at the top after climbing it once we heard a father check an offspring with the warning, "Ah wouldna go down there lad; looks like a dirty big 'ole."

It is a magnificent dirty big hole. On one wet ascent I remember happily sitting right in the slot at the top of a red chimney to belay; the water piled up behind me so tightly was I wedged. When my second was sufficiently gripped I stood up and let the flood go! . . . A friend once recently asked one of the first ascensionists, W. H. Murray (the story is in his *Mountaineering in Scotland*), about the gully. "Try and climb it in June," came the reply. "The flowers are really at their best then."

Too many feet have worn a groove down its banks, now, as they race for "the other Clachaig", so a rising traverse taking in many little crags gave me the ascent I wanted. The top of Sgor nam Fiannaidh (Feen) was bitter cold in a north wind and there had been an overnight sprinkling of snow. The weather kept dry still.

The first half-mile undulates, then, at a stride, you are on to inescapable, worn, crampon-scratched rock—all the rest of the merry way. The worn appearance testifies to its popularity, but it is as a winter climb that it comes into its own, an Alpine delight. There are some pinnacles (which walkers who never scramble will find daunting) where, one Hogmanay, two of us were blown off our holds again and again during a ten-hour, desperate traverse—an exhausting and frustrating way of playing yo-yo. Today the familiar details were welcomed like old friends and the fit body relished the succession of bumps, spikes, gullies, wee wa's that is the Aonach Eagach. At Meall Dearg the clouds came and went. A tin of pears just went. The gap beyond was wickedly cold, as cold as Sgulaird had been the opposite. The high-stepping scramble up Am Bodach, which finished the ridge, brought me to the first of the Good Friday pilgrims. There were scores coming up, so I blessed the early start that gave me the ridge in solitude. I reached the road in forty minutes. Twenty Munros. Twenty views. It was incredible. I sat looking at the marvellous post-card view down the glen.

It is justly famous, though as late a writer as Dickens could produce this: "Glen Coe itself is perfectly terrible . . . an awful place . . . scores of glens high up, which form such haunts as you might imagine yourself wandering in, in the very height and madness of a fever." Queen Victoria made one of her typical "excursions" to this spot in 1873, a visit notable for the cleg-like attention of a newspaper reporter—whom John Brown was rather itching to deal with.

David had dropped off the bike, and I used it to pech up to the Ladies Scottish Climbing Club hut at Blackrock. A tussle against the wind, as usual, gave ample time to study the filthy mess deposited by the lemming-like motorists. The waterfall in the gorge was just a trickle. Easter tents clustered round the cairn of the fold of Meannar-clach where in the old days the plundered cattle were gathered. Lochan na Fola, as you pull on to Rannoch Moor, is the *loch of blood*; tradition tells of a local squabble over the sharing of cheese in which the fray was so vicious that all the participants perished!

The Buachailles were set on the right and on the left the Devil's Staircase took the old road to Fort William over the hills to Loch Leven. This is a Caulfield Road (*c.* 1750) *not* a Wade Road as everyone thinks. The Kingshouse was the old changing house. The road through the glen was made only in 1786 and the present motor road, a wonder in its day, in 1932.

Blackrock is very old, its walls six-foot thick, deepset in the Moor. Past it runs the old military road, above it, the paraphernalia of ski facilities. The Dollar crew were parked outside and the Northumberland Climbing Club within. The *Light Brown* seemed to have run out, though, for they vanished off to the Kingshouse, Scotland's oldest licensed establishment.

Kenneth's nappies hanging on the line had frozen solid before we turned in.

Saturday 13 April THE END OF THE BEGINNING
"An inconceivable solitude, a dreary and joyless land of bogs, a land of desolation and grey darkness . . . a world before chaos . . . its elements only rock and bogs with a few pools of water."

So Dr John Macculloch described Rannoch Moor, but he libels it a bit. I love its wide emptiness, its wild skyscapes and crying birds, and have criss-crossed it many times: on foot, ski, canoe and skates! Much of it lies about the 1,000-foot level and in size it would take the Lake District nicely—not that any such swop would be contemplated by either side's advocates. The Moor drains partly east and partly south-west.

The peaks I would traverse today form an odd watershed, for one side of them drains to the Etive complex while a few feet away the drainage eastward takes waters through Loch Ba, Loch Laidon to Loch Rannoch and the Tay, and eventually the North Sea. Yet these hills perch above the sea waters of Loch Etive. There is quite a drop to the south where the Achallader hills form a big barrier and this trough takes waters from the east of the Moor to Loch Tulla down Glen Orchy, to Loch Awe and so to the sea on the west coast. The West Highland Railway swings up to skirt the east of the Moor by this natural line but so difficult was it in places to find a bottom for the railway that it is floated on rafts of brushwood. You may catch a glimpse of a sign saying "Soldiers' Trenches 1745", which refers to a reclamation scheme—but the soldiers suddenly found some fighting to do that year and never returned.

Loch Tulla is a beautiful loch. But enjoy your view of it from the road just now for there has been planting between road and loch, with sad lack of imagination, and all you will see ten years hence will be a barrier of trees. Old roots in the bog show that once the Moor was forest—the old Caledonian Forest which our forefathers destroyed.

Loch Ba, on the Moor, appeared in one early map as Loch Ball, which told where the cartographer came from. Coire Ba is one of the largest corries in Scotland. My cluster of Munros today rimmed it.

As you pull up on to the Moor from the south you will notice "the Rannoch Rowan"—a sturdy tree to the left of the road which grows out of a big rock like a flower pot. No doubt a bird dropped a seed in the cracked rock and ever since it has thrived, safe from deer and sheep. None of us would dream of passing without giving our friend a wave. Many old sheiling ruins still have a struggling rowan beside them, planted for luck, to keep away bad spirits. "The Rannoch Rowan" always seems to me to be the spirit not only of the Moor and Glencoe but of all hill adventures.

The old military road skirts the moor to the west and heads from Blackrock to Kingshouse. Blackrock is a "hut" of character. From its door I looked out to a moonlit, frozen dawning, loud with grouse and with the shadowy passing of deer. The custodian was Mora McCallum, a name from the Munro list—but more regarded as a hard-person equally at home on the Etive Slabs. Having watched her on Rhum I only hope she realises how bad she is for male egos. I thawed a hole in the frost of the Dormobile windows but every one was asleep so I wended off up to the ski slopes. For the only day of the trip, I had an ice axe.

Meall a' Bhuiridh gives good ski-ing (weekends and holidays) and my day's route is sometimes done on the boards by the ski-mountaineers. The *hill of the roaring* is perhaps not inappropriate for a ski mountain.

I pulled up under the lift, frozen footprints in the mud making a staircase. Coire Pollach (porridge!) was happily frozen too. I relished cutting steps straight up the snow to the summit. Eight o'clock with a silver *peso* of sun shining through the smokey-cold Moor. Another superb day, almost frightening, much too good to be true. I set the far corries ringing with a yell of glee and slid off down to the col and the hoary ridge up to Clachlet's corniced flank. Clach Leathad is a big whaleback; the new metric tables have switched the highest point to Creise, though. I chose a spot in the mile of cornice, chopped up to it and had fun beating a way through. Snow bunting seemed to be fascinated by the glittering chips, chasing them down the slope below where the lochan was frozen, and those on the Moor, hundreds of them, glittered like sequins.

I glissaded down to 2,300 feet again. Before the pull up Stob Ghabhar I had a break and lay sunbathing. A tumbling array of icicles set off a complaining ptarmigan who had been sunbathing in the line of fire. Stob Ghabhar was still in winter array, very imposing today, leering over its corrie loch which was half frozen, and cracked like glass. Four lads from East Kilbride were on top—only the second lot of people I'd met since Chocuill. Stob Ghabhar is the *peak of the goats*. Shepherds encourage goats in the hope that their presence on the crags will help keep the sheep off them. Later we would add Carn nan Gabhar by the Tilt, Lochnagar above Deeside, Sgor Gaibhre of Loch Ossian, and two called Carn nan Gobhar overlooking Strathfarrar—all Munros. I left this goaty hill in a 1,000-foot bum-slide.

Stob a' Choire Odhair (Corrour) is a sort of afterthought but like many lesser hills next to big brothers it has the finer view. From it I could see four parties all labouring up to the summit I had just left. The early start again. You cannot lose with it: if it is a foul day and becomes worse at least you might gain one summit before being driven off, if it improves you are high, ready to make a day of it. I have never seen the sense or fun in boozing stupid at nights and missing the best the next day. There is a certain malicious joy in being clear-headed and happy when everyone else feels as foul as they look. It is a good time to sing, bash about in boots, or drop the pans down the stairs. . . .

I was torn between desires to linger or to descend quickly. No rucksack, fit at last and not overhot, it was a day all joy. I had a good look at tomorrow's array and set off at a trot. A stalker's path (not on the O.S. map) drops quickly to join the main path down the Allt Toaig (not on the O.S. map either) and I was soon at Victoria Bridge where I had seen the V.W. from a long way off. There was nobody there but as soon as the tea was ready they rolled up. Such timing takes years of practice, or a natural talent. Nearer Inveroran we set up camp by a meandering stream.

I padded about in bare feet. The final hectic planning. From tomorrow I was on my own; the back-up of Dormobile and family ended. It had worked out very well and if the sun had been hard on me it made life easy for Marina and David—Kenneth only needed to be dumped in the nearest river or sea!

The statistics of Section I could finally be totted up: 142 miles, 49,050 feet, which averaged 2,050 feet per Munro per 6 miles. These

11 days had taken me over big brutes, often starting from sea-level, so any "average" was misleading; east of the A9 the miles would increase but the footage drop considerably.

Ben Dorain, across Loch Tulla, where I would set off tomorrow is a hill forever associated with Duncan Bàn MacIntyre, one of the great Gaelic poets. It was the subject of "Farewell to the Bens", written after his last ascent—when 78—one of the most famous of all songs of the hill. It had over 550 lines and yet Donnachadh Ban (*Duncan of the Fair Hair*) could not write, his work being dictated to the Rev. Dr Stuart of Luss, and published in 1768.

MacIntyre was born poor and served as gamekeeper or forester; in Glen Etive he wooed and won the bailiff's beautiful daughter; in the '45 he, perforce, served Campbell interests rather than those of the heart—and ended in the cookhouse. He was to retire ultimately from the Edinburgh City Guard. All the time, he had been composing: songs of hunting, of loving, drinking songs, soldier songs, lampoons and eulogies. At a ceilidh, he could recite thousands of lines of verse by heart. Burns or Scott never met him in Edinburgh, yet, in Gaelic tradition, he is every bit their equal. We've had stamps for Burns and Scott, yet 1974, the 250th anniversary of the birth of Duncan Bàn MacIntyre, could hardly have been less noticed.

He was one of the earliest to *express* feelings for the mountains. He toured to help sell his books; and was noticed in Fort William singing from a volume held upside down! He died aged 88 and is buried in Greyfriars' Churchyard in Edinburgh, but his real monument is this landscape: the soft waters of Loch Tulla, the red-barked pines and the yellow cone of Ben Dorain.

I went to give mother a ring from Inveroran Inn, one with a history going back to droving times, when the route from Skye and Lochaber came down over the Blackmount. William and Dorothy Wordsworth had a second breakfast there after coming from Kingshouse. "The butter not eatable, the barley-cakes fusty, the oatbread so hard I could not chew it, and there were only four eggs in the house which they boiled as hard as stones."

After a supper brew at the Dormobile I gave a casual goodnight and goodbye and crawled into the tent. It seemed so undemonstrative, yet I was bubbling inside. Excitement kept me from sleep and I lay reading till all hours, snug inside the sleeping bag though my hands froze. Frost-pollen dusted the walls of the tent. Even when I blew out the candles and lay in the moon glow I was still aware of the tingling world without: a coot calling and the throbbing pulse of snipe drumming.

> "Spring is come home with her world-wandering feet
> And all things are made young with her young desires."
>
> FRANCIS THOMPSON

II

LYON AND LOCHAY

"... alone I climb
The rugged path that leads me out of time—
Out of time and out of all,
Singing yet in sun and rain,
'Heel and toe from dawn to dusk,
Round the world and home again.'"

JOHN DAVIDSON

Sunday 14 April   A SABBATH DAY'S JOURNEY

The cold had really battened down overnight and the tent was furry with frost crystals both inside and out. The ice rattled in the water-carrier. I made the last meal in luxury: from now on it was the small tent and minimal gear. There was no sign of life from the Dormobile as I patted it goodbye and set off for Bridge of Orchy. The thousand eyes of night had closed, so nobody saw me steal away to my solitary hills. C. S. Lewis writes: "Most of us, I suppose, have a secret country." Mine might not be so adventurous as Narnia; but at least I was gloriously free to set off into it.

The hotel and station were both silent. Yet what memories! Two friends of mine once slept in the station "Gents" (carefully going outside to pee) and gave the station master heart-failure in the morning. Three of my kids once were allowed to use the "Ladies" when their tent had gone up in flames, an accident due to the primus being *outside* the tent. Stoves, Gaz ones especially, are one of the biggest hill hazards and they were all thoroughly trained in primus procedures. As a last resort they had been told simply to put a hand under the stove and throw it outside. I only saw this done once, at Bridge of Orchy. The flaming missile came flying out the door of a tent—and went straight into the tent opposite.

Here too we once endured 80 hours of deluge (three days and nights), the worst I think I have ever known. Mr Macdonald came over from the hotel to offer help only to find everyone all right: two snoozing in the first tent, two playing chess in the next, two brewing in the next—

who offered him a cup of tea. We all went over to the hotel kitchen later and sat watching "Dr Who" while we supped bowls of soup. It is touches like this which make or mar hotel reputations. I have a very definite list of those I recommend and those I most certainly do not. I recommend Bridge of Orchy.

Beinn Dorain is seen as a fine cone rising above the railway as you come over the pass from Tyndrum. A gate leads from the station right on to its lower slopes. The name is *hill of the otter*—a beast found throughout the hills, much more than people realise. We once met one on Christmas Day on Beinn a' Ghlo—undulating through deep snow at 2,000 feet up. Ravens are resident here on the crags and were calling as I passed on up the north ridge. The hard snow patches and rims made for easy walking and the lochan was a perfect mirror of Sellotape-tin blue. Last time on the summit three of us had fallen asleep watching a sunset.

The view today was outstanding; among the very best ever, anywhere. I named over a hundred peaks and apart from the Buachailles and Aonach Eagach all the Munros to date seemed visible, even the tent-shaped summit of Ben More. In the sun and cold everything was bright as crockery.

This was a great contrast to the Ripleys' trip. Alan had gone to the doctor from Bridge of Orchy. It was suggested that swelling ankles were caused by iron deficiency. Brian wrote on November 11th: "We had decided earlier that if we couldn't do these five peaks today, we would have to pack in as we were getting too far behind schedule." Their log was brief: "Tried to get up Beinn Dorain. Turned back at 3,000 feet. Wind gusts must have been up to 80 m.p.h.—and hailing heavily." They gave up even trying to crawl, and once down pitched their tent inside a sheep shelter. 1,325 miles, 377,850 feet, 13 weeks and 230 Munros lay behind them. It must have been heart-breaking. It was as well not to have known these details as I sat on my sunny peak.

Beinn an Dothaidh (Doe), *hill of scorching*, all too literal today: I have never been sure whether the summit is as shown on the map or the point along the rim. The north side has some good hidden winter routes. There is a wide view out over the Moor of Rannoch, and Loch Tulla today was burnished from weeks of sunshine. The next peak along, Achaladair, and the next again, Chreachain, have two tops each, both facing boldy out to the Moor. Behind them, like a ball held in a

II LYON – LOCHAY
IV TRANS TAY – TUMMEL

fist, is Mhanach (Vannoch) which also has two summits the statutory mile apart. This awkward outlier was my aim first, then Chreachain, and Achaladair. Contouring to the col for Mhanach was too steep for comfort but at the peaty col I could at least leave the sack—with a label saying the owner was returning, please do not remove.

The ascent was up slopes running with melt water. Beinn Mhanach, *monk's hill* (which is perhaps why there is a large white quartz cross near the cairn), is most easily done up the Auch Glen, since Gorton Station on the Moor is no more and the Glen Lyon side is moated with a Hydro loch.

I had a brew at the sack, for the softer snow was tiring. Wending on up the burn I had a session of most erotic imaginings—reaction perhaps to the monastic existence, but one which was never repeated. We are adaptable creatures I suppose.

It took sweaty contouring and much burn-crossing to lodge on Chreachain's western top, a Meall Buidhe, one of three such named that I was to cross in 24 hours. Figures on the prow of Achaladair had a Bonington-like *contra jour* brightness. The Moor was bright with the glitter of a thousand pools. Chreachain, 3,540 feet, was the day's highest, a cone which can be seen from afar. A deep bite of corrie on the north side has a textbook lochan at its foot, a campsite for the dreamer with the cliffs above it, a view over the Moor and old Crannoch Wood and the toy-town railway below.

I overhauled two lads from a Glasgow youth group whose tents could just be seen near Gorton bothy. They had been swarming all over the hills but these two had lingered on high. They were puzzled at the derivation of Beinn a' Chreachain which is the *hill of the drinking shell*. Alas, so much like this has vanished into the past. It needs a resident community to maintain traditions.

I mentioned an odd accident I had had, not very far from their camp down on the Moor. I tripped over a guy line and a wee toe "snapped just like a twig" (so I was told). It was a bit of a nuisance as we had just arrived there to explore the Moor (the Rannoch Rush, *Scheuchzeria palustris*, grows here and in Poland and nowhere else in the world), so it was simply ignored—a hole cut in a gymshoe gave it freedom, and thus shod, I crossed the Moor twice and climbed this group of hills. A week later I hobbled into hospital back home and was immediately told to "Sit down, sir, no walking on it, just rest! . . ."

It was too hard to explain; but a real row came later when I pleaded

c

not to have it plastered as I was off to the Pyrenees for five weeks' climbing. It rapidly developed into a—"you must"—"you mustn't"—"you must" confrontation. Compromise: I went off with a bandage sprayed with something to make it firm (but not bulky) and this could come off once there—after all, a boot was as good as anything to hold the toe in place. It worked quite well.

A chunter down again, then up the very edge of Beinn Achaladair, *hill of the mower*, which gave some scrambling on bulging granite, happily in the shade. Carpets of purple saxifrage and a mountain blackbird nest were interesting. I descended Gleann Cailliche, the *glen of the old woman*, which drains these hills into Loch Lyon. An eerie passage or two about this glen can be found in Duncan Fraser's *Highland Perthshire*.

I wish I had read it beforehand; perhaps I too could have paid my respects to the eternal lady and her never-ageing family. I innocently passed Tigh-nam-Bodach, though I did notice the evidence of the old shielings: sad stones that told of summer songs long gone before the assault of the sheep. The sheep were obviously still there: the whole glen had been burnt, so I walked through a dirty, dry cloud of dust. Groups of deer went crackling off along the brittle, charred slopes.

Each spring and autumn in the eighteenth century, the people of Meggernie and latterly Chesthill came and went the score of miles from these high pastures, as folk did to the upper glens all through the Highlands. Then the pattern broke and the blackface sheep came. The lowland cities and Canadian prairies received the exiles, and the landlords grew rich from their people-cleared glens.

The only person remaining is the old Caillich who gave her name to the glen unknown centuries before. . . .

> "Tigh-nam-Bodach, living all her lone,
> Born of water, turned to stone."

I soon left the Allt Cailliche to contour—rather endlessly across those dirty slopes—round into Gleann Mhearan, a gateway glen, east of Beinn a' Chreachain. In the old days this was quite an important through route from Glen Lyon to Rannoch Moor. It was easy to envisage "caterans and raiders, drovers and packmen, Prince Charlie's men and Hanovarians passing through the defile" (A. E. Robertson).

In 1810 Thomas Telford proposed a road from Killin to Glen Spean (estimated cost, £15,360) which would use this pass—70 years before the railway was to snake round under today's hills and on by the same route to Loch Treig and the Spean.

I pitched my tent by the dwindling Mhearan burn at the junction with the Eas Fhiuran which would give my continuation east tomorrow. Today had been quite enough: 7,400 feet and 13 miles, a scorching Sabbath day's journey. Since it was Easter Sunday I broke from my daily Bible readings to go through the Easter accounts in the Gospels. Very vivid. And vital. Above the camp was an area full of hundreds of splayed roots and white, dead trunks. They rose out of the black peat like something out of C. S. Lewis: sculptures come alive, contorted and groping like starved memories of far off times reaching for the pitying sun of today. I dreamed of them under my frosty shroud that night.

Monday 15 April   BUIDHE, BUIDHE AND STUI

As soon as the sun left Gleann Mhearan the cold swept in like a tide. I took the Gaz stove to bed and soon had tea and porridge ready while still comfy—so much for roughing it. Fingers stuck to the tent pegs and the tent folded like stiff cardboard. Wordsworth could have been thinking of this hushed and secret place when he penned

> The silence that is in the starry sky,
> The sleep that is among the lonely hills.

The only sound was the dawn chatter of grouse, the very epitome of peace.

The first Munro, Meall Buidhe (Boo-ee) lay seven miles off, as the craw flees, but a wheen loner as the gangrel gangs, for another Meall Buidhe lay between. It was a Corbett which I had not been on, so was a bonus. A corkscrew route beside the wren-loud burn took me up out of the deep freeze and at once I found long-johns impossible. Changing out of them I knocked over my brew. The high moor teemed with deer —which came galloping past. Frozen bogs and snow again made for good going to the Corbett, where I snuggled in beside the cairn for a lazy hour.

Golden plovers were calling and there was the incessant summer *twee twee* of pipits. Long streamers of cloud were escaping from Loch Rannoch up on to the Moor. Ben Nevis was clear, and never have I seen it day after day like this. One day clear in ten is the usual. I heard, and then saw, a train caterpillaring round the edge of the Moor: the morning down-train for Mallaig. For once the sight did not give me itchy feet. A snipe began drumming and a brace of ptarmigan dawdled past. It was full spring "come laughing to the hills at last" (W. K. Holmes). A grinning dog fox trotted by only twenty yards off and never even noticed me. The train pulled out of Rannoch Station and became a faint grumble in the distance.

I roused myself from the lethargy of my perch and went down by an odd, deep slot, choked and overhung with snow, then pulled up the emptiness beyond. In the middle of nowhere I picked up the tracks of a vehicle—not even ghillies walk now it seems—and later I heard a vehicle coming but when I breasted a shoulder and could see for miles, there was no sign of it, and nothing appeared. A phantom vehicle? Nonsense! Or was it?

In a glen I could name there is a house set back from the road and reached by a narrow, fenced-in track on which you could neither turn nor pass another vehicle. The farm folk were expecting visitors and sat looking out into the winter night for their arrival. At last a car pulled off into their half-mile drive, headlights weaving through the trees. Then the lights vanished; and no friends arrived. They felt a bit worried, yet if anything had happened surely someone would have walked up for help. Before they could do anything another car swung into the drive and they watched its lights come steadily all the way up. It was the expected friends—and they had seen no other car. Twice more that winter they spotted lights turn into their drive yet nobody arrived. A neighbouring house also saw them, asking who had visited, when nobody had. No tracks were left on the muddy track. Explain it who will.

At one o'clock I reached Meall Buidhe, busy chanting French vocabularies, another intended regular activity which never succeeded —there was always too much of interest. Two unsuspecting lines of deer crossed ahead, stopped, sniffed and then took to their heels. A second later a fox trotted into view. He saw me, gave a splendid double take, and also shot off.

The Munro Buidhe I remember from a tough trip in poverty days. Joe and I hitched to Bridge of Orchy station one Friday night, then took the morning train to Gorton and reached the summit by a long flog over the Moor. We dropped down to Glen Lyon and after rescuing a lamb from a cattle grid, spent a miserable night, soaked through in a sopping tent. On the Sunday we crossed to Glen Lochay and traversed Beinn Chaluim to Crianlarich, then hitched home to Fife. Car-bound days cannot equal such doings. The sheer hell of that night. The look on the girl's face in the Crianlarich Hotel when we asked for second afternoon teas. Such weather was the normal for April.

I dropped down Coire Pharlain to the loch but it was oven hot in the corrie and a golden pool in the burn was irresistible. I struggled out of clammy garments for a real bath: soaping and diving in several times and drip-drying in the sun. Some April! Pink pincushions were on the larches which framed the loch. The Stui rose across the dam, seamed with shadows I was glad to see. There was no passage across the top, so it was down and up. A Glasgow family yelled something about it being "a grand day for a wee walk . . .".

Stuchd an Lochain (The Stui) is a well-scalloped peak which fills the view looking up Glen Lyon. An ink-spot lochan lies hidden in a northern corrie. The mile round its rim was grassy and soft so I left my boots behind with the rucksack and enjoyed a barefoot romp. What anyone would make of the tracks across the snow patches. . . .

One of Scotland's earliest recorded hill ascents was of the Stui in 1590 when mad Colin Campbell of Glen Lyon ascended it. The description of the corrie rim "beetling over a deep circular mountain tarn" (Lochan nan Cat) is accurate. One wonders at the rest. Having driven a herd of goats over the cliffs, the Campbell tried the same game with one of his attendants, who only escaped by his quick wits.

I left the cairn at 6.30, yet at the back of seven was knocking at the keeper's door at Cashlie, in Glen Lyon, to the south. Glen Lyon is steeped in history as befits the longest glen in the country. It gives a cross-section, almost, of all history, geography and everything else. From my route down I could see the sites of at least four of the many ancient forts which tradition associates with Fionn, whose legendary home was here in the days before history.

Here too is the Bhacain, a stone shaped like the head of a hound, to which Fionn tied his great hunter Bran: Bran of yellow paws and black flanks and a chain of pure gold. Here too one of the several "testing stones"—to prove an aspirant warrior's strength. The Bhacain had another use they say, for under it would creep the young lassies of the glen, seeking its mysterious powers before heading to the fearful low-lands for the harvest time. They did not have The Pill in those days.

The terriers brought out the keeper and I thankfully received my parcel. I mentioned the odd coincidence of two Buidhes in the day, each with a fox; Mr MacDougall was, I'm sure, glad they were not his concern, but no doubt the word would be passed on.

Half a mile down the road lay tiny Stronuich Reservoir, and a swaying, slatted bridge let me round it to where the Allt Laoisich came down in a noisy waterfall. As so often, there was only just time to whip the tent up and take a photo of the site before the light faded. A gargantuan meal followed, for most caches had one tinned meal at least. Tonight it was hamburgers, carrots and sweetcorn—plus pears and creamed rice, plus the usual soup and coffee. "Roughing it"?

Many years ago, a gang of us were tramping home down all the miles of Glencoe to the hostel, when we were stopped at a lay-by. A card table had been spread with a lace tablecloth and on it was arranged a dainty afternoon tea: delicate china, silver teapot, cake-stand—the lot. Enjoying this was a minute, ancient aristocrat of a figure, dressed in black in the style of Queen Victoria herself, watched over by a uniformed chauffeur. We chatted away amicably and did not refuse the offered sandwiches. The crusts had been cut off, naturally, and a frilly doily edged the pile. As we parted, she said, "Well, it was so nice talking to you boys. I do so enjoy roughing it."

It became a bit of a catch phrase.

Tuesday 16 April   THE FOREST OF MAMLORN

"Forest" perhaps needs explaining, for you will find few trees on these hills. A thousand years ago, yes; it was all forest, the great wood of Caledon. Now only a few tatty remnants of it survive: the Black Wood of Rannoch, Crannach Wood, bits of Speyside and Dee, by Loch Maree. . . . For the rest, skeleton branches rising from the peat bogs are all the signs remaining. With the destruction of the woods went the last wolves and robbers; though it might be argued that these survive now in the cities under cover of the concrete jungles.

The sporting estates of the Victorian era used the term "deer forest" and because these often followed natural boundaries, such as groups of mountains, the term has stuck: you have the Mamore Forest, the Forest of Atholl, the Forest of Mamlorn and so on, which may, or may not, have trees and may, or may not, have deer.

"Maim Laerne is the King's Forest—very rich in deer, lying upon Brae Urchay, Brae Lyon and Brae Lochay" an old account tells. These braes were, and are, a tangle of peaks, steep and broken, threaded by deep passes and tricky rivers but access is easy by car now, from the east, up Glen Lochay or Glen Lyon. A Hydro road links them over the pass of the Lairig nan Lunn but is kept inviolate by locked gates. It would not do to let the public, whose taxes built it, enjoy a natural round drive!

I woke to a clammy world of fog and set off up my river in a dewy wetness. Sheep loomed large as elephants and deer "broke, and went outraged and sniffing into the dark wind". After an hour, however, I broke through the cloud into the sun. I left the tent spread to dry and gradually discarded garments on the way up Meall Ghaordie which is generally a lumpy and unimpressive hill. A quartz vein breaks through near the summit. I could hear the dogs at Cashlie giving tongue, the noise filtering up through the valley cloud.

After fetching the tent, the seven miles west to Heasgarnich probably gave the hardest going so far: very rough, deep heather with endless peat bogs and schisty crags—and hares and ptarmigan forever exploding at my feet. At one stage I sat for a long time watching deer which were browsing just below me, and then spent half an hour at a pool which seemed 10 per cent water and 90 per cent frog spawn. It was teeming with frogs, but at my first step they vanished. Slowly, eyes would rise above the water, but it took twenty minutes of immobility before they ventured forth again. For days, now, the dried-up peat pools had held shiny dollops of spawn. Mating was in full swing here. Two, gripped tightly together, went swimming off with legs kicking in perfect co-ordination. I finally scattered them all again when I could no longer contain my laughter at one frog which simply could not co-ordinate its legs into a breast stroke.

This happy procrastination could not put off the next pull, but again it was for a bonus Corbett, Meall nan Subh, 2,638 feet, a frustrating series of knolls, bogs and detours. How you could be sure of it in mist, I don't know. It had gone noon, so after crossing the Hydro road (Lairig nan Lunn) I lunched on Beinn Heasgarnich's massive slopes.

I paddled in the burn happily; then created a David Livingstone sort of hat to protect my ears which were slowly frying in the sun. Heasgarnich is a big brute of a hill, a heartbreak sometimes, but I have always been lucky with weather and company.

I first plodded up it during an S.M.C. Meet along with Messrs Gorrie, Fraser and Hartog. The last was recovering from frostbite acquired on the Mustagh Tower trip, Barclay Fraser was to climb with me in many foreign countries, and Charlie Gorrie was soon to teach at the same school where he was nicknamed Beinn a' Chlachair—because it sounded like a single malt. We had taken in this hill from Braehead on a Killin to Skye trek and also on several day trips.

The whole hill is a gentle-sloping chaos: peat bogs and fast streams. I followed up the Allt Tarsuinn. It was lined with perfect camping swards and I passed on sadly. A scarp turned the river into tumbling falls. It was cruelly hot. The burn rose in a lochan only 200 feet below the summit so must be one of the highest, and the glaciers of Heasgarnich must have been among the last to disappear. It was a relief to break over the snow rim to the cairn.

I wrung out the sponge pad from my back and dealt with a melted mess of chocolate. Ghaordie looked a thousand miles away. Chreachain dominated the other side. The sun glared into my eyes as I walked off round the rim.

I left a questionnaire. It was found the next weekend by Erland Flett who had just moved into the flat of another friend, Robert Aitken, who himself was to find a questionnaire in July on Lurg Mhor. Erland I later met in the Atlas and we shared a flooded Dormobile refuge in Marrakech. Scotland is still a comparatively small world. There are more climbers in Manchester, for instance.

The ridge down was steep and solid. The col had the name Loch na Baintighearna on it but there was no loch—just an excess of peat hags. They were dry and easy to cross. I brewed and spied out Creag Mhor above. Could I do one more Munro?

Several years ago when Ian and Mary McLeod had just started climbing we had climbed Heasgarnich out of valley cloud, rather like today. It was in January, but so mild for weeks that we left axes behind. We came down to the col to add Creag Mhor. Its north-east flank is usually a sopping, hanging garden in summer. In those inversion conditions we soon found the wet had turned to ice and the very steep, mixed ground was highly dangerous for novices. To climb down was the more dangerous alternative so we went on up, right cannily, till we found our way barred completely by a band of rock-hard snow, the remnant of a cornice. There were rude remarks about the value of certain mountain certificates!

When in doubt, eat. My jammy knife gave me the answer and I turned to work on the snow band with it. It was easier than expected and I soon had a staircase spiralling up to the ridge. I crept down again to carry up the dog and the other two gaily ascended after, with all the confidence of ignorance. They would not do it so casually now!

Having avoided supplying Benny Humble with some statistics that day I was a bit cautious now, as I sat, again with no ice-axe. But I was up and down in an hour. The snow was soft, the crags illusory, and without the pack the going just felt blissful. I landed right at the slim cairn, circled north to the first snow gully and bumslid down a thousand feet to end 50 yards from the gear.

I followed down the Allt Bad a' Mhaim, contoured and finally pitched on the 1,000-foot contour which I hoped would keep me above valley clouds. It was another delectable camp. (Did I ever have one that was not?) By the wending River Lochay curlews were bubbling, one of the greatest of all wild sounds. Pied pipers and snipe added their contribution and wheatears were about. This was perhaps the "essential silence" that Stevenson mentions.

Wednesday 17 April A ROOF OVER MY HEAD

Peewits and curlews woke me in the morning again, disembodied voices calling through a clammy mist. I could hear the birds' wings as they went off from my route up the river into the folds of the hill. The grey stones of a dead village seemed unspeakably sad in that shrouded emptiness. History is a long tale of the many imposed upon by the few and the tragedy is that so many of the many do not care.

I hoped for three Munros today: *Malcolm's peak*—Beinn Chaluim— to the west of this pass, then Meall Glas and Sgiath Chuil to the east. It would be a real challenge to do Ghaordie to Sgiath Chuil in a day. It would be much harder than the Mamores for instance. Any takers?

Chaluim is a finer peak than most descriptions would hint at. As a winter hill it is at its best. Again I suppose I have been lucky with the day and the company. If you want to be different do it from Auch; oddly enough you see it to advantage from near Bridge of Orchy. I left my rucksack among a dead forest of pine stumps behind the dead village and climbed up into the mist. The crags of Stob a' Bhiora might repay winter exploration; today they were a barrier which I tried to outflank but ended by climbing on the easy side. The weather became lighter and warmer, and on the eastern prow of Chaluim it cleared.

The view was fantastic! Yesterday's cloud had been merely ankle deep, today the thick whiteness wrapped up to the very throats of the hills. A blazing, pulsing, cloud sea reached as far as eye could see at about the 2,000 ft level, the inversion to end them all. Out of this white world rose the detached heads of all the great hills. I raced to the summit in a panic of disbelief and then sat to marvel.

Perhaps it would last till Meall Glas! I did some rapid christies down the snow flanks and plunged into the clammy clouds again. The compass seemed a sad thing in that romantic setting and it was used impatiently, if dourly, to find my gear. I followed a burn up Meall Glas but it was a doubtful navigation aid as it had innumerable forks not on the map. However, after a scramble up some garnet-splattered rocks the cairn broke from the cloud a hundred yards off. I was just too late. Patches of blue appeared overhead but even a long meal stop failed to stay the steaming, rising flow.

I went along to a minor top, then down and across the sea of bog which forms the watershed. Somewhere in the mist a shepherd was calling to his dog. It cleared on the way up Sgiath Chuil, the *back wing*, but the view was quite tame and ordinary. I sat on the knuckle of summit rocks and wrote some letters, brought my log up to date and left a questionnaire again. It was not found for over two weeks which is perhaps judgement enough on this dull hill.

My first visit to it was anything but dull. Robert and I were young and ignorant then, which is my only excuse for our day of fiascos. His mother had dropped us up Glen Lochay and fixed a tea-time meeting in Glen Dochart. We made our way up Sgiath Chuil without difficulty. The O.S. unhelpfully cut off our map not far to the south but going that way we could hardly miss the River Dochart so this did not really matter. (I was using the same map today. The price on the front said 1/6d.)

Not long after leaving the gale-blown summit shots rang out (it was October) and a bullet passed so close that we threw ourselves flat. We did not "hit the dust" so much as the mud—black, slimy, peaty stuff. We carried a fair quantity of it on with us, as we made a cautious, C.C.F. trained right-flanking movement to get behind the enemy. Eventually we hit some scrub. There were people on a zig-zag new road, so we had some more crawling about. At last it seemed clear. We felt we had done not badly for the first time under fire. We did an "over the top" sort of charge down a shaly cutting, on to the road, giggling and tumbling down—to land at the brogued feet of an imposing woman who bulged and bristled all the way up to her deerstalker hat.

Her immaculate tweeds contrasted somewhat with our grimy army surplus.

Her eye alighted on my trailing length of scarf.

"Is that a Dollar scarf, boy?"

It was either that or St Mirren, and as soon as I opened my mouth I would betray which; I confessed it was.

"Ah! My children go to Dollar . . ."

We parted most amicably. War games over, we cut corners down to the Dochart which here does a fair imitation of the Limpopo. After casting up and down we had found neither bridge nor shallows. After an hour we gave up and reverted to the C.C.F. stuff. Carrying our boots and clothes aloft we made a chilly, bellybutton-deep crossing. From the other side we could see round the next bend; there, to be sure, was a bridge.

Still only half dressed we were distracted by a thrashing among the whin bushes on the bank, and found a ram stuck with its horns entwined in the fence. It had bled its forehead. We struggled with no success and retreated much pricked and battered. Still in bare feet I set off across two fields to call at what looked like a shepherd's cottage. The fields had recently held cattle. They also grew ambushing rosettes of thistles.

Fortunately there was a shepherd so we gave him that problem and turned to ours which we now decided was to forestall Robert's mother calling out a search for two overdue walkers. We thumbed like mad. A lorry stopped almost at once.

We babbled out our story over the next mile or two as we charged along.

"What hotel was it you were meeting in for tea?" the driver asked.

"Luib. Why?"

"Ah weel now, Luib's back the way. Yon's the Lix Toll."

We did not receive any further lifts however hard we exercised our thumbs and Robert's mother, like Queen Victoria, was "not amused".

History, fortunately, only repeated itself in broad outline today. I could see perfectly clearly where Auchessan lay, with a bridge over to the main road, but even from a distance I could hear the bustle of heavy traffic on the road. I did not fancy dodging along it for five miles. I would stay on this side of the valley.

That was a mistake. First I had a temper-fraying tramp through dusty, clawing heather, then a new track led away *uphill* again, directly into the hot sun, only to hand me over to the purgatory of new forest plantings. I was above Loch Iubhair (*Loch of the yews*, another site of Fingalian legends) and between it and Loch Dochart there seemed to be a chance of crossing; the stinking, dangerous road suddenly appearing benign and welcoming. I struggled down only to find the linking river was twenty yards wide and about as deep. To add to the torture a boat lay on the bank—the other bank. I could not see if it had oars. I was quite prepared to swim over for it, then fetch my clothes and rucksack. But my problem solved itself. A shepherd began gathering in the field opposite. I slunk away. I would not appeal to him; like most I was readier to be taken for a thief than a fool.

I went through my repertoire of invective, which spans from Arabic to Zulu (they say travel broadens the mind). I passed a ruined house. Out in the loch was a ruined castle. It had been captured once by the MacGregors in mid winter when they simply walked out over the ice and surprised the occupants. Each winter whooper swans return to it. It is an idyllic spot, especially on the other side. I battered through decaying woods, then climbed a small hill, then crossed a last marshy mile to the viaduct for Crianlarich.

It was a weary and sun-battered traveller who reported to police constable Kaye who had a parcel of goodies. I staggered up to the hostel with it—a juicy meal: tea, milk, fruit, coffee went with the actual food, all quickly made out of tins. The hostel was an old barracks of a place, the military atmosphere maintained by the temporary warden. He had the pots sized off from the left even, and he tested the heat of the range by spitting on it.

There were several hitching Aussies and South Africans, three noisy lads planning Ben More, a quiet couple and Peter and his Paw from Lanark. It had an old-fashioned hostel atmosphere. I washed my underwear and went out to watch the sun setting on Chaluim. I gave it a wave—only it was not a wave . . .

Thursday 18 April   CRIANLARICH STILL

I was first up, at eight o'clock, which was after all a long lie for me. Mops were duly issued by numbers and I was paraded off to swab the ablutions. I was given permission to hang my washing on the line while away for the day. With my flannels rolled down and a pullover on I could pass as a tourist. The shop was helpful and kept my purchases till 4 p.m. when the barracks would reopen. I had a day free. A twelve-hour pass.

At the station I sat in the café and read the paper. A train came in and there was a brief bedlam. I went down to the hotel for further festering. I had given David a ring the night before to fix up meeting Barclay and give a list of "wants". This was a statutory rest day and tomorrow was an easy day too. I was half tempted to add Ben More and Stobinian, but the left tendon was playing up a bit. A rest would ease it, which it did; I had no further complaints—apart from a pair of fried ears. I do not think I have ever been so sunburnt. I had lunch in the hotel and then lazed the afternoon away by the river, reading. Morale was fine and there was little to do. Section two was over, the tally now 74,000 feet climbed and about 207 miles walked.

Grapefruit juice; fried steak with onions, tomatoes, spuds and corn; gooseberries and creamed rice; real coffee . . .

The trio had done Ben More all right, Peter and his Paw had been up An Caisteall—in self defence I told something of my recent doings. A Kenya medic and girl friend swelled the ranks. At ten to eleven the lights flashed. A Scots voice muttered something about Barlinnie. At eleven the patrol came round and the lights went out.

III

FURTHEST SOUTH

"To every man there openeth
A way and ways and a way.
And the high soul climbs the high way
And the low soul gropes the low
And in between on the misty flats
The rest drift to and fro.
But to every man there openeth
A high way and a low
And every man decideth the way his soul shall go."

JOHN OXENHAM

Friday 19 April   CAMP IN THE KING'S FIELD

The walk from Crianlarich west along Strath Fillan was on tarred roads, so I rose early to make the trip before traffic took away any of its enjoyment. This really gave me an extra lazy day, as Barclay Fraser was coming up and I wanted to do the Laoigh group with him.

The glen is named after the seventh-century saint who completed the work of conversion here. A piece of his crozier (the quigrich) and a bell from the priory (the bernane) are two of the priceless relics in the National Museum of Antiquities in Edinburgh. The bell was stolen by an English traveller in the seventeenth century and the crozier ended in Canada with the last of the hereditary custodian's descendants; so their survival is something of a miracle.

This and some fourteenth century history filled my mind as I walked along enjoying the prosperous strath scenery—something I was not to see much of in the weeks ahead. The bridge was in its usual battered state. It seems that some motorist is always knocking it down quicker than the squad can repair it. I crossed and turned up to camp in the King's Field—Dail Righ. The O.S., as with many historic sites, keeps this one a secret. It was annoying to find local litter dumped there but even that turned to the good when I found some interesting old bottles which were collectors' pieces.

Robert the Bruce retreated this way after his defeat at the battle of Methven (near Perth) in 1306, but then met the MacDougalls of Lorn who turned him back to Crianlarich. Somewhere near Loch Dochart he was ambushed by three scouts while protecting the rear of his small party. He managed to kill all three foes, quite a feat in itself, but had to part with his plaid in doing so. Its brooch became a MacDougall family heirloom till they were burnt out, in 1647, during Covenanting troubles. It vanished, but turned up 178 years later in Campbell hands! Bruce made many journeys among the Highlands and Islands and is a really great figure of history, despite the tarnish of popular legends.

Barclay rolled up in the afternoon in his V.W. conversion—which had previously helped provide a base for a fine climbing trip to Corsica. We had climbed together in the Atlas and Andes as well, all since Barclay had "retired". He brewed, and then acted as chef while I ploughed through the mail, glanced at the newspapers, looked at Tatras slides and decided I could not really accept a wedding invitation for the next day.

I was up late by candle light, still nibbling away at little things. The new lightweight trousers and jacket had come from Tiso, which took away a few more pounds of the weight that went everywhere with me. It was Chay Blyth who said: "My formula was simple—careful planning, attention to detail, hard work, the right tools for the job, and a big slice of help from Up Above."

With which I would agree entirely.

Saturday 20 April QUEEN LAOIGH

A friend of mine who has an odd habit of sexing his hills always talks of Beinn Laoigh (Lui) as female. If this is so, then she is a queen among hills. It might also explain why for the first time on the trip the hills were clouded thickly—but perhaps this change was retribution for sweeping the extreme south anti-clockwise, since it is always more propitious to progress *car deseil*, or clockwise.

I had risen at six to dash off the odd letter while Barclay dealt with breakfast. We set off at the back of nine, crossing to join the Allt Coire Dubhchraig at a remnant of old Scots pine wood. There is a great deal of planting all round this group of hills. There was once quite a settlement by the Eas Anie but it has gone completely. The scars on the hillside are old lead mines. Several companies made and lost fortunes mining here before the workings finally closed in 1923. The Campbells once wrecked the mines in 1745 as they were then run by an English

Jacobite, Sir Robert Clifton, but you can still pan for gold by the King's Field.

Apart from one waterfall our route held little of note, and the melt water and snow soon soaked our feet. It was an easy plod, apart from trying to keep up with the galloping Fraser. Beinn Dubhchraig failed to give a view though it stayed dry. We headed for Beinn Oss, *hill of the elk*, which hints at the antiquity of our hill names. It is a rockier hill: mica schist country again. The top just failed to clear so we ate on the col before Laoigh. I left my rucksack there too before the climb up to 3,708 feet, which makes Laoigh queen indeed over this corner of the kingdom.

Laoigh is a double headed peak with a rim edging the glaciated *corrie of the winds*, Coire Gaothaich, to the north east. This has been a popular winter climbing peak since the 1890's when every slight rib and gully was dutifully pioneered.

After some conversation, we had to "twine"—Barclay off down the north and I to the south—after adding Beinn a' Chleibh, a small afterthought to Laoigh, being just 3,008 feet. It deserves its name, *hill of the basket*. It is a real outlier if you have come from Cononich side yet hardly worth a trip on its own. The Oban road approaches are well defended by plantings. The summit has several cairns to confuse you in mist. After this pilgrimage I flanked back across Laoigh's skirts to my rucksack on the other col and set off on to new ground—something which always raised fresh enthusiasm.

I was soon below cloud level and having to take off my shirt again. To the south lay an area of gentle watersheds and a maze of bog and stream which the Hydro have tapped and led into a complex scheme. Despite these man-made incursions it is an area with a feel of wilderness. The bogs were dry for once and made walking easy on the fibrous hags. The whole area was alive with deer. I have an African cousin who once doubted if Scotland had any "wide, open spaces". I wished he was there to watch one herd charge off, scattering some silly sheep, splashing through a sparkle of river and streaming into the far distance until they became a mere feel of movement. As most of the herds had hardly bothered to move to let me by, I was quite puzzled at this obvious panic and its cause.

I had intended to drop down to Glen Fyne and do a sackless ascent of Argyll's Beinn Buidhe the next day, but the lure of a high camp was too great, and as by now fitness was so built-in that weight did not

III FURTHEST SOUTH

matter, I decided to stay up. I followed an aqueduct which was tapping all the side streams of a glen and actually taking the water back over the glen's watershed to drain into Loch Shira. Near the loch I saw what looked like a cave but proved to be a split boulder. In its lee I pitched the tent and thankfully got into bare feet while the billy boiled.

Glen Shira was once home for Rob Roy when the rest of Scotland was made too hot for him. Neil Munro set his novel *Gillian the Dreamer* in the Glen too. At its foot is the castle which is the seat of Clan Campbell.

I had not seen a soul since parting from Barclay but the loneliness was no hardship as some warned it would be. It led to a quiet routine and a blissful contentment. I usually had tea ready by the time the tent was up. At the lunch stop I soaked dried vegetables and these would go on to cook along with potato, macaroni, rice or some other stodge, plus the meat, usually tinned for value. Soup would clean out the dish and I would finish with apple flakes or some other fruit. This night I had a mix of eggs, cheese, chicken, macaroni and three veg—so skipped the soup.

I watched the sun down behind the *hill of the fairy*, Beinn an Sithein— grey shafts of light and banners of cloud. Gillian was not the only dreamer in these parts . . .

Sunday 21 April   REST AND BE THANKFUL

Six o'clock seemed too raw to rise so I slept on a bit. A sneaky wind "annoyed the stove" as my log put it. The hills were cloud-capped. A big burn gave a pleasant scramble up through the shambolic schisty landscape. A nesting pair of dippers scolded me out of their territory. Above a lonely corrie the north-east summit poked through the mist so I skirted it to gain the ridge beyond. Everything was exaggerated in the billowing vapours and I had an enjoyable plod up to the trig point, though, sadly, no vuidhe.

Beinn Buidhe has quite a personality and is not a bad wee hill. Glen Fyne and Glen Shira are more normal routes in to it, but the way from the Lochy to the north should now be avoided owing to plantings.

I retraced a bit, then broke down the steep, craggy slopes of the summit ridge to gain the extensive upland boggy miles. The black peat was marked by thousands of deer tracks and the beasts were mincing about as I walked through their area. I followed the glen down behind

Newton Hill to reach Glen Fyne—which runs down to the loch of the same name. I stopped at the upper limit of the trees in the burn to delight in the view. The spring flowers were all out now: primroses, violets, celandine. An eagle was working the high slopes and later, below, I saw three buzzards.

There was also a field of cows to go through; these I did not mind but I was not so sure about the big black bull with a ring in his nose. Loch Fyne was a return to sea level, which I had left at Loch Leven, Glencoe, and would not meet again for many weeks—not until Knoydart. Even working up the North West I saw remarkably little of the sea. Some day I will have to go on a coastal journey to make up for it.

I had a pleasant lunch at Cairndow Inn, with its cosy atmosphere. Keats and his friend Charles Brown had been there in 1818. The poet was then 23 and had less than three years to live, yet did a tramp of 642 miles in 42 days from Lancaster to Inverness via the Burns Country, Loch Lomond, Inveraray, Mull, Iona, Ben Nevis and Loch Ness. Coming here they had already done fifteen miles before breakfast, hoping to stop at an inn called "Rest and Be Thankful". They found this was only the top of a pass, not an Inn, which lay here, five miles on. Ben Nevis was quite a good effort for the period. You can guess the weather from the lines Keats wrote about it: "I will climb through the clouds and exist."

My walk was a lingering one for Kilmorich Church, white and clean-lined, delayed me; it is octagonal in shape. Then the gardens of Strone House needed to be looked at. They were a fabulous explosion to my moorland eyes: spring bulbs, geans, azaleas. I walked up lengthy Glen Kinglas. The old road ran parallel with the new and gave safer walking.

I once acted as a courier on tourist buses laid on for the American navy which was visiting Oban. The circular tour brought them here, and a stop was made for the men to photograph some highland cattle. ("Say bud, why do all your cows wear winter woollies?") I assured them that the beasts were quite docile despite appearances and a few hardy souls went up the hillside to take close-ups. Highlanders are docile. They are also curious; so ambled forward to meet the sailors who paused, then retreated a bit—which only encouraged the cows to come on. In no time at all the sailors were running pell-mell for the fence with the cows lumbering after. Nothing I could say would convince them I had not deliberately fixed the whole thing.

At Butterbridge near the head of Glenkinglas I pitched the tent in the lee of the old bridge, brewed—and fell asleep. It was the Rest and Be Thankful after all. The shepherd was not at home so I set off at 5 p.m. to add Beinn an Lochain, another Munro. It overlooks Loch Restil and is a craggy, twisted peak with a double summit. There are some quite big crags and, on the north side, debris from a colossal rockfall like the one which holds the famous Shelter Stone in the Cairngorms. I wended off across the face to make some fun and came upon the decapitated body of a lamb. A fox had been before me. The view on top was dreich and grey for once and the restless buzz of traffic hauling through the pass of the A83 was a constant reminder of things I had almost forgotten. I had a look to the Arran hills and the Paps of Jura before running down in one fell swoop—delighted to see a smoking chimney.

The Beatons had been away fishing. "Too dry" was the complaint for that game. He was not too pleased to hear of the fox. I retreated with my parcel to enjoy the goodies of a tinned meal. The first soup was a bit of a disaster for I made it, not with mushroom, but Horlicks' powder.

Big Ben Ime made a bold shape in the night sky. Headlights waved across its lower slopes like feelers as the weekenders poured off back to Glasgow. And still it had not rained this trip! The cars thinned and the valley bottom became gruey cold and dead—as dead as the dead sheep by the roadside.

Monday 22 April   THE ARROCHAR ALPS

I had a short and easy day as I particularly wanted to spend the night at a beautiful spot I had seen years ago. I left camp in a brittle blue morning, and had walked on the road for only a few minutes when I was offered a lift.

There were lay-bys in plenty but no litter bins and in the end I had to bury my things deep in the wood, piling on stones to ensure that they were not dug up by animals. A Land-Rover was going off up to Abyssinia and I gave the driver a bag of extra food to leave with the Beatons. I found a cool channel to "burn-up" again and eventually left it with a nice back and knee climb: back on rock, and knees on old snow wedged in the gully. I left my rucksack below Ime and went off to do Narnain first. It is a hill with some climbing but is overshadowed by the scope on the Cobbler across the valley. For wet days, though, it can offer some titillating subterranean routes. You can actually climb right through the hill. In one of its tighter spots one of my lads once managed to jam his climbing helmet and in his struggles ended up dangling from this rather unusual "chock".

The Arrochar Alps are riddled with caves and howffs of all sizes. Some overgrown gashes can provide booby-traps every bit as dangerous as crevasses. A night in a cave here is admirably described by Alastair Borthwick in *Always a Little Further*, possibly the funniest book ever written about the hills. These hills were very much the playground of the Glasgow lads in the hard days of the depression. Keats' cry: "I will climb through the clouds and exist" would have found an echo of sentiment round their howff fires.

This group provided a surge in climbing standards, and in the whole outlook of climbing, which is all too often missed in the histories of the game. John Cunningham was doing hard climbs here before certain folk-heroes down south were ever heard of. Jock Nimlin was the main pre-war pioneer, then later names like Cunningham, Smith, MacInnes appeared. They seem to have a remarkable survival record.

It was possible to make Narnain's truncated plateau by climbing on the flanks a bit. The Cobbler stood across the way in dramatic shadows. Its earlier name was Ben Arthur, for this is yet another area which lays claim to the Arthurian legends. At the cairn I found a clean hanky and a pair of woollen socks. Some one must have known my needs exactly.

In pre-nylon days four of us once took an awful pasting on these hills. Our tents were at Loch Restil, and back at them we stripped and dived into sleeping bags, dumping all our clothes into a blanket. This sodden bundle we weighed at home the next day. It averaged that we had each carried down ten pounds of water, and in those days any child could tell you a gallon of water weighs ten pounds.

Beinn Ime, the *butter mountain*—perhaps to balance the Buttermilk Burn which flows down to the torpedo station on Loch Long—is the highest in the group, though it fails to produce anything exceptional. Its best feature is a stepped east ridge down which I had once taken a party from Ardroy, our county's Outdoor Centre at Lochgoilhead. Another group had been camping at its foot and I said then that I would do likewise some day. I set off for it now.

I managed to find a good place for a standing glissade off the north ridge and left a swinging track of eight linked turns like some giant skier. I pitched my tent in a nook, up above the valley, so it was part of the view: an ochreous, secret place that looked out to the knobbly hill of A' Chrois. It was only midday.

Sun and shadow battled it out and I moved in and out of the tent to match, like an alpine weatherpiece. My log entry ended: "Little new this section as so well known of old. Write home. Wash undies. Go through the Route Book changing odd things for the better—lots of time walking to think about it. Feet fine, tendons no bother now. Ears like fried spam though! A bath would be a treat. Sponge over chilly. A slow chicken and rice meal. Day just goes."

Tuesday 23 April   DOON THE WATER

Ben Vane was a mere 1,400 feet above the camp, which I left rather thankfully. It had been a lumpy, sloping site and I seemed only to fall deeply asleep when it was time to get up. I went round over the north flank so that I could leave the rucksack and then nip up and down the peak. A little reedy pool reflected the snowy bulk of Beinn Ime like a galleon half seen through bottle-glass, a bronchial redstart was praising the sunshine; altogether superb—and morale reacted accordingly. From the summit Buidhe looked just like the Fife Lomonds in outline; the Cobbler appeared to have an elephant standing on top; Loch Lomond was smitten into silver. Ben Vane may only scrape home as a Munro by three feet but like many a Corbett or lesser peak the view is all the better for that. Very seldom do the big hill summits give the best views. Here, there had been interesting folds in the mica, and the summit is littered with wavy plates of it. I've seen inferior sculpture at the Academy!

I collected the sack and bundled down to Loch Sloy with its soiled, man-made alterations: a dam with a drought-lined loch, double rows of pylons, scrap concrete. . . . The water is led through to the Inveruglas power station above Loch Lomond, a scheme opened in 1950, the Hydro's first.

The heat of the concrete in the sun seemed to be attracting a plague of black flies, and crossing the dam was like something out of a horror film. I was waving my hat in front of my face in an effort to see. The gutter was half an inch deep in dead flies. At least they did not bite and they soon dropped off once I was on the slope beyond.

I left my tent tied to a pylon to dry, then set off up Ben Vorlich. To distinguish it from the Perthshire Vorlich, near Lochearnhead, it is referred to as "Argyll's Ben Vorlich" though it is in Dunbartonshire and both names, I suppose, will go with regional changes. W. K. Holmes in his gentle book *Tramping Scottish Hills* has a chapter headed "Argyll's Ben Vorlich". W. K. H. was an old man who befriended our gang of enthusiasts when we were youngsters roaming the Ochils from Dollar. Our outlook owes a lot to his teaching.

The way up from the dam leads to some areas of fallen rock which are a weird sight. The Shelter Stone is a pebble in comparison; here, you can climb right into the bowels of the earth it seems. The final slope is a real contrast, the trig point standing almost indecently stark from the green slope of grass. There is another summit 100 yards to the north. Take your pick.

The eastern approaches are long—and beware of the Little Hills; they are an endless succession of bumps and tops. From the dam Vorlich was just two hours up and down, even with some fun among the "Narnia Boulders". There was nothing left to make a brew so I set off down the Hydro road to the banks of Loch Lomond. The glen was full of displaying wheatears, bobbing and flitting their white rumps and darting up into the air for love. Interesting that the old English for this bird is the apt "white arse" but the Victorians changed it when that word had slid down the scale of propriety. In Gaelic it is *clachoran*— little one of the stones.

On the heights the only sign of spring had been the posturings of the ptarmigan, but walking down Coiregrogain it was flaunted in the vivid larch, the uncurling bracken fronds and the extravagance of flowers.

I reached the road at Inveruglas. In 1753 James Wolfe (of Quebec fame) spent some miserable weeks building the road here. He had little good to say of place or people. The tourist boom was still to come, soon enough for Smollett in *Humphrey Clinker* to write, "This is justly stiled the Arcadia of Scotland; and I don't doubt it may vie with Arcadia in everything but climate." Today it was Arcadia, even in climate.

I went down to the Caravan Park and of course the McNivens were at lunch, but he kindly came and showed me where the canoe was waiting. When we turned it over there was some confetti which boded ill for the parcel. It was a mess of polythene and string with only the tins surviving. So no brewing there. A can of coke soon went, though!

I sat by the loch to tidy things up and do some food planning, then paddled off for Tarbet at 1.30. An unwanted jar of jam I donated to the nearest caravan. The commuting owner took my mail to post in Glasgow, which would puzzle the recipients. The paddle down the loch was enjoyable though very hot and the glare off the water was as bad as sun off snow. Although only 20 feet above sea level, Loch Lomond is over 600 feet deep off Tarbet, and has the largest surface area of any British loch.

It is strangely divided into a highland and a lowland section: the former fiord-like, narrow and long, the latter open and covered with woody islands—which gave rise to legends about "floating islands". Its waters supply a whole range of needs—even as far away as Grangemouth on the Forth.

I looked at Wallace's Isle and Inveruglas Isle—the latter has the ruins of a MacFarlane stronghold which was sacked by Cromwell. This was MacFarlane land in the olden days when they had a reputation akin to Rob Roy's, and the moon was known as "MacFarlane's Lantern".

Neil Munro once wrote a description of pulling an oar that went something like "at the end of the first mile you think you are going to die, at the end of the second you decide to keep on till you do die, at the end of the third you find yourself looking round and enjoying the scenery." At that stage I was nearing Tarbet, and pulled in to the slip.

Fruit, milk and rolls were the tit-bits. I stocked up well to replace the mousey items. I also spent a very hot and bad-tempered hour trying to contact Dollar on the phone. Our vaunted G.P.O. improved services at one time gave me an engaged and ringing tone simultaneously.

Tarbet implies a town on a narrow neck between lochs; here it is the neck to the sea at Loch Long. In 1263 Haakon made good use of this position. His son-in-law, Magnus, sailed up Loch Long (the *ship loch*), dragged his longships to Loch Lomond, then went plundering south back to the Clyde. The subsequent Battle of Largs ended the Norse expansion. Haakon retreated to Orkney and died the same year. The Hebrides were ceded to Scotland's Alexander III.

The south end of the loch was rich even then, so was always a target. In the seventeenth century the MacGregor raids on Colquhoun lands were so vicious that they were finally proscribed. In the eighteenth century the famous Rob Roy had a house at Craigrostan until ousted by the Grahams and forced into lawlessness. Rob Roy was at the Battles of Killiecrankie, Glenshiel and Sherrifmuir but died before the "45". He travelled beyond Rannoch, even raided in the far Buchan lands, and also lived in Glen Shira under Campbell protection. He actually died in his bed—but he had taken out an insurance of seven sons.

The canoe was well-loaded when I left: sleeping bag and tent aft, food in front, rucker between my legs, and camera and boots down the side. It was an old canvas kit construction which I had bought for a fiver ten years before. It had been off the West Highlands many times (a great aid in Munro-bagging too) and survived rivers like the Tay and Tweed. I would not swop it for the best of new plastic models. The change in routine was enjoyed and the canoe cheerfully went slap-slap-slap into the hurrying waves as I crossed to Rowchoish on the east shore.

The Ferris Bothy had no water handy so I chose an enchanted spot by the shore to camp. The air was loud with bees, for gean, gooseberry, sycamore and blaeberry were all in flower.

I washed the tins again before opening them. The cream had gone off with the weeks' cooking in the canoe. The strawberries were all right! It would be interesting to see what became of the parcels which had been simply buried in the wilds. I had presumed polythene would have discouraged mice. I had forgotten to buy tea at Tarbet.

I lay only in undies to watch the sun set behind the Cobbler. A quivering highway of gold led across the water. A pair of merganser were briefly shadowed in it. A child's voice came clear across the loch. A train pulsed and died. My daily portion was Romans VIII with its great closing affirmation; the perfect rounding off to a perfect day.

Wednesday 24 April AND UP AGAIN

Colonel Hawker in 1813 noted that ladies making the ascent of Ben Lomond sometimes took a piper with them so as to dance on the summit. Perhaps Sir Hugh Munro took his flute.

Lapping instead of running water was a novel sound on waking. There was a riot of woodland birds calling, too, and I thought I might just hear the first cuckoo. No sooner the thought than the familiar pirate call came across the loch. It was summer!

New roads and plantings were not on my map; but then dealing with plantings is one of the games walkers play. It is a game with a high frustration content and should be in the M.L.C. syllabus. I used a craggy bit where the trees could not grow. A dead goat was discouraging—and a dead woodpecker a delight, or at least its feathers were with their polka dots. I took three feathers back to sew on my hat, so they did the furthest south to furthest north and were duly left on Ben Hope to puzzle northern ornithologists.

Ben Lomond is one of the most popular hills in Scotland and has long been so, though it is no longer regarded as the second highest, as it once was. From some of the accounts of early ascents one wonders why it was attempted. Stoddart accorded it "surprise, arising almost to terror . . . one side forcibly torn off, leaving a stupendous precipice". Can this be the same douce hill up which Tom Weir, like some cherubic Pied Piper, led his laughing gangs of local school children?

Thomas Wilkinson describing his tour of 1824 was obviously a convert. "Mountains and their accompaniments are among the finest specimens of the sublime." Writing of Lomondside, he describes "a female who was reaping alone; she sang in Erse as she bended over her sickle; the sweetest human voice I ever heard; her strains were tenderly melancholy and felt delicious, long after they were heard no more." Wilkinson sailed across the loch and arrived on the summit with six men, six women, a black servant and a pony with provisions. Hardy John Macculloch, 10 years later, brought the hill down to reality: "its ascent is without toil or difficulty, a mere walk of pleasure." That was obviously pre-Forestry Commission days. He met two lassies who had gone up alone—and enthused about their shapely legs.

The favourite speculation concerning the name is the old British "Llummon", meaning *beacon hill*, which would be appropriate both for it and the Fife Lomonds. Odd that a Loch Leven lies below the Fife Lomonds and that that was the older name for Loch Lomond—which still drains to the Clyde by the River Leven.

Rowardennan gives the great trade route; but I perforce was doing it from the north side of Ptarmigan Hill, a bloody-minded sort of ascent: sweating up fire-breaks and with a melancholy cuckoo going like a perpetual clock. The view was soft—as if seen through a Victorian varnish-tinted spyglass. The fourth top was the summit.

Back at the tent I procrastinated: wrote up the log, watched a coal tit, found lots of reasons for lingering. However, the good book is adamant: "Ye have compassed this mountain long enough: turn you northward" (Deut. 2:3). The same writer mentions "that goodly mountain"—perhaps he had the Ben in mind, this southmost of the Munros. It had a certain milestone quality: I was now embarked on the south–north trip as well as the larger.

I paddled off with heaven "a fair blue stretch of sky" again, beyond surprise at good days, now. The dazzle was almost soporific. I kept in the middle of the loch. Inversnaid was a landmark with the white hotel bright in the sun. Of Inversnaid were written some of the most quoted of all lines about the Scottish hills; unexpectedly by Gerard Manley Hopkins:

"What would the world be, once bereft
Of wet and wildness? Let them be left,
O let them be left, wildness and wet;
Long live the weeds and the wilderness yet."

Hans Christian Andersen came through to Inversnaid from the Trossachs to sail up and down the loch. The Wordsworths and Coleridge went in reverse order—and called on Scott going home. This was before *The Lady of the Lake* and all that, so gives interesting literary speculations.

A bit along from Inversnaid there was a bold CAVE painted on the rock. This was not a Latin imperative but a crude signposting of Rob Roy's Cave. Bruce had used it in 1306. I went on to land on Island I Vow, a name which had long fascinated. Later Ronald Laing wrote me to say it was murdered Gaelic: Eileann a' Bhogha, *island of the bow.*

It was a small islet—about a bowshot from the shore. Orchids and hyacinth made a scented carpet under the jungle of trees. A chilly barrel-vaulted cell was all that remained of the castle, built by Mac-Farlane of Arrochar who was rewarded for leading 300 Highlanders to the battle of Langside against Mary Queen of Scots. They used this castle when the one at Inveruglas was sacked by Cromwell's troops. The isle was girt by a sandy shore due to the low level of the loch. It would have been a perfect camp site but I had to push on: the next reach is a memory of cows and cuckoos calling from opposing shores.

I put in to collect a parcel from the Ardlui Hotel. It was lunch time so I went into the bar. A lanky lad in a deerstalker was the only other occupant. He had been there in February when I delivered the parcel.

Loch merged imperceptibly into river, the Falloch. Oss and Dubhcraig rose ahead. The holiday paddle was over. I was in the highlands again. I managed to end just one field away from the Inverarnan Hotel where I had arranged to leave the canoe with the Campbells. They were in the throes of re-opening after big alterations—and hoping to build up a climbing clientele again, for the hotel had been a famous one under the long rule of the Girvans.

I ate a colossal meal before starting uphill, and relished the first tea

I had had since camping under Ben Vane. Ben Vorlich was a pleasing peak through a screen of trees. The browns of winter were passing.

> A sudden shout of white
> In Winter's waiting wood:
> Come Spring and see—
> The blackthorn out.

The Ben Glas Burn was reduced to straggly strands, its falls bearing little of the suggested resemblance to the Grey Mare's Tail. The sun was hard in the west; Laoigh's cone split the rays into streamers of silky light. The slope eased and Glen Falloch vanished; instead, ahead, the peaks of tomorrow circled a valley warm with evening. I pitched the tent quickly by the brand mark of an old sheiling: a grey rectangle in the brown hide of heather. A wing of over a hundred geese flew across the yellow sky, straining and calling for the lonely north. Tomorrow they would fly over Ben Hope. In the last light I sewed the Ben Lomond woodpecker feathers to my hat.

Thursday 25 April THE FIRST HUNDRED THOUSAND

That was the footage total by the day's end. I was now thoroughly fit, and deeply content. Not since childhood had I so relished a spring season. The magic of the sun almost swallowed me whole. It no longer burnt. Perhaps the whole joy lay in being untrammelled; for we so seldom know that freedom these days. Just opening one's eyes, and ears, first thing in the morning, became important. How familiar the sound of water; the erratic burble of grouse. Man is so often an alien in his own country.

Strangely, the notes I read that morning, written by dear Rev. William Still of Aberdeen, took this theme too: "alienation is theological, between God and man; sociological, between man and other men; psychological, between man and himself; and ecological, between man and nature. . . . The first Western man to speak of alienation was not Rousseau, nor Hegel. It was Augustine, and then Calvin who used the concept to emphasize that the problem of sin and evil was not just theological but rational—a breach of man's relationship with God entailing a breach of all other relationships." God so often chooses to speak from the mountain tops; but He will never shout.

When I poked my head out of the tent it was to see the valley white-washed with hoar. Day exploded over Chabhair and I was off at seven into the brightness. Lochan Chabhair was reedy and on the castled ridge above another turquoise pool reflected the clear sky. Beinn Chabhair (Havar), *peak of the antler*, is a rough pile of minor crags and bumps. The purple saxifrage was over: lying tatty as a discarded garment. From the summit I could see eastwards: the only new ground, the rest had all been done—quite a daunting thought.

I went on down to the col beyond; one with a Coire a' Chuilinn on both sides. Near ridges framed Queen Laoigh. I skirted some quite big crags to gain the col the other side of the next Munro where I pitched the tent to dry off the hoar, brewed, then went up *the castle*, An Caisteal. Twistin Hill from Derrydaroch is the most popular route of ascent, but it is a long way over many bumps. All this group need respect in mist or winter. They have some good things but just fail to fire the imagination.

The weather was chilly and breezy back at the tent so I hurried on over Beinn a' Chroin, which is double topped (the name means *hill of the cloven hoof*), with its east summit the higher. On it, years ago, Derry Dunsire won his 102 Munros, the most by any Braeheader before leaving at 15. Ali Smith had 100. A score or more left with 50 plus, always an ambition and resulting in a presentation and various things at school, and from me, a dinner in a luxury hotel. Who says Munro-bagging is not competitive? If two kids had the same number of Munros they would count "Tops", rather as football teams counted goal averages, to fix their league positions.

The east side of Beinn a' Chroin is twisted, so the burns overlap rather than set off from a single col. The Ishag, going south, is another that changes its name perpetually: Ishag, Lochlarig, L. Doine, L. Voil, Balvaig, L. Lubnaig, Leny, Teith and finally Forth. North flows the Falloch to double round to Loch Lomond and the Clyde, while just over Cruach Ardrain, the next Munro, the streams join the long chain ending in the Tay. Three great estuaries all start in this group. Being in the heart of things I stopped for lunch and an hour lying in the sun.

I have read of several dedicated long-distance men, who would all have had a fit at this sort of behaviour. They set themselves rigorous miles per day and nibble chocolate as they walk rather than break the rhythm. They are welcome to their approach! I cannot afford eight bars of chocolate a day, anyway. My spot was so quiet that the wind in the grass sounded quite noisy. (Civilisation's decibel level was hard to bear at the end of the trip.) A beetle crawling up the rock beside me was noticed because it was *heard*.

It was too early to stop for the day so I went on again. There was never a shortage of further hills. The three I had done form a natural trio and the next two were a natural pair: Cruach Ardrain and Beinn Tulaichean. I reached the saddle between them by cutting round under Stob Glas which is quite a craggy bulk, with winter, if not summer, routes on it. I went up the Cruach, the *high slopes*, first.

It is a "goodly mountain" from any angle; the horseshoe on the Crianlarich side being the popular circle of route, though the start is made difficult by plantings of trees.

I met people on top. We chatted, and finding one lad had worked with the Hydro at Rannoch, we revelled in mutual enthusiasm for that area. This led him to ask if I, by chance, knew Hamish Brown.

We repassed going to and from Tulaichean and my wee Rollei had some foreground for once. I half thought of going on for Ben More and Stobinian but was content to rest below them on the col. A flash flood had gouged out a great gash down the hillside under the cliffs of Creagan Dubha. The *black cliff* was well named, a deep cleft in it would make a winter route. I did not linger under it: there was a nice, clean big boulder among all the old mossy ones.

I pitched the tent twice, for as soon as it was up the wind changed 180°, a dirty trick. It was a site remembered for its tipsy wheatears. For the first day in ages I had seen no deer. Just sheep. As I was in early (5 p.m.) there was ample festering.

Slowly the hills had clouded and the weather felt warm and muggy. The early cirrus had become hill cloud. It looked like rain, as Noah said.

Friday 26 April   TO BONNY STRATHYRE

It did not rain that night as expected. However, I was not far above the camp before I was into swirling cloud, so followed the snow edge of the south-west ridge to the cone of Am Binnean or Stobinian as it is more often called. Even with a cagoule on, the wind felt bitterly cold. Blue glimpses tempted me to linger but eventually I went shivering off in self-defence. No navigation problems, the ridge down was rimmed with iron-hard snow. Stobinian, I have noticed in several winter visits, is always much more icy than Ben More, its twin to the north. Stobinian's cone has a sliced-off look which makes the pair unmistakable when seen from elsewhere.

Ben More is just the *big hill* (it is 3,843 feet) and the col between it and Stobinian is merely Bealach-eadar-dha-Bheinn, the *pass between the hills*. Ben More was clear, but Stobinian stayed in cloud longer. It is a thrawn hill, but obviously popular, for it was the dirtiest I had met—every cranny stuffed with papers and cans.

It had been one of my first Scottish hills. On it that day I had found some white heather, seen my first long-tailed tits, and, in a wood, had the alarming experience of being mixed up in a herd of deer who had winded, but not seen, me, and who went charging off to leap right over my head where I lay on a bank. The normal way up, from near Ben More Farm, takes the north-west ridge which is bounded by a corrie which holds snow well into summer. In the 1890's a climber slipped on hard snow down this corrie and was killed—one of the first recorded climbing accidents. The hill produces some big avalanches at times.

The worst accident on Ben More was an aircraft crash one winter. The plane hit just below the summit—fifty feet up or to either side would have cleared it. There are still tiny fragments lying about. I picked up three links from a metal watch-strap.

Scott wrote, "On high Ben More green mosses grow", and cutting down from the bealach between the hills I found myself bogged in some of them. After a brew I took the burn down to Inverlochlarig, where I arrived among a scattering of guinea fowl. Not long after, cutting across fields, I came on a shiny black bird standing by a burn. It seemed to have no head, till after some yelling on my part, it unfolded and became a cormorant. It must have been tired for it sat tight.

I was following the south shore of the two lochs leading to Balquidder, to avoid the tarred road on the north shore. Loch Doine was boggy and plantings had destroyed the old path—it is high time we had legislation to control *all* changes of land use. The path still ran along by Loch Voil, a delectable reach with the Braes of Balquidder across the water. I crossed the hump bridge to visit the shop; and to pay respects to Rob Roy who is buried here, at the old churchyard.

I left the village in a gaggle of kids quarrelling their way home from school, but they slowly dropped away as I walked the old back road to Strathyre, through the woods that ring another *hill of the fairies* (Beinn an-t-Shithein).

The Ben Sheann Hotel made me welcome. They had a parcel. Suddenly life became hectic again. I rang Robert Elton, due to bring mail, to see if he could come 24 hours earlier than planned. I then rang my brother David to fix up delivering the wanted supplies. I repacked a bit—and washed everything I could. (Washing and wearing everything at once presented certain problems.) Finally I splashed, happy as an otter, in a bath. Hotels do have some good points after all.

I carried out food from the parcel and ate in the woods. Since the camp in the King's Field another week had given eighteen further Munros. Now I would begin to work into the heart of the land, up to the Cairngorms, then the Lochaber sweep, then on to the Great Glen. It was a bit frightening. There was such a long way still to go.

IV

TRANS TAY AND TUMMEL

I'm just a donnert gangerel
On a by-way through the murk
But I ken the yett that's best, ma bairn,
An' its toll I dinna shirk.

It'll tak ye ower some muckle braes
And ower wi snaws an' frost
But in the back end o' yer days, ma bairn,
Nae guid thing ye'll hae lost.

Aye, there's mony paths tae tempt ye
But only yin be best;
So tak the ane ma bonnie bairn—
'Tis a hunner o' the rest.

Saturday 27 April   AND THE RAINS CAME TUMBLING DOWN

Tea in bed was quite normal I reflected, even if eight o'clock was not, and the bonny lassie bringing it in was a decided improvement. Most of my clothes were hanging out of the window. I had had quite a bath the night before. Being above the kitchen and the room being blessed with conversational piping I wondered what they had made of my exuberant use of hot water. The smell of bacon and eggs lured me down after some packing and a hack at the growing beard. It was a pattern of hotel use that was to become familiar.

Strathyre is a pleasant corner, at its best today in the spring sun with the chestnut spires dropping petals like snow. The village used to have the odd name of "Nineveh" when it was just a crofting community. It changed with the coming of the railway. Now the railway has gone. The west side of Loch Lubnaig is good walking—away from the rat-race of the road. I wandered about taking photographs, and in the shop could not resist buying a tea called "Green Gunpowder" as it was one we had often drunk in Morocco. The Inn provided conversation and coffee; recently redecorated by the Betteridges, it had appliqué-work pictures of the planets, done by a school girl, which I really liked. The

D

antique shop was hard to resist. Mr King had pinned a notice on the door requesting visitors to "call at the wee cottage if out".

I had just returned to the Ben Sheann Hotel when Robert Elton arrived: another old S.M.C. worthy. In Morocco, at 69, he knocked-off five 4,000-metre peaks in a week, and I was recently reading of a route of his done in Ardgour in 1927! He was to leave for Crete in three days' time. We lunched together and then while he went for a walk I used his Dormobile as an office to deal with the mail. The first slides of the trip, from Mull, showed that the new Rollei worked well. The replies to three questionnaires came too, and I suddenly felt I had been away some time.

The Walk started again in the afternoon with a wander down Loch Lubnaig, a pretty loch: a bend in the middle gives two views for the price of one. Even with a tarred road alongside, it was quiet, and I felt "Healthy, free and the world before me", in Walt Whitman's phrase. Which is why I walked so innocently into a meteorological ambush. Just before I left the road, lined with blackthorn and primroses, Robert drove up, his car full of pussy willows and new larch branches.

The forestry folk as usual had kept their doings secret from the O.S., and I had a bit of scrabbling about before gaining the right of way through to Glen Ample. Some hens in plus-fours told me I was trespassing. There now "went up a mist from the earth and watered the whole face of the ground". It rained in a very determinedly damp and dreary manner, which later turned to a porridgy sleet. Just short of the col I found a corner tucked in beside the burn, so quickly pitched the tent and piled into bed. There was a certain novelty watching the sleet sway and dance across the landscape. Later in the trip rain became a dominant feature, terribly depressing at times, but ultimately accepted and in the end just ignored if need be. The trip finished with as long a run of pernicious weather as it had started fair.

Robert had brought fresh food, so steak and onions, Marina's weekly baking, spinach, and fruit were relished. I also found I had brought on a bit of cast iron decoration which I had meant to leave in the car. Here it was as useful as an ashtray on a motorbike, so was dumped, sadly. There were odd things found, or hidden, all through the trip, which may or may not be collected in the future. When I blew the candle out the rain was still coming down hard and a poor moon was hirpling among the clouds, hurrying the day away.

Sunday 28 April AND THE SNOWS CAME FALLING AFTER

I was as cosy in the sleeping bag as a cat inside its fur but as there was no pretty maid to bring tea I perforce had to uncurl and stretch. When I stuck my nose out the tent it was to find it had snowed overnight. As my last memory had been of accelerating rain, like horses breaking from trot to canter to gallop, the snow was a surprise. The walls of the tent were streaming, but it all ran into the ground. I blessed Dave's ingenious tent design.

I had a long, contouring rise to follow, with odd crags to go round. The sheep had broken trail quite often. I was still walking with eyes in pockets—one brief glimpse down to Loch Earn was all the view I had. I was sorry Stuc a' Chroin could not offer better, for as an opportunist youth it had been my first ski Munro.

I had planned to meet a friend in Glencoe on the Friday night, but got as far as Glen Ogle to find the road blocked and had walked back to Strathyre before giving up and crawling into the woods to sleep under the trees. It snowed all night. I remember the brilliance which one candle on a tree-stump produced on the silent, delectable bivy. On the Saturday I thumbed a lift to Edinburgh and trained home. I knew the local climbing club had a bus trip the next day, so joined them, taking skis. These were a new toy, and having done Largo Law and then White Wisp it seemed a natural progression, for the third day on the planks, to do a Munro. We all set off from Lochearnhead for Stuc a' Chroin, myself with the climbers' rude remarks about skis chasing me ahead. They found me asleep by the cairn, fair trakit, but there three hours ahead of the plodders. I had only had piste bindings and shudder at the memory. We must have been fit once. As all I could do was traverse and "sit-down turns", the descent was quite hilarious. The long traverse down Glen Ample still let me in hours ahead again. There and then I became a convert to ski mountaineering.

There was no sunbathing on the top today. I was forced well along above Coire Fhuadaraich before it was safe to cut down to the col. The new snow and the old cornice-rim barred progress earlier. My hands froze as soon as I took them out of my pockets and my eyes streamed in the cold wind. I dropped down the lee side and left the rucksack, then went up a sheltered rake and along the fence to the top of Ben Vorlich. As the next storm seemed due it was a case of walking round the trig point and off down again.

At the rucksack I cowered in a cranny to eat while the storm blew past. I could see a line of figures on the slopes of the Stuc, at odd moments their voices came loud and clear down the wind. Most ascents are made from Loch Earn so I was looking down the wrong side, so to speak, not that I could see much of the well-named Gleann an Dubh Choirein. It runs down for five miles then curves round east to become Glen Artney, scenery Ochil-like and douce, though once a royal hunting forest. Scott's *The Lady of the Lake* begins here with the well known lines, "The stag at eve had drunk his fill . . . in lone Glen Artney's hazel shade."

The clouds followed me down the glen, the rain forcing me into sweaty "skins". Ruins galore told of past life in the valley. A right of way leads over to Callander—one I had followed as a schoolboy on a cycle and not seen since. The tracks grew surer and after stark Glen Artney Lodge the landscape became tamer. I had a brew where a bridge crossed the Water of Ruchill, sheltering under it until the rain stopped.

My log cried that "down the glen seemed all uphills", but the nine miles of tarred road were quite enjoyable. Fields of pampered sheep gave way to fields of pampered cows. Cultybraggan camp brought back memories of C.C.F. days. Comrie was very welcome. A new bungalow suburb had house-names like "Fairhaven" and "Dunroamin". I went into the Royal Hotel for an hour's break over a vast pot of tea. The village was Sabbath-quiet.

I wandered on up a brae towards Glen Lednock: up past Twenty Shilling Wood and Pollyrigg. The road is squeezed in between hill (topped by the Melville Monument) and gorge (pot holes, The Devil's Cauldron). Above this wooded slice of country the glen opens up into a noisy strath, with cushies in the trees, pheasants honking, curlews chasing and yelping, redshanks, peewits and pied pipers—a real cacophony. The glen had a prosperous air. The school was newly painted white. From Invergeldie I followed the old track up the side burn. One cow turned out to be a bull and I nearly went screw-eyed trying to keep one eye on him and one on my feet on the gooey path.

I tucked my tent in by the burn and was glad to take the boots off; today and tomorrow gave about forty miles, half of it on tarred roads, the longest I would have to face. My feet were unmarked. It snowed hard for an hour and then for the rest of the night gave a right *helm o' weet*. I was reminded of a lad on Rhum who declared that if the rain was custard and the rock was pudding, he would happily eat his way up the hills.

Monday 29 April A PEAK AND A PASS

I had little encouragement in the morning. Storms chased each other's tails down the funnel of glen. Dennis Gray writes in his autobiography: "Climbing is not easily analysed, partly because both its motivations and its rewards are so variable." I went off into the snow showers quite happily, though I am sure others without the motivation or reward would have thought it daft. Churchill climbed Monte Rosa—and never went near a hill again; yet we see severely handicapped people driven to them compulsively. John Emery, who had lost his toes from frostbite in the Himalayas, told how it "moved and excited beyond description". The basic thing is that it does do just this, at all levels and skills and in all the variations climbers play. Let all respect each other.

My game satisfied me today. It sometimes felt like snakes and ladders with its ups and downs, but provided I played on I had no doubt the square marked END would come. A track up the glen helped, then the hollow of a burn let me sneak up out of the wind. Once on the heights I blew along in great style.

Innumerable hares would break and run, spraying up the powdery snow from the heather. We wrote brown tracks through the grey wilderness. Ben Chonzie (or Ben-y-Hone as it is pronounced) teems with hares as few other places—I have counted fifty at one time. There were a lot of grouse too. I met a mountain blackbird (or ring ouzel), a species which seems to be increasing. This is the *hill of the deer cry*.

The toil of snow-covered heather gave way to blaeberry and then moss and stone. A hoary cairn turned out to be a grouse butt, but a fence led to the top. A cross of old fence stabs, stones and posts, all hoary and glowing, looked just like a Friedrich painting. There was no view down Loch Turret, nor to Lawers, which is seen at its best from here. Previous knowledge was welcome as I scurried off.

My hat was pulled down and a hanky tied over my nose to keep off the stinging icy particles. I went along the plateau and down the long flank to another new track. As I trotted down it eased off. A skylark was singing its heart out in the mist, very much the "unbodied joy" of Shelley's poem.

Plans to keep to the tops and traverse them to Loch Tay were abandoned. I brewed at the tent and then took the pass I had once used with a bike twenty years before: up by Sput Rollo to a reservoir. The fall was lowly, humbled by the weeks of no rain. Sandpipers, the singing heralds of summer, went past silently—probably wishing they had stayed in sunny Morocco. The loch in some ways improved the view. I nearly stood on a grouse nest: eight grey eggs and one ruddy one.

I have always maintained passes are as satisfying as peaks (and more rational) and this one, with its feeling of being a portal to the Tay, is a good example. Its descent by the Finglen had many tempting camp spots. Woodcock and cuckoo flew past as I descended to the Inn at Ardeonaig. The setting has a rich, English quality to it, a contrast to the heather above and to the many ruins left from the evictions in the 1820's.

Tenpence produced five big cups of tea. The room was a collector's den: carved iron tables with brass tops, an old gun, real and converted paraffin lamps, a miner's lamp, prints, an array of stoneware including several "pigs". I set out again at 5.30 for the eight miles of road to Killin, arriving at seven, without any aches or pains. A roadside notice said: "No fishing beyond this fence." As the loch lay half a mile away it conjured up images of mighty castings. Firbush Point and Fiddler's Bay were two nice names. Lawers showed white in a brief clearance and Tarmachan made a backcloth to the falls at the west end of the town. The island below the bridge is the burial ground of the Clan McNab.

McNab of McNab at once conjures up a painting by Raeburn. This chief, Francis, b. 1734, stood six-foot three and his hat another foot. He backed up a wedding proposal with the enticement that he owned the most beautiful burial ground in Scotland. He never did marry, but his numerous progeny fought on many a battlefield. (Three at Waterloo.) When he died in 1816 he left debts of £35,000. The Highlands were bled to try to maintain the chief's show in fashionable Edinburgh or London, the people were cleared for sheep or deer—a state which remains to today, financial gain for a few owners being still maintained as right and proper. The people were betrayed, their land stolen—and they do not forget, though, tied into a feudal system, they can do little about it.

To revert to the McNabs. One tale tells how a party was robbed as they returned from Crieff, by the McNish of Loch Earn. The McNab had twelve sons, so he gathered them all, and hinted darkly: "The night is the night if the lads were the lads." They scurried off with a boat to Loch Earn and rowed out to the enemy stronghold to slaughter all there and return with the chief's head. A bearded head appears in the McNab arms.

It was a Killin minister who first translated the New Testament into Gaelic, his son, and successor, translating the Old Testament. The church and hotel stand in a corner of the sleepy town (main industry, tourism). The church was built in 1744 but replaces an older one. Its seven-sided font is unique and could be a thousand years old. The most interesting relics are the "Healing Stones" of St Fillan (now in the old tweed mill) which are very ancient and said to have unusual powers. From here, westwards, the whole valley is steeped in religious lore.

I went into the Youth Hostel and had it almost to myself. The Peevors had a parcel for me. They lit a fire and we sat before it and set the world right. I was glad to have the road bit over. Its saddest element had been the toll of wildlife: I had seen a slaughtered squirrel, mole, several hares, various mice, a shrew, a pheasant, a lamb, a hedgehog, a grouse, a frog and any number of unidentifiable bits of fluff and feather. At eleven we took our yawning ways to bed. In the food locker I found a slip of paper giving a curious example of racial prejudice. Perhaps it was left by an American. It analysed us all: "The Scots, who will keep the Sabbath, and anything else they can get their hands on; the Welsh, who pray on their knees, and on their neighbours; the Irish, who don't know what they want but will fight each other to get it; the English, who consider themselves a race of self-made men, thereby absolving the Almighty of a great responsibility."

Tuesday 30 April KILLIN TIME

A day when I was quite glad to do nothing and rest afterwards. A writer in 1799 used the term "a gloom of settled vapour", which described the weather well. Another writer declared "as for climate, there are nine months of winter, three months of spring, and there is no summer at all." Which just shows how little things change; an article in a recent Swiss magazine about climbing in Skye ended, "Hélas! la réputation de l'île ne ment pas: il pleut!"

Killin is an old site. "Cill Fhinn", the cell or burial place of Fingal, some would have it, with a stone behind the town marking the spot. The

Campbells arrived in the fifteenth century when the king rewarded Sir Colin with the Barony of Lawers for helping capture his predecessor's assassins. Finlarig was added in 1503 and the Campbells flourished as they were wont. Black Duncan "causit saw akornes and seid of fir therein, and plantit in the samen young fir and birk anno 1613 and 1614", for which we are grateful to this day, Tayside being leafy rather than barren. Just to the north, in Glen Lyon, in the eighteenth century, the first larch in Scotland was planted. So were beeches, and Glen Lyon remains a specially fine sight in its autumn colours. The Campbell power has now gone, the last Earl of Breadalbane sold much to the Hydro Board. The McNabs are named back to the time of David I, but gained some notoriety at the field of Dalrigh where they tried to capture Robert the Bruce. All good stuff for the tourists.

I was brought back to earth by hearing my name yelled. It was Brian Hall who had once been at Glenmore Lodge and was now Warden of Stirling University's centre on Loch Rannoch. I lunched at the hotel which reflects the importance of Killin as a fishing centre. Inertia led me back to the hostel. In the school porch some girls were trying out dance steps while others produced "mouth music"—quite oblivious of the spectator.

Chris Peevor and I sat by the fire and talked the night away. Solitude can be sweet as honey—but try living on honey only all the time!

Wednesday 1 May   CIRCUITS AND BUMPS

> "We shall grow old apace and die
> Before we know our liberty. . . .
> Come, let us goe, while we are in our prime;
> And take the harmlesse follie of the time"
>   HERRICK

That came over the radio in a May day selection! The local cuckoo had roused me at seven. I went off, down by the lochside, passing the Campbell ruin of Finlarig shrouded and greened over on a knoll. There is even a hanging tree. The local courting couples alone go near it.

Paddle steamers used to ply up and down the loch but they and the railway station are all gone. Finlarig Power Station alone was new to me and I followed its pipeline up the hillside. The map happily showed a path but there were so many animal tracks that I was not certain whether I found it. I cut up through small crags and over boggy wet to gain the contouring Hydro road. I went into the mist which swirled and scattered like water stirred up by passing oars. Killin through the clouds was like Keswick seen from Latrigg.

I followed the road round to the lairig where the public road cuts over to Glen Lyon and found a tailor-made camp site of a tiny sward in the loop of a burn. A notice about stalking on Tarmachan asked walkers to contact the factor—at Brechin. The other side of the road is National Trust land: the Lawers range which I would nibble at today and go over tomorrow. The Trust, with its honeypot ideas, has brought thousands to the hills here, with the result we have the country's only paint-spotted route along the hilltops. There is an unsightly eroded track, sleepers over the bogs, a visitor centre . . . an incredible lack of conservation from a body given land to keep for the nation. Lawers is famed for its Alpine flowers so on the summit is a notice to this effect and people, with no botanical interest, go off to see! It makes one shudder. The same approach is seen in Torridon and Glencoe.

The western arm of Lawers has a couple of Munros and after a brew I headed off for them, with the idea of circling round to Meall nan Tarmarchan. Meall Corranaich is the *bracken corrie hill*. As I went straight up it, the cloud scampered ahead and it was actually clear on top. I arrived dripping. Lawers was very white, with its height of just under 4,000 feet. I rimmed on old snow, along and down to the col, and on an easy pull up Meall a' Choire Leith. Azalea was in flower. An asthmatic golden plover wheezed ahead. This is a peak only the wayward Munro-bagger is apt to go for, but it has a good view being out on a limb over Glen Lyon. There is a great deal of Ben Lawers facing north and few walkers know it.

My first-ever juvenile trip brought me here. From my home at Dollar I had cycled through the Trossachs and crossed Loch Lomond to the Arrochar Alps, then pushed up to Crianlarich (Ben More) and on to Killin. I did Meall nan Tarmachan from the lairig then started off down to Glen Lyon, at that time on an unsurfaced road; no dam either. A tyre blew out but I was welcomed to a Scripture Union camp at Bridge of Balgie and the next day, while the bus brought a new tyre from Aberfeldy, I joined a mass assault on Lawers up these golden shoulders on the Glen Lyon side. The next day Schiehallion was done on the way to my own camp at Blair Atholl—and another Munro-bagging addict had been born.

Heading for the lairig road I found a delightful waterfall that made a picnic spot. I happily fell asleep there so had to go skelping on when I woke as I was expecting visitors at 5.30 at the tent. On the ridge up to Tarmachan I found a broken Stevenson's Frame which was odd. The way up was all lumps and hollows, lochans and snow flanks—some steep enough to need dodging. Bad weather had been blowing in again from the west and the fangs of the fine western reaches of Tarmachan soon vanished. The summit was bleak; streaming mist, which silvered garments at once. The snow rims forced me well round before I could break down. The tent was reached at 4.30. At 5.20 Ann Winning, Peter Miller and "Bramble" arrived, having driven along from Aberfeldy after school. We sat in the car in the rain drinking chocolate, recalling many familiar situations.

Ann had taught at Braehead for several years. Peter was one of her Breadalbane climbing protégés. Could he join me for Skye? Knowing them both, I was happy enough, though I had hoped for a solo trip of the Cuillins, but that would depend so much on weather: *la réputation de l'île*, etc. "Bramble" was Ann's new Jack Russell puppy: still at the stage of being all prickles and piddles. . . . When they drove off I demolished the fresh food they had brought, then read their Sunday papers. Ann had been asked if she could let me have an old pullover and took me at my word, delivering one liberally splattered with paint. Worn outside-in it looked respectable, I hoped. Daylight fizzled out like a dying candle.

Thursday 2 May   LAWERS TUSSLE

The wild night led into a wild day but eventually I packed up the camp and squelched off. Beinn Ghlas had a deal of slobbery snow on it but it was from the col beyond, for the Lawers ascent, that it became deeper, and conditions quite vile. I slithered or slipped often enough, and now and then hail showers would have me withdrawing into my waterproofs like a tortoise. The cairn felt an unhealthy place to linger, as my hair tingled with electricity. I took a bearing and slithered off quickly.

After crossing an unimportant bump I headed up the sharp, pointed, Top of An Stuc, a summit for which I already had a healthy respect. Years before we had crossed it after days of rain, when it had suddenly frozen to become lethally slippery. It is steep and shoots off into flanking corries. To the south is the finest rock face profile I know, much better than the Merrick one. From yesterday's western arm I had seen a rake flanking An Stuc which I was able to find even in today's storm. It led to a feared problem: the snow rim of the corrie head of the Fin Glen. This was so wide that it was not possible to look over without going to the edge and that was not on, as there could have been a soggy cornice. The light had the dazzling white quality associated with conditions of white-out. Seeing anything was difficult.

I said rude things and began to grope upwards, vibrams proving most insecure on schisty slabs all plastered in slobbery snow and the tent pole making a rather poor alpenstock. Each step had to be gingerly tested. In the cutting wind it was not pleasant work. Gusts would swing me round violently. The heavy pack seemed twice its weight. Willy-nilly I climbed An Stuc.

I took a bearing and set off again. The descent was steeper and gave another tussle. Despite the wind, bare hands had to be used to deal with the mixture of rotten schist, ice, mud and snow. The slope ran away down into the glaring white, but, visible or not, I knew too well how far I would go if I slipped. In these circumstances you just don't! With hindsight I reckon it was the most dangerous bit of the whole trip.

On the col I went through that peculiar sensation of bringing life back to frozen fingers and then used them to stuff food into my mouth. I felt so bloody I decided I might as well go on—conditions could hardly become worse. Meall Garbh was reached over its endless rough bumps. Meall Greigh lay away south, and my descent to Glen Lyon was northwards, but the rucksack could not be left or it might never be found again. So I had more dogged compass work and even felt satisfied to end bang on the desired cairn. I back-tracked and swung round and down till I could stuff the compass away knowing the water I splashed through could only lead to Glen Lyon. I came out of the cloud at 5.30. It broke up, and a bold patch of blue appeared. Wet feet pounded down soft, wet slopes, the route all blissfully downhill. I paused on a knoll with a glittering view right up the glen: silver snake of river and rich green of fields running west to vanish in an explosion of cloud and sun triggered off by sunset colours.

At Rorromore I greeted a shepherd and collected two ewes who would walk on ahead and not let me pass. At Balnahanaid I collected a great flock of rams who were plainly hoping for a hand-out. When the shepherd drove up they soon swopped their affection. I crossed the bridge to Camusvrachan.

Dr Fulton had converted an old church into an attractive house and garden: Cille Fionn. She was at home, luckily, though my first greeting came from a Yorkshire terrier and a Dachshund with one eye. (In my log I wrote it down as a Dachstein with one eye!) I collected my parcel and was let out by a gate at the back which led straight on to the hillside.

I wandered up through a larch forest until I found a perfect ledge perched above the burn. But I had little time to relish it: I was over 1,000 feet and the cloud base was at 2,000 feet. Darkness came pressing down with the clouds. I soon crawled in and started a glorious feed. Weight would be easiest carried internally, I decided.

Friday 3 May   LAID DOWN MY HEAD, TOMPHUIBIL

A junction in the burn just above the camp tempted me to take the west fork, hoping to add a Corbett before turning east along the run of Rannoch Munros, but a real lashing of hail and snow was easiest dealt with by turning my back on it so I was battered up on to Carn Gorm. There were big herds of deer everywhere.

This group of hills I knew well because their northern slopes drop down to the Black Wood of Rannoch where Braehead School had had a bothy at which scores of boys and girls were first introduced to camping and the hills. The Black Wood is a superb remnant of the old forests that covered Scotland once. Some of the pines are 200 years old. Much was burnt to try to displace the lawless men who took refuge in it, such as the local "Rob Roy", a Cameron known as "Sergeant Mor". After Culloden he had gathered a band and they had refused to surrender themselves, their arms or their tartan. The old mansion at Dall is now Rannoch School, originally modelled on Gordonstoun. To the east is Carie where the Jacobite Robertson chief, in 1746, had his house—and brought to it General Cope's carriage after Prestonpans. As there were no roads west of the A9 it had to be carried bodily over rivers and bogs and braes.

The previous knowledge was useful again and I was able to keep going even when the icy showers came whipping in. The first week in May is rather known for being dirty—thereafter the best weather of the year normally follows. The next Munro was another *rough hill*, Meall Garbh, it was followed by a long, rocky waste. The fences are not navigational aids. Carn Mairg is the group's highest summit, a rocky one. An old iron ladder stood over the wreck of a fence, an odd reminder of the wealthy days in the past. I skirted Meall Liath to slope down to the col for Creag Mhor, the southern outlier which so dominates lower Glen Lyon. It has two tops and provides the usual doubts, for whichever you are on the other appears higher.

Many snow patches, contourings and flounderings later I was dropping into Gleann Mor, the secret valley moating Schiehallion to the south. The peak showed as a long ridge, not the classic cone as seen along Loch Rannoch. The peak's symmetry tempted the Astronomer Royal, Maskelyne, to conduct experiments on it in 1774 to try to determine the earth's weight and mass.

Isaac Newton had suggested experimenting with a peak whose mass would exert a pull on a plumb line held nearby. Several decades passed before the Royal Society backed the experiment in Britain. Finding the right mountain was the first task. There were no maps to help. The technical details are beyond me, but the experiment needed 43 different sightings on stars, and the measuring of angles to one three-thousandth of a degree of accuracy. The ten-foot telescope would take a week's work for twelve men to shift round the hill. Two years of surveying went into determining the hill's shape—then the calculations began. Their astronomical clock, after adventures in St Helena, Schiehallion, the U.S.A. and in the Ben Nevis Observatory, now resides in the Edinburgh Met. Office. Hutton, another F.R.S., one of the surveyors, was the first person to link similar heights on a map by lines—so Schiehallion saw the birth of contours which are now taken for granted.

Gleann Mor has some limestone so shows up as bright green among the heathery browns. The river has carved out weird channels, and I nearly fell into Uamh Tom a' Mhor—Big Tom's cave. I pitched the tent to dry it off in the breeze. Deer, very grey in colour, moved past on stilted legs. I set off at four o'clock to add Schiehallion, and at six I was off again, having been up and down, brewed and packed up. It was a real treat to romp up unladen—and without contending with vile conditions.

Schiehallion is the *fairy hill of the Caledonians*. It is Rannoch's local showpeak so we from Braehead had been up it with many school gangs. Its north flank is a great sweep which in winter can give good practice in crampon use. The view today petered out before the hills of Glencoe but the loch winked a friendly eye. Dunalasdair Reservoir was low and I hoped rain would not cause it to rise suddenly, for this often wiped out many birds' nests. Kinloch Rannoch is misnamed, for Kinloch means *head of*, yet it sits at the foot of Loch Rannoch. On a clear day you can see from North Berwick Law to Lochnagar to Ben Nevis from the summit of Schiehallion.

Descending the glen the deer gave way to sheep. I hit the old Wade road at White Bridge and collected another parcel from Mr Forest, the roadman, who has created a fine garden beside the high and lonely miles he maintains. We chatted till hunger drove me to excuse myself. Near the top of the pass at Tomphuibil I found a secluded spot among disused quarry workings. There is an old ice-house nearby. I pitched with the door facing Schiehallion. The poet Thomas Gray had the cheek to call it "that monstrous creature". It was after eight when I began brewing and I was lying there in blissful ease when a roar and pounding feet betrayed a visitor. David grinned in at the door.

He dumped a pile of mail on me and said to come along to the Dormobile for coffee. This was an unscheduled meeting. He and Marina were taking the bike to Kincraig so that I could have it to get over some dull A9 road stretches later on. Always an opportunist, I said I would be happy to use it on the morrow. At the Dormobile I scrounged fresh bread, bacon and eggs. Kenneth was in the back "sleeping". Marina produced coffee and Turkish Delight. They had gone to leave mail with Mr Forest, only to find I had just been—a day early. David soon guessed where I would be camping.

They had come up through Aberfeldy which has the most famous of all Wade bridges. It has even appeared on a British stamp. This pass is at 1,270 feet, then drops to the single arch of Tummel Bridge before heading over by Dalnacardoch to the A9 line. I walked home to the coldest night of the trip. The stars were pulsing in massed array and there was a big, blowing moon. The black-headed gulls called all night on the loch.

Marina wrote later to say the next night they were back at Rannoch. Kenneth refused to go to sleep and kept pulling the curtain aside to look along the road for his uncle who appeared at the oddest times. "Eesh-eesh" was as near as he could get to Hamish and this he kept repeating. At home, too, a telephone call would have him grabbing my map board and tracing along the magic pins that marked the route.

Saturday 4 May   CAM' YE BY KILLIECRANKIE, O?

I was brewing early in self defence, for the cold was dagger sharp. The tent pegs stuck to fingers—not usual in May. A gigantic sun soon throbbed in the haze and before most folk were awake I was spinning down to Foss and Loch Tummel. Boats were moored on top of their reflections. Schiehallion took on its cone shape, trailing a cloud like a volcano.

Beyond the mirror of loch I crossed the Coronation Footbridge. This whole area has been laid out with paths and tracks and the Hydro have created lochs which look fine in the woodland setting. Ben Vrackie and Ben-y-Ghlo form a mountain backcloth, well seen from the 130-foot-high new bridge over the Garry. It cost £300,000 in 1968. The railway viaduct, over 500 feet long, cost £5,730 when it was built.

The nature trail (N.T.S.) showed a ruined chimney where Robert the Bruce rested after the rout at Methven—a day lost partly by Pembroke breaking a sacred tradition and attacking the newly-crowned king on a Sunday. They went on to capture and kill Bruce's brother and they grabbed his wife, daughter and sisters from the sanctuary of St Duthac. Two of these royal ladies were hung in a cage from the walls of Berwick.

Gilpin called Killiecrankie "an ample specimen of the sublime", the sort of praise it has endured ever since. With an ever-changing A9, Wade's old road, the railway and pylons all squeezed into the defile, besides the river, it holds its sublimity wondrously well. The N.T.S. have a small centre with a display on the Battle of Killiecrankie—another where a dead man won the day. Dundee's highlanders routed Mackay's troops, winning the day for James II, but Claverhouse himself was mortally wounded. Macaulay has described the battle, and Scott of course. Rob Roy was taken along by his father and had his first taste of fighting there. The highlanders were unable to pass Dunkeld despite their victory, and the loss of their leader resulted in the campaign fizzling out. Only a haunting song remains—and up in Blair Castle you can see Bonnie Dundee's breastplate, with a hole in it.

I collected a parcel at Killiecrankie Hotel and waited there for the Broons to catch up. I was chatting to a couple who turned out to be from Dollar, and who knew us as schoolkids. The miles up the A9 to Blair Atholl were not enjoyable. I booked in at the Tilt Hotel and started the usual game of trying to wash and wear things at the same time. I spent the evening with Dewi and Maggi Jones who had once worked at Fife's outdoor centre and now lived at Blair Atholl.

The Atholl estate is another which has a long tradition of tree-planting, one duke being known as "the Planting Duke". Timber for shipbuilding was important to the area and the introduction of iron hulls a disaster until the railways came with their call for sleepers. By 1830 over 140 million larches had been planted. The trees at Bruar Falls had been planted following a visit from Robert Burns. The poet had left some verses, speaking through the Bruar Water, pleading for trees. The castle is open to the public, and is interesting. On our first visit six of us, kids, were thoroughly spoilt by a nice old guide (rather to the resentment of a bus group he was meant to be leading) and it was only later we found that he was the Duke of Atholl himself. During the "45" the castle suffered what was to be the last ever siege in Great Britain, an odd one as the Jacobite leader Lord George Murray was besieging his brother, the earl. The Dukedom was conferred in Queen Anne's day.

I had my usual mail-and-logistics evening till late. I wrote to Mike Keates with new ideas which would allow the last two weeks to be done without having to carry the tent. Whatever people like to believe, attention to detail is one of the essentials of success. The slog before this trip repaid that care by giving freedom from care. If the human animal could just keep on walking, all would be well. This section had given a stormy 26,000 feet in its 94 miles.

V

THE SOUTHERN CAIRNGORMS

"Let the mountains bear prosperity. . . ."

PSALM 72:3

Sunday 5 May   BRAIGH COIRE CHRUINN-BHALGAIN

I finished off *The Story of San Michele* over tea in bed and for the early walk had a Flashman tale. Tea in bed was not what it could be with the A9 traffic snorting past twenty yards away. Nor was the breakfast up to tent standard. The greatest pleasure was dry, snug, clean clothes.

I read up the Tilt and Fender roads. The rich landscape of greens and browns was one I knew well. Flashman was deposited in a bothy where I left the tarmac. I had bought *Weir of Hermiston* in the village. I was having a snack in the hut and watching a peewit bowing his rufous rump at me when I slowly realised the hill above was crawling with people: pinpricks of colour, those polluting identikit colours, that stood out against the burnt hillside darkness.

I crossed bogs and ascended by a line of grouse butts. The slopes were a grey and brown jig-saw of heather, burnt over the years to encourage new growth. There is a false summit to Carn Liath and as I topped it I found a female squatting before me. Movement being the thing one notices, I simply turned and admired the view for a few minutes. The true summit had a bus load of visitors from the old "Scotsman" club, now the "Ptarmigan Club", out on their first-Sunday-in-the-month trip from Edinburgh. I regretted my late start, another hotel drawback, for with so many people on the hill the sense of solitude vanished—and so did any chance of seeing much in the way of wildlife.

I had forgotten what a fine group this was: big brown and grey domes, clean-honed by the wind, runny with screes and seamed with deer tracks. It was a hill group I had been on more often in winter. Once the wind was so powerful that I took a photograph of our party "leaning" on it. Another intensely cold Christmas Day our eggs froze solid at camp, and at 2,000 feet up we met an otter out for a bit of tobogganing. The farmer was on skis.

Today was bitter cold so I soon went on. There were people all along the ridges: some had taken only single tickets up Carn Liath, but others went on for the other Munros: Braigh Coire Chruinn-Bhalgain, the *slope of the round, bag-shaped corrie,* and Carn nan Gabhar, the highest, at 3,671 feet. Beinn a' Ghlo (or Ben-y-Gloe) covers all three in a group name. They stand as a solitary bulk bordering on the lowlands. B.C.C.B. had quite a picnic collection of folk but the atmosphere was rather from Jerome K. Jerome as people cringed behind the cairn, or each other, in an effort to avoid the searing wind. The last Munro lies beyond a substantial col so I left the sack by a long and very visible snow runnel and went off for it. As the group name means *hill of the mist* I was taking no chances. Never leave a sack without some sure marker.

I came back over B.C.C.B. Always another Munro after all—and the shortest way down. (1974 ended with 344 Munros, a yearly tally I am never likely to equal again; the figure for 1969 was 206 and most years straggle to the 100.) I suddenly had the hill to myself, and almost breathed a sigh of relief. Though the company had been enjoyable one of the loved aspects of Scottish hill-going is the solitude. Our own Braes o' Fife Club tries not to go in a party of more than four or five. Above that number all sorts of dissatisfactions creep in. We also try to discourage the hideous belisha-beacon clothing which we are conned into wearing. (I know it is in the name of safety, but you can have a bright poly bag hidden in your sack till you want to be seen instead of becoming part of the human pollution problem. The same criticism goes for tents in the wilderness.)

Several hundred feet of standing glissade took me well on my way down to the great cleft of Glen Tilt. The rest was brutally steep grass. For once the River Tilt gave no problems and I hopped over to the road. A rainbow spanned the vee of the fault line. I crept under a bridge for a shower, left the sack there and went a couple of miles down to Forest Lodge.

The keeper, Mr McGregor, benign and unshaven, had a food parcel. We had a wee crack, then I went up the glen again. Many are the tales of this stalwart figure confronting unauthorised motorists who have dared the potholes of the private road up the glen. Once we were brewing at the Dormobile after a day on the hill when he stopped to check on us. (We had permission.) I had fished some nice red granite stones out of the river for a garden dry-stane-dyke. These were eyed. "Aye, aye, there's some folk just climb hills but others now, mun tak' the hill home with them!"

Fitness allowed the addition of a heavy parcel to go unnoticed though I lightened the load by the weight of mandarins and cream. A fit body is a marvellously casual thing. I ate up the miles to the head of the main glen to camp by the Falls of Tarff on a bright sward. Last time up there I had led a cycling gang through to Braemar. Where the track became a mere slot I caught a pedal and fell down the bank, bouncing alternately with the bike, till it landed splash in the river; I stopped one bounce short.

Today I was furious to find the site disfigured with litter, half-buried compo tins, bare stone marks and stove burns—all the signs of Army activity. Tins had been pushed into molehills, hidden under the nearest stones, or simply thrown into the river. It took an hour to clean up the place before I could feel relaxed in it. I threw dozens of boulders back into the river: campers should never leave them where tents have been: the grass looks as if it had chicken-pox after a few years. I like my camping to be as secretive as possible: known to none at the time or after.

Craig Dhearg caught the evening sun, lighting the translation of its name in almost neon extravagance. The sound of the big river dominated the site: river and falls. I concocted the first curry of the trip. A quarter of the tally had been done. A month had gone by as casually as river flow.

The Tilt is one of the oldest of through routes. It narrowly missed being linked up with the Lairig Ghru in an English-type long-distance jamboree track, the brain-child of the Scottish Countryside Commission. The route was all worked out, and a massive report issued with all the details, before any users heard about it. After a terrific outcry the scheme was dropped. Some consultation *first* could have saved a great deal of money and effort. It was even suggested that sometimes the path would have to be closed in the interests of stalking. It would have been fun seeing the Commission trying to "close" a right-of-way as old as any in the land.

In 1847 a botanical professor had had the Tilt barred to him and the ensuing lawsuit clearly showed the right of way. In Scotland we try to keep a sane balance, respecting each other's interests and rights. We

V SOUTHERN CAIRNGORMS

Miles
0 1 2 3 4 5

Glen Geldie

Dee Valley

Braemar

To Main Cairngorms

Glen Muick

Conachraig

Mount Keen

Glen Mark

10/5

Glen Lee

Ben Tirran

11/5

Loch Muick

Broad Cairn

Lochnagar

White Mount

Cairn Bannoch

Jock's Road

Capel Mounth

Broadownie

Clova

Glen Clova

Glen Prosen

Dreish

9/5

Mayar

12,13/5

Cairn an t'-Sagairt Mor

Glen Collater

Tolmount

Tom Buidhe

Cairn of Claise

Glen Isla

Glen Callater

Carn an Turc

8/5

Glas Maol

Creag Leacach

Glen Cluanie

Devils Elbow

Spittal of Glenshee

Glen Shee

Carn Aosda

The Cairnwell

7/5

An Socath

Carn a' Gheoid

Glen Ey

Carn Bhac

Beinn Iutharn Mhor

Glas Tulaichean

Carn an Righ

Carn nan Gabhar

Braigh Coire Chruinn - Bhalgain

BEINN A'GHLO GROUP

Carn an Fhidleir

An Sgarsoch

Ring of Tarf

5,6/5

Carn Liath

Beinn Dearg

Carn a' Chlamain

Glen Tilt

Blair Atholl

4/5

JR77.

do not register rights-of-way as in England but are given freedoms which we value. Were they all cut and dried everyone would lose a great deal. So there have been very few cases like the "Battle of the Tilt". The 1975 Scottish Mountaineering Club Journal had an article on this and allied tales, "Stravagers and Marauders" by Robert Aitken, which is good reading.

The glen itself is full of history and old ruins: whole villages lie tucked away in side valleys, telling of what past? Pennant on his tour went through to Braemar in 1769 and called the glen "the most dangerous and the most horrible I ever travelled". James VI stayed there as the guest of honour at a specially-built wooden lodge and enjoyed a massive deer drive. Pools for fish were created. As a final flourish, on his departure, the lodge was burned to make a huge bonfire. One hears little snippits like this and longs to know more. The glens were not always empty.

Monday 6 May THE RING OF TARFF
"Willy-needy, willy-needy, willy-needy . . ."
The call of a summer piper woke me to a cold morning—cold enough for me to take the Gaz stove into bed and read *Weir of Hermiston* for an hour before starting to brew. Long day or not, it was nine before I set off.

I scrambled about taking photographs of the falls as they foamed in the sun. The Tarff supplies the bulk of water for the Tilt which beyond here lies in a remarkable slot of trench. The falls are among the best in the land but seldom seen, as they are far from any road. It has been suggested that the upper Tilt flow has been reversed and that the Tarff waters once flowed to the Dee. The Tarff, crashing out of its gorge, has always been a hazard to travellers between Atholl and Deeside: the Belford Bridge was erected in memory of a drowning in Victorian times. The bridge is a perfect period piece, spanning the pool into which the double fall tumbles. It is a great spot.

I explored upstream—where there is a higher fall—and then flanked upwards along a series of "little hills". The country is misleading: small and simple on the face of map and landscape, but the miles contort and the hours pass in remarkable fashion. Heather braes and black bogs ensure the Ring of Tarff is no stroll. It is wild mistmoor, unlived-in, lonely as a sad heart, the silence more crashing than any sound could be.

An Sgarsoch and Carn Ealar, the *fiddler* (Fhidleir), are not among

the more exciting of Munros, though their isolation will probably
add something to their acquisition. For instance, in 1908 Munro
and Walter Garden dined at Blair Atholl, then drove and walked
up to the Belford Bridge, which they left, already well soaked, at
9.40 p.m. The Tarff was in spate. To read a compass they had to
shelter under a coat. Sgarsoch's summit dome was chaotic, the cairn
hard to find in the rain, dark and cloud. As they were "unable to keep
their powder dry" they could see neither map nor compass. Ealar was
abandoned and they simply steered into the wild north wind to drop
down to the Geldie. It was unfordable for many miles and they
staggered into Braemar at 10.20 a.m. They had a certain style in those
days. Another S.M.C. party in 1903 did this pair and Chlamain
starting at 2.30 a.m.—so as to be sure of being "back for dinner" at
Blair Atholl. They walked on dried peat bogs, all too glad of such
conditions.

Today I had it not bad myself. The hills are a good pair from which
to view the Cairngorms. The valley mists had streamed off into
invisibility. Only Nevis remained hidden. The hills of Glen Etive could
be named. A day of infinite things: glossy, moleskin mountains and
happy animal activity. Surely too good to last.

Ealar is the meeting place of three counties: Perth, Aberdeen and
Inverness, or as would be on the morrow, three regions: Tayside,
Grampian and Highland. There were large herds of deer all day. They
trailed muddy tracks across the snow patches. By the time I had
followed down to and then trekked up the Tarff I was ready to envy
them as they lay on the snow. I paddled and rested a while, then
pushed on for Beinn Dearg, a granite-pink cone which takes a bit of
coming-at from any direction. Combined with Chlamain it gives an
excellent introduction to bumps and bogs, about which the map
retains a coy reticence.

Both Ealar and Dearg received questionnaires. Alan Smith of
Glasgow found the Ealar one three weeks later, and also one to the
north, on Carn Cloich-Mhuillin, which is comment enough on these
hills. He had tramped up from a camp at White Bridge, wearing
swimming trunks. Dearg's was found after a week by a gang with
Eddie McCulloch from Dundee. He made rude comments about bogs
too.

Carn a' Chlamain remained. It was Queen Victoria's first Munro—
the first of quite a bag. She would have made a notable patron for the

L.S.C.C. I reckon. Her journals and letters written in Scotland are well worth reading; she ranged widely and did more than any one else to remove the old wounds of 1745. In 1842 she was the first monarch to visit the highlands voluntarily and freely since Jamie Six beat it off to London.

Carn a' Chlamain is the *cairn of the gled* or *kite*. From Dearg it is reached by devious means, ease of approach being in proportion to cunning employed. I did not linger on top as the weather was sneakily turning raw. I was eventually caught by the bogs—flying off like the victim of a judo expert and thumping into a gooey spot. I carried a fair bit of it away on my clothes.

The yellow strath rang with the crying of plover and curlew, giving a loneliness to the one building standing, the Tarff Bothy—a man-made, geometrical shape among the flowing river and brae curves. An old A.A. Hotel sign hung on a gable. I brewed, and had a dram, signed in the register, and went down for a wash, removing the mud. The clothes dried before I was back "home". I deposited my Stevenson and took a blood-and-thunder. Still, a two-star howff.

I read most of the way back, walking down, or tripping out of, deer tracks. The path shown was illusory. The new dirt road came over a gap to end at a stable. The Ring of Tarff is a fine round largely in retrospect.

Tuesday 7 May   THE GREY WASTELAND

If no hill is dull, some are certainly less entertaining than others. This section of the Walk would probably have my vote as the least notable of all. Luckily the animal spirits seemed high during the long, grey miles.

The upper Tilt gave a trouble-free crossing. I read my way up the slopes on to the ridge above Fealar Lodge, the highest and one of the most remote in Scotland. In 1822 the shooting tenant won a remarkable wager: midnight to midnight to shoot 40 brace of grouse, to ride to his home at Dunnottar (near Stonehaven on the east coast) and back again. The shooting took four and a half hours, then the 140-mile ride was accomplished, with time enough to descend at the end to Braemar again for 10 p.m.

The cropped heather led easily up to Carn Bhac which has an area of graded chips and blocks of quartz that look as if they have been combed. From there Beinn Iutharn Mhor was an unexpectedly fine sight:

a snow-filled corrie topped by an almost-perfect cornice. Just one portion had fallen to streak down to the lochan—the sort of flaw a child weeps over when building the dream sandcastle, and a bit falls down. Iutharn may mean *hell*. Bhac is *peat banks*.

The dip between the two Munros is very boggy. The ascent was runny-nose cold. I ran down the other side and flanked to reach the col for the *king's cairn*: Carn an Righ. It was such an easy ascent that I went off into a day-dream and, when I reached the summit stood completely disorientated as I was faced with a massive Beinn a' Ghlo which I did not recognise at once. I have had the same feeling in a tent, waking, and for a moment not knowing where I was.

I traversed deer tracks up Gleann Mhor, made some chicken drinks and then went up and down Glas Tulaichean, the *grey hummock*, at 3,445 feet the highest of these plain hills. The clouds were rolling in so I took a bit of old fence iron and descended direct back to the sack. The top few hundred feet gave a standing glissade, the rest a glorious bumslide—the nether regions kept dry by a bit of polythene sacking, which also reduced the coefficient of friction considerably. Two ptarmigan stood resolutely in my line of fire, trusting in their camouflage no doubt, but while they had changed to summer the hillside had not. They only burped off in the nick of time. At the foot of the slope I nearly had a repeat—with a hare. Obviously the speed of sliding humans was not easily judged.

There are some extensive bogs at the head of the glen and an odd, round, dug, pool which puzzles as to why it is there. Over the watershed lies Loch nan Eun, a favourite wilderness campsite of mine. Several of us from Braehead once met there coming in from different routes, quite a good night exercise. On another occasion Edi Crooks and I had to dig through eighteen inches of ice to reach water. Today a ring of acid-whitened stones showed where someone had pitched a tent on the peat itself; flat ground is hard to find, I suppose. The loch's name means the *loch of the birds* and its two islands were raucous with nesting gulls—2,550 feet above sea level. At 3,050 feet a few days later oyster-catchers were calling by Loch Etchachan, and under Bhrotain lies the *loch of the black-headed gulls*. Hardy birds all.

Sadly I left the chance of camping by *lapping* water (Loch Lomond was the last such site) and went on another couple of miles to lodge by the usual *running* water of a burn under An Socath. The sky paled to a delicate blue and the bovine bulk of Gheoidh and its odd "horn" of

Carn Bhinnean glowed in the sunset. The grey wasteland glowed. It is a country of browns and ochres and blues often, with great sky character. When it is grey, it can be in tones that no camera could ever touch. They are hills to camp on and see at dawn or dusk.

My lonely spot was at 2,425 feet, set in a slot by a burn which flowed underground for much of its length. There was just time to pitch and eat—a big hoosh of everything thrown in together, a meal spiced only with need. The company and setting were both agreeable.

A transistor radio had tempted me as an extra but it was a gadget, so was left. A book did not depend on dodgy mountain reception. I did miss music though. (Between trips I drive everyone mad at home by making up the loss.) Braehead gangs were quite likely to come stomping back to camp singing a chorus from *Aida* and on trips to Ireland we sang and climbed equally, thanks to Kirsty Adam. A photograph of us with the kids on a summit found its way to Morocco one winter there, local friends saw it and jumped to the conclusion this was my wife and family. Such fecundity, of males especially, made my reputation soar in their Islamic regard. I have not had the heart to shatter the illusion.

Alas, music on the Walk was limited. Water Music all too often. Sometimes one dreamed of Handel's Lager or Bach's Bass in B. Minor . . .

Wednesday 8 May   THE DEVIL'S ELBOW
An Socath was just above and gave an airy ridge walk. The new Tables have switched the Munro from one end to the other. A *south* wind was so bitter that I had to don a cagoule on top of all my garments to keep bearably warm. It was an excuse for a second breakfast before striking camp, then a burn down and a burn up gave me Carn a' Gheoidh, the *cairn of the goose*.

A small lochan had been blown nearly dry, and Loch Vrotachan had white horses and the spray sheeting off over the heather for a hundred yards. The wind rushing out of the corries to the south made it quite a tussle to rim round. Years ago I had an unforgettable experience here. It was a day of big, billowing clouds—explosions in slow motion. The clouds suddenly parted and a long corridor of clarity led the eye down glens and ridges southwards to the Lomonds of Fife and Arthur's Seat. The corridor was only a quarter of a mile wide, yet I could see seventy miles. While still marvelling at the view a flock of about thirty white ptarmigan burst from one wall, went sweeping round in the sun, then swooshed over my head to vanish in the cloud again. When I turned from following their flight, the corridor had closed.

On the Cairnwell (Scotland's easiest Munro with, or without, the chairlift) the anemometer was "fair going its dinger" and everything was well guyed down. This is Penguin Country and nothing looks so soiled and sorry as ski machinery and markings in their summer nakedness. Ski-ing has its valid claim but needs careful management. So much had to be learnt the hard way in Scotland. So much does not seem to have been learnt at all. The grim scraping of bulldozed tracks over the hills with little thought of the result is typical; there are some dreadful eyesores, not just the tracks but erosion caused by bad siting. Nor is any planning needed for tree planting, so views of great beauty, and importance as a tourist attraction, are wiped out by unthinking afforestation. It seems quite fantastic that there is no control over the drastic change of landscape use. The machinery for planning control exists, but it seems the vision does not.

Our mountain heritage in Scotland is both precious and fragile. Even bodies like the National Trust who have been given parts of it to protect seem unable to resist the "development" urge. At times I am tempted to say "to hell"—"I've had it good"—"there are limits to one's fighting powers". But can we allow the future to blame us for the loss? This is every man's fight, and in particular, it is a fight for the young; but then, I wonder if they know how to fight. We have all been trained to hold our hands out with open palms.

I came back down the Cairnwell along the snow fences, full of past memories. Most of our girls' parties learnt to ski here. The area I had been over in the last two days is all great ski-touring country, a side of mountaineering that deserves to be far more popular.

Two fishermen were battling through to Loch Vrotachan: the *loch of the lost skiers*. We yelled a greeting and I blew on up Carn Aosda, an unpronounceable Munro (try "Carn Oosh"), which is in danger of being demoted as the skiers wear it down. It is only 3,003 feet: bottom of the class. Down on the road I went into the café and indulged in three hot pies and three cups of coffee. The manager, Mr Patterson, had a parcel, quite a bit of which I left as a thank offering. I rang Jim Donaldson at Braemar and then Marina at Dollar. Kenneth, aged two, answered first as usual with his gurgly conversation but I managed to get my message through: "At Cairnwell. Next phone from Braemar

Sunday or Monday. Alarm if not, Tuesday. Checks: Thursday, Glendoll Y.H., Saturday, Mr Robertson, Spittal of Glenmuick where also John Lawton meeting noon, Saturday. If I do not arrive, pass things to Mr Robertson. Wants: new anklets, Suppletect, a book, writing materials." Peep-peep-peep went the machine. "O.K.? Ta! Cheers."

That was typical of the safety system operating. I fled the sound of a juke box but on the hill was overtaken by a Caterpillar and Land-Rover going up in tandem. Some hills is definitely not lonely.

The Cairnwell pass is 2,199 feet, our highest main road. The famous Devil's Elbow just below it is, alas, no more, being superseded by a foul, steep brae which is much harder on cars. This has been a major route to Deeside from time unrecorded. It was built as a military road in 1749–50. St Rule, with the relics of St Andrew, crossed it to join the Pictish king Angus I Mac Fergus in the eighth century. Legend is even older.

Down Gleann Beag, above the Spittal of Glenshee (an old hospice), lies Ben Gulabin, a hill connected with the Fingalian hero Diarmid Mac O'duine. He slew a monster boar on the hill but chanced to knock his foot on a bristle, which tiny wound led, eventually, to his death. If this sounds a bit like the Achilles story, it probably is; Celtic and Classical mythology have several links. In 1644 the Cairnwell saw a battle against a cattle-lifting party from Argyll. A famous Braemar archer became the hero of the fray but had the misfortune to return home with an arrow sticking from his own posterior.

I could see the Elbow as I flanked out to Creag Leacach. A band of snow had frozen in the sharp south wind and I had to cut steps with a slice of schisty rock to cross it. A wall undulates along to the top. In the mist the summit bump can be difficult to be sure of; they all look the same. The wind bullied me along and up Glas Maol. A mitt on a stick decorated the cairn. (One time it was an onion on a stick.) I dropped down to collect my sack, left before Leachach, then contoured into the lee-side corrie to look for a camp-site.

I crossed several burns and in the end pulled up, crossed the Monega Pass track, and dropped down into the next corrie. It proved a veritable wind tunnel. The next again was less draughty. I chased some deer away and pitched by a burn. It proved a noisy, uncomfortable night: the tent sloping, the ground lumpy and the wind scratching endlessly at this poor bellyfold among the hills.

Thursday 9 May   DRIESH AND NOT SO DREICH

The tent proved itself overnight. The wind was very wild, giving it periodic thumps while careering down the corrie. I cringed as I heard them coming. Previous disasters with nylon tents were still much on my mind.

I had had two epics of high camping with the water pouring in at about a pint per hour, and winter has many hours of darkness. The sewn-in ground-sheet had been very effective; it had let none of this water out. I might as well have slept in a bath. I took the present tent with great scepticism, but came to have great faith in it. Sure, there was condensation, but it ran down into the ground, for the tray-shaped groundsheet was held off the walls by elastics. Simple and effective. (This also meant one could pee without going out; a vital benefit once sealed inside on a midgy night.) The only thing I took a long time to become used to was the noise; a breeze rattled it, sounding like a gale.

Here though there was a gale, and a dreich, grey morning when I crawled out. Not far up the burn I passed a much better site.

Once over the corrie rim it was really wintry, the wet far colder in feeling than any of the hard frosts of April. From Cairn of Claise I set off into featureless country, gentle-sloping, streaked with snow, milky with mist. Contrary to opinion it is easy ground like this that is hardest for navigation. Anybody can navigate along the Aonach Eagach; but try the Cairngorms, or here, or Kinder. That is where you really have to be accurate, just when the mind is dulled.

A corrie rim came on schedule, and another bearing took me past a ruin to the top of Carn an Tuirc, within a minute of the estimate. Such accuracy always gives a certain element of wonder that navigation actually works. The wilderness beyond was treated with simplicity: minimal bearings: the first one beastly cold as it led into the wind, the second a long leg of forty minutes to a fence I had marked, then along it through a lunar landscape of tussock, snow, bog and brae. Dotterel crouched or scampered off, a snipe went like a squib, ptarmigan sat stolidly and pipits flitted past, slicing sideways in the gale—a strangely animated, avian wilderness.

The fence came four minutes ahead of schedule, then a clearance showed me the paps of Tolmount and Tom Buidhe. There can be few pairs of Munros so easily collected as this couple of Siamese twins, yet they are not to be scorned either. Jock's Road, the famous pass from Glen Clova to Braemar, lies just beyond, and twice during my lifetime, groups have died struggling over it in winter blizzards. Easy is a relative term.

So much is relative. I happily left my rucksack on a fencepost to do Tolmount, something I often did. Yet I have seen categorical "Never leave your rucksack"—just as I have seen "Never go alone"—statements which are, when unqualified, highly irresponsible. It is quite wrong to lay down *rules* for the hills; basically the hills don't play by the rules and their evil has to be matched with cunning, with gumption, not a set of procedures which ultimately fail. Common sense is not part of the M.L.C., though. Experience is still the sum total of our near misses.

The miles beyond Tom Buidhe are savannah-like, a comparison I found apt with the deer streaming off like antelope. There were brief clearances of weather so I hurried along to cash in on them in case it clamped down. I ate up the miles to the Fee burn, then, with Mayar ahead, relaxed. I actually dropped right down into a peaty hole where a burn ran underground and in that shelter had a cosy brew. The map showed some fine names: I'd passed Kilrannoch, the Burn of Fialzioch and the Dun Hillocks, while west lay Finalty Hill. Unfolding the map I found even more speculative names: Dog Hillock, Horse Holme, Shank of Inchgrundle, Loch Brandy, Naked Hill, Meg Swerie, Badhappies, The Witter, Hill of Saughs, Trusty Burn, Boustie Ley and Watery Hill—and that is but a sample.

A party passed over Mayar just before I reached it. Navigation had not been difficult. Helpful fences more or less linked on to Driesh. I added it and returned, dropping down to the valley by the Shank of Drumfollow, into the forest and over a fallen tree which is now highly polished by the passing of many walkers' breeches as they take its short-cut to the youth hostel. There I found my parcel, and a store, and the Browns at the farm sold me creamy milk and fresh brown eggs. Life felt good. There was also a one-inch map of the way to Mount Keen, which I had posted as I had found it only at the last minute. I was to be glad of it.

A gang of Alyth boys and girls came in to see the hostel, having crossed Jock's Road. Dan Smith, the warden, sounded like a guide to a stately home—which to an extent he is. The hostel is a white shooting lodge set among vivid forest. It was built at the turn of the century. An early owner had tried to close Jock's Road to the public (and the

Mounth path to Ballater) but ran up such a bill over the litigation that he had to sell out.

I had the hostel to myself, so Dan and I had a good blether, he being a hillman too. He leant me a *Climber and Rambler* (always makes me think of a rose-grower's magazine) which had one gem, describing hut life: "We seemed to do nothing but saw up wood to keep the fire going to dry out clothes we got wet sawing up wood."

I slept poorly, all too aware of a growing roar of river as the rain poured down in the night.

Friday 10 May   FURTHEST EAST

It was a bleak dawning. A curtain of rain fell in front of the window; giving a feeling of despair. Only well on in the walk did I learn not to be depressed by filthy weather messing up my plans. I think it was the wearing return to more logistics when things could not go to plan that drained me; at least I had a clear decision here: I was staying. A huge breakfast and an hour with a needle, then at 10.30 the rain switched off and the valley choked itself with clouds of steam. Perhaps I should go.

I left at noon. The Bachnagairn road was all washed-out worms. A redstart grated beside the turn off for the Capel Mounth path but I went on to pass the Capel Burn by the bridge, as the path would certainly give no ford in that spate. I followed this old drove road of zig-zags up into the cloudy tops. A county boundary led all the way to Mount Keen and I hoped there just might be a fence along it. There was no fence. A new bulldozed track simply led me a hundred yards into the murk and left me there on the edge of the bogs.

I floundered through them, then took the Allt Darrarie west of the aptly-named Watery Hill, deciding this would be better than heather and bog bashing. It was. I crossed it at once as it was in spate and soon became quite deep. After two miles following it down gently, I turned up a side stream (when it swept off for the Spittal) then a fork—and I was well committed to the moors of madness. I had read "to navigate up there you're either a fool or an expert". I did not have much doubt of the former. I had better become the latter.

At the last shelter I ate egg rolls, brewed and had a tin of oranges as morale-booster. My cutting was like a trench on a battlefront. It sounded nasty overhead. My gully petered out later and left me by a green and slimy pool. This bit of countryside is full of great holes and sinks, ditches and mounds, hollows and hags; and the constituent peat itself ranges from firm cutting-cake, to meringue glacé, to watery Chantilly. It is as if two giants have had a battle, their only weapons being an inexhaustible supply of Christmas pudding, then having tired of fighting they had taken hoses and given the scene a good wash down.

While I had brewed I had reduced the required bearings to two. It was not a day for the niceties or finer points of navigation. The first leg was three miles, the second a shade less and should bring me to the cone of Mount Keen. Even the fool could see it was going to be fun— you could not take more than a dozen steps in a straight line. You would have to go to the Ruwenzori to find bog like this.

I aimed for a nick on the skyline, at the limit of visibility, but am unaware of having reached it. The cloud came down and it began to rain, hard, as it did to the end of the day—except when it was sleeting and snowing—a biting horizontal battering from the flank, just the thing to cause navigational "drift". I played the endlessly repetitive game of taking a bearing of something on the verge of visibility (edge of hag, boulder, tuft of grass), then making for it round, through or over any obstacles that lay between. These were often considerable, and always slaistery. (The Scots often have a word for it.)

Somewhere in this Bunyan bog I found a Met. balloon and while trying to collect it the ground caved in and I landed in a stream ten foot underground, all tied up in balloon, guys and bits and pieces. I climbed up out of my crevasse with the recording label which was duly dispatched. The balloon had left Shanwell in September 1973. I described the incident so was a bit put out later to receive a massive box asking would I be so kind as to send the whole caboodle to them. I was tempted to send them a six figure reference and a spade.

The day was unique. I actually revelled in it, even at the time. Only the irrationality of my ploy was justification for being there at all. It would have been easy to escape down to the Water of Mark and then up to Keen tomorrow, but having taken up the fight, I was determined to stick to it. What climber likes to waste height already gained?

The variety of bog was amazing: solid or oozing, smooth peat and broken hags, hillocks, banks, deep-cut burns, swamps, lochans, even dry rocky sections. There seemed to be little life—and most of it dead, so to speak, the bleached bones and scraps of hares and ptarmigan. Such landmarks as there were (the Burn of Fasheilach one) came as expected, then, after hours of teasing away, the new bearing which made only one difference, the sleet battered on the starboard bow instead of abeam. Bogs. Bogs. Bogs. Some were deeply worn. The ground began to rise steadily, gravels broke through a bit, and a cairn, the first man-made object apart from the stray balloon, was strangely evocative.

The last bit seemed interminable. There were some very gooey bits, black lochans almost. A pair of hare's legs, furry and obscene, perched on a tussock. A post appeared on my casting line, then several more. They marked nothing in way of a path but after rising on to heather slopes I found the Mounth track to Glen Tanar.

It began to snow properly. The wind was bitter—and from the south again (deflected by the summit cone, perhaps). I became white with hoar. The summit granite jumble was very welcome. I rammed down a bar of chocolate and left a note on the wrapper at the cairn, the eastmost Munro. I ran like a madman off the summit to regain some warmth. I had reached the summit within ten minutes of the time guessed back at the hostel, which, in retrospect, rather pleased me.

The old path, called *The Ladder*, had been smashed up into a vile Land-Rover track but I was soon down into Glen Mark and pitched in the lee of a dyke. I just got the meal on when dusk came down like a curfew. As I had no candles I lay snug in the flea bag cooking by the light of the stove. The rain and hail battered the fabric an inch above my head. There was almost something of arrogance in being there. The margins are never wide and sometimes they are very narrow. It was an arrogance mingled with humility.

Somewhere in the day's madness I had clocked up the first 500 miles, and I had made a west–east traverse, though the purist might argue for Banachdich and Skye, Ben More and Mull being slightly east. But I was now on the way for Keen-Banachdich, in any case.

Mount Keen has one of the earliest recorded ascents of a Munro: July 1618. The Mounth path was then in use, and no doubt there had been scores of ascents; however, it fell to the Water Poet, John Taylor, is his *Pennyless Pilgrimage*, to record one: ". . . when I came to the top of it, my teeth beganne to dance in my head with cold, like virginal's jacks; and withall, a most familiar mist embraced me round . . . withall it yielded so friendly a deaw, that it did moysten throw all my clothes." I knew exactly what he meant.

Saturday 11 May   VISITORS FROM DOWN UNDER

I started the wettish, westish wending early the next day. The journey up the Water of Mark was enjoyable. I cut one loop of river by the

a Sir Hugh Munro

b The first ever Scottish Mountaineering
   Club Meet, Dalmally, 1891 sees Sir Hugh
   Munro, in kilt, and other stalwarts
   outside the hotel

c The Long Tradition—Sir Hugh Munro
   (beard and bonnet in back row) and
   other Scottish Mountaineering Club
   members at an early Meet of the Club

d The Long Tradition—Sir Hugh Munro
   (on right) and friends "on the hill" in the
   early days of the game

a Rev. A. E. Robertson—first man
  to complete the Munros in 1901

b John Hinde, who led several
  R.A.F. long-distance Munro
  treks in the 1960s

c Sandy Cousins at Cape Wrath
  at the start of his big trek in 1971

d Brian Ripley, leader of the 1967
  attempt on all the Munros

Hamish on Ben
More, Mull; the
start of the Long
Walk

Glen Etive:
Marina and
Kenneth with
support camp
established

a

b

b

a The Cruachan–
Chochuill groups seen
from the east; the first
mainland camp was on
Beinn a' Bhuiridh, the
leftmost bump

b Blackrock Cottage, the
L.S.C.C. climbing hut
with the Buachaille
Etive Mor behind

c

c The early support
team: brother David
and his wife Marina
(with the dog Kitchy)
at Loch Ba on
Rannoch Moor

Beinn an Lochain
from Ardkinglass

"Grampian" type
scenery near the
Cairnwell road,
itself over 2,000
feet in altitude; a
view from Glas
Tulaichean

a A view from the top of Lochnagar, looking down the Black Spout

b Cairngorms: Cairn Toul seen across the Lairig Ghru

c A famous shelter—the Corrour Bothy in the Cairngorms

a

a A' Choinneach and
the Saddle beyond
Loch Avon in the
Cairngorms

b Hamish looking
down the cliffs of
Ben Alder

b

a

a Gleouraich–Spidean Mialach beyond Loch Quoich; seen from
Sgurr na Ciche

b Knoydart—over Garbh Chioch Mhor from Sgurr na Ciche to
the saddle of Gulvain

Earn Stone from where I could see up to the cloud-capped dome of yesterday. Maybe it never clears up there, a perpetual Wuthering Height. From a side stream I joined my starting point of yesterday. The nick lay on the skyline. My footsteps marked across a black mud patch. A good stalkers' path criss-crossed the stream down by Creag na Slowrie to the Spittal of Glenmuick where I had a meeting planned with John and Penny Lawton. He was an Australian doctor whom I had first met in the Alps. A spell at Edinburgh was giving him the freedom of Scotland.

I hung the tent from a tree and went off to Mr Robertson, the keeper, to collect a parcel. John Hinde had done the same on one of his long treks. John, Penny and a Chinese friend arrived at 3 p.m. They were off for a holiday in the north. A shower saw them on their way. The kids watched fascinated as a line of stags stuttered its way through the pines. Later the herd passed my camp in the wood opposite, grazing their way slowly past and out of sight. I lay reading my mail all the while. Marina wrote saying that the telephone only needed to ring and Kenneth would rush to my itinerary board calling out my name. My log mentioned an orgy of fresh food again. The bubble and squeak of roding woodcock was the last sound coming through the hush of mist.

Sunday 12 May   NO CLOTHES, SORRY CAN'T COME
"Up at six and off at seven" was almost automatic by now. The fair dawn spluttered out all too soon. I went up Conachraig hoping the clouds would clear and give me a view of Lochnagar. No luck.

On the path I overhauled two lads dressed like lost fishermen in oilskins and big boots. Fifty yards at a time was all they could manage before steaming up and stalling. Did I know where the Red Spout was? They sounded sceptical when I said it would be full of snow. I hastened on into the clouds speculating that their errant way was a more valid experience than that of assembly-line production. Being lost is a much more effective way of learning than being led, or being churned out by the instant mountaineering industry with its questionable practices. It is not unknown for teachers to do the M.L.C. merely as a bit of paper which might give them an edge in job-hunting, or to get more money. Their mentors play musical chairs, juggling salaries and scales, creating departments and bumf. The whole system is open to question. I remember meeting a gang of trainee teachers on a hill

E

above Rannoch Moor. The view was superb yet they arrived and slumped down with all the enthusiasm of potato sacks. Nobody commented on the scene. Nobody looked at a map. Nobody said much. Nobody trained anybody in anything. After a statutory five minutes they filed off in their identi-kit rigs. And these were the potential leaders of kids.

The ascent to the plateau was quite an icy scramble. On top, tracks led through snow and melt to Cac Carn Mor, whose cairn many take for the summit, which is actually on a bit, Cac Carn Beag (the Mor and Beag are the wrong way round). I installed myself in the summit rocks and was just tucking into bacon butties when another boarding party scrambled up, a couple plus an older gangrel who seemed all artificial limbs, and blind. I can hardly think of anything more remote from the institutionalised mountaineer than Syd Scroggie. They had come up from overnighting at the Glas Allt Shiel, once a favourite haunt of the mourning Queen Victoria.

Some years before, three of us had met Syd on the long road up to Derry Lodge. He was alone. We chatted a while, a conversation punctuated by his comments on this and that bird which he heard, and which we neither saw nor heard. Now on Lochnagar he was able to describe the view though we could see nothing but mist. And he trotted out all the bearings while we were still groping for compasses. Only when well away from the summit did it clear so that I could see down to Deeside, and the lochs and woods that Queen Victoria knew as "the bonniest plaid in all Scotland".

White Mounth is a dull dome of a Munro: a snow-soggy bump today. Next comes Carn an t-Sagairt Mor which has two cairns on top, fifty yards apart and both decorated with pieces of crashed aircraft. I went on round the deep trough of the Dubh Loch to add Cairn Bannoch and Broad Cairn—almost back to Jock's Road in my sweep. It is all rolling granite plateau country, great on ski. The Dubh Loch reminds of Loch Avon, a deep-set, crag-bound, black ribbon of water. Instead of the Shelter Stone Crag there is Creag an Dubh Loch (with climbs as hard), instead of the Feith Buidhe, the Allt an Dubh Loch and instead of the Stag Rocks there are the Eagle Rocks. Climbers must enjoy the old S.M.C. comment on the cliffs as "overhanging rocks which are manifestly impossible".

I rewound my route over "Taggart" and dropped down to Loch Callater. Gulls blew like confetti up the loch, nesting safe on an island as usual. The road was covered in stinking diesel oil and two caterpillar vehicles came up, one driven by a lad who must have been all of fifteen. I passed the miles singing hymns and psalms—it was the Sabbath after all. The golfers and cuckoos on the golf course eventually shamed me into self-conscious silence. The Youth Hostel, a fine granite building, stood on the edge of the town, very welcome.

Seeing it nestling in the trees reminded me of a sermon we once had under the pines there. The Rev. William Still from Aberdeen talked to our youngsters for an hour and a half—and held them enthralled. Reality, in any aspect, can only kindle. It is today's tragedy that reality is so glossed over by the puerile, the facile and the plastic.

Mrs Ewan has been the happy warden at Braemar for so long as I can recall. I had a shower and then went round to spend the evening with Jim and Sheila Donaldson. A dainty meal in a house seemed an incredible luxury. Mountain pictures by Alf Gregory and Tom Weir were on the wall, pages of the latest Munros Tables lay ready for revising. Jim is the keeper of the facts and figures. They had a parcel for me. Jim did the Munros back in 1961 and has probably skied more of them than anyone. When I had left the parcel in February he had a leg in plaster to prove it. Their hospitality was much appreciated.

I had a gigantic washing of everything, once back at the hostel, so retired to the dorm draped in a blanket. An hour later Mrs Ewan crept in and shook me awake. Jim was on the telephone asking if I would like to go out on a search for some folk missing on the Feughside hills. I whispered my apologies. I had no clothes—I had washed every stitch to the extent that I "lay between the lily white sheets with nothing on at all".

Monday 13 May QUIETLY FLOWS THE DEE
The missing trio had been found, suffering a bit from exposure, but Jim was back for breakfast. A large gang from Inverness Academy were in at the hostel last night. They, Gordonstoun, and Braehead used at one time to be the gangs one met on the hill—in the good old days. The tradition still lingers it seems. The type of noise was familiar. Youth is certainly the time to start.

I prowled about Braemar a bit then reccied the Dee down to Braemar Castle without finding any spot for easy wading. The river was still high, so I would have to make the detour to the bridge. The castle sat sunnily among the larches by the river, quite an historical place, it is open to the public. The Invercauld Arms now occupies the site where the standard was raised in 1715. A garrison was maintained at Braemar up till 1831.

Back in the village I watched a craftsman working with horn. Braemar is a prime tourist spot in summer, of course. The Aberdeen accents were still obvious, not yet overwhelmed in the babel of summer tongues. I once heard a local climber query, "Fa' did ah fa' fa' times?" And had I not come in past fields loud with teuchats calling? A house had a plaque mentioning that it was here Robert Louis Stevenson had stayed as an invalid in 1881, and written *Treasure Island,* which made his name. Reasons of health brought Queen Victoria to Deeside, too; she had considered Lagganside but a summer monsoon there, and word of the drier clime of Deeside, brought Albert prospecting to the east.

I had intended an early night but two Tasmanian lassies easily prevented that. It was a calm evening and we only fell silent as dusk shuttered down on its silver glow. Looking back, what could have been a dull section of the walk had gone quite pleasantly if not quite without incident. The plateau-like landscape had brought the average height per Munro down to about 1,400 feet, compared to over 2,000 feet at the start. Braemar itself is over a thousand feet up. It would be interesting to see what the main Cairgorms would give.

VI

THE MONADH RUADH

"But we sleep by the ropes of the camp, and we rise with a shout
  and we tramp
  With the sun or the moon for a lamp, and the spray of the wind in
  our hair "

JAMES ELROY FLECKER

Tuesday 14 May BACK TO THE SINGING HEIGHTS
"Say, is that an English breakfast?" The hitch-hikers watched, all
eyes, as I ploughed through cereal, a mixed grill, fruit, tea, toast and
marmalade.

The morning had a glitter like crystal at a banquet and for once kept
its splendour. The clean town and tidy landscape seemed as if it had
just had a spring clean. Braemar Castle had obviously been painted
in to complete the filming of some romance. The eye led from the valley
richness and the brightness of the Dee up to the combed greys and
browns of the vast moines and mountains. The Cairngorms. The
Monadh Ruadh.

I had picked up one of Molly Weir's books, *Shoes Were For Sunday*, and
read it walking down the miles of road to the Invercauld Bridge and on
up beyond. At one stage I walked straight into a gate (and apologised)!
After the walk I was doing a programme with Tom Weir and mentioned
reading while walking and my apologising to a gate. He at once asked
what book I'd been reading and of the scores I did read it had to be one
by his sister.

The old bridge over the Dee had its postcard backcloth of Lochnagar,
the Byron image of

> ". . . the crags that are wild and majestic!
>   The steep frowning glories of dark Lochnagar!"

Patey parodied this into a song,

> "Gasherbrum, Masherbrum, Distigal Sar,
>   Are all good training for dark Lochnagar"

which became set in my mind all the way up the Slugain path. I had a brew once past the ruins of the old lodge. A pool reflected the snowy rims of the high hills. I had a last look back down the secretive path to the feudal landscape and went on into the folds of the hills.

Cairn Toul was a familiar shape. In the south the snow corrie of Iutharn Mor stood out. The path led on under the big corries of Beinn a' Bhuird. Coire na Ciche comes first, only losing impressiveness when Coire nan Clach, the *corrie of the boulders*, appears beyond. I put a foot in a bog. Washing the stocking at a burn, I saw the glitter of an eye and found a pipit nesting under a tuft of grass. It had five eggs of warm, spotted loveliness. I hurried on. Deer were lying along a snow rim above. Somewhere above Clach a' Chleirich, the *Clergyman's stone*, the path ran out and it seemed a hard haul up to the Sneck, the 3,200-foot col between these two eastern giants. Once I left the rucksack progress was like levitation. The sun glinted on a vehicle down by the Avon river below the Slochd Mor, as the valley on the other side is called. The col had a cluster of wind-sculptured rocks which could have been quite at home in a modern art collection.

North from here is some of the emptiest landscape in Britain. Go astray and you will go twenty miles possibly before seeing a habitation. I doubt if that could be done elsewhere. The name Avon derives from Ath-Fhinn meaning *Fingal's ford*. The hero's wife is supposed to have been swept away and drowned near Inchrory. The point at which the Lairig an Laoigh path crosses the Avon is still called Ath nam Fiann.

Ben Avon, though 3,843 feet, is soon reached from the Sneck. It is a great plateau with many strange "warts" or "barns" of granite. The summit is one, Leabaidh an Daimh Bhuidhe, meaning the *couch of the tawny stag*, though if you search, all you will find is two wind-carved sea-lions, one with a basin in its head. Several of the tors have these hollows carved out by the swirl of grit and water. (On Ben Loyal in Sutherland I have actually had a bath in one.) I spent half an hour clambering on the Henry Moore shapes, then sat on top enjoying sun and view. Lochnagar looked a bit further off now. Morven to the east and Ben Rinnes to the north act as outriders to the big hills, the better viewpoints for not being Munros.

I went down, collected my sack, and up the other side to rim round the big *table* of Beinn a' Bhuird. The Dubh Lochan was a white lie to its name as it reflected the snowy cliffs. The summit, 3,924 feet, was at my end. These two big hills plus the four of over 4,000 feet form the "Big Six" of the Cairngorms. They have been done on skis and they are a pretty good summer walk.

The south summit lies two miles on, with the wound of a Land-Rover track up it; just one of many inflictions disfiguring these clean heights in the name of ski-ing, which the snowless winters have shown for folly. I suppose these two hills have the best of defences in a lazy society—long miles of necessary self-propulsion.

From Beinn a' Bhuird I could see the warts on top of Beinn Mhead-hoin and also the Barns of Bynack, two other areas of weathered granite. I dipped to 2,750 feet on the Moine Bhealaidh, the *Pass of the moss*, and on its vast, ochreous, flat sweep, pitched the tent. It was another site I had dreamed of for years. Instead of dashing off for the Munros at either end of it, I sat to enjoy the sunny hours of evening. The hot day had caused some sweaty chafe again. To sit was bliss. The deer browsed towards me unconcerned, grouse came noisily down like distended helicopters to pitch in the heather, and the saddest song of the hills, the golden plovers' call, was a constant background. It had been a day with the gathered perfection of a symphony.

Alas, contrasts come in all ways, the night was made foul by something I had eaten. In our local dialect I was "minging" and did not enjoy the company one little bit, however fine the setting.

Wednesday 15 May   A WINDY WINDAE

I was up early, in self-defence. I buried deep a suspect packet of dried onions. It was back to raw winds, but thankfully dry. I had heard a skylark singing above the tent long before six-thirty, when I set off. Beinn Bhreac was a gentle walk to the south end of my plateau, but I had not gone far before the tent was simply swallowed up in the vast sweep of this empty reach. What a contrast say to the site under Ben Lomond! I tried to capture the atmosphere on slides. Beinn a' Chaoruinn lay to the north of the site and I did both these Munros before returning for breakfast. By then I was fit to live with again.

I had left a questionnaire on the latter. It was found by a fellow-member of the A.B.M.S.A.C. the next day, James Walmsley, who wrote a kind note back. He mentioned the late Willie Docherty in it, a person known now to a decreasing circle of friends, one of that passing breed of "gentle giants", modest and kindly who yet did mighty deeds in the hills. He published privately a trilogy listing some 900 summits in the British Isles and including dozens of large, pullout panoramas which must be unique. Having heard of our Braehead doings, he very kindly had given me a set. We became friends. He had an encyclopaedic knowledge of the hills, despite having nearly lost a leg in the war and having a wife helplessly bed-ridden. At the top of his house he had a prophet's chamber lined throughout with framed panoramas.

W. K. Holmes (author of *Tramping Scottish Hills* and volumes of verse) was another of this sort who had befriended our gang when we were kids at Dollar. He was the only adult we met in the Ochils, we thought him rather fine, though goodness knows what he thought of us banging in six-inch nails for pitons on routes in the out-of-bounds quarry. He came and watched, though—his example meant a great deal, I can see now.

The hills are peopled with all these past memories, enriching, encouraging. How could I possibly be bored? Oh, can I plead, for the taking of the heritage in full; do not be a specialist, the mountains are worth so much more. Read, and look, and go and go to the very end. It is all joy.

The Cairngorms are divided north–south by two great passes, the eastern, the Lairig an Laoigh, the *Pass of the calves*, lay just below this moine, at this stage a deep trench across which I looked to Coire Etchachan. North and south of this corrie lay my next two Munros; I therefore had to drop steeply down into the pass before starting the day again, so to speak.

On the slopes of warty Beinn Mheadhoin I found a hole which looked as if it had been caused by lightning or by a meteorite, for it was too fresh for the work of Cairngorm hunters. The barns were like piles of platters—fascinating weathering. A ptarmigan flopped off its nest at my feet and tried to lead me away with a mock-injury display. I hurried on for the wind was icy cold and the eggs would soon chill. Sometimes I have only been saved from standing on nests by the sitting bird's blinking eye. The camouflage is perfect. Dotterel, too, sit tight, often to their grief, rarity making them prey to the inane egg-collecting mania.

Mheadhoin's summit is another barn, and not for the first time I reached it on hands and knees, the wind making balance difficult. From it I could look straight down on Loch Avon. The scene was still like something from the arctic. I was sad not to be using the famous Shelter Stone (by the next morning I was to be doubly sorry), probably the most famous howff of all. There used to be a visitors' book. One brief entry took our interest; it said, "It moved"! Nearby the Cairngorm Club was founded—the first club in Scotland.

Not so long ago a body was found near the Shelter Stone. It had lain for some months, yet nobody knows who or why. Forty years ago, on Ben Avon, another body was found in a burn, and its presence there is still unexplained. On a rock upstream was laid out a razor, brush and other toilet items; an attaché-case held pyjama trousers and the like. His identity was never discovered, nor why he should have been up there dressed in city suit and bowler hat. There have been something like sixty unexplained bodies or vanished persons in the Scottish hills, since records have been kept.

The Cairngorms are among the most-used hills now, yet off the beaten tracks you can still be very much alone. From Mheadhoin down to Loch Etchachan there is now a path. This loch, sited at 3,050 feet, is the highest large spread of water in the country. Lean trout survive in it and pied pipers were calling round it today. My first acquaintance with it had nearly been my last for I had managed to get adrift on an ice floe. In winter it can be iced over for weeks—I have crossed it on ski. Today the ice still rimmed it and the wind was throwing the spray far up the slopes round it, reminding me just how wild and inhospitable these hills can be, modest though they may seem in area or height when compared with foreign ranges.

Derry Cairngorm lies out on a limb and gives some good boulder-hopping practice. It is probably the least-visited Cairngorm summit, and one of the best with its view of the Lairig an Laoigh, Glen Derry, and the cliffs of Sputan Dearg and Lochain Uaine. Every other loch seems to be a *green loch* in these hills.

I hopped my way back off Derry Cairngorm and dropped into Coire Etchachan where there is a small concrete memorial hut built in 1954. In the book I found the name of a local lad, Pat Heneghan, and of Gordon Mackenzie who had been with me in the Alps a year previously. A mouse was often mentioned—or was it a shrew? From there I dropped down into the Lairig and followed it through to the Fords of Avon where there is another wee shelter with a book. Syd Scroggie, met on Lochnagar, had been there. So had Robert Aitken, an old climbing partner.

The ford was just a ford, fortunately, and I crossed dry. The shelter was welcome and I sat out of the wind relishing a brew. The howff has a garden of compo ration tins.

I was tempted to stay the night but, high wind or not, the call to push on was stronger than sanity. I pinched a candle, left two paperbacks and wended up to Loch Avon, which I could hear long before it came into view: the waves were crashing on its red sands like a sea. A toil up boulders, heather and juniper took me to the Saddle and I dropped down the Strath Nethy side hoping for a lee. There was none, but after eleven hours on the go tendons had had enough, and I pitched the tent.

Thursday 16 May   WIND ON THE LEFT

The night produced a Cairngorm roarer, the big wind whamming up the glen into the tent which cracked and banged so that sleep was really impossible. A bivy bag would have been much less noisy. The night stayed dry, mercifully, though, after midnight, it blew so hard that I half-dressed and half-packed in case of an emergency exodus. At 5.45 I rose thankfully. Neither candle nor stove could cope with the wind inside the tent, so after a tepid breakfast I crawled out again to battle the flailing canvas into a packable bundle. Leaving the gear I staggered up the slope above for A'Choinneach, a minor Munro.

My course up the slopes was erratic as the wind landed blow after blow, eventually sprawling me on to the granite gravel with an unexpected lull. Loch Avon, below, looked like a sea torn by a storm from some unlikely film. A'Choinneach was dull enough to merit a questionnaire. It was picked up two days later by Peter Mackay from Alva (like Dollar, an Ochils hillfoot town), who was then on Munro 100. He climbed, he said, to get away from people who ask him to fill in forms.

Bynack More, a better Munro, was reached almost at a trot, the wind pushing me up its flank. Cairn Gorm was spouting smoke-like clouds of its own making. I had wanted to visit the Barns of Bynack, a group of tors big enough for some climbing, but decided I had plenty to do as it was. I reckon it took twice the calories to fight my way down to the Saddle again, into the wind, than it had to sail uphill with the storm. A roof over my head was a dream. Two nights without sleep had me yawning like a zombie.

It would be easy to believe in the *each uisge* on a day like this, for the loch had a hundred wild horses kicking on its black surface. Toiling up the slope on the other side of the Saddle, even with the extra weight of the rucksack, I was twice knocked over. I traversed above a shallow corrie to leave my burden on the slopes of Coire Raibeirt, then spread my jacket like a sail to help me up Cairn Gorm. Two dotterel with flickering legs went speeding off, and just a minute before reaching this most popular of summits I found a fine cluster of Cairngorm stones in a block of granite. I hid it, took a bearing and paced the distance from the cairn. Months later I returned for it—and could not find it.

The largest Cairngorm ever found—two feet long—can be seen at Braemar Castle. It was found in the eighteenth century on Beinn a' Bhuird after the Cailleach nan Clach, the *old woman of the stones*, had dreamed about it. A 50 lb monster was found by the Feith Buidhe by John Grant of Ryvoan. It went to Queen Victoria, Grant receiving £1 per lb for it, quite a sum in those days.

Cairn Gorm is one of the most visited of summits. It now has an erosion problem, a chair-lift, a café and such like. The name has come to be given to all the hills, replacing the kindlier Monadh Ruadh—the *blue hills* replacing the *red*. Speyside is the tourist magnet. On the A9 at Aviemore there is even a road sign marked "Cairn Gorm". This is a corner of Scotland I try to visit only during the odd days of the off season. There are worn paths connecting all the popular tops and routes, as in the Lakes, but equally, go aside a wee, and it is all yours. The Monadh Ruadh is still finer than the sum of the ants who crawl over it.

The tourists are not new. One of the attractions used to be that Macdhui was regarded as the highest point in the British Isles. While working on notes recently I was glad to see that a new book by Campbell Steven had come out, for it tells quite a bit about early visitors to Cairngorm. *The Story of Scotland's Hills* (Hale) gives many fascinating historical accounts and is a must for anyone wanting more than just topographical information. Another comprehensive book is that by Adam Watson and Nethersole-Thomson, *The Cairngorms* (Collins). Doing courses in the hills I am for ever recommending books and am usually saddened to see nobody at once note the titles. Any book can be ordered from the local library where a whole world of vicarious fun lies ready to hand. Few seem to use it!

I cringed in the doorway of the radio relay station only to cram in a Lee's Macaroon Bar, then fought back down to my rucksack. A refreshing high traverse followed, taking me round to Lochan Buidhe, the highest small lochan in the country (3,683 feet), where I went into the Curran Bothy for a brew. The floor was inches deep in ice, covered in melt and a malodorous collection of refuse. It was the first and last time I would use the place. It has since been knocked down. Hateful place, it had been the fatal loadstone of a Cairngorm tragedy. It was while trying to make for it that an Edinburgh school party had been overwhelmed by a blizzard and died on this wild plateau.

As with so many tragedies it drove many into ridiculous extremes of attitude. Climbers too readily cry "keep all kids out", yet most of them first went on the hills as kids themselves, and probably a deal more dangerously. All of us who have been at this game a long time are survivors in a way and in no position to throw stones. Yet safety has been made the latest sacred cow and the hills roped down with a load of rules and regulations. One authority had the following orders worked out: the Cairngorm plateau banned from October to April; parties to go up a hill only so long as they return by the same route; in winter they must not go above 2,000 feet; climbing, only up what they can climb down; through routes and treks forbidden, and areas beyond the Great Glen are not to be used because too remote.

The hills cannot be made completely safe. It is a pity that the M.L.C. has been regarded as a magic wand that ensures safety. It merely shows a basic hill competence, nothing more. Yet the experience and competence of climbers is seldom called upon to help head-masters assess a teacher's potential on the hill with kids. It is easier, I suppose, to rely on a bit of paper. Some naughty people, too, have proclaimed that one type of mountain activity is more "worthy" or "right" than another. But you cannot separate values, ideals, dreams, motivations, nor grade them. The hills are not there for climbers, for walkers, for skiers, for mountain rescuers, for bird watchers, for tourists, for committees, for school kids, for grannies, or even for educationists. They are there for fun—for the rising of any man's heart, whatever the game he plays. Answer only to your own heart.

These were no doubt gloomy thoughts, appropriate for the midden of the Curran, perhaps. The shelter gave a wind-free brew. I had coffee and soup and then went off still supping a bowl of porridge in an effort to gain Macdhui ahead of the mist. The mist won. By a ruined gable I donned waterproofs—it was bitter cold in the cloud. The whole region of this summit is a mess of holes and bothy ruins and the like—a reminder of the days of searching for Cairngorms. We were mercifully spared the erection of a massive cairn to raise Macdhui above the Ben, a scheme which failed due to cash shortage.

Circling down and round I came on three figures in the familiar colours of Glenmore Lodge. We loomed up on each other, passed, and vanished like ghosts. Naturally the mind turned to the tales of the Great Grey Man. Sadly I have nothing personal to relate, despite many visits in misty weather, despite even sleeping on the haunted mountain. The Lodge staff do not tell tales and the locals keep quiet on the topic. Persistent puzzles could be largely due to our ignorance, yet it is easy to joke. One wonders just what Collie, famous scientist, but also famous joker, was up to when he first admitted taking to his heels on Macdhui. That was in 1891. Since then there have been other admissions of terrifying phenomena. Borthwick touches on it in *Always a Little Further*; John Buchan (a fine climber) has a story of a similar experience in Bavaria entitled "Pan" (in the S.M.C. Journal, vol. 22, p. 41). Why, of all Scotland's likely hills, is this one singled out for such persistent tales?

Beyond the Tailors' Burn I turned down and came out of the blowing cloud. Rising in a succession of bumps the only real ridge in the Cairngorms led on to Carn a' Mhaim, the day's fifth Munro. On the col, the Ceann Caol, I found a white azalea among the many pink ones. I blew along to the summit which has a great view down into the Lairig

Ghru and to Braeriach. Below I could see the Corrour Bothy which squatted like a spider in a web of radiating paths. It was to be my shelter for the night, eventually.

First I went on to the end of the ridge which always looks higher than the real summit, then dropped down to cross the Glen Derry path to gain the Lairig Ghru well to the south of the bothy. I had a brew and emptied my rucksack. A lochan above me actually drains both ways, to Dee and Derry. I carried on down the Lairig path till opposite the Allt Garbh where I boulder-hopped the Dee rather cheekily, then once I had added a heavy load to my rucksack I more cannily chose to paddle back.

This load was a food parcel which I had buried, back in February, among a jumble of granite boulders; it proved to be in perfect condition. The sugar ran out of its bag freely. No damp at all. Untouched.

The way across to the bothy was signposted and the Dee has a bridge; after all this is the country's premier pedestrian motorway, so to speak, and the "services" have to be provided. Being about the busiest of all bothies it is often also the dirtiest. Even the deer know this and you can lie listening to them clattering among the tins and rubbish at night. The bothy was originally built in 1877, but in 1950 had to be virtually rebuilt in unfriendly concrete and non-combustible materials, a testimony to vandalism. Seton Gordon, the grand-master writer on the Cairngorms, tells a story of being in the bothy during a blizzard when his friend went out to fetch water from the burn and did not return. In the storm he had lost the bothy, and only found it again by following the sound of the bagpipes which Seton Gordon was playing for the purpose.

This great pass, which rises to 2,700 feet, is an old through route—as old as man himself no doubt. Cattle were regularly driven through it to southern markets. Raiders used it. The Tailors' Stone marks the spot of one tragedy. It is as well that the idea of creating the glorified "Grampian Way" through here has been dropped, or we no doubt would have a few more.

I joined an older man in the bothy. The statutory brew was welcome. I was bleary with the wind. R. L. Stevenson I think it was who talked about "the flaws of fine weather we call our summer". It cleared for a blink of sunset sun. A mountain blackbird was tugging at a worm on the lawn outside, just like his urban counterpart. In the middle of the night I went out and sent off a startled stag. By then the night was impressively wild, with weird clouds towering and a single beacon star bright in the vee of the Lairig. Some things you cannot spoil.

Friday 17 May WIND ON THE RIGHT

Sleep can be either consciously relished or a deep oblivion. It was from the latter I woke at 7.30. My bothy companion packed and even washed before going off to Loch Morlich, hoping to return later to go down the Tilt. I merely ate. It was nearly ten before we went our ways.

Devil's Point looms over the bothy, a thrust of crag and slab that sticks out in any view down the Lairig. The slab was not to be resisted, and rather than go up the corrie path I simply scrambled up direct. On top I nearly stood on a ptarmigan brooding her seven eggs. Dodging wet and boulder areas I gained the rim for Cairn Toul, the *barn hill*, which was again very windy. Angel's Peak beyond is another thrusting shape; Sgor an Lochain Uaine, its older name, tells that it sits above yet another lochan of common name. The loch was like a cauldron, all spume and motion. Braeriach, across the fastness of the Garbh Choire, had a weird cloud formation above it.

The Garbh Choire is one of the wildest in Scotland, a huge bite, or bites rather, taken out of the plateau which is all near or over the 4,000-foot mark. The whole rim was still corniced. Many times on the plateau I was forced into a run by the push of the wind. The infant Dee falls from the plateau, usually in a string of white which today was oddly missing. I found out why when I went over to see the fall—and received most of it in my face. The wind several times knocked me down or threw stinging gravel at me. Progression had a drunken look about it as I would stagger first one way, then rush off in another, then lean on nothing, then fall down. Approaching gusts could be seen in the spray they picked up, like miniature waterspouts. It was an entertaining way of gaining Braeriach.

The summit itself was quite without wind, but it was not quiet. A roar like the sea came from only a few feet away and the fantastic upward thrust of wind out of the corrie was creating the cloud paintings overhead. It was eerie and impressive, but a glower of grey was a warning not to linger.

It was on the cliffs where the infant Dee plunges down into the corries that one of the earliest rock-climbs was recorded in Scotland, in 1810. The Rev. George Keith Skene was tracing that river to its source and no bit of cliff was going to divert the enthusiastic scientist. The route is still in the climbers' guidebook. It was the same gentleman who finally destroyed Macdhui's claim to be the highest. His measurements gave it 4,300 feet (four feet out from the present) but his son came back with an upsetting 4,406 feet for Ben Nevis.

I returned to the Lairig by the Sron, meeting a vertical wind at the first nick on the rim and later stopping to look at bits of old wreckage from a wartime air crash. As a kid I took home from there an old flying boot with some bones in it; a precious souvenir which my parents managed to lose rather quickly. On another occasion I broke an ice-axe trying to gain some mechanical parts.

The latest two trips had been with Assessment candidates for the Instructor's Certificate, overnight exercises from Glenmore Lodge, the latter memorable in full moon on new snow that made a wonderland out of winter. You could read the map without a torch and see for miles. Not the most testing of conditions for assessing navigation, but a night the victims will not forget. My group of Instructors crossed from Glen Feshie, walked up Glen Einich and then over the plateau, bivying on Braeriach before going out via the Sron to Loch Morlich.

Today the Sron na Lairig col was devilish, and it took a real tussle to drop the 200 feet off it to the forgotten zig-zag of a path. After that it was a romp. Wreckage was strewn right down to the burn in the Lairig and if you went up Macdhui by the slope opposite you could follow wreckage there too, for another plane had crashed on that side. The Devil's Point and Carn a' Mhaim are nicely balanced seen from here and the loops of the Dee were glittering and silver; Poussin could not have arranged it better.

An hour of boulder-hopping saw me back at the bothy. I crossed well up from the bridge, which is cunningly placed to land one right in a big peat bog which has been well ploughed with a million feet. Be warned of Cairngorm bothies, they are often full, and at the best grimy, sweaty, concrete boxes. Earlier I mentioned the tragedy of the tailors: they had set out on a wager to dance, in one day, in the dells of Abernethy, Rothiemurchus (Speyside) and Dalmore (Deeside). The worst of the pass over, they perished at the spot known as Clach nan Taillear. Even the doucer Lairig an Laoigh had a group tragedy, in 1805, when five out of seven soldiers died in a storm while walking from Edinburgh home to Speyside. I have been pinned down at Corrour in a blizzard in which it was impossible to move. The bothy was a real haven then.

I kept a candle in the window and periodically warmed soup and tea water. Weekenders were expected. At midnight two winking lights appeared miles off. There was a sensation of excitement and unreality watching their approach. Figures evolved out of the glowing patches. Ian and Mary McLeod and a German teacher friend, Wolfgang, burst in; our high-spirited reunion was no doubt a puzzle to two quiet French girls who had arrived a bit earlier. Brews, beer, soup and much chatter ensured I had my latest bedding of the trip. We drifted into a silence lapped with the sound of rain.

Saturday 18 May TENT IN THE CLOUDS

The French girls snored, but they were away first. In sawn-off jeans we reckoned they would have delicately blue knees on top of Braeriach. It still rained steadily though the cloud cleared off the tops. I was telling the others of our last Braehead trip at Corrour when we had had the Army encamped about us. We had stayed on for two extra days living off their left-overs. Every boulder seemed to be hiding a steamed pudding or tube of gooseberry jam, quite apart from what we were officially given. If the Army chose not to march on its stomach, we did!

Eventually the rain turned off, so there was no excuse for prolonging our fester. Ian, Mary and Wolfi set off to traverse Macdhui while I turned for the Bhrotain group. They had the more interesting day, for they had no sooner settled into the Etchachan Hut than Wolfi spotted someone "humbling" down from the near crags: a young Marine who had completed a V.S. route and then fallen on a loose boulder. They had to evacuate him to Derry Lodge.

The Dee sang bonnily—and deeper than before. I had to paddle again at the same easy spot near the cache site. The blue milkwort was out and suddenly there seemed to be butterwort stars everywhere—as if they had crawled out like starfish from the pools. I followed the Allt Garbh which joins the Dee there, its deer-tracked gorge or the slabby burn itself giving better walking than the deep, clawing heather. Close-cropped heather above was better and took me up Carn Cloich-mhuillin, the *cairn of the mill*, the hill Sir Hugh had intended for his last as it was easy to ascend with ponies bearing the appropriate celebration-day libations.

Tramping up Bhrotain beyond, I entered cloud—and that was that for the rest of the day. My steering led to the knobbly cairn and the nearby trig point. Bhrotain and Bhrodainn, a loch in the Gaick Pass, probably derive from Brodan, the hound of Celtic lore, which chased the white stag of Ben Alder into the loch where both vanished for ever. The corrie between Bhrotain and Monadh Mor (the *big dumpy hill*), the next along, is Coire Cath nam Fiann, the *corrie of the battle of the Fianns* (Fingalians). It is sad that so many legends only linger in mysterious place names.

Both are unshapely lumps of hill, part of an empty quarter only visited I reckon by working keepers, filthy Munro-baggers, and a few other aberrant walkers. In quite a number of visits I have never met anyone up there, though I have still to go on a day with decent visibility.

Between these hills and the Devil's Point runs Glen Geusachan, once a deer sanctuary, a long glen, with slabby flanks (which might repay climbing on) and only lacking a loch to give it full splendour. An interesting lochan lies above its head, Loch na Stuirteag, which at 2,840 feet must be the highest site for nesting gulls in Britain, nor could they be much further from the sea. The name means *loch of the black headed gulls*—which certainly do make a stuirteag of a noise. The gulls nesting now are common gulls, but the name was given about eighty years ago. Before that it was the "Insignificant Loch".

Monadh Mor was reached over a bouldery col and gave typical map, watch, and compass navigation, both to reach it and for the continuation, until the snow banked down to the Allt Luineag, a mess of river dawdling in the puddles and melt. It is a wonderfully empty desolation, the home of haunting birds and wet winds. I crossed the river and cut through between a Top of 3,009 feet and lonely Loch nan Cnapan, both faintly discernible. A path of sorts (deer?) led to the Allt Sgairnich which led to a new bulldozed track. I took it for a while but then reverted to map and compass to make sure of hitting the strong, if infant, River Eidart, here known as the Caochan Dubh. The ground was very *dubh*. I found the river and followed it down to where it made a marked swing to the south-east—which let me know exactly where I was. Not for nothing is this the Moine Mhor, the *big moss*; broken country of peat hags and, higher, grassy sweeps now scarred by man's new tracks. I ran into the Land-Rover track again and as I knew where it left the plateau to drop to Glen Feshie, I gave up map and compass to follow it. A fork of the track soon landed me on Mulloch Clach a'

Bhlair just after 7 p.m. As it had rained for several hours I decided it was time to stop. In the conditions it would have been a tricky night descent to reach the Feshie. I might be a "spoilt child of adventure" in the words of Roger Duplat, but I was a canny one withal. I pitched the tent within sight of a corrie rim which bubbled over with cloud. It was crying plover country, a desolation I love. One by one four candle stumps burnt out as I scribbled the day's log. At 3,025 feet the site was to prove the highest of the Walk.

Sunday 19 May REWARDS AND THE FESHIE

Some days are good from the opening of eyes. This was one such, no doubt helped by being at over 3,000 feet already. The first brew was made while still cosy in the sleeping bag, and eating and reading made for a lazy start. Stones went into the burn and I left no sign of my stay beyond a temporary depression in the soggy grass. The cloud was tense and bright with the promise of clearing.

I groped round the rim of Coire Garbhlach, a gravelly, floral place seldom visited by walkers. The cloud teased off like cotton wool pulled from an aspirin bottle. I stood on the dome of Meall Dubhag. A ptarmigan sat in the confidence of its camouflage. Perhaps it should be my symbol of the summits, this gentle bird of the mists and snow, of bog and ridge and dew-glitter. I sat watching it a while, then read a bit, willing the weather to clear up and the sun to shine again. Impatiently I stormed over Carn Ban Mor.

Only then it cleared. Like surf sucking seaward, breaking, ebbing, clear. I gazed about the casual complex of the Cairngorms, over the green richness of Speyside, to western dream hills that were still to come. It was very good. I romped on, singing as only optimism in the sun can sing.

> "Where lies the land to which the ship would go?
> Far, far ahead, is all her seamen know."
>
> A. H. CLOUGH

Today was a day of holiday! Sailing free!

If I have dwelt on this feeling of elation, it is on purpose. The feeling of being in tune, both with the finite and the Infinite, is a vital part of the game of hills we play. We suppress the romantic only to our hurt. If I had my ups and downs, usually related to the weather, then, overall, the ups far outnumbered the downs. There would be no sense in it otherwise. The bad days of course make better copy (disasters sell best of all), and we British are so loath to appear enthusiastic about anything.

One winter, back in the days when perforce we had to exercise our thumbs, Mike Smith and I hitched up from Fife one Friday night. We had agreed to meet at a certain bridge at midnight, which, despite blizzards and one lorry arguing with a telegraph pole, we did. We walked to Glen Feshie and camped. It was freezing-the-eggs cold but gave a swinging day over these hills in just the way today was doing— except we were one Munro on that day. Looking to Sgor Gaoith today I had a feeling of disbelief. On those gentle slopes we had got lost, Mike and I, in classic fashion too. It was obviously going to clear so we were lazy about steering by compass, and tramped on in the mist. We found two more tracks, newly made, which was surprising at that early winter hour. When we joined an even bigger track we at last became suspicious and at that moment the cloud blew away to reveal everything written in the snow. It was quite amazing what a small circumference our circling track marked out, while we were quite sure we had been going in a straight line. We hurried on from the displayed track of our sinning.

Later in the year Mike and I and a teacher friend had a similar experience on a narrow ridge above the Great Glen. On such a defined ridge we were only checking every now and then as there was so little chance of straying. Yet on one check we found ourselves 180° out. We turned in obedience to the compass but our friend raised hell—he was for on. There was a right old argument until, left with no supporters, he came with the compass. Mike had just stood by grinning and saying nothing—a change for him. As we set off he whispered to me as I passed: "the Feshie hills, eh?"

Sgor Gaoith, 3,658 feet, is the *peak of wind,* a dramatic perch of a summit being a prow overlooking the long line of cliffs above Loch Einich. The group is usuallly known as the Sgoran Dubhs, for Sgoran Dubh Mor, the next bump on, though 3,635 feet, and therefore only a Top, is the dominating piece of dark architecture seen from Glen Einich. The cliffs give long ridge climbs, grand in setting, on nervy granite, pioneered by a regular Who's Who of the far off times: Naismith, the father of the S.M.C., Mackay, Raeburn the Great, Solly, Maylard, King, Glover, welcome Sassenachs, arch-Munroist A. E. Robertson—and from less distant times names like J. H. B. Bell,

H. I. Ogilvy, who was killed here, Richard Frere the writer, George Ritchie and Alistair Cram, who I was to meet on the Walk.

Pennant, in his 1794 *Tour* mentions "Sgorgave in Rothiemurchus" which is probably Sgor Gaoith. It has a "Cailleach" pinnacle to match the "Bodach" across on Braeriach opposite. The flesh and blood people of Glen Einich and of the sheilings at the head of the loch have long gone.

I pitched the tent to dry in the sun and breeze on top of the peak, and lay looking over the edge. The loch was brilliant silver—for a change. Ptarmigan were making noisy and erratic flights among the arêtes of grey rock and a herd of deer browsed all unaware not far below my eyrie. Opposite the bulk of Braeriach blocked the view, but to the south I could see Beinn a' Ghlo and the Ring of Tarff beyond the rim of the snow-patched wilderness I had stravaiged over yesterday.

In the 1780's Colonel Thornton, the famous (or infamous) sportsman, had flown his falcons at ptarmigan up here. Dotterel too. One of my joys this trip was to see rare birds, not just in the known places; but that is not something I will be mentioning. The first snow bunting nest discovered in Scotland now sits in the British Museum!

Munro-baggers are driven off the rim to descend out for a measly Geal Charn, 3,019 feet only, but on the sacred list. A group sat eating by its cairn but the finer view is over at some cairns on the rim so I paused there instead. As I continued I noticed that Schiehallion away to the south and Ben Rinnes to the north are perfect mirror images with long and short sides matching. The eye also went to the gash of Loch Ericht and its guardian, Ben Alder. It then struck me that this was the next section. The way to the west was opening. Lochaber would see the half way, mathematically, and the Great Glen the half way, psychologically. . . .

The descent to Glen Feshie takes one down through zones of boulders and deep heather—inescapable. The remnants of old pines were douce after the arid heights. I had a brew just to revel in the richness of the setting. Brewing was always an excuse for a stop—or vice versa. Wood ants were rather active and there were flying insects, while a cuckoo with a sticky "ooh" kept up its monotonous call. Nature-loving has moments when one feels like putting in for a divorce, but with siskin, coal and crested tits, chaffinch and warblers all flitting and chitting it was a delightful change. I ate the last of my food and scattered thank-you crumbs in best Stevenson tradition.

The River Feshie was bouldery and low, a mere paddle. A roe deer
barked as I set out across it. The Ripleys had a more exciting crossing
a bit higher up the river. Brian wrote: "As I was crossing the swing
bridge I very dreamily let the map slip from my grasp. It fell into the
fast-flowing waters and floated merrily away. A mad dash followed . . .
after about half a mile Alan made a spectacular dive, grabbing the
precious map but getting thoroughly soaked." All I did was nearly
stand on a clutch of large pied piper's eggs. Camouflage can be too good!
Then, once I had booted-up again, I nearly had a heart attack—a
capercailzie went clattering off.

The Dell Hotel at Rothiemurchus often has enthusiastic ornithologists staying and one guest had spent most of his time happily watching
a brooding caper in the bushes opposite his bedroom window. Only on
his morning of departure did he confide his find to the hostess. She
promised to keep quiet—and did as far as the kitchen . . . "and that
bird-watcher has spent a happy holiday doing little else but watch our
broody turkey!" It could easily be done; but turkeys do not rise at your
feet and racket off through the trees half scaring the wits out of you.

Our native capercailzies had been wiped out by about 1771 (the
last was recorded in Glenmoriston), and reintroduction at Mar Lodge
in 1827 failed. In 1837 efforts at Taymouth Castle by Loch Tay
succeeded, the original 32 becoming over 1,000 a quarter of a century
later, on that estate. The Black Wood of Rannoch birds no doubt came
from there. Introductions east of Inverness were made in 1894 and now
the bird is fairly common in coniferous woodlands.

As I stepped it out for Milehouse I was surrounded by new plantings,
trees being Speyside's other industry. Over the whole country our
treatment of trees has a poor history. Romans, Vikings, raiders and
lawmen, all down history, burnt and cut at this precious covering.
Bare Rannoch Moor has the old bones of skeleton trees across it. Only
on the islands are there remnants, safe from sheep and deer—which
man drove on to the hills (the deer's natural habitat is forest). Commercial greed just about destroyed all that was left: shipbuilding and
iron smelting decimated the Speyside, Argyll and Loch Maree forests.
After the 1745 money was urgently needed by clan chiefs aping the good
life in London. They sold their woods for cash as they sold their people
for sheep. Names such as the York Building Company and the Duke of
Sutherland were synonymous with blatant exploitation. The ravaged
landscape has been starved, burnt uncontrollably, and overgrazed

ever since. It has taken writers like Fraser Darling to stir the public conscience.

The old ways of pre-1745 were changing, but the forced peace after that date, together with the introduction of the potato, helped to create a population explosion which only the export of people could relieve. Some landlords beggared themselves trying to help their tenants, and some of the present scenic gems owe their green beauty to sportsmen who had bought their acres with cotton-spun sterling. Have a look in the deep gorges and ravines in the wilds where no fire or beast has ever destroyed. There you will find the secret, old Scotland: Scots pine, birch, rowan, holly, willow, hazel and so on.

On Rhum they are re-creating the original woodland—with results we will not see for generations. The first thing the Conservancy did on the island was get rid of the sheep. At Kinloch you can see, next to each other, areas where deer are allowed and excluded. On the latter good soil and ground cover is found.

Forgive me if I have flown off into the trees after my caper—but wildlife matters and trees matter. They are part of our mountain heritage, and as man-dependent as the rest. I would almost stick my neck out to say the Irish Munros have a beauty ours lack, for where ours rise almost always from a sterile desert of our past creating, in Ireland the hills rise from a patchwork of bright green fields. You look down on a landscape blue with smoke (you can smell it even on the tops), dotted with homes, stitched with wending roads and hedgerows and trees. Come down off our tops and you pass the refugee deer to find glens of sheep and broken walls of houses, treeless, empty. Men betray themselves in the way they have treated trees and soil.

I collected my cycle from Clive Freshwater who runs the sailing/canoe school on Loch Insh and lives next door to the Ladies Scottish Climbing Club cottage of Milehouse. He was in the throes of litigation over canoeing on the Spey, a case he was to win, though appeals went to the House of Lords. Landowners are slow to see that co-operation is the best policy. Clashing with the masses can only lead to one thing.

The shop was shut so I went up to the Ossian Hotel and treated the inner man. The contrast was savoured: there over the trees and the crying gulls were my hills, and here was I having buttered scones and cakes sitting on the lawn and throwing stones for the dog to fetch.

The girl who made the tea had the west-country surname of Rainbow.

"When I was courting Johnny Rainbow my parents thought he was a pop singer or something!"

I was back on the line of the A9 road and also back to lower altitudes: 800 feet, the lowest since Blair Atholl. Loch Insh took quite a lot of film, the reflected trees and the old church again being such a contrast. I meant to go to church but had the wrong times. I collected a food parcel from Mr Fleming, the forester, neighbour on the other side of Milehouse. He kept exotic pheasants, which explained some of the odd noises I had heard. I washed lots of clothes and hung them out. My kilt was waiting too, for it is a grand walking garb. Alas, even at the last buckle, it could not find anywhere to hang above my ankles. So I parcelled it for home, wrote a dozen letters, did some logistics, wrote up the log, cooked and ate a huge meal and went to bed and read till all hours. Life is not long enough.

> Hold sun, for just another hour of day!
> We know pale dusk's when all ships weigh
> And sail off; and the last sunset
> May be best of all—but not just yet.
> I have a thousand miles to travel, friend;
> Then sail me under, make a glorious end.

Monday 20 May THE MILEHOUSE WORM

Bookworm that is. Milehouse has a splendid bookcase. It rained most of the day so I was happy to read by the fire, lost to the world of the Walk and reality. In the evening I went to telephone David and Marina, as the next morning was my deadline for Kincraig. At 7.15 the line was engaged. I watched the speugs nesting behind the board proclaiming "Smith's Stores". It was "closed" when I had bought some provisions earlier. At 9.15 the line was still engaged despite trying to get through every few minutes. I was not very good-humoured by then. The exchange could not help. In the end I phoned Mary Gordon, two doors along from David, and asked her please to report my safe arrival —and see if they had been on the telephone for two hours and more. Of course they had not; just more gremlins in the system.

Spring had slipped into the comfier clothes of summer. I could have lingered quite happily in that rich green landscape. It was still full of bird sounds: snipe drumming, the wuthering of the peesies, the babel of the *stuirteag* out in the marshes and, loveliest of all summer calls, the sandpiper.

I lingered long before my fire at night, loath to break the idyll. Milehouse is a great wee place. I filled up the form to send off to the custodian, Ann Winning, wrote her a letter and left unwanted things in a cupboard. A last brew. A last dram of "Jura". Bed. An hour of C. S. Lewis. And then only the honking of the fancy pheasants next door and the quiet, soothing sound of the wind in the larch trees.

VII

LOCHABER AND BACK

"Life is an alternating current, illumination coming from the contrasts."

F. FRASER DARLING

Tuesday 21 May WEST OF THE A9

The evil reputation of the A9 road was thoroughly manifest today: no freewheeling, a persistent headwind and thus a bottom-gear grind all the way, and three times I was ditched by big brutes of lorries, twice just blatantly "breenging" past as if I did not exist. As "an aid to pedestrianism" the cycle was a dead loss.

My only pause was to look at Ruthven Barracks, a roofless, stark ruin with a vivid, typical history. At one time it was the home of the Wolf of Badenoch. In 1451 it was demolished by the Earl of Ross, in 1546 Locheil and Keppoch were held fast there by Huntly before being beheaded, in 1582 the young teenage James VI and I was decoyed there and captured by Gowrie and Mar, in 1594 Argyll laid siege to it, in 1647 General Leslie captured it, in 1654 Cromwell's general, Monck, was there, in 1689 Dundee burnt it. That is a selective coverage. It was thirty years after the last event that the present barracks was constructed. A sergeant won fame and promotion for a gallant defence against the Jacobites in 1746. Two days after Culloden, Lord George Murray and others re-grouped there, hopeful of renewing the fight. The Prince, however, had despaired and exile and death was their end. No wonder there is an air of sadness about the gables. It looks over great marshes and the low skyline of the rainy Monadh Liath.

The sausage, eggs and chips I had at the transport cafe at Dalwhinnie were better than any I'd ever had at hotels. I collected a food parcel and went on past the Wade bridge, through endless road works, past Balsporran, to pitch the tent just over the watershed where a roadside sign gave "Drumochter Pass, 1,506 feet". A peewit was nesting fifteen yards off.

This really is a Wade road, completed in 1729, when the soldiernavvies celebrated with four oxen roasted whole and four kegs of brandy. It links with the Corrieyairack road to Fort Augustus. Wade was "Commander of the Forces in North Britain" till 1740, but is chiefly remembered as a road builder. It was ironical that the rebels of 1745 were the first to use his roads. He built about forty bridges, many of which are still in use today. And all at £70 per mile. To appreciate the pass, climb Meall na Leitreich above Loch Garry—a remarkable series of moraines makes it as choppy-looking as sea.

I returned to Balsporran and set off for the hills to the west. A made path goes up Coire Fhar and let me reach the top of Geal Charn in an hour and a half. From the road several "stone men" give a human likeness from a moving car and many misjudge the ascent by taking the scale from them. Some are ten feet tall. The group gives easy going but the map does its best to hide the summits in vague contouring and misleading heights. There are two cairns on Geal Charn which scrapes into the list by all of five feet. It gives a long view down Loch Ericht, which, in five visits, I've seen for about two minutes in all. Today the landscape on the other side was a glitter of a thousand sequinned lochans.

The col to A'Mharconaich was teeming with deer as it always seems to be. It is a swelling slope of grass. The map shows a spot, 3,174 (small cairn) but the real summit, 3,185 feet, lies a good half mile to the northeast, at the end of the ridge. I had just escaped from this flat summit area when an inky storm came spluttering up Loch Ericht and it began to snow "upwards". There was a feel of thunder so I was undecided whether to go on, wait, skirt, or whatever. I ended doing all these things which did not make for good progress to the *top* of the hill.

"He tae Cupar mun tae Cupar." I made a cowardly race to the top of Beinn Udlamain, the *hill of the shaking*. It loomed out of the mist like an irascible porcupine, for the cairn was sprouting old fence-posts in all directions. My run down the other side scattered dotterel which went off in pantomime runs—fascinating birds.

The col for Sgairneach Mhor is very boggy, riven into peat hags. On the sweep up and round above it I found I was heading off for the wrong bump, so corrected course. It seems such an easy hill, but, again, it is easy to go astray on it. The summit is an erect and proper "stone man" on the edge of Coire Creagach, 3,210 feet, not the 3,160 spot shown on the map. Descending the rim of this corrie the rain came on for the rest of the descent. I drew into my waterproofs like a tortoise into its shell.

VIII MONADH LIATHS

VII THE A9 MUNROS

The lower slopes are always squelchy. The burn was low and easily crossed to gain the scruffy track which now runs right up Coire Dhomhain, which is really a valley hidden within the sweep of the last three of today's peaks.

I was in the tent again at 7.30 for a night of rain and traffic noises.

Wednesday 22 May EAST OF THE A9
I began the day by going up the burn by which I was camped. In the space of half a mile I found in it the corpses of a stag, a crow and a sheep. I also found a good antler which I shoved in my rucksack.

Well up on the heathery reaches of the hill I could still smell the rotten pong of decomposition and knew the worst. The antler had leaked a repulsive slime all over the rucksack—fortunately not on food, camera or logbook. There was no handy water, and in the throes of dealing with this the rain came on. Be warned, all who dream, reality often has prickles!

A'Bhuidheanach Bheag is dismissed by most as a dull plateau, but the eastern side has a great corrie, well seen from the top of An Dun in the Gaick Pass. Bheag means small, yet it is the highest summit hereabouts. There is a trig point marking the top, also a fence. (A cairn at a quartz outcrop a hundred yards to the north can mislead in mist.)

The Aonachs, Mor and Beag, next to Ben Nevis, are also the wrong way round, Beag being higher than Mor—but this is rather how they looked from below when people were naming them (it is only in the recent past that silly people started wandering about on top of the hills. Because these people were local they used the same descriptive words: More (big), Geal Charn (white cairn), Dearg (red), Ghobhar (goat) and so on.

Today's hills are in a vast area of moss and bog, but in certain lights, with piling clouds, the view can give a spaciousness unknown in lumpy Perthshire or crowded Lakeland. It is dotterel country. All day long today the golden plovers were weeping their complaint to the grey, sad skies, a sound of utter heartbreak. Squeezed in under the clouds I could just make out the Gaick Pass to the east and beyond it the even more desolate "moine" of the Ring of Tarff. The old drovers' way, the Minigaig, has to climb to 2,750 feet in crossing from Atholl to Speyside, the Gaick slices through the hills in a deep trough.

"The Loss of Gaick", an incident enshrined in folklore, tells of an avalanche disaster in this latter pass which happened on the first of

January 1800. A notorious recruiting officer and four friends were overwhelmed in a shooting bothy. A stone with a Gaelic inscription marks the spot. There is another tale, of a poor, starving family which was actually saved by an avalanche sweeping off the steep slopes to leave a huge snowball beside their cottage. When it was broken open it produced three brace of ptarmigan, six hares, four brace of grouse, a blackcock, a pheasant, three geese and two fat stags.

Today's walking gave the less attractive tops rather than the logical passes. The boundary fence can be followed usefully but I was happy to cut corners as much as possible. The fence shies off before the second Munro, Carn na Caim. It is seldom a good thing to rely on hill fences for navigation; they seldom go just where you want; nor can tracks be trusted, even on narrow ridges. Frequently their initial markings was the work of deer or sheep, and these have more intelligence than to seek out summital exactitude.

Chuaich is often done from here but the going is bad, and as I had to shift back to Dalwhinnie again from my Drumochter Pass site, I went down to the A9 direct. The shoulder below had been torn up to extract the quartz rock and the bulldozed track up to the workings is an ugly scar as seen from the A9. One more example of the need for landscape control.

Collecting the tent I pedalled down to Dalwhinnie, dry, with the wind behind, and ignored by mad motorists. The Portnastorm Cafe was visited for another dose of sausage, egg and chips, and at three o'clock I set off along the track beside the aqueduct for Chuaich, a Munro which is a useful "quickie" for the motorised walker. Meall Chuaich is a pudding-shaped lump, the most individualistic of these shapeless hills and a good viewpoint. It can be romped in an hour from the loch at its foot. I followed a new Land-Rover track for a bit and then sneaked up a slot of burn with the reward of being able to lie and watch deer grazing about twenty yards off.

I trotted down the north-west corrie, steep but not rocky, to see the water intake. There was a hut where instruments recorded the flow. A plaque said "Cuaich-Seillich tunnel, 22310 feet, completed 1940". This tunnel captures water from the Gaick Pass and feeds it to Loch Ericht at Dalwhinnie. Loch Ericht has a dam at both ends, and from its south-west end drains to Loch Rannoch which in turn flows on to the Tummel-Pitlochry series of dams and power stations—a unique multiple use of water.

A notice proclaimed Loch Cuaich was stocked with rainbow trout, and the limit of three fish must be checked with the head keeper—with a 50p per fish fine for any cheating. As I cycled back along by the aqueduct I met the keeper and chatted awhile. He was wild at the ravages of the new A9 for which the moor was being torn up beside us. "My wee birds! My wee birds! Could they not wait till they'd done nesting?"

I went to see Mr Oswald, the keeper for the Ericht hills, but he had won a prize holiday and was off in Majorca. He had thoughtfully left my parcel with his mother. After a chat I went off to pack. Food parcels! If only we could eat grass. Or heather. I phoned Dollar and also Gerry Peet, the custodian of the C.I.C. Hut on Nevis, to arrange a key for next weekend. A good round lay ahead. While in the phone box a redpoll sat on the bike. There was wind enough to blow away the cuckoo that infested the wood where I camped.

The sounds of tree-surf, of trains and traffic all merged pleasantly in sleep.

Thursday 23 May NO POLTERGEISTS
The wind died, the rain came lashing down and the blasted cuckoo began at 4 a.m. It went off at eight (the rain that is: the cuckoo went off on the hour, half-hour, quarters and much in between), and depression turned to a sort of desperation. I hung the tent to dry as I was leaving it. Originally I thought it could be left standing, but a stone's-throw from the A9 was a bit risky. The kind ladies in the shop stored it for me. It was bliss to go off on the bike down the empty miles of Loch Ericht, the grey loch trimmed with the verges of golden broom. I sat out a shower at the lodge. Above it some thirty stags stood to watch me go by, while several white garrons came cantering along beside me. Over the rise the bulk of Ben Alder appeared, bright and mottled, reaching up into the clean, shiny clouds. The freshness was a delight, the loneliness a tonic. I hid the cycle and strode on.

Loch Pattack was a fine reflecting pool. More white ponies were grazing on the alluvial greens which fight it out with the peat hags. A bridge of wobbly slats allows the pedestrian to cross, the track just uses the shoreline, sometimes in and sometimes out the water. Beyond the loch is a junction of tracks where I once had an alarming experience.

I had come through from Moy on Lagganside, heading for Culra (as once did Prince Charlie). The thick cloud, with me all the way, was stirring and about to clear. Suddenly there was a loud bang. I *felt* the blast of it, and dropped quickly to the ground cursing folk who fire guns in a fog. The clouds almost instantly rolled away leaving the brown reaches of Pattack clear. Not even an early midge stirred. There was not a soul to be seen. I suppose there is an explanation but nobody has given me a likely one yet.

I reached the bothy at Culra just before a heavy shower, so sat in it for a brew, looking out the doorway as the trailing curtains swept through the Bealach Dubh between Ben Alder and the Lancet Edge— a view instantly recognisable, the very epitome of a pass. When I set out again I found a dead deer just up the burn. It was the fourth dead deer I had seen that day.

The bothy book went back to 1966 and in it I found an entry by Brian and Alan Ripley. They too came in from Dalwhinnie and had two nights here doing in turn the groups south and north of the Bealach Dubh, before heading through it for the Ossian hills. There is a useful line of bothies linking the A9 with Fort William. At Loch Ossian is a fine, old-fashioned hostel, too, which can only be reached on foot, or by train, or by cycle. Knowledge of these havens was allowing me to yo-yo to Lochaber and back without a tent.

Slides are an abiding reminder of the day's towering cumulus clouds. I wended up towards the pass, then jumped the silvery burn to take the stalkers' path over the moors. This leads up to a pass, the Bealach Beithe, which divides Alder in two: the vast plateau of the Ben itself, the largest area outside the Cairngorms and Nevis to top 3,500 feet, and the splinter summit of Beinn Bheoil which used to have the magical height of 3,333 feet and be Munro number 111. Ben Alder's plateau shape is seen from all over Perthshire and the Cairngorms. It is as far from roads as can be, south of the Great Glen. It has good winter climbing and some summer potential—largely untapped.

My path led up to the loch in the pass, vanished, and then re-appeared beyond, only to die again at the top of the pass. Some supernatural power seems to stop all tracks to Ben Alder bothy, down the other side, for the track in from Rannoch stops, like a chopped worm, a mile short, and the lochside track from Dalwhinnie has been destroyed in many places by the raising of the water level. The good weather had gone by the time I reached the col: a grey ceiling as far as the eye could see. I returned down to the loch and up the Garbh Choire which was saturated and clammy with mist but at least provided a lee out of the storm. I took the line of a burn, then worked up ribs and gullies to the rim of old cornice. It was snowing hard on the plateau when I broke through, so I left a tiny cairn to mark my exit and tramped over the old snowbeds, head down, till I met the trig point and cairn. Ben Alder means *mountain of rock and water*, which is probably what it is made of. Bheoil is the *hill in front*—of Alder presumably.

I back-tracked without delay and by the time I was at the loch again my feet were soaking and the corrie was noisy with the sound of many waters. It cleared as I cut up and along for Beinn Bheoil, the *mountain in front*, a knobbly ridge, high above Loch Ericht, which is a great viewpoint. Schiehallion's cone was set in a halo of rainbow. The incomparable Neil Munro, in *The New Road*, could have been describing my view: "the moor stretched flat and naked as a Sound . . . all untracked and desert-melancholy . . . cotton sedge strewn like flakes of snow . . . grey like ashes, blackened here and there with holes of peat. The end of it was lost in mist from which jutted, like a skerry of the sea, Schiehallion."

From the pass I dropped down to the bothy. Sunset came in vivid yellow light and towering black clouds. The bothy stands by a lonely bay, with a solitary guardian tree, a place of character and charm.

The B.F.M.C. had had a Meet here a month before but the only food that had survived was several tins of baked beans. I had them for supper, breakfast and lunch—and was not fit to live with! My treat today was thick, *fresh* onion soup; its preparation brought tears to my eyes. I drew the rickety bed close to the fire to dry clothes. Tetley coffee bags made endless brews. The night was noisy with storm and life in the wainscot. No poltergeist activity, however.

This is no joke. I know sensible, rational, couthy, even dull folk who would on no account stay there. If you want to read of the sort of things that go bump in the night here, borrow W. H. Murray's classic *Undiscovered Scotland* (Dent 1951). To be fair it must be added that the last owner did not hang himself on the back of a door as even Murray retells. The S.M.C. Journal for 1951 had a note from A. E. Robertson: "McCook died in his bed at Newtonmore, honoured and respected . . . a very fine type of Highland stalker, level-headed and sensible." So the disturbances have nothing to do with him. I have never noticed anything in the years I've gone there, often alone, in auspicious circumstances. This is not negative evidence, however. Some people

F

just do not experience these sort of things. The bothy is there if you want to conduct personal experiments.

Friday 24 May STAOINEAG IN SUMMERTIME

Ben Alder's most distinguished visitor was the eighteenth-century gangrel Charles Edward Stuart, not that he really intended such a close contact with the wilder parts of Britain. For a week in August 1746 he was in hiding up on the hill behind the bothy (nobody knows where exactly though the map gives a confident guess) along with Cluny Macpherson, Cameron of Locheil and Dr Cameron, all wanted men. Word was brought of French ships off the Arisaig coast, and he set off from his hiding-place to leave Scotland for ever. Cluny Macpherson hid hereabouts for seven years. Stevenson in *Kidnapped* leads Davie Balfour and Alan Breck to Cluny's Cage.

The topping and tailing of the day gave that vivid colouring that is associated with wetness but it was a grey, dull day on the whole. I simply followed up the Allt Tom a' Chogaidh to the loch, a dry meander among an extravagance of peat. I brewed at the loch, but it would not clear, so I scrambled up on to Sgor Gaibhre, down to the Mam Ban and on to Carn Dearg, all without pause—and with no view. The north-east wind was bitter, so I trotted down to the old Corrour path. There were motor cycle tracks to remind that the Six Day Trials roar through here once a year, a sight so out of place as to be amusing.

Craig, Glen Affric and Loch Ossian Youth Hostels are in a remote and superior class, each in a superb setting. I would not swop one of them for a score of the misconceived Grade One palaces. At Ossian we once enjoyed meeting Hari Dang, an Indian Everest climber, who was recuperating from frostbite while acting as warden. His stories kept the kids happy and I enjoyed reading several of his sensitive, poetic writings.

A mile on from the hostel is Corrour Station and not far from it a sign gives "Corrour Summit, 1,350 feet", one of the highest parts of the West Highland line. Today's hills, and even the addition of Beinn na Lap on the other side of Loch Ossian, can be done in a day's romp between trains. My favourite hill lies above the station with a view over the Moor: Leum Uilleim, a name which sounds like the name of a hero from a legend. It is *William's leap*.

On the pretty track down to Loch Treig I met the shepherd walking up with measured stride, dog at heel. The Grey Corries, and even Ben

Nevis, cleared, showing a dusting of snow on their tops. I skipped along —in this withdrawn Walk the barometer seems to be the register of feelings, my spirits going up and down as it did.

Loch Treig was exceptionally low and even had a waterfall dashing down a little gorge that would normally all have been under water. This is part of another great water-system. The upper reaches of the Spey and Pattack are caught and led to the Moy reservoir, which in turn feeds Loch Treig, and from here a tunnel runs round under the hills to descend from out of Ben Nevis to the British Aluminium works by Fort William.

Creaguaineach Lodge and the bright valley beyond were alive with birds: raven, stonechat, tits, dipper, sandpiper, merganser, peewits, pipits, all were proclaiming that life was not bad at all. The valley was brilliantly green and lush after the spell in the browns of the Cairngorms. The dainty butterworts were out. The river glowed as if molten. Staoineag bothy beside it had recently been done up by the M.B.A. and Ian Mitchell seemed to have taken personal care of it. We were to meet later. Idiot vandals had ripped off much of the old wooden panelling. After a search I found pencilled names above the fireplace: "Gus Cameron, Jock Stenhouse, James Hunter, Andrew Hamilton, Alex Lindsay, James Marshall, Bill Drysdale, 13.3.63" and "Sandy Drysdale, Ian Routledge, Frankie Spence, John Carroll, Pete Adamson 10.10.64". It seemed impossible that ten years had passed since those visits—when we had crossed Rannoch Moor in midwinter and traversed all the Mamores in autumn. And now I was there in the fairest of summertime.

Saturday 25 May THE MAMORES

Blissful silence; no wind, no cuckoo. Even the bare boards were unable to spoil sleep. I had read till all hours and yawned my way through breakfast. It was a magnificently fine morning, one that lay lazily as a cat. Sandpipers and greenshank were calling, the Ben reflected in the river. I threw away my French vocabulary and went singing westwards up the strath. A peculiar double day it proved to be.

My first pause was by the lochan under Sgurr Eilde Mor where a diver carried on a noisy courtship not thirty yards away even though I was sitting in full view. In that empty setting it was as if the wilderness itself was crying out. Marvellous sound.

The Mamores in a day is a good hefty hike but it was put in the shade by Philip Tranter who did it and then went on to add the Grey Corries, Aonachs and Ben Nevis—within 24 hours. As if that were not enough, a woman in her fifties repeated the feat.

The nature of the ground can be gauged from the names: they are all *Stobs* and *Sgurrs*—no gentle *Bens* or *Mealls* or *Srons*—though the last peak is, rightly, a *Mullach*. A popular range, giving good ridge walking, with scalloped corries, airy crests, and ten Munros. In winter they can be superb: the Devil's Ridge, the An Gearanach tops, Binnein Mor are all narrow. The group is best done east–west, so one walks into the sunset. It is also logistically easier that way.

Sgurr Eilde Mor and Binnean Beag are both out on a limb in the extreme east, so it is good to have them out of the way at the start. There is a path linking the cols that demarcate these two end hills, a continuation of the one shown coming up from Kinlochleven. Binnein Mor, 3,700 feet, is the highest in the forest and dominates the east end, a summit thrust up by narrow ridges with sheer flanks. I lingered on it, enjoying the sunshine. It was too good to hurry and I was quite content to be what my granny often called me—a great slitter.

Na Gruagaichean, the *maiden*, has a top split into two paps with a gap of perhaps two-hundred feet between, which the one-inch map does not show. An Gearanach and An Garbhanach are both given 3,200 feet and translate as *short* and *rough* ridge. They require a bit of scrambling and in winter can be alpine in character. I was not sure which was the Munro but could not resist the fun of going along the crest and back. On Stob Coire a' Chairn I was enveloped in cloud, a change as swift as curtains dropping in a theatre, and a shock to realise it was 4 p.m. With five Munros ahead I would have to hurry. I did, and the tops were peeled off in about four hours, in thick cloud, viewless and dull. Am Bodach and Sgor an Iubhair took me west.

Sgurr a' Mhaim, the *peak of the pass*, is the hill dominating Glen Nevis. As Munro number 50 it is always a convenient yardstick. Its quartz capping can look like snow and tourists by the thousands must have slides of it at home labelled "Ben Nevis". The "bad step" on the ridge out to it is perhaps exaggerated—it can be jumped across. If you missed, of course, a couple of bounces would land you down in the corries. Back under Iubhair, which deserves to be a Munro, I took the zig-zag path down to the lochan below, a path long known to us as Jacob's Ladder. On our school traverse we had a swim in the loch and a lazy brew. Today I simply crammed in the rest of my available food

VII LOCHABER AND BACK
VIII LAGGAN

N

0 1 2 3 4 5 Miles

From Newtonmore

Loch Laggan

Carn Liath

Stob Poite Coire Ardair

Creag Meagaidh

Achallader

Beinn a' Chaoruinn

Creag Pitridh

Geal Charm

Beinn a' Chlachair

Carn Dearg

Culra

from and to Dalwhinnie

Ben Alder Bothy 23/5

Loch Ericht

Beinn Bheoil

JR 77

2,3,4/6

Geal Charm

Aonach Beag

Beinn Eibhinn

Ben Alder

Geal Charm

Beinn na LAP

Loch Ossian

Sgor Gaibhre

Carn Dearg

30/5

Tulloch Station

Inverlair

Fersit

Stob Coire Sgriodain

Cruach Dearg

Loch Treig

Corrour Station

Glen Roy

Spean Bridge

To Loch Lochy Youth Hostel

Laggan

Stob Choire an Laoigh

Stob Coire an Laoigh

Laring Leachach Bothy 19/5

Stob a'choire Mheadhoin

Stob Coire Easain

Stob Ban

Staonaig Bothy 24/5

Na Gruagaichean

Sgurr Eilde Mor

Stob Coire a'Chairn (Am Bodach)

To Mallaig

Carn Mor Dearg

Aonach Mor

Aonach Beag

Sgurr Choinnich Mor

GREY CORRIES

Binnein Mor

Binnein Beag

Sgurr a' Mhaim

An Gearanach

Stob Ban

Mullach nan Coirean

Ben Nevis

26, 27, 28/5

Glen Nevis

25/5

Fort William

MAMORES

and groped on up for Stob Ban. A lost lamb was bleating its woe in the misty corrie. Mullach nan Coirean and "home" still seemed far off.

Stob Ban is *white* from quartz stones capping it. At 2,950 on its north ridge there is a bump which is often mistaken for the summit. The way to the Mullach is partly defined by cliffs, but I used the compass a bit. The rock changes to a red colour suddenly, and the cairn is a rufous pile. Previous knowledge helped me to keep up a good pace. The descent of the long ridge to near Dun Deardail (a vitrified fort) was tedious, an impression from the previous traverse with Braehead, too. However, it led home. If you choose the right break in the trees you can indulge in a long grass glissade, of the seated variety, a good ending to a 10,000-foot day. By the time I reached the hostel I had done 21 miles.

The hostel was mobbed and noisy. As soon as I stepped into its steamy din, my face turned red with the heat. David Gunn, the warden, had food for me and George Luke had left some too—and gone off to camp. Best of all, I found Alan Boulton, one of Ann's pupils, and being well-trained he at once produced a brew. Charles Knowles had turned up from Sheffield to join me for the next day or two. Everything was far too hectic, the meal gobbled down, and bed as per regulations. Only next day did I realise that I had now passed the half way—on Am Bodach, *the old man.*

Sunday 26 May HALF-WAY PICNIC

I was glad to leave the promiscuous bustle of the international hitch-hiking brigade and wander off in search of the campers. I rang home too. David and Marina had collected the canoe, which was all right, but the life-jacket had been discovered by mice who had turned it into "a sort of yellow confetti".

As it was about ten o'clock I found George, plus Val Hadden, Bob Binnie and Tommy Dunbar still having breakfast. Charles and I joined them. They had been over the Ben and the Aonachs the day before; today, though, was "too nice to do anything". We talked and brewed the morning away. George admitted that I outdid him in both: the latter no doubt from much recent practice, the former from almost total neglect. The C.I.C. key had come in the mail, so two cars went off up the glen as Charles wanted to have his there in order to traverse the Ben from the hut. This done, we then set off up the hill, very much against the stream.

The variety of clothing, or lack of it, was amazing. I once saw someone going up the tourist path wearing fisherman's waders which I thought a bit extreme; today, the extreme was the other way: flip-flops and hot-pants. Verily, they have their reward. The quirk, however, was that it was we who received the odd looks—madmen obviously heading uphill when everyone else was going down.

We were into cloud when we turned off, through by Loch Meall an t-Suidhe. The going was unusually dry. We rounded under the Nevis cliffs to the hut. The C.I.C. (Charles Inglis Clark Memorial Hut) had been painted and modernised. Many mourn the bad old days of the coal fire when the cast-iron stove would glow red hot and climbers sat about near-naked in midwinter watching the butter melt. It had a grubby atmosphere all of its own. Now a clean, pathetic gas fire blubbered away in its place. Outside the hut I could smell fumes from the pulp mill, the distillery and some nearer sheep. City-dwelling Charles could smell nothing.

We ate to a stand-still and sat browsing through the big ledger of a hut book. It was brought up in 1971 by "D. Lang *assisted* by N. Quinn". In April of that year a gang noted their ascent of Point Five Gully as 18 hours. Two days later John Cunningham and Bill Marsh took 2¾ hours—the application of the new techniques which have so changed winter climbing. A well-meaning hand had kindly amended their time by adding a figure one in front of the 2¾. It takes a while to adjust! Sandy Cousins had stayed during his Cape Wrath–Glasgow trip. In December 1971 two climbers had peeled on Gardyloo, from the top pitch, and got off unhurt; they then fell again, this time being killed. John Hinde reported finding three men and a dog dead under the Douglas Boulder in 1972. Last year a Dundee University gang had to bivy in poly-bags outside because everyone thought someone else had the hut key. One hopeful offers a half bottle (of what?) to the finder of a lost Chouinard axe. Does he not know that McInnes combs the foot of the cliffs each year, with his dogs which are trained to find metal objects?

The C.I.C. is a great howff, even though the litter round it gives the lie to the conceit of climbers who tend only to blame others for this sin.

The hut was opened in 1929, a memorial to the son of a member killed during the Great War. The date was April the First. The Rev. A. E. Robertson pronounced the blessing and prayed that it might be a refuge in time of danger. Two climbers obligingly fell down Observatory Gully and staggered in while these proceedings were still in progress.

Monday 27 May c.i.c.

The day was a wash-out. We revelled in the comfort. Our only visitor was an Australian-German who had slept on the Ben the previous night and went off "up the creek" to cross the arête. He vanished in the storm but though Charles monitored the newspapers we heard no more. . . .

Charles is essentially a ski-mountaineer; he has probably been up more hills this way than most "climbers" on foot. We both were members of the Eagle Ski Club and had been together in Austria, Switzerland, Pyrenees, Morocco, and just before this trip, in the Polish Tatras, along with Donald Mill of the S.M.C. Recently he had slipped into the Munro habit, ticking them off in the Tables.

At the end of the last century there was an Observatory on top of Ben Nevis. During the period 1883–1904 the records produced an average of 261 gales a year (i.e., winds of over 50 m.p.h.; gusts of three times that velocity were noted). The average rainfall was 157 inches and the mean monthly temperature just below freezing. If the Ben were a few hundred feet higher Britain could have her very own glacier.

Each September there is a race run from Fort William to the top and back. The record, set in 1976 by David Cannon, is 1 hour 26 minutes 55 seconds, a time most people take just to walk *down* to the glen from the C.I.C. It is comforting to know there are others even crazier than oneself on the hills.

The day went well enough, though it was a "waste", I suppose. It was right to have one day off in seven, that is a scheme which has both human and divine authority; another day like this would hint more at divine retribution.

> I dreamed of a great mountain
> To be climbed next day
> But the rains came down in torrents
> And washed it all away.

Tuesday 28 May STILL C.I.C.

The storm went on; so did Charles who had to motor back to Sheffield. His car now lay, unhandily, at the head of Glen Nevis, so he too vanished off to cross the Carn Mor Dearg Arête.

I read the only book in the place, then cleaned the hut in self-defence. Outside I buried 26 buckets of rubbish. The noise of water had increased. A brief clearance showed the Douglas Boulder: wet and black; a later clearance showed it snowy white.

The C.I.C. is a genuine alpine hut, built of the local stone, walls six feet thick, it fits into the landscape now as if it had always been there. It fits in to the landscape so well, indeed, that one of the games climbers play is "Finding the C.I.C. Hut". You are always reaching it, with massive packs, in wind, rain, snow or darkness, or any combination of these. Luckily the prevailing wind is up the glen.

It is surprising what you can find in a hut where no food is supposed to be left. I fed well despite the extra day. The meal was disturbed by a mouse which I caught in a bucket and despatched. Its brothers and sisters came and clouted about all night with their boots on to get their own back.

A last trip outside showed it was still snowing.

'Hail, snow an' ice that praise the Lord; I've met them at their work,
An' wished we had anither route or they anither kirk."

KIPLING

Wednesday 29 May EASTINGS AT LAST
In the mousey hours I had lain working at the logistics to see how I could make up for the lost time. I reckoned it would need a bit of doubling-up, and leaving Beinn a' Chlachair to be done from the north, later, rather than on this run eastwards back to Dalwhinnie.

It was obviously going to be a day of snow showers but not bad enough to delay any further. I locked the C.I.C. at 6.30 and set off in the statutory direction of the Arête. Boulder-hopping was a slithery game and the easy line up from Coire Leis by the abseil posts was barred by sheets of ice. The steeper rocks to the left were better, giving a scramble. Cold work on the fingers, though, as snow had to be brushed off each hold. Another 900 feet of boulder-hopping led up to the highest midden in Britain, the summit of Ben Nevis.

The derivation of the name is disputed but I think *hill with its head in the clouds* is more likely than *mountain of heaven*. The Ben took its rightful place as Britain's highest peak only in the early nineteenth century and therefore has less history than many lower summits. There used to be a plaque on top (long before the present scruffy rash) which proclaimed: "Ben Nevis, 4,406 feet", then, in modest, smaller print, "Erected by the Scottish Mountaineering Club". The new maps have given it 4,418 feet and no doubt it has been metricated.

I did not wait for the weather to clear. I thought of Charles back in his Sheffield Insurance Office and went smugly off for the Arête to Carn Mor Dearg, racing along in an effort to beat the next storm. The wind was not bad. I snuggled in to the cairn and watched the trailing curtain of snow sweep across the Nevis cliffs.

An old S.M.C. member was once explaining to a novice how on very narrow ridges like the Arête the only way you could save somebody falling off down one side was to jump off the other so the rope could balance across the ridge and thus save both. Having scaled the Ben by the Arête, with his mentor, the novice said he had remembered the instruction: had the leader fallen, he would have jumped off the other side. The elder shook his head. "Och laddie, yon is a technique that is best kept for when we are using a rope."

I gave up waiting and went down the East Ridge in a swirl of spin-drift. In winter this can be a ridge of great beauty, the snow building up, not into a cornice, but a thin, wavering crest. Down at the col it was dry again. One winter, while sitting at this col, we watched a gentleman pass by, umbrella up, wearing a plastic mac, grunting away at a tune...

The flank of the Aonachs was steep and slobbery in the conditions— far more alarming than if it had involved real climbing. The plateau was windy. I left the sack and hurried to reach Aonach Mor and be back before the next blatter, for footprints are not always a reliable navigation aid. There is an almost Cairngorm-like gravelly quality to the top here, and the Aonach corries seem to be holding the snow even longer than the eastern hills these days. The next shower caught me on the col to Aonach Beag (the higher)—a shower of that evilly wet snow which makes dry, colder snow seem positively benign.

Aonach Beag is a hill I have come to respect (it has still to be thoroughly explored for its winter climbing potential). On several occasions its bald skull of summit has given trouble. There is only a tiny cairn and this can vanish in winter. On one trip its position was guessed by some orange peel which showed through the snow. I had peered into the near white-out to see my companion, Mike Smith, about to step over a faint crack line. I yelled at him to stop. It was the cornice beginning to break off. We were right on the edge. Today the summit was giving a repeat presentation of another problem.

The whole dome was icy. The angle was by no means steep but with neither axe nor crampons that was no consolation. It was not possible to contour lower, for both flanks fall in cliffs. I found a likely chunk of stone to act as an ice-axe and chipped away at the unavoidable bits. There are times when it is best to be alone.

To revert to Mike Smith, at that time a pupil of mine at Braehead. I very nearly gave in my notice after the incident, but stayed for another ten years during which time we had no genuine hill accident. The pupils were given a freedom and responsibility far greater than most. But any accident would have been my fault—I would have had to live with it. I give it as a warning to romantic youngsters who dream of becoming an instructor, leader, teacher, whatever the title. The P.E. man can allow errors on the soccer pitch where mistakes may lose goals, on the hill they lose life. You are playing for keeps.

Since the Cairngorm disaster of course the tendency has swung to the other extreme. Everything must be safe—which is not mountaineering. If we decide to take another's youngster on the hill we cannot salve our conscience by trying to kid ourselves, or the parents, that it is safe. The mountain is an illiterate thug who has not read the books and plays to no rules.

For once the cliff edge of Aonach Beag was useful for navigation. There is a north-east ridge which has suffered neglect. An old account declares, "The narrow part in the middle . . . is the most sensational of any of the great ridges outside Skye". Unlike the Aonach Eagach, you cannot park your car at the foot of it. There is a big winter route to be done up the face under Stob Coire Bhealach, the corner bump at the end of the circling cliffs.

Prior knowledge helped me to wiggle down through the cliffs, south a bit from there, to reach the col before the start of the Grey Corries ridge. It is not a good area to wander about in if there is thick cloud, not unless you have a parachute. Sgurr a' Bhuic is an odd peak of upended strata, full of holes, as you sometimes find in schisty rock. It is worth climbing for the view: being out from the main range it has the finer panorama.

The Grey Corries is an old apt name for a long switchback ridge of quartzy rock. It has been likened to a row of pit bings, but this is a slander. The corries in the north have some grandeur, the westmost being as rough as any in Knoydart. You will walk more on naked rock to collect its four Munros than anywhere else outside Skye. I recommend their traverse right through from Glen Nevis to Tulloch.

On Sgurr Choinnich Mor I met an English lad who had been camping below at Tom an Eite on the old drove road, part of the Road to the Isles. The ridge down has some slots in the strata which act as crevasses when snow-covered—I have twice seen people fall into them. I slid down old snow to the col and the best of the ridge beyond, scrambling where I could find rock, up to Stob Coire an Easain. I met another solitary figure there. On Stob Coire an Laoigh I met a family I had seen on the Nevis path. Our greetings were cut short by a vicious snow shower. I passed yet another solitary Englishman, who explained it was the Whit Week invasion. Footprints in the snow led east but I never saw the party; I thought it interesting that only one party out of all these had the gumption to travel *with* the weather, rather than suffer its periodic lashings.

The sole of my right boot was beginning to pull away. I promptly found an old bit of lace and tied it up. Just in time: ten minutes later it gave way completely. I tied a protective hanky round my face for the ascent of Stob Coire Claurigh, 3,858 feet, the highest of the range, while the storm produced what looked like ragged hail. It was quite evil while it lasted. A glimpse to the hills of June, a glimpse to the hills of April relieved the present struggle. Stob Ban is a sort of coda to the Grey Corries Symphony.

From it I dropped down to the Lairig Leachach, another old drove road from Loch Treig to Glen Spean and the west. There is a poor bothy in it, which we knew in its finer days in the past. To us it was "Payne's bothy" as he showed it to us when staying at Inverlair. He was the keeper then. He had lost an arm in the Korean War. Now, there was no flooring left and it was grubby. The book had complaints from the shepherd about folk using his "stabs"—and comments from Sassenachs asking what these were! (fence posts) A surprising number of schools had been there—Melville, Watson's, Kingswood, Aberdeen Grammar, Rannoch—apart from fellow gangrels such as Nancy Smith and Richard Wood, or instructor types like Blyth Wright or Klaus Schwartz. It suddenly felt crowded. I spent an hour retrieving bits of wire and string and tied up my boot in a glorified cat's cradle. It was another noisy mouse night.

Thursday 30 May   TRIG POINTS ROUND LOCH TREIG
Easain and Mheadhoin were the local Inverlair hills for many Braehead kids, known always as *This Yin* and *That Yin*, names transferred to a pair

of Wullie Dugs back home. The "Stob Corries" are a fine pair of hills, bounded by Loch Treig to the east and Coire Lair to the west. Their main joy is the setting, for as hills they just fail to enthuse, all the features seem just short of being good. My log dismissed them in six lines but revelled in the descent to Coire Lair with its pastoral scene of cows browsing on the bright green of grass among the brighter green of new birch growth. After the sterile days past it was as refreshing as a dram. Stob Coire Easain and Stob a' Choire Mheadhoin sound like malts.

I looked for, and saw, cloudberry, chickweed wintergreen (summer star) and dwarf cornel—a trio of exceptionally beautiful alpines. This was a bit of country we had combed with the kids, for the lodge of Inverlair was given to us by British Aluminium and we wanted to have it as a centre. It could have been a great scheme but it was strangled with red tape. Instead, we had the freedom of Scotland, which we used to the full; not that I could see it ever having developed into a placid sausage-machine, timetabling stereotyped courses, boring the staff, disenchanting pupils and soiling the very landscape which should delight —which is the end result of far too many outdoor education schemes.

We were self-contained groups, doing the sort of thing ordinary people did on the hills. Each term a programme would be produced for the next term. All pupils received this, and then applied for what they liked. They were never "sent". You might juggle a bit to make balanced parties; but then you knew the boys and girls already. They were not impersonal statistics to be suffered for a week. The trips were real too. We might be dropped, say, in Glen Strathfarrar and collected ten days later at Loch Duich—and until then we were on our own, self-contained, self-reliant, not playing at things, nor conning the kids with simulated adventure. They revelled in it and it has made me cynical about the way the Educational Establishment has developed. At Inverlair, for instance, we were banned from living in the building while working on it. Too dangerous—but we could camp on top of the Ben in midwinter. We camped outside and worked on until that was stopped —it was not right that kids should take work away from tradesmen. (So back to the simulated in the school workshop.) The teaching profession I think deserves much of the trouble it gets.

Not being based on one spot the kids came to know Scotland as a whole. They could rile adult Munro-baggers with accounts of visits to the most out-of-the-way summits. I recall one perky visitor to Inverlair asking a fourteen-year-old for his tally of Munros, he having all of fifty. The lad, embarrassed, confessed that he stood at 101. Quite a few of them have gone on to climb in the Alps and Norway and Morocco, but reward enough could be the conversation the other day when I received a telephone call from someone I had not heard of for seven years. "Hello Hamish. Do you mind yon hotel we went into when we got washed oot o' Moidart? I'm gettin' marrit next month an' I thocht it wid be a great place fir wir honeymoon."

The school has closed, but a host of memories remain. There was not a Munro they had not been on, so how could I forget?

> Doon the road we gang oor gate,
> Past the gorge, the bridge, the brae;
> Backward spy ower Speanside
> A' that bides—'tis we that gae.

So an Inverlair Song went.

The eighteenth-century house had been used as a prison for Hitler's deputy Rudolph Hess after his parachute landing in Scotland during the war. The cell still exists with its bolts and bars.

The Spean has some fine gorges and falls under the bridge on the road leading to Inverlair, but up above these today I just hopped across on the exposed pink boulders and walked along to Tulloch Station. Behind it is the old coach house which had been turned into a small outdoor centre and factory for producing tents, cagoules and so on. (It was later sold to the Army.) It was from here that my tent had come, although I had left it at Dalwhinnie I was able to give Dave Challis, its designer, an enthusiastic report. We chatted over tea, dealt with food parcel and mail; it was tempting to stay, but the sun shone and it was still a far cry to Ben Hope.

I took the forest path up to Fasgadh, wondering if Nancy Smith or Davie Glen might be there. Nancy runs a highly individualistic "hostel" there for gangrels, climbers and folk from all over the world. Today it seemed deserted. I wandered on through Fersit and up the Allt Chaorach Beag which had cows surprisingly high on it. There was also one big black bull. The observant may notice the map shows a stream here splitting into two; this is not an error, but one of the very few examples of this oddity. There was a heron by Lochan Coire an Lochain, 2,500 feet up. The corrie arms here are both Munros: Sgriodain on the west overlooks Loch Treig, while Chno Dearg lies to the east, and translates as the *red nut*, a description I thought more appropriate to myself. Between Stob Coire Sgriodain and the loch is the Fort William railway: here squeezed in by the steep slope and giving a succession of cuttings and tunnels. The railway allows good days hereabouts as you can return or start using it from a base at Nancy's. Sgriodain is the *hill of the scree corrie*.

Instead of circling back to Fersit, I went south to add Beinn na Lap. There were several cast antlers on the hill today. I dropped down to hit the head of the long trough that cuts off Lap. Lochan Ruigh Phuil on the watershed had dried out. The meandering rivers are just too wide to jump. Once across I brewed and finished off all the food I could allow that day. Beinn na Lap is the *boggy mountain*, which is true on this side, but the Loch Ossian flanks, which I went down to the Youth Hostel, are usually dry. It is a very easy Munro. It looks right into the throat of the Nevis glen, westwards, while in the opposite direction Ben Alder's bulk once again looms large. I sang into the rising wind and trundled down to the hut.

The hostel was not officially open till Saturday but the warden, Tom Rigg, made all welcome. My face "blew-up" with the heat of the room. Kettles steamed on the old range. You fetched water by the bucket from the loch. It was all a youth hostel should be. Tom had been warden there before, and told us of his days helping with the stalking and the real regret with which he left at the back end. A Watson's quartet were camped outside on a Duke of Edinburgh "Gold" Expedition while their assessor lorded it within. The wind was doing its best to blow tents and hostel into the loch. The bothy last night felt a million miles away, already. I'd had two good days of between seven and eight thousand feet, with thirty miles from the C.I.C., which felt even longer ago. The consciousness of what lay ahead seemed always to sweep the past into immediate oblivion.

Friday 31 May NEW BOOTS, PLEASE!

Dave Challis had promised to phone Dollar and pass on my plea for new boots. It was one thing he did not manufacture. I remember once throwing a brand-new pair into Loch Ossian, in despair, after they had badly blistered my feet. The next day I fished them out and they soon moulded comfortably. Drastic remedy! For the Long Walk I had broken in three pairs beforehand.

On one previous walk along Loch Ossian, in winter, the ice had been broken by a storm, and the broken wafers were piling up with a loud, continuous hissing which was most unusual. Today the heronry produced its particular noise.

A path leads past from the lodge at the end of Loch Ossian, crossing the Uisge Labhair by a bridge; but later it peters out leaving you to pick a way on for the Bealach Dubh, 2,300 feet, the pass through to Culra. Running parallel to this pass, to the north, is a line of four Munros. The hills have well-bitten northern corries and bulky slopes to the south and swoop along in pleasing fashion. Most of the tops are over 3,600 feet, and I've often watched the deer in summer come up to lie on the lingering snow patches. Today it was cold enough to wear a cagoule. I saw an eagle, a bird that had been surprisingly scarce, but then I had been much in sheep country, where there is still lawless slaughter. The first Munro, Beinn Eibhinn, means the *beautiful hill*, but it is simply a great lump. Aonach Beag is next, the highest of the group. Geal Charn (another, unnamed by the O.S.) has a wide plateau and a Top, Sgor Iutharn, *Hell's Peak*, which is the spike of Lancet Edge, the framing edge of the Bealach Dubh as seen from Culra.

A bit of care is needed to hit off the descent from the plateau to continue to Dearg. The col has corrie lochs on both sides, the one to the north with the name of Loch Coire Cheap. Carn Dearg is a rockier, scree-covered hill, with quite a brutal descent to Culra bothy. A dotterel went dashing off on a blur of legs over the red scree. Two dead deer lay in the stream which served as the bothy water supply.

I crossed the moor back to the road and retrieved the old bike. "Stowaway" was an appropriate trade name for it. Belting down to the lodge was hard on the wrists and the rough track needed all eyes; deer were smelt rather than seen in passing.

Near Dalwhinnie Station I called in at the schoolhouse and collected a parcel from the Parkins. He was a member of the local Mountain Rescue Team but was about to move south. We had a chat and I think I gave away my real ploy. I collected the tent next and was soon back at the Cuckoo Wood waiting for Lorna Marsh and Bob Binnie. I had expected them about 7.30 so had a brew made then. I drank it and several others, wrote until dusk at ten, then lay listening to the wind in the firs.

Another section was over. Twenty beyond half-way. They certainly piled up. Now I could head west, if a bit circuitously; then the Great

Glen, the crossing of which was bound to be a spur. I felt fine physically, I had had no foot problems, and was receiving plenty of mental stimulus from people, books and incidents. I ate well, slept well, and when Bob and Lorna finally turned up, I even found I had new boots, thank you. The old ones had taken me to 237,850 feet, over 802 miles for 159 Munros.

VIII

LAGGAN

There is not good or bad in the hills; just life, just death. There is only a calendar of seasons and the tick-tock of day and night. Sit relaxed and still, and the life of the hills will creep up to you unafraid, rest, and the very air will whisper wonderful things in your ear. Even the bleached skeleton in the grass will give a message of comfort, in the Word's old sense of strengthening. The strength of hills is His.

Saturday 1 June THE DULLEST HILLS IN SCOTLAND
I must admit my log book entry for the day was headed "Monaidh Liath Puddings". They are not the most dramatic hills we have. However, one thing they can offer is navigational exercise in a thick mist, particularly west of the actual Munros. I've had my share of criss-crossing them, and think they are maligned: they have a quality of remoteness and silence which their bigger counterpart, the Cairngorms, cannot offer.

I used the bike; wind and hill were both in my favour over the brae to Laggan Bridge. One lay-by had a notice saying "Beware of the adders", a good anti-parking gambit. I bought goodies from the shop and scoffed them at Crathie. I had to fix a cotter pin, and thought I had a sheep to rescue under the bridge, but it was dead: a crow was busy picking out its eyes. *Whisky Galore* helped walking up the track.

West from where I'd left the bike, you can go by Garva Bridge and Melgarve to the Corrieyairack, the famous pass over which Wade built a road (1731) to connect Aberfeldy and Fort Augustus. It goes up to 2,543 feet but is a desolate crossing. One of the first people to profit by it (a twist of fate) was Prince Charlie. Montrose came over some-where in this region on his great winter march to Inverlochy. They say it's haunted by a lone piper . . .

Today's Geal Charn was small and unpretentious: with only one feature, a fine craggy corrie on the east, above which is a sneck or window (the Uinneag a' Choire Lochain) which separates Geal Charn from its south top. I left Glen Markie at a sheepfold and hopped across the river boulders, again let off gently, then wended up Beinn Sgiath and along to Geal Charn, which has a large cairn for such a plain summit. The ascent was a bit dull and I was still half asleep after my late night. Today, however, I was, at last, doing something I'd long wanted to do—all the Monaidh Liath Munros in one sweep.

The Monaidh Liath are aptly the *grey moors*. They fall into two very distinct areas: the five scattered above Glen Banchor, which joins the Spey at Newtonmore, and this odd, solitary Geal Charn, away towards Laggan, six miles across the grey emptiness.

The cloud had lifted so I felt happy to stay high, but it would probably have been no less tiring to have cut down to the Markie again and used it as a highway. But I had my six miles of moor: empty but for monotonous plovers crying, a few deer, a few dotterel. It gave every variety of bog and brae without being difficult like the Mount Keen day. Above the final col was a solitary gate, standing like a lost sculpture by some facetious modern artist.

There is another such solitary, fence-less gate in the Ochils; sheep tracks converge for miles on it, go through the ever-open portal, and then spread out again across the slopes.

The first of my group, another *red hill*, Carn Dearg, 3,093 feet, is the highest. It is also the only one with a bit of shape: a spur juts out and forms a double-wave of ridge. Below it, and worth taking in on the ascent by its path, is Coire Lochain Dubh, a deep hole of a corrie, the crags backing its lochan, probably giving the only climbing in the whole range if someone would go and try them.

The Monaidh Liaths also have distracting fences. The next hill, not another Geal Charn, but equally meaning *white hill*, is Carn Ban which is shown with the fence passing the top; it does not. A mile further along, Carn Ballach, *cairn of the pass*, has a veritable collection of cairns to choose from.

Carn Sgulain, "a mere stony eminence on the ridge", is perhaps appropriately the *cairn of the basket*. I arrived on it with a ptarmigan brood scattering and their mother flapping about. Driving clouds and rain finally arrived, too.

A bite in the lee of the cairn and then the way led off into the storm— angling down over wet slopes to the wet col for A' Chailleach, *the old wife*, a long whaleback from which I was glad just to take a bearing and try and reduce altitude quickly.

Once off the very steep top slopes, the group became gentle and hag-ridden. I came out of the cloud—and for minutes just could not place anything, for features below meant nothing and above was hidden. "The compass is always right," I muttered, and followed it, endlessly it seemed, over bog and brae until finally I was looking down on a wee wooden bothy, just a shed—but expected—and giving some shelter. I peeled off dripping waterproofs and read for an hour till the worst of the rain drew off.

I found some old names scribbled on the wall. There was Joe and me in November 1962. *That* was a day, marvellously cold and a rosy, beautiful dawn from Carn Dearg. In May 1968, I was with Ann Winning, Tom Izatt, David McNab, John Parker, Ian Flaws, a day when snow-melt on still frozen ground made for saturation of feet. March 1971 with Andrew Patterson, Tommy Cameron, Willie Harrison and Jim Morrison. Jim had also done the Monaidh Liaths before, with Ann I think, for, with four out of five Munros done, it suddenly struck him that there was something familiar about the hills. From which you can draw the moral: keep records, or you may end doing the Monaidh Liath twice!

I made a quick descent. My feet could not be wetter, even after a slithery river-crossing. I came down to the end of the public road in Glen Banchor where I'd arranged to meet Lorna and Bob. There was no sign of them: no car, no tents. Just a friendly cuckoo calling.

Some day I will do the Monaidh Liath again (the summits, that is), but it will be on *langlauf* ski, and some day I want to follow Glen Markie and the old drove road through to Fort Augustus. You cannot exhaust the potential of even the dullest hills in Scotland.

Having finished off *Whisky Galore* (alas, the book), and near frozen by two hours' reading, I began to walk to Newtonmore. If they had broken down or something, I could sit waiting a long time. Main's Hotel would be cosy.

Half a mile down the road, I turned back again due to some sixth sense, and from the road-end went down to the river itself—and found them! I knew it was a great camping spot, but had not thought it possible to get a car down to it. They had, of course, so there was no car up on the expected bit of road. While I'd frozen for two hours, they had been lying snug in a tent less then 200 yards away.

We made up for lost time: instant coffee, tent up and a gargantuan meal of fresh everything. Next day they told me it had been a night of gales and rain.

Sunday 2 June PEDALS WEST

Perhaps it should have been "paddles west", though at four o'clock I took photos of the dazzle of sun on the birch-held river. A roe deer was grunting away across the stream when I woke Lorna and Bob with coffee. They had collected the bike yesterday, so once again I went off on it.

The wind was fresh and I was travelling dead against it. At Laggan Bridge they tooted past and I found them ensconced in the Laggan Hotel drinking more coffee. Dave Challis had left a new waterproof for me with the Camerons, who also had a parcel. A heavy shower passed.

The other pair went bombing off to the hills they had abandoned in yesterday's deluge. I had a grim struggle along Loch Laggan, which rather spoilt the enjoyment of a favourite loch. West of Moy Lodge, the length of Loch Laggan battered behind at last, I pitched the tent between road and river-cutting. Scrub birch sheltered it completely. It would be unpleasantly wild on top so I was quite content to call it a day.

Lorna's van was only fifty yards away, so I squatted in the back sorting out parcels and preparing for the next few days. I also cleared off mail that needed a reply. Some vicious squalls caused the van to rock about as if riding at anchor. Along the road, a stand of trees echoed like surf, and the sound of rushing water grew to impressive volume.

Yet it was splendid in its wildness. Who would have their mountains always tame (any more than a wife)? Wordsworth's lines always come to my mind when storms are galloping free over the land:

> "The sounding cataract
> Haunted me like a passion: the tall rock,
> The mountain, and the deep and gloomy wood,
> Their colours and their forms, were then to me
> An appetite; a feeling and a love . . ."

It was a day fought out by sun and rain, and victory was given to the rain.

Lorna and Bob came in a bit battered, scoffed some more coffee, and rushed off. One Munro had been their weekend haul. Civilisation seems in such a rush! Perhaps, at the finish of the Walk, I should just turn round and go on for ever; yet the Walk blatantly used civilisation—escapism soon comes down to earth-reality. Fresh food, company, news and mail, and the bliss of a new book in the wet: civilisation is very nice, thank you!

It was a night of gales and rain, quite worthy of Wordsworth.

Monday 3 June   THE MALT HILLS

After ten hours' sleep the storms had settled into the "showers and bright periods" beloved of the forecasters. I set off for Beinn a' Chlachair (a name which has a gurgly, single malt flavour), enjoying a chat with the Luiblea shepherd, then followed round a sweeping bend in the river which was bright with broom. The Bealach Dubh hills lined themselves up beyond a waterfall, a brief scene of delight before I plunged off across bogs white with hare's tails drying in the wind. All the ground from the Moy Reservoir to the hills, and through to the gates of Loch Ossian, is now planted.

Across the moor, I joined an old, established track which does a rising sweep round to Lochan na h-Earba. On the flank of Pitridh, a fresh scar of rockfall showed clear. The path had been surfaced with rounded river-stones and I collected a pocketful of them to tumble and polish. A stalkers' path leads through to Loch Pattack and Culra. I used it for a while and then cut across to go up the stream that led right into the wide-smiling corrie mouth of Beinn a' Chlachair.

Hopes of a typical corrie lochan are disappointed—there is none. You would hope for good cliffs, judging by the distant view—there are none. Poor Beinn a' Chlachair just fails to deliver the goods. The best route is a narrow, winter ridge on the south side.

The corrie gave shelter from the wind until I met the full brunt of it on the plateau. One bright period actually gave me a summit view and what with the peak's own plateau, Geal Charn's next and then Ben Alder's, it looked strangely as if you could just walk straight over to the cairn on Ben Alder.

Beinn a' Chlachair means *mason's hill* and much of it is bouldery. I flanked down, keeping above the level of a line of seepage. The dry spell called for lunch; then when the clouds rolled in again, I "felt" my way up Geal Charn. It is also called Mulloch Coire an Iubhair, *hill of the corrie of the yew trees,* if you do not want another Geal Charn.

The map does not show the ground well, but the summit is un-mistakable, as beyond the bouldery dome you see a cairn like a Tibetan "chorten" beside the trig point. In mist it can be hard to find. The wind was fluting tunefully on the holes in the trig point.

Back-tracking through the saturated clouds, I bore off down very wet slopes to swing up to Creag Pitridh, *crag of the hollows*. This little hill has a shape all of its own which makes it prominent from both ends of the Laggan strath. The note left on it has never been returned.

I descended by the west ridge for variety and to have a look at the rock-fall I'd noticed from below. There was more debris than expected, and some spiky overhangs and hollows such as you sometimes get in schisty rock. Wending down the rakes, I kept putting up small numbers of deer and, below, a really big herd traversed under the crags.

I collected another pocketful of pebbles as I wended back to the tent. An enjoyable, if unremarkable, day. There was time to read until the warblers in the scrub sang the evening away; then it was a fresh apple and into bed. Such a gentle ending to the day was no preparation for the foul night. My log next day simply said, "awful night, suspect the onions"—which is enough.

Tuesday 4 June COME WIND, COME WEATHER

It had rained most of the night, and I breakfasted in a mood of near despair as it went on and on. The rain could well have drowned the Matterhorn as deep as a Mendip mine—and this *was* June, the blessed month of dryness.

In an unpleasant frame of mind, I dressed and stomped off into the wet to call its bluff. From Moy, I followed a swollen torrent uphill, crossed the deer fence, and then had to go much further upstream, on beyond burn junctions, until the river reached safe proportions to make a crossing possible. I followed a tributary to Lochan na Cailliche, the bog myrtle scent rising under my feet. Slowly I began to enjoy the walk. It is never quite so bad once you are committed.

Keeping above another water-seepage level, I traversed across to the Allt na h-Uamha, *river of the cave*, which demarcates Beinn a' Chaoruinn's craggy east face and cuts it off from the Creag Meagaidh hills. I have never been able to find a cave, but the river is full of superlative swimming pools.

One sweltering day, a party of us were descending, longing for a dip, when we heard voices coming from a likely pool downstream. When we topped a rise, we looked down on a gang of middle-aged women (to be kind) disporting themselves like Rubenesque goddesses in the river. I dare not say which club I think they were. Such a quantity of pear-shaped nudity took us momentarily aback; then we diplomatically withdrew, unobserved. As we detoured off, one of my young charges grinned at me and commented, "Aw, Hamish, it's enough tae gie ye a complex fur life!"

Strangely, the river gave no problem today, though very swollen. The lee of a boulder was used to snack under when a wicked storm rattled by. The butterworts were no doubt relishing the wet: they seemed to be crawling all over the place like refugee starfish in search of the sea. Starry saxifrage was also in flower.

The ridge in the middle of the east face gave a nice dander up—as far as the wide main ridge where the storm was waiting in ambush. Beinn a' Chaoruinn, *hill of the rowan*, has an undulating summit-ridge with three tops; the centre, once a deleted Top, has suddenly become the Munro in the recent revisions.

I was glad of a new waterproof; the rain poured down as I followed the cliff edge over and down to the col, the Bealach a' Bharnish (2,686), which marks the start of the long grassy haul up Creag Meagaidh— which, like its derivation, was obscure. At 3,700 feet, it is a big brute, a veritable mastiff of a massif, with a sizeable plateau and cliffs with winter-climbing on a par with that on the Ben, Glencoe and Lochnagar.

It was a relief to see the cairn appear when and where expected. Further on is "mad Meg's cairn". Various stories are told of this huge pile of stones, marking no summit or spot of known interest. It is ten feet high, contains few really big boulders, and, as the ground is hollowed round about, some of it could simply have been dug out and heaped up. On the east side, traces of stairs mount to the top. It resembles an Inca sacrificial mound or some such monument, and might even be worth opening up to see if there is anything inside.

I let the wind blow me over to the 1,500-foot cliffs of Coire Ardair, and then followed their diminishing height to "The Window", a conspicuous gap leading through from the corrie. This particular window is famous as being the pass used by Prince Charlie on his journey from Cameron country en route for Culra and Ben Alder. It is at about 3,200 feet. The loch in the corrie is at over 2,000 feet, and from it a good stalkers' path leads down to Aberarder.

This easy option downwards made me think sourly of Steinbeck's comment—"we can do strange things when we want to . . . and nearly nothing without pressure". I went on. A brief clearance gave a glimpse of the cliffs.

The climbing in summer is scruffy, but in winter Creag Meagaidh's cliffs and "Posts" (gullies) come into their own. It is interesting to see that Raeburn (the Scottish Mummery) was early in this field—and J. H. B. Bell, during the pre-war period, with his penchant for vegetated verticalities.

Charlie Gorrie tells of climbing there with Jimmy Bell on an attempt on one of the Posts. They had been swimming in the loch and the approach was light-hearted. The redoubtable Dr Bell led off and Charlie followed, sufficiently gripped to ask if Jimmy had a good belay. "Of course I've got a good —— —— belay!" Charlie climbed on and arrived to find Jimmy Bell busy struggling into his trousers, the rope meanwhile held in his teeth!

The last person to stamp his mark here was Bell's modern counterpart: Tom Patey. His winter girdle traverse, solo, has gone down into climbing folklore as well as history.

On my first visit in winter, Mike Lindsay and I saw the second largest avalanche I've ever seen in Scotland. The largest was a vast slab avalanche off the north slope of White Whisp in the modest Ochils; not even in the Highlands.

Miles of undulating crest led eastwards; along it are strung seven Tops, two being elevated to the Munro peerage, including the first, Stob Poite Coire Ardair. The fence should not be taken as a good guide. The wind was shrieking on its posts, and the rain was belting down as I had not previously had it on the Walk—at least, not at above 3,000 feet—not the best of conditions for navigating. Fence and cliff edge are both apt to lead astray. I plodded along, munching soggy peanuts and more than ever convinced all mountaineers are daft. The rain was bouncing off the surface like ball-bearings, but at least the storm had been from behind.

At Carn Liath I left a note (not returned) and then turned to fight my way off its stony dome, a punitive experience. I ran and slithered downhill, fast, and soon popped out from under the black clouds. The Allt Coire Ardair twisted like a live snake, and I trundled down and took the path to the farm. A good amble along Loch Laggan gained the tent at ten to eight—three *Irish Short Stories*' distance. There I hung the book up to dry and devoured a large meal.

Before the meal was over, I became conscious of something odd. It took a while to dawn on me that the wind had gone; for the first time in days the land lay completely quiet. My relief was short-lived. There were midges! The first few thousand all came crowding about the tent: the original Scots mist. The site had been great for protection from the wind. It could hardly have been worse for a muggy calm and the little devils. I sealed myself in for the night. After three nights there, I knew every bump intimately.

My spirits stayed content, though, for now I had achieved all the Munros south of the Great Glen. It was a landmark, a pleasing one. Things were on schedule without too much effort. I did not like the thought of midges henceforth, but they just had to be tholed.

I had experienced hard days—like today—and had taken it all without too much complaint from body or soul. It had to go now, for so much had been done (252,000 feet, 922 miles and 68 days, to be precise). I dreaded the thought of anything that might interrupt the walk: a broken leg, say. Even after a week, it would lose genuine continuity, would become failure. And the thought of having to go back to the beginning—was unthinkable!

I lay back and watched the beads of condensation forming on the fabric above my head.

Wednesday 5 June THE GREAT GLEN AT LAST

The morrow being made of the past todays, I woke to rain—a gentle, midgy hiss of it on the streaming tent.

It was very pleasant in bed, drinking tea and bird-listening: skylarks, wagtails, sandpipers and warblers were all going full blast; blessed insect-eaters, while overhead a snipe was "drumming". I could just hear a distant rush of water. The rest was silence.

When the rain eased, I packed up and, before setting off, had a crack with the shepherd again. He was telling me of his prowess as a weather forecaster. "Ach, I aye say 'it will come tae rain'—and I've never been wrang yet."

I was tempted to call in at Tulloch or Fersit, but the dry was obviously only given while the west was calling up reinforcements. It was no time for being sociable. My single stop was for a brief look at the relief model of the British Aluminium complex of dams and catchments, which is sited by the roadside overlooking the west end of Loch Moy. This man-made loch alters in level drastically with the rainfall effects and British Aluminium's usage. Spouts on the dam can be opened one by one till, in conditions of peculiar deluge, all six may be sending jets into the gorge and the spray upwards like smoke. I've seen it once or twice and very impressive it is. Today a mere two spouts were operating.

It is from here, and back beyond the Loch Laggan cutting (where I'd been camping), that water is led to Loch Treig and then by the Nevis pipeline to the Fort William power station. It actually skirts round the foot of the Ben, maintenance being carried out by a small railway system, now, alas, defunct.

I cycled on to Roy Bridge to shop. North up the glen lie the odd "parallel roads" which I would have seen if footing it. The main road was longer, but a change. Tinkers were parked alongside the road, something I can remember here since my early wandering in the Highlands, which was done by cycle. But as I grew older, and the roads more busy and dangerous, the hills came to dominate. Perhaps the pressures of civilisation are becoming too much even for the tinkers: you see fewer on the road now. Many a brew I enjoyed in their camps as a kid on those cycle tours.

At Spean Bridge I had reached the Great Glen, the long-awaited landmark. I shopped again, and bought a light but warm Shetland pullover at the Mill. I would not feel such a tramp going into hotels in future.

Given the choice of the hills beyond the Great Glen or those south of it, I would choose the former, even though I would lose the Ben, and Glencoe, and the Cairngorms and much else: personally, I feel that the best of our wild hills lie from Ben More in Mull up to Cape Wrath. Ascents often start from sea-level, so even sub-Munros may mean far more footage than for Grampian summits. Who would swop Suilven for Geal Charn—any of them or all of them?

I ground up the brae in bottom gear to the "Commando Memorial": a dramatic bronze of three Commandos who gaze over the wide landscape to the south. This was the country where they trained, and Scott Sutherland's monument (1952) does the subject and the setting full justice. In an earlier time, it was at High Bridge, visible in the valley below, that the first shots of the "Forty-five" rang out—and the story of Scotland swept on to its sad days for the Highlands.

In any highland village the war memorial tells grimly how laird or pony-boy left the glens never to return. The trend is still away, but to the towns. The locals find it hard to obtain a foothold in competition with the affluent who want holiday homes.

> They would not let me buy
> The four grey walls and the roof of sky.

The deluge resumed, so, by the mouth of Glen Gloy, I was glad to patronise the Coach House Coffee Shop. An hour of reading saw little change and I went on by Letterfinlay above Loch Lochy. Across the water, my next bit of the Walk was hidden in the clouds, two Munros which on one occasion we reached by *canoeing* across the loch.

At the schoolhouse at Laggan, Mr Robertson had a parcel. The field-mice had been at it, and I left a trail of Millac along the road to the youth hostel. Fortunately, only that and a packet of Vitawheat had been touched.

I hung the tent up to dry in the cycle shed, washed my undies and myself, and hung the former to dry and the latter by the fire, mug in hand. The Frasers keep an immaculate and friendly hostel (he works for the forestry commission, she is the warden). A New Zealand couple on a motorbike (grand conditions for that), a solitary camera-laden Japanese and two Swiss made up the company.

I twice went up the road to try to ring Mike Keates. After the second "no reply", I went on to see the "Well of Heads" by Loch Oich (the Caledonian Canal's highest point). This is an odd monument that few motorists even notice. A base inscribed with the tale in Gaelic, French, Latin and English, is surmounted by a column at the top of which a stone hand, holding a *skian dubh,* dangles seven severed heads by their hair. The headless corpses were recently discovered in a mound by Inverlair: "The heads of the seven murderers were presented at the feet of the noble chief in Glengarry Castle" (not very politely) "after having been washed in this spring, known since as the Well of the Heads, Tobar nan Ceann." If you drop down the bank, an arched passage leads to the old well—now under the modern main road.

The "improvements" to our highland main roads are a boon to those of us who use them to reach a place where we then go on foot, but the car-bound tourist finds them merely an irresistible call to speed up again and so goes whizzing through the very scenery he had presumably come to observe. The "Road to the Isles" is now a real race track: lovely Loch Garry, the pass of Glen Shiel, the waters of Loch Duich, all flash by, so the motorists can then crowd into Kyle and squabble over parking places. . . .

I had to nip along next morning at eight a.m. (in the rain) to ring Mike Keates to tell him that the bike would be at the youth hostel. He was now my "base man" in place of the Dollar Broons.

Thursday 6 June WINDOW-SHOPPING
Fort William owes its name to William of Orange. Earlier defences were at Inverlochy Castle where the Comyns acquired the lordship of Badenoch and Lochaber in the thirteenth century. The present ruin is a four-square turreted bastion beside the River Nevis.

Inverlochy was the spot where Montrose thrashed Argyll in 1645, a battle gleefully recalled by that half of the Highlands who love not the Clan Campbell; but far more, it is a memorial to one of Scotland's truly great figures, a hero coming at the end of centuries sadly lacking one.

Montrose had taken fire and sword down into Argyll to sack Inveraray and was returning up the Great Glen when the pursuing Argyll set up camp at Inverlochy. With armies sealing both ends of the Great Glen, Montrose decided to attack Argyll. He had less than 2,000 men. They turned off into the hills eastwards—an area of featureless Monaidh Liath bog and brae—desperate in January snowfall and darkness, came down Glen Roy and, skirting the Grey Corries and Ben Nevis, fell on Inverlochy by surprise. In consternation, Argyll rowed off to his galley while his army was slaughtered.

Five years later, Argyll was to watch (from behind a curtained window) in Edinburgh, as Montrose was led to the scaffold, a man betrayed in far Assynt for money, unthanked by the king for whom he had virtually gained Scotland, perhaps one of the greatest military generals of all time. . . .

Cromwell's General Monck came to deal with Lochaber and he built a new fort not far from Inverlochy Castle—whose name he transferred. Today a Victorian mansion (now an hotel) of the same name, a few miles to the north, adds to the confusion.

The town that grew up round the fort became the present Fort William. After various vicissitudes and more recent attempts by local landowners to stamp their names on it—Gordonsburgh, Duncansburgh, for instance—officialdom finally gave in to the *vox populi*. Fort William it is, or, often simply "The Fort", as Ben Nevis is often simply "The Ben".

The town must be one of the most blatant examples of poor planning. From Loch Eil's massive pulp mill to the hideous white boxes high on the braes, from British Aluminium's pipelines down the flanks of Ben Nevis to the sprawling ribbon development down Loch Linnhe, it is a mixed-up mess of the industrial and the residential.

Compared to most continental countries, our Highland towns are desolate places in which to pass a wet day. I took the bus into the town to relish the ludicrous contrast to my walking life—and regretted it. The interesting West Highland Museum was unfortunately shut.

There is a swimming pool, so I went there.

Swimming trunks were not on hire, and I got an odd look when I replied, "Och well, can I just have a towel then, please." (With most of my clothes drying at the hostel, I was wearing my trunks.) I had a long, long hot shower (the last had been at Nevis Youth Hostel) and was agreeably surprised not to have washed off all my colour—some sunburn remained after all. A pool is a bit dull to oneself and after hearing the record of "Elvira Madigan" for the twentieth time non-stop, I'd had enough.

I called in at "Nevisport", who had supplied some of my gear, and emerged with a pile of old magazines; for the rest, it was window-shopping only. I took an early bus back to Loch Lochy. Still it rained. There had only been two really good days since I had set off from Glen Nevis nearly a fortnight before. I turned in early.

The dormitory, filled with its quota of humanity, grew intolerably stuffy, so I crept over and opened the door to create some draught. The lad in the next bed had a filthy cold, the Germans snored, the air was smelly with humanity. I longed to be back in the tent along with the rain and the midges, beyond the Great Glen.

IX

WEST TO KNOYDART

Silence of wind and of sea and of sun,
The silence that is life when life is run;
Give me silence that is the best of joys
And its questing the very best of ploys.

Friday 7 June SEVEN GAZ CYLINDERS HID BEHIND A WALL

I had a cup of tea with Mr Fraser and was off at 7.30. The loch beyond
Laggan Locks was showing quiet reflections of hills, trees and gorse
bushes. I was suspicious. Too bright too soon, will rain by noon. It
rained at 11.30, to be precise.

The walk down past Kilfinnan was pleasant. The flora of wet and
wilderness was thriving: lousewort, butterwort, bog cotton and myrtle.
The forest is mature and felling has started. In the muggy conditions I
was soon a-drip with sweat. I left the rucksack at the ruin of Glas-
dhoire, and took the old stalking path for the Cam Bhealach.

The air was fresher once out of the trees and into the cleft of the pass,
which was green and full of sheep. Two fishing boats crossed the visible
slice of loch leaving a herring bone pattern from their wakes. From the
top of the pass I angled up and round to gain Meall na Teanga (*hill of
the tongue*), the last pull up on to the ridge being slippery and steep. There
was a small cairn and then a bigger one fifty yards further south.
Meall Coire Lochain, 2,971, is the only height shown on the one-inch
map—the new 1 : 50,000 does not bother to show any.

In early days I climbed the Sron, it being the highest of the hills
seen across Loch Lochy, and because the map gave 2,971 feet over
this side of the pass, I had no idea there was another 3,000-footer. I had
faith in the O.S. in those days! The hills are pleasing, anyway, and so is
2,957-foot Ben Tee just to the north, a mini Schiehallion which
dominates the gentle eastern end of Loch Garry. For a long time my
lads had held it against me, for they went off to climb it by themselves
while I was laid low with 'flu. Conversations would begin, "When
you've climbed Tee instead of just drinking it . . ."

An obvious zig-zag of stalking path leads on to the *nose of the rough*

corrie, Sron a'Choire Ghairbh. I arrived in mist and rain. Its *rough corrie* lies on the other side encircled by the arms of this rather tame hill. A questionnaire left today was returned ten days later. Back in the forest at my sack I heated a tin of soup and had pieces, but no sooner set off to walk on south, out to Clunes and Achnacarry, than the rain belted down, a real helm o' weet again. The book went away, "skins" went on, the sun came out, the skins came off. The forest smoked and I sweated. I read along the red-surfaced track: a Nigel Tranter historical novel.

The Chattingtons, at the forestry houses, were not at home so I sat under the trees by the Dark Mile, among the heavy-scented hyacinths, and read for an hour. Then I met Mrs Chattington, so soon had my parcel. With a bit to go an offer of tea was actually refused!

My rucksack suddenly felt very heavy, for it was a hefty parcel and even allowing for a good meal from tins there would still be a lot of weight to carry during the days ahead.

The Dark Mile is a fine avenue, hemmed in by towering hillside plantations, the branches drooping over the road draped with moss. D. K. Broster uses "The Dark Mile" as a title in her trilogy of romantic novels set in this area after Culloden. They are still popular enough to be found in paperback. The *Mile Dorcha* leads to the east end of Loch Arkaig where a river pours down from Gleann Cia-aig (pronounced "Kaig") with a fall into a deep black pool overlooked by the bridge. A path up the glen is a good approach to the Loch Lochy hills.

In August 1746, towards the end of his wanderings, Prince Charlie spent two weeks in hiding in this area, "in sundry fast places", including a cave now lost in the forestry plantings. I found a fast place among the big trees and went through my parcel. No wonder it was heavy, there were far too many Gaz cylinders. I ate a huge meal from tins, buried some food in the forest, and hid the surplus Gaz behind a dyke where it could be found easily by the next weekenders. I continued past Achnacarry for the south side of Loch Arkaig, still able to read on a rough road.

Achnacarry House is the home of Cameron of Lochiel. The Duke of Cumberland laid the place to ruin in 1746 and the Commandos, during wartime training, accidentally tried to burn it down again. Restored, it is still the home of the present Cameron clan chief. Here is mature parkland and wild wood, forestry plantings and birch, set among

G

flowing rivers and loch scenery: a few miles along, when I'd left the last struggling Scots pines, the heather and bare corries were wild and empty. The transformation from Great Glen westward by any route is startling.

People were fishing in Loch Arkaig. Children in a "Wendy House" among the trees peered curiously at me as I peered curiously at the strange wee house. Where the River Mallie flows into the loch I was met and escorted by a great mob of curious cows, a sight which obviously amused the occupants of a passing Land-Rover. With my noisy escort bashing about in the bog and myrtle I turned up the glen, leaving the long loch, for it is trackless.

The south shore forest of Loch Arkaig was burnt during the war and the scars still stand in gaunt, dead trees. It is now being replanted—the workers commuting daily across the loch by boat from the switchback road. I found a quiet corner of the river and hoped another herd of cows, just up the glen, would not find the tent. The remnants of old Scots pines (some 300 years old) and new plantings made it a delightful spot as a pale evening sun shone down the glen.

I demolished another meal and worked out the needs ahead, for it was possible, with the petrol crisis, that Ian Mitchell might not arrive from Fife at the weekend. The wind died down after supper. The midges came out. I went in.

It had been a good day again, over 20 miles. The "human animal was happy" as Rebuffat puts it, and was I not into the land beyond the Great Glen at last, westing in starless summer to the sea and all that was best?

Saturday 8 June   WEST, WHERE ALL DREAMS LIE

Six-footed rather than four-footed beasties were about in the morning. It was bright and fresh, with eiderdown clouds and brief slips of blue. Wouldn't a dry day be nice for a change! I off-loaded two pounds' weight by leaving a jar of honey and a pot of jam perched on a boulder by the track. I would like to have seen the reactions of the finder.

The old pines died out and the glen became, slowly, more barren, of poor grass and sedges, of bracken, and at the end of the track a semi-derelict cottage which would make a fine bothy. The upper reaches of Glen Mallie are much wetter, the river narrower and fringed with alders to the last. The going, as I slowly sauntered upwards, was so easy that I just carried on reading. I was still aware, though, of the lengthening corridor of view back down the glen—and of the fresh, yellow light of returning summer. It was as if the hills and glens had had a thorough washing and were now hung out to dry. They smelt fresh. They looked clean. Ah, that wonderful additive, the sun!

An odd wall ran up over the col to the Allt Screamhaich, whose corrie, from above, was a rock-rusted cauldron, flecked with tiny pools. Each pool had a little lawn and each lawn made a bed for a few deer. Even though I zig-zagged up, outlined against the sun, they failed to move.

A steep bouldery slope brought me to the summit of Gulvain (or Gaor Bheinn), where I went round and round the cairn gaping at the view and clicking away till I'm sure I had photographed a 360° panorama, all good.

The West was a jumble of spiky summits and deep-cleaving valleys—there was nothing soft or rounded. To the south east Ben Nevis stood out as a bold shape, shrinking the Mamores with its height. Bidean, Starav, and things beyond Etive were all blue and edged with sun. South lay the massed array of hills forming quiet Moidart and Ardgour —perhaps the largest tract of rough mountain country without a Munro. The length of Loch Shiel quivered below its guardian hills. Up this loch Prince Charlie sailed from Moidart to raise his standard. A monument to the event stands beside the road. The Streaps (2,988 and 2,916)—again not Munros—were etched starkly; they are among the very steepest of all hills in Scotland; bare Thuilm lay behind. The Cuillin were there, saw-toothed, beyond the piled blocks of Knoydart and Ciche, beyond the one touch of softness—Glen Dessary. Sgurr Mor took its high, double-topped, stance beyond Glen Kingie, in front of the Saddle and the Glen Shiel ridges, in turn before the Affric ranges.

Yesterday's hills seemed almost tame compared to this western mob.

My tent was draped over the cairn to dry off, while I prowled round it and round again to look and look at the panorama. One fault with nylon is that it retains overnight moisture until really aired like this. If it goes up unaired, the interior is damp, a problem yet to be resolved by manufacturers.

I left a questionnaire behind. Patrick Simms, the Secretary of the Ross-shire M.C. found it, but added he was off back to "native Ireland after five years' Munro bagging". He discovered the note only a few hours after I'd left it, having come up Gleann Fionnlighe from Loch Eil and traversed the South Top—the normal route for most, but my descent route to Glen Pean can be used in reverse: a crafty, back-door approach. The name means *back-shaped hill*.

I went down the very steep flank to a col where I kept a bit to the north so had many ins-and-outs over the gashes cut by streams—hard on the ankles. There was a wee loch near the watershed and once down the glen I had a picnic, and a paddle in exquisitely cold water. The glen is dominated by the Streaps, hills you would have to bargain quite a few Munros to equal.

A 500-foot pull took me slanting up easy slopes to cross the ridge and drop down the rake into Gleann a' Chaoruinn, which must be one of the oldest through routes in a district where north–south communication is singularly difficult. It leads to a fine pass (1,586 feet) hemmed in by the steepness of Thuilm and the Streaps.

Strathan at the end of Loch Arkaig could once see a score of shepherds gathered for the shearing. Now sheep do not pay. Lochiel has sold off glens here, and private forestry is the new thing for Pean and Dessary.

There were figures at the bridge across the Pean (just east of where the Allt a' Chaoruinn joins it) but I had the glen to myself. I collected the odd bit of bog wood for the bothy. A new forestry track was coming in along the slope above, which I found saddening, as this is probably the finest pass in the west and its obliteration by trees would be an act of vandalism. Let us hope the owner, Mrs Jean Balfour (Chairman of the Countryside Commission and a keen conservationist), has these dangers in mind.

The finely-sited bothy shows well the sort of work the Mountain Bothies Association is doing. It had been pointed, re-roofed and good windows inserted, so is now weather-proof. The upper rooms are still panelled and cosy for sleeping, and downstairs (stripped in the past by vandals), though barn-like and bare, has a fireplace. The work done partly with funds raised as a memorial to Wilf Tauber.

There were two sleeping bags. Ian Mitchell I'd expected, but with him was John Lawton whom I had last seen at the Spittal of Glen Muick. Ian was then the M.B.A. membership secretary and a great bothy fan. They, unfortunately for me, had been on the hills I had on my list for tomorrow, so even with friends around, I would not have hill company. Fresh food was much enjoyed. We sat by the bothy fire and I enlightened John (from Australia) and Ian (from England originally) about the doings of my ghost—Prince Charlie.

It was at the house of Donald Cameron of Glen Pean that Prince

Charlie began his foot-slogging in the months after Culloden. That mismanaged February affair lasted only 30 minutes (the barbarous killing that followed it went on for months, earning Cumberland his nickname, "Butcher"). The Prince fled, by horseback, to Loch Oich that same day, to Glengarry's castle, the "Rock of the Raven", then on the second day by the Dark Mile and Loch Arkaig arrived here. He went on foot through to Morar and sailed to the Isles. It's a story walkers should follow on the map, once they know the Highlands. It was an impressive journey. Later, returning from the Isles he was to come over the shoulder of Thuilm, possibly even over its summit, for his party skulked on top watching Glen Pean and Glen Dessary being "beaten" by the redcoats all day before they sneaked down in the dark, traversed Carn Mor's long ridge which rises to 2,718 feet, crossed Upper Glen Dessary and lay up again somewhere on the Ciche side the next day. The next night they descended Coire nan Gall to a "fast place" at the head of Loch Quoich—where we'll take up their route again.

Sunday 9 June THE FINEST PASS IN SCOTLAND

The forecast had been of sunny periods and showers but reality was giving a deal too much of the latter. John and Ian were cutting over the ridge of Carn Mor to visit A'Chuil bothy in Glen Dessary before walking out to Strathan for the long drive back to Fife. We all took photos of each other and set off—up opposing hillsides.

Before beginning my uphill stint I wandered up Glen Pean as far as Lochan Leum an t' Sagairt and managed to cross with a running leap. (All the rivers in Knoydart can be desperate in wet weather.) The reeds were bending to the breeze and the pattern of reflections was very pretty. Crags and trees crowded down to the water's edge and the pass beyond was a deep "kloof". With the ochreous grass colour you could almost have filmed a western there.

It was a no-messing-ascent of Sgurr nan Coireachan, aptly the *peak of the corries*, for this slope enfolds many a secret, deer-filled corrie. It is craggy and wild, with tumbling burns dodging down its flanks. The bothy shrank in size as I rose and Loch Arkaig, every now and then, had its silver light shut off by the grey damask of curtaining showers. On the summit these were giving a touch of snow. Cow-wheat, thyme and bedstraw were all in flower.

Turning east I lost the best of the view (the east–west traverse is better), but had the showers pushing me along the many ups and downs leading to Sgurr Thuilm, or Sgor Choilean, *peak of the holm*. Keep to the crest between the Munros: contours do not pay. (You may find unusually large *books* of mica.) These hills are bulky big brutes but present no real problems.

The big curve of the railway viaduct at the foot of Glenfinnan and the monument to the '45 were both quite visible—and the bewildering pile of mountains beyond. The viaduct is historically interesting as being one of the first to be made of concrete, by Robert McAlpine, who pioneered the Fort William–Mallaig line. Now we take it so for granted, then it was a new-fangled material (though known back to Roman times). This railway is a vital line for hill-goers, for both south and north of it lie great mountain tracts which can be circled without having perpetually to return to a car. A boat from Mallaig into Knoydart is another good starting method, walking out eventually to train back to the start.

I went straight down off Thuilm: steep and a bit slippery underfoot. The sun came out again. I staggered into the bothy with both rucksack and arms full of bog wood, and found a Professor of Logic and Metaphysics installed. He had come from St Andrews to see the bothy: Wilf Tauber had once been a pupil.

I procrastinated over a "sort of" meal. I was not wanting to leave at all—a not uncommon experience this trip. Perhaps the schedule was a necessary discipline; but there was a subtle thrall in the very things I was seeking to flee: telephones and motor cars—the perpetual safety factor.

I left odds and ends of food by two new rucksacks lying in a corner, perhaps they were the figures I'd glimpsed on Thuilm. I noted my doings in the bothy book. An entry there from a Canadian explained his great-great-great-grandfather had left Glen Pean in 1794 for Ontario.

Not being an enthusiastic reader of guide-books I did not know that the better side for passing the loch in the pass lay to the south. "The loch *can* be passed by a laborious ascent on its north side" which I proved: climbing first above cliffs that dropped directly into the lochan, and then descending down shattered crags and trees, rather in the manner of a Tarzan with rucksack. A dead goat lying below was discouraging.

That fun over, I was intrigued to find the pass wending on for well over a mile: corner after corner with a central twisty stream and steep, rocky slopes, hemming it in. The season was progressing. Pipits' nests now held young instead of eggs. Hot, raggedy sheep stood to watch me pass.

I came on an area (like the entrance to the Lost Valley in Glencoe) where a cliff had fallen and filled the glen with boulders. Wending through them I suddenly came on a lost lochan: a small, jet, reflecting pool, delicately set among vivid birch and boulders, wine-coloured in the sun. Above towered a bold edge of cliff. This whole miniature landscape was a complete surprise.

The big pass just to the north is a bleak place in comparison, even on the sunniest of passages. This may only be 400 feet of pass—but it has no superior anywhere. Beyond it lay the watershed and a glimpse of Loch Morar. A crazy gate marked the start of a good stalkers' path and a singing descent through wild scenery led to a tame valley-bottom where there was the usual ruin marking old prosperity and another lochan—an unwinking yellow reptile eye of colour. Round a corner was Loch Morar. I was puzzled by a view of hills far to the west. They looked *very* familiar, but I could not place them for some time: the Rhum Cuillin.

Loch Morar is separated from the sea by a river, only three hundred yards long, leading to a sea bay of brilliant white sand which continues, bay after bay, by Traigh to Back of Keppoch. The loch is over a thousand feet deep, the deepest fresh water to be found in Europe, and you would have to move west beyond the Outer Hebrides, and off the continental shelf, to find a comparable depth in the sea itself. Like Loch Ness (over 700 feet deep), Loch Morar has a reputation for harbouring a beastie of some kind, by name of Morag.

This is country associated above all others with Charles Edward Stewart, for in South Morar he landed and escaped in 1745 and 1746. I think part of the reason his story has been so romanticised is that it was the last flash of a way of life which the rest of the country was already rejecting: Stewart finery and Hanoverian plainness, religious bigotry and the new liberalism. Perhaps by being rid of the Stewarts, we were saved a French Revolution later. What remains sad was the harsh way the social changes came about, and the way the land and its people were forsaken, broken, and cleared, right up to this present century.

Anyone expeditioning in this wild west must be camel-like in self-sufficiency. Since Achnacarry I had not passed an occupied house, and to escape from here would entail a hard day south or west, northwards I would simply run into the Rough Bounds of Knoydart, a landscape even more isolated and empty.

I followed the path among the grassy knolls to the edge of the loch, picking up the odd bit of wood for a fire. The amount of plastic was surprising, even here. I was also keeping a look out for bigger finds. Back in 1746 a treasure of 35,000 louis d'or was brought up the loch and carried through to Glen Pean into the safety of Cameron country (money for the rising, typically arriving *after* Culloden). It was thought to have been buried by Loch Arkaig, perhaps at Murlaggan, if it reached that far. Anyway, it was made so safe that it has not been seen since. Two possible reasons could account for that!

I passed an old, disintegrated landing stage, and there, tucked into the hill with a lawn of wild grass running down to the loch, was a cottage.

Oban had a forsaken look about it. Great steel shutters and plastic gutters and piping obviously showed a determined and recent occupation —yet it stood empty, the wind already having stolen a few sections of roof. Kinlochmorar, the house on the opposite side of the loch, had dark windows, empty like blind eyes, another deserted spot. Both buildings had solitary rowans not far from their doors. Rowans were grown for luck in times past, but luck has long since deserted the glens. Only the odd gangrel stravaigs this way, or the odd boat plouters up the loch. It is as desolate—or peaceful—a spot as you could desire.

"The chip-chip-chipping of a snipe and the mocking call of a loon flying west; these were the sounds of evening." So I wrote in my log and added, prosaically, but sucking encouragement from bare mathematics: "A hundred Munros to go."

Monday 10 June   THE LOWEST EBB

> "And when he was up, he was up,
>   And when he was down, he was down."

It was too warm a night for good sleep. I spent much of it *on* rather than in the sleeping bag. Mice were scrabbling about in the panelling of my bare room in the empty house.

The loch was calm when I rose at seven, but the dull sheen of gun-metal grey had an ominous look about it. I set off wearing just a Damart vest and nylon shorts to try to reduce the volume of sweat expected. While I was busy dealing with a craggy headland opposite the cottage, the loch crumpled into ripples and a drizzle began.

Campers by Kinlochmorar had their belongings scattered in the ruin and, trustingly, a bottle of malt lying! This once large two-storeyed house was falling down—odd furnishings, even a double bed, were still *in situ*, but by a year later vandalism had reduced the interior as if an I.R.A. bomb had been thrown into it. Oak, sycamore and rowan protected the building and a straggle of narcissi told of past affection.

I was faced with another dramatic pass now: Gleann an Lochain Eanaiche. Above it lay Sgurr na h-Aide, a narrow ridge, which seen, end on, from Glen Dessary, or along Loch Arkaig, is often mistaken for Sgurr na Ciche. The slopes of this flank rise at a continuous forty-five degrees for over 2,000 feet. Carn Mor, the other side of the glen, is steep as well, but lacks such crags and slabs on its long eastern shanks.

There was an excellent path up the glen which gave easy gradients. The river plunges at times through some good gorges, tumbling wildly down in successive falls, and carving out holes in the rock, then at other stages meanders gently along. Lochain Eanaiche was a lonely spot.

A bit further on the path degenerated into a foot-track and eventually just traces of beast-track. The ground rose only another hundred feet in over a mile up to the watershed (*c.* 750 feet), a narrow gut (like a small fault) which makes it different from any other pass I know. It ended with the burn twisting down from the left in a splashy fall; then there was quite a dip to link with a meandering burn which flowed to join the River Dessary.

By the top of the pass the rain had come on hard. I was dripping with sweat inside my waterproof top and bottom, though still clad in my minimum. The atmosphere grew colder, but the physical effort of breaking round to the Mam na Cloich 'Airde path kept me warm. Not for the first time I now put a foot in a bog and drew it out black to the knee. I could not be wetter below knee level, anyway, so a walk in the next burn cleaned it.

The rough going slowed me down and I began, suddenly, to feel ridiculously cold. A brief clearance showed the hills ahead (which I was hoping to climb) plastered with snow well below the 2,000-foot level. The rout was complete. Their ascent would have been madness in the conditions, and my state had suddenly become serious: I had become very cold indeed. It was time to camp.

Finding a dryish bump on that blasted weather-scoured col was not easy. Most of the ground was inches deep in water, at just the time I was in a hurry. I eventually chose a knoll where the underlying rock wasn't too close below the thin skin of moss and lichen. Then I found I'd left the tent pegs back at Oban.

"What sort of crazy game was this? It was ridiculous. Time to pack in. It was just not worthwhile. I must be donnert. Daft." Such were my feelings as I grovelled about collecting piles of stones for holding the tent. At least I had the poles. My hands and legs were numb with the icy wetness by the time I got the tent up. Thank goodness it was simple to erect.

At the back of noon I stripped off everything and crawled into the sleeping bag to thaw out. It took half an hour and a couple of brews before I stopped shivering. I was too near ending up as one of Ben Humble's statistics to be amused—even in retrospect.

I ate the last of my bread. My two tea bags were stewed to death, and raisins were counted out one by one. I did have an evening meal spare, though, plus emergency chocolate etc. I could survive a delay, and a cache lay at the foot of the pass. It was loss on the schedule that worried me. I had a tryst at Loch Quoich dam for the weekend.

Perhaps I should make for Inverie and phone, make a meeting at A'Chuil or Kinbreak, then catch up beyond. If these conditions went on, Knoydart would be impossible. I worried myself into the deepest "low" of the trip, needlessly too, for I was only a few miles from friends who could have looked after me for days, and Inverie had a shop.

It was the numbing cold, I suppose, that depressed. It is no fun recognising in oneself the symptoms of an exposure case. I quote the outpouring in my log fully, partly because it is the only such to be found there, and for the sake of truth.

"Storms blast through periodically. Tent a bit drafty and noisy of course. Very wearying. Toughest area of all with difficult lines of supply and communication—and this November weather at its worst. (Still cold in sleeping bag yet last night sweating.) Heights barred by blizzards and valley driving rain and flooded wildly. Oh, it would be nice to pack in—but can't. Must hang on or even retreat and come again. It is so good when good, or even reasonable, but apart from the last three days it's been pretty awful for weeks. It is June, damn it. My shoulder tells the weather: the wet cold sets it gnawing away like a beast. Read a bit and early to kip. Morale low."

Tuesday 11 June   ROUGH BOUNDS

"He who would make a journey must first make peace", says the old Chinese proverb.

The next morning seemed bright very early and the atmosphere had reverted to the stuffy warmth of Oban. A good sleep had worked wonders. I was away at 7 a.m. (I thought) and only ended at 9 p.m. (I thought), so had a long day, which closed as wet as the previous one but with morale high again. The setback had acted like a sharpener on the edge of determination.

Sgurr na Ciche, the *pap-shaped peak*, is the highest of the Knoydart summits. It has a special place in my affections because it was my last Munro, the first innocent time. That was nearly ten years ago and done just days before going off for my first winter in the High Atlas. I had come west by train to Glenfinnan and tramped through between Streap and Thuilm (mostly in the dark) to bivy in a filthy ruin by Loch Arkaig. The next day, via Glen Dessary, I had traversed to Ciche, in tiring snow conditions and then walked out to Glenfinnan again the same way, into darkness again, just in time to catch the evening train to Glasgow.

Now, I skirted up via Coire na Ciche to the bouldery gully descending from the col between Sgurr na Ciche and Garbh Chioch Mhor. This is as good a line as any from the Glen Dessary side if doing Ciche first or on its own. The approaches from the north have been barred by Loch Quoich; direct from Loch Nevis the ridge is very long.

There is probably no mainland ridge as complex as that beginning on Ben Aden, taking in Ciche, Coireachan and along to Sgurr Mor. The going is rough in the extreme: bare mountain rock: ribs and ridges, walls, slabs, gaps with the navigation tricky due to all the tormented twists and turns.

Perhaps it is as well that so much of the best does lie far west and north, and often far from civilisation; people tend to have served some apprenticeship before they wander into these regions. Loch Nevis, to me a place of sunny peacefulness (or "gey weet" peacefulness) has *frightened* people not used to the isolation or grandeur.

From the col at the head of my gully, the Feadan na Ciche (Ciche's whistle or chanter) the route proved surprisingly easy. Not altogether trusting the compass I left tiny "stone men" along my route: skirting up left on steep grass, gaining the crest, then left again—all fairly natural lines between the steep walls which looked huge in the mist. Pockets of snow still lay inches deep but on the whole it had been stripped off almost as quickly as it was plastered on.

The Ordnance Survey deserve a reprimand for the mess they have made of this summit. There are now *three* trig points, in various stages of disintegration! I wended back, tumbling my wee markers as I went, and had soon reached the Feadan. Some day Ciche will give me a view.

A long hogsback ridge—a hedgehog ridge—lies between here and the next Munro, giving two summits: the Garbh Chioch Mhor and Garbh Chioch Bheag—the large and small rough paps. You will not get over them without using your hands and if you try you can use your hands a fair bit. I found quite a good rake along the south flank and on it put up an eagle, who gave me one cool look before dropping into the clouds.

A ptarmigan family broke and scattered at my feet, one of the chicks rolling head over heels down a slab. How the mother bird finds them all later is a marvel—or perhaps she doesn't. You often see a dozen tiny bundles of fluff, but in July there are usually just three or four in the exploding flight. The mother beat her wings against my legs. I took a picture of her against the lichenous rock which showed her marvellous camouflage. Sitting birds just do not move sometimes, and you may only notice them because they blink an eye.

Navigation on the Garbh Chioch is made easy by the presence of a wall. To the north is Coire nan Gall which is precociously slabby without giving real climbing. Prince Charlie came up from Glen Dessary and descended into it in the dark. From the Bealach nan Gall the west ridge up Sgurr nan Coireachan proved easier than expected. I simply did an up and down it, and then turned south west from the col: a slanting line which eventually led more or less back to the tent site.

The descent gave quite a bit of slab and rock, and many a hanging-garden gully. Marsh mallows, globeflower, roseroot and saxifrages loved their wet recesses while eyebright and thrift kept to drier parts. Thrift is Virgin Mary's Pillow, *Cluasag Mhuire* in Gaelic. Deer went off constantly, usefully showing where to break through the odd difficulties.

Glen Dessary was all dollops of sunshine and shadow. It once had a Wade track (not a road), and Cumberland established a camp there. Miss Jenny Cameron of Glen Dessary had led her men to Glenfinnan on a white horse, no doubt by the pass under the Streaps. The three cairns at the head of this pass marked the meeting of Lovat, Glengarry and Locheil lands. The latter alone is left and he recently sold Glen Dessary to the woodmen.

I collected the tent and began the diverse delights of the descent from the Mam na Cloich 'Airde, the *pass of the high rock*. Even in this bleak spot I found a ruined shieling. A fenceless gate marks the watershed. I crossed a river, pulled up—and then the plunge down to Loch Nevis truly began—as dramatically as opening a door.

The path is built up in tight angles or curls down in fine sweeps. There is one rushing stream crossing it, about which I was concerned, for one wild November, when I was escaping from Knoydart, I very nearly drowned in that spot. It was surprisingly easy today though requiring a certain amount of "leaping from rock to rock".

I crossed to have a look at Finiskaig: the roof had fallen in from neglect and as the M.B.A. had offered to do it up at their expense, such neglect is sad. As a bothy it had been the only place for miles where emergency shelter could be found—a possible life-saver. A geologist was camping by the ruin.

The tide was well out and still ebbing I was glad to see. The map is correct in showing the path running between the tide lines as it rounds the head of the loch. Great areas of sand are bared at low tide and this is an area loved by wading birds.

In the 1920's an S.M.C. Journal account describes a round trip from Glasgow: train to Fort William, sail in to Inverie, and then via Sourlies east to Spean Bridge, train back to Glasgow. Quite a weekend. The cost was thirty-five shillings. (Sourlies is now fully restored as a bothy which makes a very useful haven.)

The Carnoch river flows into the head of the loch beside a large area of green patchwork pieces cut by little channels. If you *have* to pass at high tide you may have some scrambling to do: the crags, like the head of Loch Morar, fall steeply to the shore, or sea.

Coming in by steamer, passengers are ferried ashore by rowing boat to Camusrory. Crossing the Carnach can then be a problem. I remember once, on the boat, telling tales of this fearsome river. Another passenger was all ears, too, and chancing to land with the first boatload, set off over the brae before we had all assembled.

When we topped the rise and could see the Carnach I was relieved to see it was not in spate, and by going a little way on we crossed without even taking boots off (the only time, ever, to date). Coming downstream again we met the other passenger pulling on his breeks and still in bare feet. We received a somewhat dirty look! Like every river between Loch Quoich and Glenfinnan the Carnach can be desperate or impossible, something visitors normally never consider elsewhere, but vital in the wet west. The bridge shown here on the map does not exist.

I waded across the Carnach mouth easily enough, but felt my feet were very soft with so much wet and sweaty walking. Ben Aden, up Glen Carnach, had a foreground of Camusrory ponies.

Tony Montgomery moved here and had established one of the best little outdoor centres, first for Barnardo's, and then as "The Travellers Trust". However, lacking the big backing of education authorities, services or the like, it cannot compete and the centre is doomed in its present form.

Here people "travelled", experiencing something of the reality and riches of adventure. They might go off on ponies right through to the Cairngorms—or sail off to Rhum or the Cuillins—or trek through the Rough Bounds. A wonderfully dedicated staff has, over the years, ensured that participants gained the maximum from their experiences: experiences far more valid than in most centres in dull areas where the same old stuff is churned out year after year.

Tony was away on his honeymoon when I called. Nicola Pilkington, a well-trained lassie, produced tea before David Smith turned up. David had long been a fixture here, and one of the pleasures of passing Camusrory was to look in to see him or Tony.

My food parcel was there all right (52p postage); and, if I had to lose tent pegs, the neighbourhood of an adventure centre was probably the place in which to do so. I refused further tempting offers of hospitality and, with the black cats seeing me across the lawn where the lupins were still wrapped with seaweed from a January gale, I turned to the highway again. A blessing on all such kindly folk.

I wandered up to the old ruins of Carnoch—once a keeper's house, now a shell. Charles Inglis Clark, his father, Walker and Jeffrey stayed there in 1913, having walked in from Glenfinnan. Their doings are worth reading up in the old S.M.C. Journal (Vol. XII, p. 297) for the similarities and differences to today's adventures. Some of their photographs are interesting: Kinlochquoich Lodge having since been drowned under a Hydro scheme.

The excuse of removing some weight from the rucksack had me pausing to demolish strawberries and cream. *That* was quite a morale-booster too. However, to balance the renewed zest for living, came the realisation as to why the Clunes parcel had had so many Gaz refills; this parcel, being posted, had none. I had one left and the next supply lay by Loch Quoich dam! It might have to be the old wood fire again: at least there were trees in Knoydart. But that would be a problem for the next day. I still had a pass to cross and a peak to climb, and the next dose of wet stuff was coming up the loch.

The path goes up in well-made zig-zags (not as per map) and the whole area here is craggy and wild (which the map does not indicate either). I had to don skins so was soon sweating away. The smir turned to steady rain and then to equally steady heavy rain. I plodded on up with the wet running off me in sploshy streams. Cuffs and feet were soon wet.

The Mam Meadail was a gruey spot, utterly bleak and completely saturated. I dithered. Having toiled up, Meall Buidhe was immediately above. If I did not do it now it would mean a further day, and a sea-level start. I sheltered my tent and things among a large group of boulders and set off upwards. It was *only* wet, the warmth removed the dangers of the day before.

It is an interesting peak to do in poor visibility; this side especially bears little resemblance to the old map contours. After breaking up through a lot of crags, I ended on a long narrow ridge which did not exist on the map. However up is up, and none of the dips were large enough to go astray on. At the east top I was on familiar ground and edged round the rim of cliffs, Creag Dhearg, which the map shows well down the corrie. The summit is a spacious green one, but I lingered only long enough to stuff a macaroon bar into my mouth.

Meall Buidhe, and its western friend Beinn Buidhe across the Mam, are both fine viewpoints, the latter probably the better with its broader seascape and a view perhaps of Sgurr na Ciche, at its sharpest, mirrored in one of the many lochans. One of the best of hill rounds is the combination of Meall Buidhe and Luinne Bheinn.

Coming down in my cloudy wetness I overshot the turning-off point on the non-existent ridge. Suddenly it "felt" wrong. I had run out of remembered features and markers. Back-tracking failed to help so I began to slant down and just as suddenly it "felt" right again—and sure enough on a boulder I found two perched pebbles left on the ascent.

Up and down from the col took two hours and another two passed before I was done for the day. The descent of Gleann Meadail is another piece of Scotland I have yet to see despite several visits. The saturation continued all the way down the path. Trees "moved" among the smoky valley mists and a rickety bridge took me over to the memorial on the road. Rushes stood silvered with the wet and the scent of the wild hyacinths was strong. On up the glen the myrtle gave a sharper, spiced scent—reminding of food!

It was already gloomy with dusk, and most of the light went as I tramped the road miles to the Dubh Lochain where there is an old cottage used by the estate as a boathouse. It was smelly with recent fibreglass work and the floor was largely wet, but in the black wet night I took the option and just spread the tent on a dry patch and slept on it instead of in it. Every stitch of clothing came off to drape the walls. I heated mince, sweet corn and spinach and had a couple of brews. It was bed I wanted.

My watch had stopped the previous night and I'd wound it at breakfast without noticing: hence, all through the day, I was running two hours out. Which was just as well; for it gave me Meall Buidhe. I was back on par.

Wednesday 12 June   ZIP

Concrete floor or not I slept well. The first glimpse of day was not encouraging: the weather seemed to be carrying on as it was, last thing. My island of dry in the middle of the floor had shrunk.

I was not wanting to be discovered; one may take being thought naughty but not silly. I pitched the tent in the lee of the ruin alongside. I doubled Alpen and halved tea to save precious Gaz. I guessed it to be eight-thirty, set my watch at that, and went off up the slope directly behind the bothy: a route to Ladhar Bheinn used more than once before.

It is quite a straightforward line from the Dubh Lochain side, though at first sight it appears barred by Sgurr Coire Choineachain. But the alternative, to go round that summit, is six or seven miles longer. Choineachain is a fine viewpoint; it is the hill you see immediately above Inverie when you sail in from Mallaig—and the Mam Suidheig, the dip behind, is a natural line.

I was soon soaked below knee level: "Euch" was my log comment. A wren came and made noisy comments too, and the usual cuckoo flitted past until a gang of pipits chased it—going, as you might say, hell for feather.

A large, but still dappled, calf went yelping off and a disapproving grunt came from the hind up the hill. Another was mooing like a cow. I had obviously hit a favoured calving spot. The calves are beautifully camouflaged and the hind will leave them for most of the day. Perhaps this is why her milk is six times as nourishing as a cow's.

Mam Suidheig is rather cut by peat bogs, but deer tracks allowed a gentle slant to be made down into Coire Torr an Asgaill. Not too much height is lost before crossing to the skirts of Ladhar Bheinn.

A fox leapt from a jumble of rocks and trotted across the hillside. As I was carrying no gun he seemed to cock a snoot at me. His presence I reported later, so word could be passed on to the keeper. I still giggle at the face of the keeper in Glen Lyon when I told him I had bumped into two foxes that day, and the relief when he found that neither had been on *his* ground.

I dropped to just under the cloud level, but had it again, like an irritating blanket on a hot night, all the way up the long slopes of Ladhar Bheinn, *the forked mountain.*

Ever so slowly the cloud began to move, a welcome change from the static wet of the last twenty-four hours. I plodded on. The trig point appeared and I was soon on top. There was no view—on a hill with a view as fine as any.

Ladhar Bheinn (the most westerly mainland Munro) is an impressive hill from any side—even the grassy southern slopes will impress, if not depress, with their length and steepness. Walkers not used to really wild country would be well advised to keep to this southern side for an ascent: either my ascent or descent route can be taken. They both drop 2,000 feet in half a mile.

The "obvious" ridge line from the top of Mam Barrisdale is complex and gives scrambling, and in winter can be a proper climb. The north-east corrie (Coire Dhorrcail) is one of the most splendid corries outside Skye. A path leads up into it and you can gain the ridge above. The summit ridge is all of two miles, a narrow crest in places. It is worth saving for a good day, both to see the very fine view and to ensure you find the summit. (The trig point is not at the highest point.) Tom Patey did some winter climbs in the corries.

The hills hem in Loch Hourn as dramatically as any fiord in Norway. I once canoed across from Arnisdale in November to climb the peak from the north. It was a raw, sunless spot, even on the good evening I landed. The next day, after camping overnight, I climbed up the fine northern ridge—thick mist all the way but of course this was no worry ascending, the top was known and had to come in due course. It did. Descending, however, I wanted to swing off on a curling ridge westwards to add a lesser summit beyond the Mam Li. At the appropriate place, estimated from several factors, I did so, and worked very carefully by compass. I became puzzled, for the lie of the land bore no resemblance to the expected, though, as little could be seen in such knobbly rough ground, I could have been anywhere. Eventually I gave up and just took a bearing due north for Loch Hourn. I came down below the cloud about two miles from, and at right angles to, where expected.

This was very bad for morale. It was quite incomprehensible, what's more. Chewing it over later I came to doubt the compass, but on other hills subsequently it worked all right—I was still using it on the Walk. Subsequently I learnt that there is magnetic variation on Ladhar Bheinn's north flank.

The bothy at Barrisdale is equipped and run by local people. Most week-days a boat plies to and from Arnisdale taking mail, and children to school. The next best approach is by walking-in along Loch Hourn from the head of the loch: a path without equal in Scotland. At times it is built up on naked rock above the sea like something in a Himalayan gorge.

I flanked down in tight zig-zags for over 2,000 feet so was glad to stop and take a quick photo of another deer calf lying motionless on the grass at my feet, neck outstretched, big eyes moist under their lashes. In the river, a dipper family was splashing about like a gang of Braehead kids. Stonechats were about again. At Camusrory yesterday I had noticed a stonechat on the bird table. Two other calves broke from cover to go screaming across the slope. A slope to avoid in June it seems!

Folach was another ruin, but of a comparatively modern building. Where fenced off the grass was green and bright. It was hard to imagine Knoydart well populated. It was Macdonell land, and the clan suffered as a result of the '45 like everyone else. Many emigrated to Canada. Glengarry was the seat of the chief, and it was to maintain a position in Edinburgh and London that so much of the land was bled. Raeburn's portrait of Macdonell of Glengarry in the National Gallery in Edinburgh appropriately forms the cover of John Prebble's *The Clearances*.

In 1840 the then chief sold out, except for Knoydart, and emigrated to Australia. In 1846 there was still a population of 600, but potato blight and the failure of the annual herring migration caused famine, and further poverty drove away many of the survivors. The chief returned to die at Inverie in 1852, but his widow has earned a special place in the hall of infamy for her brutal clearing of the estate the next year to make way for sheep. It would fetch a better price, cleared, when sold to a southerner. Four hundred people were driven from the little hamlets, their homes broken down or burnt under her personal direction, and then they were shipped like cattle to a waiting transporter, the *Sillery*, generously supplied by the government to take them off to America.

A few lingered on, living in constructions of sacking and turf, eating shell fish—and dying in the winter. That was the Clearances.

Today, an Ardrishaig firm were busy with yellow monsters chewing up a "road" which at present was all squelchy black mud. The Allt a' Mhuilinn led steeply down to Inverie through woods and rhoddies smelling of honey. The boat was chugging its friendly course into the bay and the usual group of people had gathered at the pier for its arrival—a scene as much part of Western life as fish, midges and wellington boots.

Sailing from Mallaig is possibly the finest way of reaching Knoydart. *The Clansman* once gave me an unscheduled landing on a remote shore simply by edging in so that I could leap from the bows on to the rocky shore.

The Ripleys when they landed at Inverie met a very unfriendly reception: the third week in September not being a diplomatic visiting period! They did my yesterday in reverse to end at A'Chuil in Glen Dessary, sleeping on corrugated iron sheets to keep themselves off the sheep droppings. Fortunately, the M.B.A. have saved that vital haven.

The shop had a fine selection of wine and I loaded up with all manner of fresh goodies: cheese, milk, tomatoes, bananas, rolls, butter and cakes. They had no meths, no paraffin, no Gaz, and no ideas—but my eye lit on packets of Zip firelighters. I bought two, and some tins of food for quickness—and "because they were there". (Who eats dehydrated when there are alternatives?)

I lacked a book for the tramp home and it seemed a long road in the stuffy heat and with a load of tins. The white houses strung along the bay always look attractive and the big house in its green setting has none of the misplaced flamboyancy of so many mansions. Inverie is lush with big trees and green farmlands, again giving the sense of contrast which was such a part of the Walk.

On the knoll near where the Mam Meadail path branches off, there is a monument which, in Knoydart, gives the Clearances story a modern appendix. The monument is to the late Lord Brocket's father. That Lord Brocket was the landowner at the time of the post-war land-grab; his name lives on, in the lines of a popular, not very complimentary ballad, if nowhere else. He had sacked people at will and generally made life intolerable for the local folk, some who had worked there for generations. An approach by locals for land was rejected and when "The Seven Men of Knoydart" tried to grab land for crofts, they were interdicted. A few years later Lord Brocket sold the estate anyway. Perhaps it is time for this feudal system to end. We have to cull the deer, but there could be a better system.

It was only a mile or two from the monument back to the loch and the tent. The estate road finishes there and the path on to the Mam Barrisdale is an old, excellent pony track. Patches of blue appeared in the grey clouds like lost pieces of a jigsaw.

All the tracks in Knoydart exist as shown on the one-inch map. Where they are shown as ending they usually do, and the reason is that to continue is probably impracticable. Many buildings shown fell into disrepair during the war. You go in to Knoydart prepared to be self-contained. They might not have Zip firelighters next time! This is not beautiful country but it is highly dramatic, very rough and blessed with the silence of remoteness. Saint-Exupéry defined silence as God's cloak spread out upon man's restlessness.

I'd never met anyone all day till I came on the road works, nor was I to meet anyone again, on subsequent days, till the weekenders arrived at Loch Quoich. With soap and soap powder from the cache, I washed undies (and myself) vigorously. Had I known the characteristics of Zip firelighters I would hardly have bothered. Cooking on them left dixies, hands, face and tent liberally covered in soot. A huge meal, extravagant and enjoyable, ended with oozing butter and jam pieces and fresh milk. A meal makes amends for many things. A touch of sun shimmered through the leaves of the tree growing out of the ruin—a change from yesterday's grey hours groping into black night. It was great not to be pushed for once. There was time to write home, to cut nails, to catch up on the log (the 1,000 miles up today)—and indulge in the old Knoydart game of chasing ticks, for which being alone had certain disadvantages, no offers of "you do me and I'll do you". The wind dropped and the midges swarmed out, so it was into the tent early. Mountains bring forth a peculiar joy which makes us willingly pay the coin of sacrifice and suffering to obtain it. Knoydart had proved a "high" even if the day before had been the lowest ebb. The walk would go, surely: the hills might trip me up, break me, kill me—but otherwise, now, they would not beat me.

Thursday 13 June SUN ALL THE WAY
One titbit from the past cannot be omitted: this was the famous S.M.C. "Yachting Meet" of Easter 1897. The ship was intended as a base for the Cuillin, but the weather drove her from there to Rhum and then to Knoydart.

The Meet report is exciting stuff—such as ascending Ciche, from Inverie, against the tide clock and the ship sailing. Raeburn was on his first Meet, and besides Sir Hugh (with his flute) were Bell, Boyd, Brown, Brunskill, Douglas, Gordon, Howie, Maylard, Ramsay, Rennie, Gibson, Robertson and Ling. Quite a talented gathering. Imagine if the ship had sunk!

Meets have deteriorated since those days. The original account ends, "And now being safely off the hills and steaming for the open sea, the mirth prevailed—the pipes were brought on deck, and the President (Munro), in all the splendour of Highland garb, footed it deftly through the Highland Fling—and reels were danced—a fitting termination to the Meet."

A heat-wave switched on at sun-up. Camp was soon cleared. Despite eating to a state of tightness, various items were surplus, so these, plus unwanted Zip firelighters, were parcelled up and left, with a note giving them to the finder, on top of the boat in the bothy. My last act was to gulp down milk kept as a treat. I found the last mouthfuls lumpy and a check showed some big black slugs.

The Dubh Lochain was like a mirror and Knoydart lay in un-believable peace, yet I was walking through the wettest region of the country. Knoydart weather does sometimes prove bloody marvellous instead of just bloody. In six miles I shot off a complete 36 exposures, a spool of slides I've never equalled for variety: the reflections in the loch, footsteps on the sand, striped slopes of rushes, bobbing clumps of bog cotton, hands of "bloody fingers" under the trees, a birch in a golden blaze of back light, Luinne Bheinn lifting all too high, and Choire Odhair deep set, the roughest corrie in all the rough bounds. . . .

Knoydart seems a remarkable place for its beetles. Yesterday and today gave a bigger variety than I've ever seen before. A cast from some bird of prey was made entirely of beetles' cases. There were a lot of frogs too. And there are the ticks. Before dressing I'd removed several more of these unwelcome creatures.

Mam Barrisdale is 1,450 feet and I reached it feeling puggled. However, with a breeze of sorts, the next miles were merely hard work, not an intolerable sweat bath. On this sort of trip you "mun dree yir weird" as it comes.

Luinne Bheinn to Braehead kids inevitably ended as "loony-bin". Perceptive lads. To be fair, they had once suffered a Knoydart heat-wave too. We toiled up from the Dubh Lochain and then from the pass set off for Ladhar Bheinn—which explains my route of yesterday: there is more to Ladhar Bheinn that the O.S. cares to admit. We reached the top in a state of collapse and, as I wrote in an account of the trip for a certain well-known magazine, "there we drank our bars of chocolate". It was stolidly altered to "ate our bars of chocolate". (The same editorial pencil once substituted "bottom slide" for "bum slide"—which took years to live down!) That Braehead trip had been our finest ever, for it was part of the "Killin-to-Skye Trek". We dropped down to Loch Hourn from this pass and had to go miles up the loch before we found water to drink: every stream had dried up.

I brewed on top of Mam Barrisdale. The dominating peak beyond was Sgurr na Sgine, next to and more dramatic than the Saddle. Strange, for it also plays this trick when viewed down Glen Shiel.

It was possible to skirt the first bump before the real hog's back of ridge. There were rocky bits enough for scrambling but I was too laden and too hot to be very enthusiastic. Two eagles in succession passed just twenty yards off, soaring along like birds of fire in the dazzle of sun. On another visit I very nearly landed on top of one when careering down the ridge.

I forgot to leave an intended questionnaire note on the summit and was far too happy on the east top to go back. An oozing "jelly piece" seemed much more important. My good intentions of adding Sgurr a' Choire-bheithe had melted in the sun. A swim in Lochan nam Breac sounded better. A big herd of deer going through the Bealach Unndalain thundered by fifty yards below me.

A path wiggled down and by cunning use of rakes and ledges led to Lochan nam Breac. Here I had a sandy bay to swim in, to soap and clean self and clothes, to brew while things dried again. Noon was wrapped over with blue and tied with sunshine. Luinne Bheinn was framed between the rocky bulks of Ben Aden and Druim a' Chosaidh, looking unreal and remote already. Such afternoons are made for minimal effort, and that aquatic.

Lochan nam Breac is a collectors' piece: dramatically wild and lonely. My route had carefully been planned to include it. Eastwards, through a gap, the sight of the spike of Sgurr Mor, reminded that there was another day to come, and eventually I pushed on rather than camp there by the loch. Tomorrow might be worse, even hotter.

There are two streams flowing into the loch at the east end which start as one burn. Only in two other places do I know of burns which split and flow off on independent courses; but this is the weirdest, for the Allt Coire na Cruaiche here splits like a T-junction, one arm flowing quickly into the loch and the other setting off in the opposite direction, taking four times the distance to join the same loch.

The remoteness of this spot is emphasised because Loch Quoich (pronounced: Koo-ich), when dammed, flooded all the old approaches from the east. The water level is higher than the watershed, so there are small dams at this end above Lochan nam Breac. This had left the spot untouched but drowned a whole group of shooting lodge and tenant housing further east. You can try and guess the site from the paths that once converged on it, and now plunge into the loch.

Royalty once stalked here, and at drowned Glenquoich Lodge under Gleouraich but that glory has departed. So have trees; the road to Kinloch Hourn passes dead remnants and midge-loved splatters of rhododendron (which signify dead mansion houses as surely as nettles point to ruined cottages and rowans to vanished shielings). It is nice to meet the herd of Highland cattle by the loch, and there are sheep and stags which hopefully eye every car in winter for a hand-out. I practically had to push one out of the way to hide a cache back in February. Speculatively I eyed across the silver water. Food lay over yonder. Double caches and folk coming up tomorrow.

The Great Glen with its massive forests of pine seemed years distant —yet still lay just a day's walk away. Scotland's glory is this eternal contrast. The varied climate, underlying rock, geographic site and so on give an endless fashion parade of form, colour and vegetation. If tonight I was to lie in poor shoddy, tatty with bogs, then in two days' time I would as likely be camping under a monkey-puzzle by a glen of leafy livery.

Loch Quoich was very low and several islands had popped up. It took a hectic bog-hopping diversion to cross the mouth of Coire nan Gall, that slabby bay where I met Prince Charlie's route again; perhaps the most incredible part of his 22 weeks of wandering—longer than this trek of mine and with man as well as mountain set against him. The kilted charmer of the romantic tale came out of Coire nan Gall as a wretched fugitive: thin and hungry, in tatters, and weather-worn and probably as demoralised by midges as any man ever.

He and his company had come down here in the dark, what is more, to a "fast place" at the head of Loch Quoich. That evening they climbed Meall an Spardain to watch the troops below in Gleann Cosaidh. They skulked across and up the Leac na Fearna ridge on the other side—still within the cordon. Descending Coire Beithe in the dark they at last made it through the enemy line somewhere near Loch Coire Shubh and escaped up Coire Sgoir-adail after a day spent hidden right above Loch Hourn where they could see the Redcoats all day. Another night's work took them over the Bealach Dubh Leac to Glen Shiel and eased the pressure.

Later I would use that bealach to gain the Cluanie Ridge from Glen Shiel, and two nights hence I was to camp by Loch Coire Shubh.

One of the outcomes of the 1745 was the mapping of the Highlands. Neither Prince Charlie nor the Redcoats had maps, which is hard to envisage today with our superabundance; hence the Prince's constant search for and use of "guides". In 1747 an infantry detachment arrived at Fort Augustus and spent the next eight years surveying. Roy's map was the result, one with which he himself was not altogether satisfied. He had not had the best of instruments and was limited to too tight a budget. It sounds familiar today. He was a youthful twenty-one when this work began, and it was a year after he died, in 1790, that the Ordnance Survey was founded. They of course began at the other end of Britain: the first O.S. one-inch map was of Kent, in 1801. Now they are in the throes of metrication and a huge re-surveying programme with air photography, helicopters and other modern aids. British maps have always been, basically, among the best and are likely to remain ᴑ: which is why we love to find them erring!

Shaking loose of the bogs, I slowly contoured up and round to enter the next glen below Sgurr Mor. A grassy knoll on top of a boulder above the burn was an idyllic camp site, only spoilt, briefly, now and then, by jet planes diving through all sorts of unlikely passes and taking one by surprise.

The meal was made on the sooty horror of firelighters again—a simple meat, veg. and macaroni—a culinary task not particularly enjoyed. There would just be enough left to make a brew in the morning. The first peak was right above—deceptively close until a line of deer crossed its upper slopes and gave the true scale.

There was time to splash in a small pool under a fall—and to read, snug inside the sleeping bag. Oddly, lying in the tent I was actually missing the sweep of Grampian scenery—perhaps because I read Karen Blixen the other day, and now *A Story Like the Wind*, by Laurens van der Post with its evocative picture of the spacious African scene. That was where I first consciously realised that mountains and landscape played a vital part in my dreams and reality. I'd have been about seven at the time, a refugee from the Japanese sweep through Malaya and the battering of Singapore, so even then was aware of the dichotomy of man's evil doings and the marvels of the wild, open hills. *Jock of the Bushveldt* and the tales of the Great Trek were heady stuff, though it was then too that Gino Watkins and Shackleton were placed on their respective polar pedestals. All of which remains.

The Africa in my blood is very disturbing. (Am I not blood-brother to a Zulu chief with the scar on my wrist to this day?) It desires the veldt sweep of ochreous miles: the Grampians. Here I missed it, yet in the Grampians the other voice called. The blood of the Celt is strong, too, and where wild crests fall into the lochs of the west and the sun sets like blood in the sea, there I would most long to be. It works too on the larger scale: in Scotland I plot and ploy for the next trip abroad— but no sooner away than all the dreams are of home hills again.

The murmur of the stream and the occasional grunt of a hind, the flaring gold of a sunset, the glow of a body hot with sun: the day had been well filled with the small things of immeasurable joy. Like the Psalmist I was inclined to "live while the sun endures".

X

QUOICH—GLENELG

"If you have dwelt in the secret heart of the mountains, beholding the full glory of their revelation, as they unfold their signs and wonders from the going down of the sun to its uprising, nothing can efface the memory of such nights."
—JULIUS KUGY *Alpine Pilgrimage*

Friday 14 June SOUTH SIDE

The first morning sound was the blatter of rain—a surprise after such sunshine. One assumes the good days will go on for ever.

I followed the burn. The path shown up Sgurr Beag continues right along to Sgurr an Fhuarain, though it has deteriorated. On the east ridge of Sgurr Beag it actually breaks into a stone staircase, a relic deserving preservation by the N.T.S. as an example of a feudal sub-craft of the stalking hey-day.

Sgurr Mor is a great hulk of mountain and one not easily reached from a road-end for the normal Munro-bagger. It seemed a good place to leave a questionnaire. Ron Hardie (from Crail) and two others of the Fife Mountaineering Club picked it up two weeks later. Ron was at 269, and not long after he succeeded in finishing his Munros. There was something rather eerie about leaving a note in such a place and it being found, as happened several times, by someone I knew.

Leaving the summit of Sgurr Mor the cloud rolled in, and all day it rose and fell just above walking level. A dozen sheep, wild and un-tended, went down the ridge before me. It was for these brutes the humans were cleared from the glens—and now they in turn are a financial liability, often neglected and running wild, unless, as in Knoydart, simply cleared in their turn.

Down below I could see the bothy at Kinbreack, a restored stable. Fifty yards along from it the "lodge" slowly rots and falls—a roof gone here, floors gone there, the whole a mass of sheep droppings, even up the crumbling stairs and in the rooms where once the wealthy patrons slept in the stalking season.

Glen Kingie, which moats all this day's mountains to the south, is a desolate spot. From the bothy door down there, these hills form a wall as far as eye can see, east and west, yet there is no feeling of being shut in. It is a wide strath of ochreous grass and wild sheep. You can sit by the bothy door with the tang of wood fire in your nostrils, blue smoke clinging to the ground, snipe drumming in the sky and waders calling mysteriously from the river verge, enjoying the held-breath of a summer's night, utterly at peace.

But first you would have to reach it. No road goes to the door and the easiest path is a rather imaginative O.S. gesture. If the river is in spate the Kingie can be an impossible barrier and Loch Arkaig is a long way from anywhere. Man seems to have given up the glen. Perhaps here, as in few other places, you will find solitude. Months may pass without an entry in the visitors' book.

Kinbreack bothy, like many, has been done up by the Mountain Bothies Association: a small corps of hardened individualists who love the wild and lonely places. They don't go in for much publicity—solitude is one of the benisons of bothy life—but quietly, with land-owners' permission, the M.B.A. has saved many an old building, sometimes with incredible physical labour.

Bothies give a roomy shelter, instead of the confinement of a tent—and without a tent you can carry its weight in food, giving more days in the wilds without having to re-stock.

Sgurr an Fhuarain (2,957 feet) is a Corbett, its ascent a long grassy slope. The great crag markings on its east face are exaggerated—there is nothing different there from scores of nearby hills which get no markings at all, Sgurr Mor for instance. I left the east ridge by a path and then cut across to another which zig-zagged on to the steep end of Gairich, which, after that, was a gentle walk among endless deer and bleeping plovers. Gairich means the *mountain of yelling* which no doubt I did one December morning with Eck Rollo and Ian Moreland, when it gave the last Munro of the second time round.

Gairich has fine corries and a big south gully, but they are all too seldom in winter condition. The east ridge has one narrow bit. Over the moors I took a path down to new plantings and then joined the old right-of-way from Lochan to near the Quoich dam. The path eventually goes into the loch, the Hydro being no respecter of paths.

I searched about for sites by the dam and then pitched on a breezy knoll above it, quite invisible from the road yet covering it in best Commando fashion. The cache I'd hidden up a burn told its tale from afar: a confetti of plastic and paper betrayed its ravished state. The tins were safe enough, though breakfast misfired due to the labels having come off: spinach and Nestlé's cream made an odd combination!

I was very glad to see Gaz cylinders, and was soon tucking into stew and carrots, strawberries and rice—all tins of course. Before supper I walked up the road and made the dreamy occupant of a Dormobile jump when I asked the correct time. A morning rendezvous depended on it, and for days I had been on guesswork.

Clouds poured over Gairich all evening—a strange effect which no other hill was sharing. I sat in the evening sun and read. It was not perfection though: my buttocks were covered in red ant bites. Somewhere, I hoped, Bob Binnie was on the road. I finished the log and turned in. The next entry would have to wait until Monday. Life for the next few days would be busy.

Saturday 15 June   THE QUOICH HILLS

I slept the sleep of the happy ones. There was breeze enough on rising to keep the midges away and by nine I was at the dam to meet Lorna and Bob: an appointment which once seemed so unlikely to be kept.

The next two hours were hectic. I used the car wing mirror to slice off some of the facial jungle. We also took some black and white pictures of the tent and doing various things—like digging up the cache by the Alltbeithe bridge and dealing with mail at the car. I hate publicity yet, perforce, need it.

There are times when one is happily cut down to size. Some of my girls once gleefully reported a conversation they'd overheard in an Aviemore supermarket where two men had ultimately decided it could not possibly be me after all as "surely he could afford decent breeches."

"We'll buy you a needle and thread, sur, for a treat," they offered. Another time, rock-climbing at Aberdour someone came up and said I must be Hamish. After I admitted it, he added, "I thought so. I recognised the dog."

After sorting out food, films and maps and replacing odd garments and making a parcel for Dollar, we returned to the dam to pick up the Long Walk. I set off towards Loch Fearna, while Lorna and Bob drove several miles west, first, as they had to circle back to the car. We met at the loch where I was busy answering letters.

There were loons laughing away on Loch Quoich, and I wondered if one of them had watched me bury the parcel down by the bridge. It had been found by mice but only the chocolate had gone. It seems as irresistible to mice as to children. I was worried, however, about the cache in Glen Strathfarrar. That one would be vital. Obviously I'd have to assume chocolate and all non-tinned items had been destroyed and carry replacements.

Cloud came and went but it remained dry which is enough to ask of Quoich. Bob went bouncing off while Lorna and I followed at a rational speed. We lunched late on top of Spidean Mialach, the *pinnacle of wild animals*. A note left here, decorated with rhododendron blossom, has not come back.

We wandered down to the col as cloud rolled in and were glad to find a zig-zag of path up beyond. We also found a coupit sheep and gladly left ex-farmer Bob the smelly job of righting it. We also enjoyed Bob's disbelief on the south-east top for he had assumed it was the summit—which now appeared half a mile off—magnified by mist to twice the distance and height. Gleouraich has *uproar* as its translation.

We separated here: Lorna going down to Loch Quoich by the south-west ridge and we two, bent on the third Munro, off for Alltbeithe to the north-west. Lorna's way off was down another quite remarkable made path: perhaps my favourite among them all. On it, "King Edward's Butt", tells of departed glories.

We had a path down too—once we found it. We had a bite before crossing the river to Alltbeithe and then cut over to the River Quoich direct, rightly judging it to be low enough not to cause trouble.

We took the path up Coir a' Chaoruinn, but it is certainly not kept up, and the good one zig-zagging up to the Am Bathaich ridge is much better. Having done the circling ridges, though, I wanted a new way. A great rockfall had strewn boulders down the slope and even across the burn. We wended up the steep slopes beside them, enjoying the rough craggy scenery, to arrive almost at the cairn of Sgurr a' Mhaoraich, *peak of the shell fish*. We also ran up into cloud again, so the dramatic view down Loch Hourn was missed. Munro regarded it as the most beautiful of all highland lochs, but I find it too shut in. Dramatic, remote, wild are perhaps better words than beautiful.

As we were not going to receive view or sustenance on top we angled off with the compass. Romping through the mist we set off more deer. One went for a mighty *skite* and left a long scar where it had slipped. Deer often seem infallible but under many a crag you will find the remains of a past accident. Eagles have been known to start them over cliffs.

We crossed the Allt Ban high up, and from the lip beyond could see down to the road and the lochs. Lorna's bright orange tent stood out vividly, mine was invisible. It was a steep drop down but seemed to go fast and at 8.45 we were in—a good romp behind—and a midgey purgatory ahead.

We piled in for tea, protected by a smoking Moon Tiger and lay gossiping for ages before facing the beasts again. My tent was free of them, but at the price of having a sweat bath as soon as I lit the stove. Through the thin fabric it was possible to see the seething millions crawling over everything.

Unhelpful bumps and the heat made it a weary night. Midges can bite through a sheet liner, I found. Later I crawled into the bag when it cooled. There was a drumming of rain.

Sunday 16 June HEAVENLY HELL

Climbers are long-suffering beings, but they have their rewards now and then. There are individual days which are all joy. They often come unexpectedly and unplanned, and for them we will endure much, for, when we have them, we are kings awhile.

They are usually inexplicable, for wonder is secretive and personal. We may mumble over a pint in a pub, "Aye, a great day", leaving it both said and not said. Thank goodness something defies analysis. Wonder? Beauty? Revelation? Poor atheist with no God to praise!

The neb of the morning passed me by and it was a quarter to eight before I set off. I woke the others and left some food. It was a drumlie sort of day with little promise beyond much walking.

Loch Coire Shubh lay like a grey puddle among the dark hills. Knoydart country this: bulging bellies of rock showing through the rotting skin of grass. Oddly, on each side of the loch stood a monkey-puzzle tree.

I contoured round on the path while the road and river both fell madly down to the flats of Kinloch Hourn: a strange touch of green farmland at the head of the loch.

Here in the past a population lived by farming, fishing, timber, smelting, boat-building and even a little mining near Glenelg for silver, lead and copper. In the eighteenth century herring fishing was flourishing: boats crowded in the inner loch here so you could cross their decks from shore to shore. 30,000 barrels a year were produced, then the herring vanished, deserting old, established routes and impoverishing much of the western seaboard. Arnisdale decayed, and now most of its string of cottages belong to the white settlers—absentee holiday-homers. In 1836 the population was 600. It is a grim tale, the misery completed with potato blights, typhoid and vicious Clearances—as in Knoydart.

On that Braehead "Killin-to-Skye" trip we came through Knoydart to round Loch Hourn and go on to Glenelg by part of today's route. Camping at Loch Hourn we woke in the morning to find the farmer had unexpectedly left eggs and milk at the tents. We did many treks, and the tougher the kids had it the more they seemed to enjoy it. There was no "simulated" adventure; if you broke a leg in Knoydart you were in for a rough ride. They knew it—and did not break legs in Knoydart. Youngsters are fitter, better co-ordinated, and safer than adults realise.

Adults set out brainwashing their own children from the earliest age *not* to be adventurous. "Don't do that, darling, you may fall and hurt yourself!" Children naturally climb trees, the tragedy is that adults do not. Much of the adult world considers all mountain activity a form of adolescent irresponsibility—to be curbed and controlled if not banned.

Kinloch Hourn today lay silent and grey. I leapt the Allt Coire Sgoir-adail quite easily. It is real river, quietly draining the vast soggy cirque—up which Charles Edward Stewart floundered heading for Glen Shiel—and then plunging down to Kinloch Hourn in a series of rough slides and falls. A path led through a gap to the woods of the estate house. It dipped, then rose again, to twist up behind another bump and then split, with branches taking separate bealachs to Gleann Beag and Glen More, great walking routes both.

By the time I'd reached the river which drains the Saddle to the south, the sun broke through. I brewed, finished off my book and dried the tent. It would have been an idyllic site to stay but my route continued on up a side stream to the Bealach Aoidhdailean (1,550 feet) with only a tracing of path. The view back gave a series of V-gaps, all in line, one inside each other, right to the start seven miles away.

A few miles down the other side led to Gleann Beag, but first there was Beinn Sgritheall (Sgriol) and between it and me lay two Corbetts with their distinctive drops all round.

I believed these could be skirted. North of the first was the Druim nam Bo, the *ridge of the cows*, which surely implied grass, for cows don't climb rough stuff, and the flank of the second was only half a mile wide, and though steep, memory recalled clear deer/sheep tracks across it.

So it worked out. I was soon on the col below Sgriol. The slopes seemed to be full of deer calves: some cowered and some fled bleating for their maws. Sgriol was a peak we always associated with school trips to Sandaig (Gavin Maxwell's Camusfearna, where his ashes are scattered on the grass of broken dreams) and though a long approach from that western side, it was our usual one. But the least-penal route from Arnisdale is to come up to the Bealach and along the crest, as I did today. It is a bit rough up on to the east top but after that there is a green ridge of pure delight.

Loch Hourn widened into the Sound of Sleat below, the isles of Rhum and Eigg were surfacing from a haze into the sun and in every direction one saw an extravagance of mountain scenery. Beinn Sgritheall is king of the little hills and not only my opinion. "The view remains in my mind as perhaps the most beautiful I have seen in Scotland . . . every stroke of the oars of a boat on Loch Hourn could be plainly heard, and the note of a dozen cuckoos shouting in all directions." That is Sir Hugh again.

I found a pure white thrift on the way up, a new mountain flower to me in its colourless form. Milkwort, lousewort, more campion, these are not uncommon in white form—caused by chemical deficiencies in the soil I'm told.

An English lad was already on the summit. He seemed to know his view. And what a view! Every aspect pleased:

Rhum, Mull, Jura, all the "country" of Knoydart, Moidart, Ardgour, Creag Meaghaidh, the Grey Corries, Nevis, Bidean, the hills of yester-day, the Glen Shiel ridges, Affric, the Lapaichs, Sheasgaich, Fuar Tholl, Torridons, Slioch and beyond, Applecross, the Cuillin of Skye and the Outer Isles. If I named off a hundred peaks on Beinn Dorain, I think I beat that here. I would not have swopped it for any mountain view in the world. It was also a formidable array. Had I done well till now, the view of summits northwards, all still to be climbed, was enough to sober anyone.

The English lad set off down to his car on the Loch Hourn road and I suddenly felt smug and superior again: my day progressed in a great sweeping tramp westwards, his had been a circle from and back to a car, as had been Lorna's yesterday.

a Hamish with the
Challis tent and
folding Raleigh at the
Morvich camp site

b The lowest ebb of the
trip was experienced
in this pass between
Knoydart and Glen
Dessary

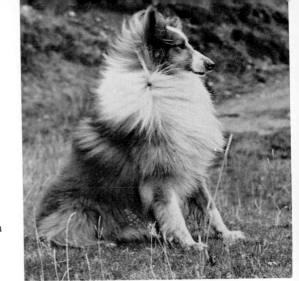

a "Kitchy"—Hamish's dog which
climbed all the 3,000-foot peaks in
the British Isles

b

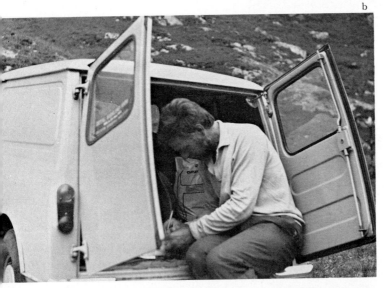

b Lorna's van by
Loch Quoich;
Hamish deals with
fresh food, mail,
films, etc.—a
welcome ritual if
always a rush

c

c One of the early
summer joys of the
Long Walk—
frequent meetings
with red deer
calves

The training
schooner *Captain
Scott* in Loch
Linnhe

Inverie, the only
village in remote
Knoydart

Tea outside the tent near Loch Hourn

Knoydart—Luinne Bheinn seen from the boathouse at the Dubh Lochain

Ben Sgriol from the prehistoric hill fort of Torr Beag

Skye—a view along the ridge from Sgurr Alasdair

The pinnacles of Sgurr nan Gillean from Garbh-bheinn over the
bump of Ruadh Stac

Glenelg and the Glen Shiel hills seen from the brae of the Bealach
Udal after crossing to Skye

The Five Sisters of Kintail across Loch Duich

Loch Duich and far Ben Sgriol seen from the Gates of Affric

I remembered to leave a questionnaire at the cairn; it was found four days later by John Hartley from Birmingham who also wrote a long letter. He was aware of the Munro disease, and wrote: "I look on the Munros as a lifetime's ambition, but not one to achieve as soon as possible, at the cost of pleasant days, which is what we go for. I like to think there is enough in Scotland to last me a lifetime. . . . Nobody visited Sgriol on the summer days between our visits: south of the border I have counted over 150 on the summit of Helvellyn during a Friday in April.

"It's fascinating to write and know the recipient only as a name. You, sir, might be a schoolboy having just tasted your first Munro, or you might be at the height of your career. I met Lord Hailsham on top of Macdhui in 1972."

I was loath to leave the summit, but with ten miles still to go, the day's darg was hardly done. A small vee of wake followed a buzzing boat up the loch. Loch Hourn and Loch Nevis have been, rather imaginatively, translated as the *Loch of Hell* and the *Loch of Heaven*. Physically and meteorologically that is usually apt.

Just how indented the west coast is, can be seen in the fact that between Ardnamurchan and Loch Carron it twists for 350 miles while the comparable distance up the Great Glen's fault line is 80 miles.

It was only later that I heard of another mountain event on this day. It was the 150th Anniversary of the Edinburgh Academy, and the school climbed 150 Munros as part of the celebrations. Sgriol, being a solitary, distant Munro, was not done, but parties were busy on the Glen Shiel switchbacks, and Colin Turner and party were opposite on the Cuillin.

Rather than simply retrace along over the east Top again, I cut down into Coire Min where a clear lochan was surrounded by paint-spotted sheep. The stream from it, the Allt Mhic a' Phearsain, becomes the Allt Srath a' Chomair before ending as the Amhain a' Ghlinne Bhig. Sgriol rose in a mixture of shadow and silver, bold prows out of dark shadow and flanks glittering with sun.

I cut the dog-leg only to find myself on crags above Gleann Beag, but even that was fun, teasing a way down by half-secret animal tracks and paddling joyfully over the river. A brew was very welcome. I covered six miles down Gleann Beag to Glenelg in an hour and ten minutes which was a fairly pleasing end to a twelve-hour day. It was a glen I knew well, milestoned by old *duns* and Pictish *brochs*, shaded by hazel

H

scrub and bright with yellow seggs. I walked with past company down to Eilanreach (lovely name), and along to Glenelg—which the kids would always ask you to spell backwards. I walked into the doup of the day with heart glowing as well as face. On days like this it was good to be Scot free.

Glenelg was as quiet as ever—watched over by the bronze angels of its ornate war memorial. The church is hidden among the trees (the first one here was founded by a hunch-back monk from Beauly) and the main street has a grassy, timeless untidy air. At the far end lived Dr Catherine MacInnes. A note for me was pinned on the door, but she was in and we were soon chatting away over coffee. The offer of a bath and a bed was not refused, the rain and midges having joined forces again as dusk fell.

I opened stacks of tins and shoved away plenty calories. Catherine leads the local rescue team (consisting mainly of forestry lads) and Ladhar Bheinn was one of their stamping grounds. I was delighted to hear that they had several experiences of navigation going astray on the magnetic northern flanks of that peak. The doctor obviously enjoyed a good crack with someone who was not a local patient!

She told a story of Jack Thomson at Glenmore Lodge out with a gang from Glasgow on the hill. One girl, rollers in her hair and all, girned about being tired, to which Jack replied: "Och well, lassie, I'll just stand you on your head and wheel you along."

It was after midnight when I collapsed into bed—stockings and vest washed, self bathed and the room strewn with gear and the contents of food parcels.

The rough wooing of Knoydart was behind. Skye lay across the water. I could even see it, though whether glad or not I don't know. They say here, "if you can see Skye it is going to rain. If you cannot see Skye, it is raining already."

XI

SKYE

"All the winds that blow on that far and happy isle may bring rain, and most make a habit of it."

JOHN BUCHAN

First Skyeman, at bar, in October: "Aye, Donald, it's been raining since June."
Second Skyeman, after deep thought: "Just so. Just so. *Which* June?"

Monday 17 June DELUGE DAY

There was regret at leaving comforts but Skye was a lure as few sections could be. I went over to the shop, packed, pieced the bike together (Mike had dropped it off) then had coffee with Catherine; a procrastinating start. Behind lay 188 Munros—1,059 miles and 297,500 feet.

I walked past the Bernera Barracks which are identical in layout to the Ruthven Barracks at Kincraig. *That* felt decades ago! A garrison was kept here for fully thirty years after the Forty-Five.

The Kyle Rhea ferry plies this swift passage. On both sides are identical old buildings which were once Inns. The redoubtable Dr Johnson stayed there in 1773. In the cattle-driving days Skye beasts were forced to swim the channel. Daniel Defoe wrote of this trade in 1726 while on his "tour". My interest crossing today was a school of porpoise. The ferry swept across quickly but the rain caught it halfway.

I sheltered a while but it was obviously no passing shower so I walked on, pushing up the brae. The Bealach Udal rises to 870 feet, in a couple of miles, a brutal slog at any time. Now I know why it is called a *push* bike. I sweated and battled in the deluge until ready to despair, a yelling misery. Glen Arroch beyond had me pedalling *down* it.

I passed one of Scotland's scenic refuse dumps—there are quite a few carefully laid out so that every tourist can get a view and a sniff. About 200 gulls were arrayed round this one. By Breakish I was peckish and by Broadford I'd had quite enough. It had rained without stop all the way and the gale had been entirely contrary. I was a day in hand, anyway, if I needed to justify stopping.

An efficient young girl signed me in to the Hilton (guest house) for bed and breakfast. I went along to the Hotel for afternoon tea—and stayed for dinner. It gave me a chance to catch up on the log book, back to Loch Quoich days. A couple came in who had motored all the way from Killin in the deluge.

Skye weather is apt to be unreliable. It suffers from a sort of emotional instability: one day all sunshine and sweetness, warmth and kindness —the next throwing a tantrum and viciously attacking anyone daft enough to go near.

I recall just one episode from Braehead days. The wind had blown a booming, dry gale for half the night and then produced a Nilotic flood. At four we were conceding victory to the elements. The girls were perched on top of saturated sleeping-bags calmly frying eggs with the water lapping half-way up the primus tank. "All mod. cons. Running water in every tent," somebody yelled as they shoved a brew in my hand. The trouble was it was not running. Sewn-in groundsheets were merely creating paddling pools. We took our essentials and fled. Sligachan Hotel gave us a garage to live in, while we fetched the bus (which limped along on a borrowed motorbike spark plug) and we then retreated first to the bakery in Portree, and then to Broadford Youth Hostel. At Portree, however, I was called to the Police Station and told my father had died suddenly—and began a bitter journey home by bus, train and hitching. My brother from Hong Kong reached home before me!

My log was not encouraging; the incessant rain and Broadford's complete lack of facilities for the visitor rather depressed. Everyone was expecting me to finish and so few knew anything of the pressures. Who, these soft days, puts up with rain and roughing it for weeks and months? Water can wear away stone. I wrote: "Keep it cool; sit it out and battle on. It is such a battle, not physical, but is sheer mental effort." I had no option but to be flexible. The tree that cannot bend before the storm just breaks. I expected that there would be ups and downs. It is just another—acceptable—face of adventure. My remedy was at hand: a good dinner.

The meal was one of the best of the trip. I recall it all clearly: Iced melon cubes; Fillet of haddock, Mornay; Roast leg of pork and apple sauce, boiled and croquette potatoes, green beans, cauliflower, cress, gravy; Sherry-trifle and cream; Coffee—and *Faisca* to drink.

Broadford Hotel will long be remembered for its hospitality that wet

THE CUILLIN OF SKYE

Sgurr Nan Gillean
To Sligachan 21, 22, 16 Camp
From Sligachan 18/6 Camp
Dubh Lochans
Red Hills
Clach Glas
Putting Green
Blaven
Loch an Athain
Loch na Creitheach
Camasunary
Sgurr na h-Uamha
Druim Hain
Harta Corrie
Coire Riabhach
Sgurr na Stri
Bad Step
JMCS Hut
Lota Corrie
Bidean Druim nan Ramh
Loch Coruisk
1916
Am Basteir
Basteir Tooth
Bruach na Frithe
Sgurr an Fheadain
Coire na Creiche
Coir' a Mhadaidh
Sgurr a' Mhadaidh
Sgurr a' Ghreadaidh
Sgurr na Banachdich
Inaccessible Pinnacle of Sgurr Dearg
Sgurr Mhic Coinnich
Sgurr Thearlaich
Sgurr Dubh Mor
Sgurr Dubh na Da Bheinn
An Garbh-choire
Gars Bheinn
Loch Scavaig
Sgurr Thuilm
Coir' a Ghreadaidh
From Youth Hostel
Coire Lagan
To Youth Hostel
Inaccessible Pinnacle
Coir' a Ghrunnda
Sgurr Alasdair
Sgurr nan Eag
1916
2016

Glen Brittle

N

0 1 2 3 4 5 Miles

JR 77

night, then back to the rather stilted atmosphere of the guest house. It was a wild night of storm.

Tuesday 18 June SLIGACHAN

> Like a pale King of Tarshish bringing his gift
> The sun came slowly to the courts of Day.

It had rained itself dry. The day eventually became bright, breezy and midge free.

The coastal road wends in and out of several lochs and over many braes but was not bad going. At Luib someone had painted "Vote Labour" on the rocks—with *blue* paint. Scalpay and Raasay in turn lay off-shore, the latter island unmistakable from any angle with the sliced-off top of Dun Caan, its highest point. Boswell danced a reel on its flat, grassy summit.

At last I came round under Glamaig—and there were the Cuillin: the warrior peaks standing quietly waiting, ready to ambush one with new experiences. They are a great sight. Nestling below them is Sligachan, itself a great sight.

The historic whitewashed hotel beside the old pack bridge, the few trees and rainbow dashes of water; these give a perfect foreground to the Red and Black Hills. Generations of climbers have been based on the hotel or camped across the road. The hotel had the Coruisk Hut key and other bits of mail. I was reading it when Peter found me.

Peter Miller was sixteen and one of Ann Winning's keen lads from Breadalbane Academy in Aberfeldy. We had fixed this meeting at the Lawers camp site. He brought more mail, via Ann, and by the time we had pitched tents up from the bridge, played a few games of darts and gone round finding lost tent pegs (you can aye tell a Fifer) it was happily too late to do anything except eat and sleep.

There are times when the old Sligachan pack bridge fills to its cap-stone with the rush of water. (When it does that you use your return tickets.) I hoped we were not in for a drubbing. The Ripleys had had quite an epic while doing the Ridge in the day: bad visibility, rain and greasy rock, trouble on Ghreadaidh and Mhadaidh and coming off Gillean on the wrong side to add a three-mile walk out.

Had I been alone it might have been tempting to do the ridge, but Peter was new to Skye—and I was playing a tortoise game.

> Much at ease with space all round,
> Peace in heaven, in flesh, in ground.

The overnight promise was not fulfilled and we set out only at 8.30. The hills were cloudy but we had to gamble on the weather. I 'phoned the police to explain empty tents, a precaution against trigger-happy mountain rescuers.

Glen Sligachan never palls. Peter almost went off up the wrong side of Marsco as everyone seems to do first time. Redshanks were calling and golden plovers. Bog asphodel, the flower of August, was in bloom already. We passed "Eric's Pool", so I told Peter of a heat-wave carry-in when we'd stopped for a dip. Eric alone did not go in. He came running up to push someone else in, but was heard and dodged just in time. Like a caricature in an old movie he went rushing on, back pedalling in mid air, and plopped into the pool—fully clothed!

Loch an Athain was where we had always camped. The expected summer-piper (sandpiper) was flitting round the edge of the loch. We hid most of our gear in the heather, and "burned-up" towards Blaven. The rain came on. The deep heather soon saturated our legs. Heather is *not* common in the west (outside the fanciful song-writers). The air was revoltingly hot and stuffy.

On the col between Blaven and Clach Glas is a small area of mossy green known as the "Putting Green". On a previous trip one of our lads, David McNab, had reached it first and excitedly yelled down to me to hurry. Expecting an accident or something urgent I gasped up the screes to join him. With a proprietary sweep of the hand Nabby said, "Is it not great?" So much for those who would declare the kids have no aesthetic reasoning. We looked down to Loch Slapin where the white Torrin marble under the shallow waters had made a brilliant turquoise pattern. No view today, though it was still an impressive perch.

The traverse of Blaven–Clach Glas is one of the finest bits of Cuillin traversing: pure Alpine rock-climbing. Beyond Clach Glas and some minor tops the "Black" Cuillin suddenly abut on to the crumbly pink granite of the "Red Cuillin". One takes liberties on gabbro that would be undreamt of elsewhere.

Blaven is the odd Munro off the main ridge, a portentous postscript to the gabbro galaxy. (It is occasionally tacked on to the traverse of the main ridge and called "The Greater Traverse" but it is in no way a true continuation and seems a pointless and artificial addition.) Walkers are best to keep to the long ridge from Camusunary or the Loch Slapin side.

The route on from the Putting Green is complex, wriggling in and out of avoidable problems and climbing one or two steps. The first small one of these gave me the jitters after so long off rock—greasy trap is demoralising at the best of times, so Peter tiptoed up further right and I crawled after. We had a lead each up the next step and were soon on the path to the trig point. Blaven is the best place to see the whole range of the main Black Cuillin. Sgurr na Stri above Loch Scavaig is also an exceptional viewpoint.

Blaven is a Norse-Gaelic name: Bla Bheinn, the *blue mountain*. It was first ascended by the poet Swinburne and Professor Nicol of Glasgow in 1857—perhaps the third Cuillin peak to be climbed. Rather than descend the way we had come, we went along over the south summit and down the ridge a fair way before taking pot-luck on the notorious west flank. This is complex and riven, full of scree gullies, and areas of slab, pinnacles and undercut edges, just the place to throw Peter in at the deep end: a bit different from nice, clean, safe, roped climbing at Craig-y-Barns! I wondered if Peter knew Mary Stewart's story *Wildfire at Midnight* for its thrilling climax is set on Blaven on the very place we had come down.

We must, briefly, recall the "Coruisk Affair", perhaps as a warning, for the whole character of a place can be so easily altered when, as here, the army built bridges and roads and threatened to blow up the "Bad Step" with dynamite. It was all dreamed up in the name of safety and facilitating rescue operations when seas were too rough for boats, but at no time was the Mountain Rescue Committee of Scotland consulted. The scheme only came to light when the Army made a request to use the hut.

Tom Weir made the percipient comment at the time that the hut itself was an intrusion which altered the quality of remoteness. The planners went ahead despite vigorous protests from all who knew the area: two suspension bridges were slung across, at Camusunary and Scavaig, and a perfectly adequate path from Straithaird was turned into a horrible Land-Rover track. After the opening ceremony the

V.I.P. party preferred to *walk* the track. A trooper watching one vehicle, was heard to comment, "Any injured climber in that would be dead by now." An officer defended the road with, "It's only a good weather track."

As far as I know no casualty has been taken out by the track yet, and the Scavaig bridge was swept away the following winter. We noticed a few traces as we crossed by the boulders, reaching the hut at 6.30, a ten-hour day which had taken the total of feet ascended, so far, to 300,000.

After supper I sat up till all hours, for I discovered a copy of Eric Shipton's *Upon That Mountain*, a book which has influenced so many of us. I lay awake a long time thinking of this great explorer, his simplicity and his vision, and I'm sure went on the better for it, refreshed and with resolve hardened.

Thursday 20 June TOPS TO GLEN BRITTLE
Over breakfast we watched a rapidly-advancing frontal system, and lingered in the cosy hut until 9.45.

We crossed the Mad Burn. It was high but not in spate. It can be an effective barrier to the hut. You can imagine climbers' feelings on seeing the hut only two hundred yards away—and beyond reach. We followed it upwards and then took the gap to the Garbh-Choire, so very aptly, the *rough corrie*.

The sky at dawn had been as frail-looking as tissue paper but had soon dissolved into sodden tatters—now the shreds were thrown in our faces! We lowered ourselves through holes among the boulders and crawled into a completely dry haven. Through a small skylight we could see the rain sweeping past: horizontal and vicious.

The black walls hemming in the corrie would appear, stark and streaming, in brief clearances, then vanish into the grasping clouds. We enjoyed it while in the safety of our howff but feared for the future as we scrambled on up the corrie in extravagant "boulder-hopping"— the boulders were sometimes the size of double-decker buses. Eventually the pale, ultra-rough, rock of "The Castle" towered above us. On one side a fallen block makes a hole through which you scramble to cross the col itself. Easy enough scrambling along the ridge took us up Sgurr Dubh na Da Bheinn, from which the Munro, Sgurr Dubh Mor, lies off to the east with a good gap between. It is usually skipped doing the Main Ridge, unless also taking in all the Munros.

Skye is walking country for the more expert: for those who are prepared to scramble a bit and not be intimidated by exposure and complex route-findings (the compass, remember, is useless on the tops). Skye is Valhalla, Mecca, the Ultimate. . . . As even rock-climbers will admit, Skye wandering can be fun on an off-day.

Sgurr Dubh Mor ("Scooby Doo" to my irrepressible pupils) is not easily reached from Da Bheinn. A left-flanking rake leads off down, but you must scramble up again for the col. Take the right flank from there, and, on the final tower, zig-zag up right, then back, to ascend the prow itself. The ridge up from Coruisk gives 3,000 feet of rock climbing of a slabby sort almost from sea-level to the summit. "Doing the Dubhs" is a classic not to be missed by the Climber.

We popped through the hole back under An Caisteal and traversed it for the long ridge out to Sgurr nan Eag. The few problems can be by-passed on the west. Several bumps have false cairns.

The way up Eag from Coir a' Ghrunda has few difficulties though the beaten-way seems to lead straight into a booby trap slot on which I've seen quite a few victims struggle. Nearly everywhere in Skye you can get round most problems, a lesson Kitchy was to teach us as, time and time again, we would look for the dog to give him a lift up a step, only to find him gone, and then grinning down at us. Even Kitchy had a special delight in Skye scrambling, his only problem being that his pads wore through after a week on rough gabbro.

We returned along crest and flank, skirted An Caisteal again to collect our sacks, and dropped down the bouldery flank to lunch by Loch Coir a' Ghrunda. The scene was of varying shades of rain which stopped for our brewing, and the clouds began to break up. As it cleared we began to add potential peaks to our day's plan. Gulls came swooping in to join us—eerie flights in the mist, piercing calls, and splashes in the steel-smooth surface. Oatcakes and cheese, jam pieces, K.P. nuts, raisins, biscuits, Bournville—we did well enough not to grudge the odd crumb to our birds of fair omen. After all we could see Alasdair with its grey scree skirts and shawl of mohair mistiness.

Sgurr Alasdair is the highest Skye summit, named after Sheriff Alexander Nicholson who made its first ascent in 1873. He was a Skye man, a journalist, barrister, and Gaelic scholar. His first route was the descent of the West Ridge of Gillean (Nicholson's Chimney) when he was thirty-eight.

When doing the Main Ridge a quick diversion is traditionally made to include Alasdair. The gentle walker is faced with the famous "Stone Shoot", which is the longest scree run in Britain and purgatorial in ascent. Alasdair deserves better and a reasonable way can be made from Loch Coir a' Ghrunda to the col linking Alasdair and Sgumain. Alasdair looks downright impossible from the col, barred by a small cliff, a famous *mauvais pas*, strictly for climbers with long reaches and good Policies. The rest must make along right, to the first rather obvious and worn chimney, and climb it. The steep, gravelly looseness above is probably much more dangerous. The top is a fine viewpoint: both of the other hills, and also of the blazing seascape. The feeling of being perched above the sea makes this end of the Cuillin an extra joy. The ridge between Da Bheinn and Alasdair was the last bit to be explored. It includes the Thearlaich–Dubh Gap and is to be avoided by the walker.

We had a clear, soft view from the top of Alasdair. The polluting brightness of waterproofs pin-pointed figures all over the place, all rushing up things now the day was improving. It is difficult to start early in Skye, I don't know why, but in June it hardly gets dark, anyway.

With no wind the midges will chase you to the top of Alasdair. Rock-climbing under those circumstances is apt to drive one to the verge of insanity. Midges are no joke: I have seen fine streaking performed by innocent swimmers who knew not what they did; I have seen pedestrians cross the road to avoid a blotchy, bitten friend (muttering something the while about the infectious diseases hospital); I have seen strong men weep, and children cry.

Sgurr Alasdair was the dog Kitchy's last 3,000-foot summit in the British Isles. He was a Shetland Collie, the colour of autumn birch leaves, and had spent much of his life on the hill. He was very much the mascot of Braehead School and it was apt that his last Munro was achieved on Braehead's penultimate expedition.

Peter and I found Thearlaich a greasy rooftop. Peter did not like the loose rock on the descent to the Gap under the seemingly vertical prow of Sgurr Mhic Choinnich, *Mackenzie's Peak*. Climbers will tackle the prow by King's Chimney but the scrambler need not feel cheated; Collie's Ledge is laid on for him—possibly the most sensational situation the British walker could happily get himself into. Apart from the initial step to gain the ledge even the dog can do it unaided so it is *not* difficult at all.

Collie's Ledge leads back on to the ridge proper but by-passes Mhic Choinnich's summit, so we had to wend along up slabby rooftops to reach it. Peter and I had taken two hours from Alasdair and were surprised to see it was 7.30 p.m. Skye days go like that. We would have to hurry if the youth hostel was going to be our home that night. It lies well up Glen Brittle.

We reached it at 9.30—a weary Peter was having quite an introduction to Skye—having bombed down and out past Loch Coire Lagain hardly pausing to look at the wall of Sron na Ciche—the best of all climbing cliffs in Britain. The Cioch was throwing its elongated shadow across the face and the colourful dots of climbers could still be seen on several routes. One of my unfulfilled dreams is to bivy on the Cioch!

Peter and I cut across the grassy lower slopes by the Eas Mor, the *big waterfall*. The grass off-loaded its share of ticks on to our legs, so we had a body search before turning in. We bought stacks of tins and had a stupefying meal, feeling flushed with the romp down and the heat of a building. It had been a twelve-hour day. How different its ending from the start, beginning in rain and despair, ending in sun and delight.

Friday 21 June THE CENTRAL, HEATED, COOLIN

John Buchan, writing in *Blackwood's Magazine* (June 1906), describes the magic change. "You awake one morning to a clear rain-washed earth, a pale-blue sky, a thin chilly wind from the north, and an amphitheatre of gaunt black hills. Thereafter for a week or a month the weather is flawless, and you spend days in an enchanted world of essential colours, infinite distances, and an air as pure as leagues of hill and ocean can make it." He knew Skye well of course—and the realisation of its unique character: "the essence of Skye climbing is the extraordinary feeling of space, of endless waters, and illimitable fields of air, and man himself set on a small rock looking out at immensity . . ."

The heat of the renewing sun could be felt in bed. Skye was playing extremes again. We bade farewell to Mrs Taplin, the warden, at 8.30, soon wished we had been off hours earlier. It was a day of "grillade".

Tramping up Coire na Banachdich had us wringing with sweat. We were glad to stop for drinks, and we filled all the available bottles. Even my log seems to have become dehydrated: "whaleback rocks, scree and rubbish lead up Dearg." Sgurr Dearg is the Munro which has brought many dreams to grief, for its summit is not just the expected top of the ridge but a long, stuck-on fin of rock which overtops it a bit. It is still called the Inaccessible Pinnacle—or just the Inn. Pinn.—and for some walkers it is all too aptly named. Sir Hugh Munro himself never managed to scale the Inn. Pinn. and one wonders how many hillmen have followed him in having done all the Munros bar this one and possibly a personally-chosen final one?

We dumped most of our gear on the ridge and skirted down along under the sheer west wall of the flake: it is vertical for over 100 feet from the screes to the top, then steep ground, screes and crag tumble in confusion down to Coire Lagain. The east flank falls precipitously down to the Coruisk side. Just the wafer of rock remains: 60 feet high on the short prow facing the ridge-top of Dearg, bulging out in a slight overhang, and perhaps twice that length up the back ridge—the easy way, with which we were content today.

The odd hold wobbles a bit as you tip-toe up; the crux requires a right big toe on a very small hold, and that digit of mine occasionally fails embarrassingly—ever since I broke it bird-watching in Morocco. We led through in small "pitches" to gain the maximum fun out of it.

We sat about on top for a while, then rigged an abseil off the steep side: our doubled line only just reached the foot.

During a typical Braehead circus here we once had fun with the dog. Everyone had been climbing up and abseiling off in various directions. The last enthusiast was abseiling off when voices were heard coming from that west wall. Eventually a hand appeared and a head peeped over—to find a dog sitting there watching him. The head vanished.

Animated discussion below was followed by a brief look once more by the leader, and a clearly audible "There is so a ——— dog on top!" followed his second withdrawal. The last two of us quickly abseiled off and boys, ropes, dog, all vanished. The top was still empty when we left. I would have given a lot to have heard the conversation when both climbers reached the top!

From some angles the Pinnacle looks like a squat clown balancing a banana on his nose, for a few oddly-shaped boulders are perched on the chunky summit, and are useful for abseils.

We were watched as we abseiled off: early as it was the mobs were arriving. We ran a free information service for a while. Some lads from the hostel were a bit surprised; nascent Munro-baggers, they had not realised "things like that were involved".

We skeltered down the rubbishy flank of Dearg and on for Sgurr na Banachdich. The numbers operating along the ridge have now caused a plethora of paths, useful or otherwise, all over the Cuillin. In thick mist some of these can be quite misleading for even the false trails have had so many on them that they look like useful routes. Banachdich has paths now which outflank many of the ups and downs. But don't be tempted to outflank all the fun!

The very easy "tourist route" comes up via Coir' an Eich. The derivation of Banachdich is *smallpox peak*—possibly from the pock-marked state of some of the rock. It is also called Sgurr na Banachaig which is the *milkmaid's peak*. Off Banachdich, the paths leading down scree and scrag on the west are correct. (A misleading track goes east, if you want to go west, so to speak.)

There is another distracting path, which goes horizontally across left, where straight up is best, on Sgurr Thormaid. This is named after Professor Collie: *Norman's Peak*, a rather modest sub-summit for the greatest of the early explorers. Beyond here the interminable central ridge beckons: Ghreadaidh and Mhadaidh, the Munros, like two jagged hedgehogs meeting nose to nose—all spikes and bristles for we poor fleas to make our way along.

I can never recall the details of this central part of the Cuillin. Their remoteness tends to draw climbers much less often, and every Munro seems to have several tops to it—complex, endless bumps to try to recall after twelve hours of sun or twelve hours of wet groping. It merged, today at least, into a sunny, tip-toe memory. Peter had now adjusted to the peculiar Skye situation of romping about unroped above big drops and the dry rock was greeted with zest.

There was a roof-top down beyond Sgurr a' Ghreadaidh (pronounced Greeta), the *peak of the thrashing* [*winds*], double-topped and good non-stop scrambling. In the heat and "merely Munro-bagging" we were not loath to do our share of flanking. Off Ghreadaidh we were soon faced with an odd rock hunk which is turned on the left. We then crept down and in under a disintegrated dyke which would have been a fine bivy site with its view down Coruisk. Its cool shade was bliss. We even had all we needed to make a brew.

We scrambled back up round and headed quickly up Sgurr a' Mhadaidh (pronounced Vatee), 3,012 feet, the *foxes' peak*. ". . . among the rocks we went, and still look'd up upon the sun . . ." From Mhadaidh we flanked down towards the Thuilm saddle but at the right level (where the rocks run into scree) we swung back into Coire na Dorus—for a known water supply. It was warm but we gulped down pints of it and filled the bottles again.

We went down the screes a bit and then took a traverse line across to the col. The cliffs of Mhadaidh from here are arranged in superb long buttresses—corrie scenery as fine as any in Skye. It deserves better of the rock climber.

Traversing Sgurr Thuilm is a good route off. It is an easy descent by Coire na Dorus. From the Thuilm bealach we dropped down a bit on the Coir a' Mhadaidh side, then doubled back under the cliffs and by a succession of rakes and screes and slabs reached the corrie floor. An easy way—if you can find it—and with skyscraper ridges soaring overhead. It is one of my favourite spots in the Cuillin.

We went on round under Sgurr an Fheadain with its famous cleft of Waterpipe Gully, one of the great gullies from the early days of climbing. Green Coire na Creiche betrayed its cattle-gathering past. Creiche almost looks like crèche. It means the bovine equivalent. Tradition has it that Macdonalds and Macleods once clashed here on a raid and virtually wiped each other out.

Beyond it, a rising path took us to the Bealach a' Mhaim. The vivid, cropped, grass slopes were lively with rabbits. The col itself is wide and bold, with a little pool. It is on the old highway from Sligachan to Glen Brittle, and if you have not yet been to Glen Brittle try to reach it on foot by this historic path for your first visit. It is comparable to reaching Zermatt over the hills rather than up the railway.

The descent to Sligachan was all joy. The Allt Dearg soon becomes a bubbling stream with endless turquoise pools.

It seemed years instead of days since we had left Sligachan to start culling our Cuillin Munros. Several other tents had surrounded our pair in the interval. We drank and ate prodigiously till it grew dark. The midges had a session when the wind dropped. My last memory was of a cuckoo. This one, to be different, had a three-note call.

Saturday 22 June THE PEAK OF THE YOUNG MEN

Yesterday we had been a bit overwhelmed with the sun, so today we set off early—a quarter to six—while the sun was still handling the world gently.

We went back up the Allt Dearg path. This morning the sun was shining straight into its churning tubs and falls. A river of champagne, but we had no time to drink. A gentle wander took us up the long Fionn Choire, probably so called from the great areas of light-coloured gravels.

Bruach na Frithe, the *brae of the forest*, is one of the easiest of Skye Munros, and the only one besides Blaven which has a trig point. The O.S. obviously have limits as to where they will hump cement.

We had gone up tightly under Sgurr a' Fionn Choire to leave our sacks. Two people were just setting off from their bivy by the corrie's high water patch—worth knowing, for it is almost the only reliable water to be found near the Main Ridge.

There is a section of ridge between the Bruach and Mhadaidh which does not have Munros and is probably the least frequented of all. Bidean Druim nan Ramh has a complex triple summit where the ridge does a twist, easily lost in mist, and before the Bruach there is one of the lowest cols (2,494). It is the make or break section of the traverse. Suddenly, on Bruach, you see all the last peaks, you know there is water, and faith springs again.

For Peter and me the day's summits were black shapes set against the sun; but a pushy east wind held off something of its temper. It is quite a view: the Bhasteir Tooth, like something hammered out of molten metal in some Iron Age of creation; Gillean, rising like a totem pole from the giddy, dancing ridges that swirl out from it, and Uamha, the last, least, and loved end to it all. There is nothing quite like Skye.

By the time we had dawdled along to the Bhasteir Tooth the two from the bivouac were starting up Naismith's Route. As we had only a line (we were not supposed to be climbing, we had to keep remembering) we dropped down on the Lota Corrie side to take the "easy" diversion —an obvious break upwards, and then rakes and dykes back to the Tooth.

Naismith's is the straight climber's route and only *Difficult*—but you begin with a traverse across the wall before going up the vertical face above, so it is beautifully exposed.

W. W. Naismith is a famous name from the past. What M.L.C. victim has not heard of his "Rule"? It was Naismith who really moved things leading to the founding of the Scottish Mountaineering Club in 1889. He was a man of deep Christian faith who had been climbing since he was fourteen (Ben Lomond), but it was within the S.M.C. he produced his notable leads: the traverse of the Cobbler, Spearhead Arête, the eastern traverse on Tower Ridge, and this face route on the

Tooth. He refused to be elected President of the club but will never be forgotten as its "father figure".

The Tooth is a quite incredible "Top": a slanting roof set above vertical walls, as unique a perch as the Cioch, a sphinx among the pyramids. Sometimes the loose stones on the roof-top slide down and block a hole which is the exit flue of a remarkable route—King's Cave Chimney. This route begins on the Sligachan side of the Tooth in a slot which soon becomes a real chimney, so you actually wiggle about inside the mountain—like a barium meal—till you pop out right on the summit roof.

Not being a Munro made it doubly appreciated. Am Bhasteir, the *executioner*, is the Munro. The tooth simply leans out from it like some decaying denture. There is no direct route between them—yet! A by-pass is made on the right with an awkward undercut little chimney the only problem. Peter was romping it all now, another willing victim to the lure of Skye.

The long easy ridge off Am Bhasteir is slabby and gravelly, so security is not at its best, wet or dry. The crest is better even with one awkward step. Not an easy walker's hill.

It was with a certain sadness we traversed along the well-worn trail for Gillean's West Ridge; this was the last of the Twelve Apostles. Our Skye days began so dubiously and had given such lingering pleasure. I led the chimney up to the ridge and Peter the traverse of the Pinnacle. We then coiled the line.

An Inverness quartet bombed past, having romped along the ridge —a casual weekend ploy. What a difference to someone at the camp site last night who had only done Alasdair, by its Stone Shoot, and on the strength of that planned to do the ridge. "Do I need a rope?" he had asked. . . . This is the beauty of Skye: to some it is the ultimate of ambition, simply to gain the vital summits; to others, the whole Main Ridge can be a romp of a day. All find it good.

The West Ridge is fascinating. It ends by threading the eye of a needle, the ridge merely the thickness of one block of gabbro. To the left the Pinnacle Ridge raises its four tops up towards the summit. Bright figures, like spiders, seemed to be spinning thin webs as they tangled ropes along the final peak almost directly below us. Sgurr nan Gillean is the *peak of the young men*.

It is the last Munro but, like Sgurr nan Eag at the other end, there is a lesser bonus top to mark the true end of the ridge—better in this case for, while it is a walk to Gars-bheinn, Sgurr na h-Uamha, the *peak of the cave*, has a last wee surprise up its sleeve.

The quartet got us to photograph them on top; and then asked which was the way off! The Tourist Route is notorious—for this conjures up the gentlest of ascents normally. But not here. The way is long and hard and not a few have found it a very full day on its own. My log simply catalogued the descent, "Ridge, rubbish, moor and bog." The bogs were dried and cracking again. A pool of yellow spearwort acted as a reflecting pool for Marsco. It was all heat haze and shimmer. The early start had been rewarded.

I took a bath in the river. The white hotel among the whispering trees, the old pack bridge, the familiar Gillean-Bhasteir crest, it is a scene which can hardly have altered since Collie's day.

It was to Sligachan that Collie retired—and there he died—in the grim days of the Second World War.

In 1886 he had come to Skye to fish, but became hooked on the Cuillin which were to become a passion. In the next two seasons he climbed every summit, often with John Mackenzie of Sgurr Mhic Choinnich fame: a sort of Young-Knubel combination.

As Skye was a war-time restricted area, Sligachan must have been a quiet spot. The last glimpse we have of Collie is from the pen of a young man, Richard Hillary, in his book *The Last Enemy*. Hillary, a young pilot, was there convalescing, and not long after writing this classic story was killed in action. He and a friend, Noel, were at once attracted by the austere beauty of the setting.

"We were alone in the Inn save for one old man who had returned there to die. His hair was white but his face and bearing were still those of a mountaineer, though he must have been a great age. He never spoke, but appeared regularly at meals to take his place at a table tight-pressed against the window, alone with his wine and his memories. We thought him rather fine."

The two young pilots went off and had an epic on Bruach na Frithe in the mist, thoroughly enjoying it. On the way down they even fell into a pool in a gorge where they had gone astray. To their after-dinner tale the landlord's sole comment was "Humph"—"but the old man at the window turned and smiled. I think he approved."

I am sure Collie did.

Peter packed to go off on the evening bus. The hotel was full, so instead of a dinner I had to dream up a meal of left-overs; soup and apple flakes mainly. The sun left the site all too soon; the red colours ran up the Red Hills, the last slanting rays came streaming through under the bridge. I lay writing this and watching the little incidents of camp life. There was a very definite "end of holiday" feel to it. Skye is so uniquely different that these last few days seemed quite divorced from the rest of the Walk. Tomorrow it would be back to the office, so to speak.

Sunday 23 June THOU SHALT NOT CYCLE ON SUNDAY
Wind-direction averages never favour the cyclist: in a land of westerlies I set off into a strong east wind. The landscape was devoid of people, Broadford a ghost town, Kyle deserted. Breakfast had been apple flakes and twice-brewed tea bags, at which my stomach was complaining, but at Balmacara, the Kyle Stores provided welcome fresh food and drink. I struggled on to Dornie, effort rather subduing enjoyment, for the colours were vivid and the whole landscape decked in the sort of green one associates with bad taste in clothes. I sprawled between road and water where I could see Eilean Donan Castle on one side and the view out of Loch Duich on the other.

Eilean Donan must be the most photographed building in the Highlands, though few people now enjoy the view down on to it, possibly the best angle, for the new road speeds them along the lochside. It's an ironic twist of fate that this bit of fine road was engineered by hillman extraordinary, Philip Tranter, the first man to have done the Munros twice. He died in a car crash on the way home from climbing in Turkey. Had he lived, who knows, he might well have been writing this book! An all-round mountaineer, based on the West here, he was the driving force of the Corriemulzie Club with its famous "feich trips" and pioneering climbs in the remoter regions.

The history of the castle can be found in many books including Seton Gordon's *Highways and Byways in the West Highlands*. This great writer has given us about forty books over the last fifty years and few have such a love for the hills and wildlife. Like Collie, he had retired to Skye.

I was away in my day-dreams when I became aware that Peter was talking to me. His parents' caravan was parked a hundred yards off. I had a job to persuade them I really did not need a full three-course lunch. The morning of fasting had become a day of indulgence, and it was a bloated climber who wobbled off. From the bridge I could see a glimpse of the wild hills beyond Loch Long. The bridge was built in 1939 so that "puffers" (coastal steamers) could get through into the loch. A hundred years ago 200-ton schooners were built here and the local "parliament" met down on the slipway.

The Five Sisters had drawn a veil about their heads but the scenery was still jewel-like. At last I pushed into the National Trust camp-site at Morvich at the head of Loch Duich. Donny McLean had three parcels for me: a cache left by Mike Keates, a weekend box from Ann Winning (she had been unable to wait) and left-overs which I thought I had off-loaded on Catherine McInnes. I was not going to starve.

XII

THE BIG GLENS: SHIEL, AFFRIC, FARRAR

"In the Highlands it is mountain after mountain, mountain after
mountain, for ever and ever."

THOMAS WILKINSON

Monday 24 June SADDLE SORE

After Skye, this was intended as a rest day but the goals and the gods
sent me off instead. Rest could come with the next deluge; if the Shiel
ridges could be done dry it would be a great help.

The wise were up, for, as on so many summer mornings, the touch
of glory had soon gone, replaced by a middling green opulence. Even
the loch was green with the forest reflections—while in the eye of the
view lay the mote of a red fishing boat. It seemed a long way up to the
quarry which sits as such an eyesore right across the road through a
glen so important to tourists.

A little after ten I took a useful stalking path upwards. I'd bought a
paper and read of Scotland out of the World Cup with no lost games, of
the Lions walloping the Springboks, of Wimbledon and of the F.T.
Index at a new record low. On average I thought I was well out of
things.

It was a day for pants-only again. I was muzzy with a cold and on
several occasions sent sheep skelping off across the hillside with my
sneezes. Like an Eskimo, my contacts with civilisation had given me a
bug. The path ended on the ridge which hides the Saddle from the foot
of Glen Shiel—however fine the peak appears from up the Glen.
Beyond lay Coire Caol and the rocky ramparts of the Saddle with its
famous Forcan Ridge which gives some scrambling.

I cut across the corrie today, to keep out of the sun. It was dark and
cool. A hind, lying by the burn, had died while calving, a sad sight.
Rocks gave some scrambling and I went up the steep north ridge where
the ground was shiny with black mica. The other side of the ridge has an
even finer corrie; Loch a' Choir' Uaine was low from the dry weeks of
April. An eagle was working round the headwall in easy flight and
passed fifty feet below.

The ridge ends in a definite "top" which is the summit. Along another thinly curved ridge lies a trig point, which is slightly lower. Today I did both to avoid any possible ambiguity.

The Saddle is only 3,317 feet but dominates the south side of Glen Shiel with its configuration of five crests and several deep corries. It has its place in a Top Twenty. Just below the trig point, on the south side, you may find a pool for a deliciously cold dip. Very few summits provide this service where it is most wanted—at the top. I wrung out my sweaty pants, washed them, and by the time I'd eaten my pieces sitting on the lawn, they had dried. The pool was still rimmed with snow so a brief paddle was enough for today.

The view was very clear: one of the best of the trip. Ladhar Bheinn dominated but much else fused from propinquity. Rhum, Eigg and Skye were all lined like a fleet in the Minch. Loch Hourn had not a ripple on its placid depths. Sgurr Mor was big, Sgurr na Ciche, for once, poor. It was possibly the view of the Walk's "crux": entering Knoydart had been the most depressing day, the Rough Bounds had restored, Sgriol gave the finest of all views and the Cuillin had been a holiday delight. As I sprawled in the sun on the Saddle I began to feel really confident: only a disaster could stop me now. I was beyond reach of depression or despair—which was perhaps as well, as it proved.

A south flank down, a wet traverse of the col, another rising traverse and Sgurr na Sgine, *peak of the knife*, was soon added. There are two tops, the eastmost being slightly higher.

Faochag, the *whelk*, is a Top, sited nearly two miles back round the corrie rim to the north. It is easily recognised from Glen Shiel: the brutally dominant and simple cone next to the more complexly-designed Saddle. Sgine is tucked away out of sight, except for the walker coming over the Mam Barrisdale in Knoydart.

Sgine's north ridge I have come to call "Concorde Ridge". Alan Moreland and I were descending it one winter: a steep, narrow ridge but not technically demanding. Fortunately we had roped-up for with no warning there was an indescribable sudden double-bang. Alan virtually let go with the shock and slipped off his holds briefly. My heart nearly stopped a second time as I heard the fearful sound of a wet snow avalanche. Being on a narrow ridge no avalanche could have hit us even if the conditions could have produced one; but reflexes work quicker than rational thought. This second shock revealed itself in a vast flock of terrified ptarmigan. The sound had been the noise of their wings.

I don't think the Saddle–Sgine day has ever let me down, summer or winter, it has always blessed us with sun, a tradition I was glad to see maintained. I dandered down again. On Sgine I'd seen *white* moss campion. Years before I knew of white forms, I had found a white milkwort on the Saddle and cursed all my ineffectual flower books which gave no picture of it.

It was roasting in the tent. Odd conditions for Christmas Pudding. French voices from next door added a touch of unreality; imagination was happily working an Alpine camp-site out of it. Good coffee, fresh fruit, and other luxuries were consciously relished knowing the lean days to come. Jimmy Watt, from Edinburgh, an old gangrel and C.T.C. man, had walked up the road with me in the morning; now we sat chatting in the golden evening. We had similar wedge-shaped tents; dwarfed among the tourists' frilly "cottages".

My day of sun had taken its toll and I went to bed glowing and hot: Saddle sore all over!

Tuesday 25 June SOUTH SHIEL SWITCHBACK

The trouble with writing about a big switchback of ridge is that memory tends to blur the detail. I still cannot recite the names of these peaks, never mind remember the details, despite several traverses. It was another sun-smitten day—almost too sunny.

There were midges on waking. Just dashing out and away from the tent left my legs with a score of bites, and that was at seven o'clock. The Bealach Duibh Leac, the *pass of the black slab*, is 2,400 feet and just one bump along from where I'd been on Sgurr na Sgine yesterday. It is an old right-of-way over to the head of Loch Hourn. Prince Charlie slipped over it after breaking through the Knoydart cordon. He then headed up the glen for a well-earned respite beyond Conbhairean. Of that later. The Glen Shiel road was built by Caulfield, Wade's lesser-known successor.

The Scottish hills are criss-crossed with rights-of-way. I always feel the Scottish Rights of Way Society and the Mountain Bothies Association are two bodies all of us who use the hills ought to join—they both do so much for us that a small subscription is only a right return. A. E. Robertson, the first "Munroist" and founder member of the Scottish Rights of Way Society, has never been equalled in knowledge of the subject; but if he saw the need for such a society all those years ago, how much more is it required today.

I had a path to follow so immersed myself in *Ring of Bright Water* and only looked up when the mew of a buzzard or the tumble-song of a lark caught my ear. The streams were tepid and too low for any swim. The path became sketchy but eventually landed me on the Bealach whence I followed the wall up and down and along to Creag nan Damh, the *rock of the stag*, a summit of many false summits.

Sgurr Beag, the next bump, not being a Munro, was traversed on the

south, from col to col, laziness rewarded with finding a stream—welcome water, though warm. Sgurr an Lochain is higher and the view expands to the fullness one always thinks of in this district of great ridges. Ben Nevis was in view again. I began to feel I would never break away from its familiar shape. On Sgurr an Doire Leathain, *peak of the broad thicket*, I left my book by mistake. I'd been reading on the move again—and lazing at cairns over the book. I dropped in search of water but warm peat pools were all I found, as I skirted along to sit in the shade of a crag and demolish some tinned raspberries and Chicken Supreme. Scissors made a messy substitute for a forgotten tin opener. Beyond Sgurr Coire na Feinne, *peak of the Corrie of the warriors*, skirting on the grassy south flanks I found a welcome trickle of water again.

These slopes lead down like massive limbs to the man-made arm of Loch Quoich. The bridge on the Loch Hourn road was clearly seen—black against the silver shine—while figures passed westwards on the crest above. I wonder if they found my book? Having lost one paperback (which I'd read often, anyway) I fished out tomorrow's and started it, another sailing story, *Dove*, by Robert Lee Graham who set off *when sixteen* to sail round the world. I was soon jotting down quotes: "One learns from the sea how little one needs, not how much" . . . "I'd want him [son] to love nature. I'd want him to love animals, mountains, clean water, sea life."

It was an easy pull up the next Munro, Maol Chinn-dearg, the *bald red top*. I envied the deer in the deep shadowy corries; there was no shade on the crest. The poor beasts were puzzled by the noise of my passing, looking nervously all round—but not up. Aonach air Chrith, the *shaking height*, was reached by a narrower ridge with rocky steps. Two very pink bodies were lying asleep by the cairn but woke when my cold shadow fell on them. They *said* they were traversing the ridge. Below the next col, for the third time in the day, I found welcome water to the south: quite a large stream—even shown on the map. It oozed out of the earth as warm as if held in the mouth for minutes. It was liquid though. I flanked a bit and was soon on the curl up to Druim Shionnach. A dark hare, with white front feet, went dashing past—set off by a couple with two small children who came whooping up from the north ridge on to the *ridge of the foxes*.

The continuing ridge (roughly south-east) is a narrow, broken crest which gives a surprise to visitors. Once, ski traversing, I recall swivelling round on it with tips and heels both sticking out over space. The map does not really show that sort of narrowness. The sweep down and up beyond is gentle, and suddenly, it is over, the Cluanie Ridge, the south Shiel switchback. Creag a' Mhaim is a rather adolescent swelling to end such a day, the *peak of the pass*.

Deer shot out of all the shadowy corners as I flanked down. The rough going by Loch a' Mhaoil Dhisnich (my sneezy state could say that fine) led to a good stalking path and I was soon walking with the whirling, crying peewits across the bridge to the Cluanie Inn. This old charge house on the road to the west is where Dr Johnson decided to keep his famous journal. He went down Glen Shiel and over to Glenelg.

(Descending the other side of Mam Ratagan he rode two horses turn-about!) He had lots of things to say about the Glen Shiel hills—none of them polite. The Inn snuggles into the sweep of landscape as old buildings do.

My purchase of seven Cokes took their entire supply. I drank two, had one with an excellent, plain dinner, and the rest were saved for the morrow's likely sun-beating. I enjoyed a wallow in a bath with musical plumbing, and read there, and in bed.

Some thought to statistics gave me 36 Munros from here to Achnashellach and 34 beyond. So this indeed was a big section. Oh, if it could progress like these last two days! The sun had made my thighs tender: "rare" I think is how a chef would have described them. I'd carefully kept a shirt on to protect my burden-bearing shoulders.

The seven-mile Cluanie Ridge gives a haul of seven Munros. It never falls below 2,500 feet in six miles, and perhaps only on tomorrow's side of the glen, or on the ridges of Affric and the Lapaichs beyond, can there be its equal for length and height. It was a 6,850 feet and 20 miles day. The S.M.C. guide book, I see, says the traverse is "best done with two cars"—which must be rough on the suspension!

Wednesday 26 June   THE BROTHERS AND SISTERS RIDGE

A real bed was a luxury but nevertheless I was off at 8.30 after a good breakfast—surely a record for an hotel. I took the east bank of the Allt a' Chaoruinn Bhig, a pleasant, tumbling stream, gouged out of rock in places with here and there silvery waterfalls. For a while there were swarms of long-legged flies.

The A' Chralaig group to the east was holding back a great ocean of cloud, but now and then waves of this brilliant white mass would break down the slopes towards me. It distracted the eye all the way up little Ciste Dhubh, the *black chest*. A black bog-pool was full of floating, tattered bodies of moths—like confetti in a dirty street puddle.

Down in the glen to the north is Cam Ban bothy which was done up as a memorial to Philip Tranter. An entry in its book read, "Did the Five Sisters of Kintail today"; another hand had added, "Bloody sex maniac". The name "Five Sisters" is often used loosely for the whole north Shiel ridge but it really belongs to the western summits which appear as regular paps when seen across Loch Duich. We have long given the eastern tops the name of the Five Brothers of Glen Shiel. Brothers and Sisters combine to give another great day.

I finished *Dove* as I wended up the next Munro—and realised time was pushing on if I was not. Ciste Dhubh curls away north from the main ridge and is more often than not excluded by those traversing the ridge. Sgurr an Fhuarail is named on the map, but the Munro is not: Aonach Meadhoin which lies a bit further on. The ridge off it was narrow and nice. Sgurr a' Bhealaich Dheirg is the highest of these brothers. Its summit is a big cone of a cairn stuck out on the narrow north ridge—with an odd 100-yard wall leading to it. The map rather implies a plateau.

Looking west, Saileag, the *little heel*, is hardly noticed, though its southern slope must be one of the steepest and most even gradients in Scotland. A traveller in 1803 passing down Glen Shiel wrote of the slopes as being "an inclined wall, of such inaccessible height that no living creature would venture to scale it". Yet no doubt locals had. The Bealach Lapain implies an old pass. I left a note and it was found the next day by Michael Scott from Ayrshire who gave his "reason for starting" as "too old for anything else".

Sgurr na Spainteach is the *Spaniards' peak*, a name recalling a Jacobite sideshow on its slopes in 1719 not far up from the now by-passed Telford Bridge. This minor rising, which included a contingent of about 300 Spanish soldiers, ended before it really began, in a long and disorderly skirmish on just such a June day as today. One feels a bit sorry for the poor Spanish yokels. We are told that Rob Roy was involved too—far from his usual range.

It was near where I left the road yesterday that Prince Charlie (as fugitive) had lain hidden behind a boulder for all of a long, grilling, summer's day. Be warned, this is not normal Kintail weather. "The Cluanie Curtain" is the local name for the grey sweeping rain more often met with as one nears the region. Today it seemed in reverse: the east still dammed back like a great white wave.

Sgurr na Ciste Duibhe, another *black chest*, is quite a rugged peak and takes one on to the Sisters. Sgurr na Carnach is rough and not being a vital Munro I flanked it a bit which led to complications. I *smelt* goats without actually seeing any. The day was both hot and clear. I could see both Ben Nevis and the Cuillin. Jets flew through Glen Shiel; like tiny models. The hills at this end start on sea level and rise with brutal steepness, one reason why most prefer to travel east–west.

Sgurr Fhuaran, 3,505 feet, is the highest on the ridge. It is a superb viewpoint, lording over much else in the vicinity. I sat on top and drank the last of my life-saving Cokes, enjoying that great peace which only the restless know. This is the central and grandest of the Sisters: beyond again lie Sgurr nan Saighead, 3,050 feet, newly promoted to a Top, *peak of the arrows*, and Sgurr na Moraich, 2,980 feet, *peak of the shellfish*: scalloped corries and ridges not to be missed.

Today, however, I explored a direct route down to Glen Shiel: 3,500 feet in a mile and a half. I returned to the col and then traversed up a bit to hit a shoulder south of Carnach where I knew there was a steep rake. This led down all right, the careful study of yesterday paying off with an easy line of descent which took an hour. The river merely required boulder-hopping.

It was too late for the shop, but a vast meal was soon demolished back at Morvich. Sleep was painful: burnt thighs and a cold. And my boots were disintegrating again.

Thursday 27 June DOING LOCH DUICH
I had reorganised the original Walk plan to enable the big Shiel ridges to be done unladen, now I was having an off-day: all this a conscious gathering of strength for the long trek to Achnashellach. There would be no helpers, the heaviest rucksack, and only one reliable parcel on the way. I was not unduly worried, willing to take what the hills gave. I felt I had already been pushed to the limit. Anyway the mountains were and are my environment. I was going neither with eyes shut nor starry eyed.

Fraser Darling wrote *Island Years* while recovering from a broken leg, the result of an accident while going down a field to milk a cow; yet he had climbed and canoed and caved among Hebridean islands for years. As he warns, "danger may be in the illusion of safety". More *walkers* die accidentally than *climbers*. More die on the casual afternoon descent than when fighting uphill. The commonest cause is the simple slip. In all the Walk I had only the odd slip—fewer I reckon than in any week at home, that most lethal environment of all.

A bad cold seldom makes for good judgement so I relied on the homework already done and after a long lie set off in holiday mood to "do" Loch Duich.

Task one was dealing with food. I could hardly squeeze into the tent for assorted boxes. Soon one was packed with what would go with me, another with tonight's meal and a couple with what would be left, along with the bike, for Mike Keates to pick up some time. I paid for the camp-site, to ensure an early start on the morrow, then wandered along to the shop. It was coping with busloads of animated tourists. I fled down to the Kintail Lodge Hotel for coffee, stayed on for lunch and then coffee again: there was lots of mail to clear off. The day was warm again: green, grassy summer now. A red fishing boat bobbed on the tourist-blue loch beyond a row of white foxgloves. The tide was high and the thrift heads were bobbing like corks in the foamy water. Pied pipers were rushing about like busy waiters and a heron stalked the burn, every now and then stabbing into the water with his great beak.

Back at Morvich I prepared another vast meal. The Ripleys, coming out of the north, had shopped gleefully and eaten to a similar state of "bloatation". After the feed I began my next book, *The Man in the Iron Mask*. At ten to eleven I remembered I had not phoned Mike or David/Marina. I dashed down to the phone box and eventually contacted them. Mike would meet me at Achnashellach and would bring replacement boots. I had bled a finger, broken a pair of scissors and somehow wired my soles on to the uppers last night. They would have to do till then.

A crowd of us, walkers, pot-holers and such like, gathered for a late brew. In June it is very hard to turn in before the last kissing colours leave the slopes. We sat looking at Fhada and A'Ghlas-bheinn—my gateway into Affric on the morrow. As so often, I turned in feeling a great content. I recalled and repeated the grace spoken at our first Braes o' Fife dinner:

> For wir bonny bit peak and a guid climb too,
> For a dram o' the malt and a brew or two,
> For friend, and ficht, and a' the blaws that wind may blaw,
> And a' the saws that evening gangrels saw,
> The guid—and bad—and the just so-so
> Hill days and holidays. . . .
> Dear God,
> Forget not the earth where aince you trod
> And tak the thanks o' men and mountaineers.
> Amen.

Friday 28 June THE GATES OF AFFRIC

The great glens running east–west, north of busy Glen Shiel, have a very different atmosphere from that well-known, well-used area. They have the emptiness of being far from the beaten ways of man, shut off into a huge area, strath and ridges in bewildering quantity, the highest summits north of Ben Nevis, far from the sweep of sea. Again, it is so different from anywhere else in the Highlands. This changing from one area to another had the same quality of refreshment that one enjoys meeting old friends. I set off for this new and vital section in good spirits. The Odyssey has a line that set the mood: "Past the gates of the sun and the home of dreams they went".

The Gates of Affric for me are the peaks of Beinn Fhada (Attow) and A' Ghlas-bheinn—or at least the pass between them, the Bealach an Sgairne. I would climb the peaks and go through the pass into Affric. A rapid-fire cuckoo began at three in the morning to make sure I was wide awake and away in time.

Both these peaks appear from Loch Duich: Fhada as a massive, notched, wall and A' Ghlas-bheinn seamed with long gullies. Affric can be reached up Gleann Lichd under that south flank of Fhada, but Fhada has superb corries facing the other way. A little lochan at 2,000 feet on Fhada's southern slopes must be one of the oddest sites for a camp (in deep frozen winter) I have ever had. The extreme left, looking up, shows Fhada's crest as deeply dented. It is. There is one *mauvais pas* which can bar walkers, but it gives good scrambling, and ridge-walking at its best.

A mile from Morvich I left the tarred road—for probably the longest mileage during the Walk. I was also carrying the heaviest rucksack: it must have weighed at least 35 lb. I read my way up Gleann Choinnea-chain, the gentle path, for once, not doubling as a burn. Above the zig-zags I perched on a knoll for a break, then left the load, to take to A' Ghlas-bheinn, which is pronounced something like "Glashven", and usually dismissed with little good said of it. All of 3,006 feet, I suspect it suffers from grudging Munro-baggers, simply thrown in with Fhada or done on an off day, so dismissed or forgotten.

This is a pity for it is a complex little hill and has a splendid view. I have a Christmas picture of a party sunbathing on it. I do not have pictures of another Christmas when we battled in a blizzard up the long ridge from the pass. I had warned of many false summits (someone claimed there were sixteen), and going up we had one side plastered, coming down, the other, so we ended in an icy armour. Kitchy spent most of that day in my rucksack and I was just glad he was a Sheltie and not a St Bernard. On two different trips we have been glad to splash, like speugs, in the pool a mere stone's throw from the summit. No, I will have nothing said against A' Ghlas-bheinn!

North of this peak are the Falls of Glomach, reached from either Loch Duich or Glen Elchaig, east lies Loch a' Bhealach and the boggy strath of upper Affric, all dominated by the Kangchenjunga of Scotland: Sgurr nan Ceathreamhnan. South is the spectacular side of Fhada, west the glitter of Loch Duich and a hint of far Cuillins. Who could ask more?

Knowing the long ridge of A' Ghlas-bheinn I decided to flank first, then head upwards. At once I became snarled up among crags, then barred by a slot of gully. It was not even an easy mountain it seemed. While messing about like this I was attracted by the angry calling of hoodie crows and then saw an eagle flying with one in its talons. It dropped the dead bird over the pass so that it fell like a black rag, and the eagle then swept casually up over Fhada, the rabble of hoodies yelling after but unable to match its pace.

I scrambled up a burn to Loch a' Chleiridh. Even at 2,600 feet the water was warm. It was no wee summit pool but one of Olympic dimensions. I had a swim, of course, then followed the natural lay of the land up to the ridge and along to the summit. The Torridons suddenly looked near, but, like the Ben, they would do a fair bit of advancing and receding before they were actually reached.

I had a picnic back at the rucksack; eating till I felt as bloated as a full moon. A side path, not on the map, breaks off to skirt round into the Fhada corrie, going on through green bays and ending on the low saddle of Meall a' Bhealach—a spot where I had a welcome pause. In autumn I have perched there in the rut with every hillside covered with deer, the stags roaring mightily. It was as if they were all crowding in, knowing it to be N.T.S. property and their hides safe. The view looks straight down Gleann Gniomhaidh into Affric. I wandered on peacefully to Fhada's beacon of a trig point.

The Sisters of Kintail faced me over the depths of Gleann Lichd: sunny crests and black, shadowed glen. They used to be known as the *big hill*, Beinn Mhor, which balances Beinn Fhada, the *long hill*. Tiny dots of colour were coming over the Plaide Mor as the plateau is called: lucky people who would have the great westward view clear today.

I romped off down, peeling off layers of clothes, as a cook might strip an onion, regretting that Attow did not have a high lochan too. I collected the heavy rucker and went through the pass, quite a defile, to find myself in Affric. The pass is at about 1,800 feet and part of an old route. St Duthac used it in the eleventh century and there is a well named after him just down the east slope a bit. Loch Duich is Duthac's Loch. The path dropped down to Loch a' Bhealach which is very nearly on the watershed for it does not flow to Affric as expected, but north, then round to the west to help feed the Falls of Glomach.

These are frequently praised as being our highest and best, which they are not. I am often amazed that visitors go into superlatives at places pin-pointed in their guidebooks—and then miss their equal or better simply because there is no sign saying, "Marvel here!" Perhaps it is as well. One of the problems facing climbers who write about the hills (as I am doing now) is to balance enthusiasm with giving away what one would prefer to keep secret. Fortunately I am covering the Munros, a well-established treadmill, though even here I take care *not* to mention some things about some areas. Elitist! No, jealously conservationist. Bodies like the Scottish Countryside Commission would "promote" a "wilderness experience", which is a very contradiction in terms. Experiences are not promoted. You cannot teach an appreciation of beauty. Glomach is fine, and let us leave it at that.

I walked right down the upper reaches of Glen Affric dryshod, which was a novel experience. Various ways-in converge: mine through the Gates of Affric, the Gleann Lichd path up by the Cam Ban bothy, and the pass from Loch Cluanie, perhaps the most direct. On the slopes of the Mulloch where the last-named drops down there is the wreck of an aircraft. A propeller has been built into a bridge near the hostel. I strolled over the meadows to this haven accompanied by a puffing herd of cows. The hostel is an old "iron" lodge: green-painted corrugated iron, with fine wood-panelling in its rooms, the door a bright red and the usual guardian rowan nearby. It was one hostel you could be sure not to meet the plastic-soled, international bums who swamp the roads in summer. It is a far cry from the bob-a-night atmosphere. You have to go to the bothies to find that these days. We are told that today's youth expects higher standards, that we must conform to international ideas; but I wonder who says so. Youth? I suspect hot water is more attractive to the middle-aged committee men who run such things.

I dropped my armful of bogwood at the door. A lark was nesting less than ten yards away. The warden welcomed me with a cup of tea—

perhaps there is hope for the old association yet! Bill Lockyer was a student at Strathclyde University. His bednights that spring had ranged from zero to twenty-two. There was nobody else just now. The Ripleys had been there and been told the hills were "out of bounds" (during the stalking season) but they, perforce, went—so had their cards confiscated.

Alltbeithe was an old lodge, and many early accounts by the S.M.C. founders mention staying there. They were gentlemen climbers given the hospitality of gentlemen owners. It was a very closed-shop world. In volume one of the S.M.C. Journal, Munro, himself a landed gentleman, tells how best to bypass the bothy on Mam Sodhail where watchers lived all summer for the sole purpose of warding off sheep, both four- and two-footed. He carefully spells out all the rights-of-way. It sounds very modern. There is a paper in a later volume which takes the S.M.C. humorously to task for thinking this area "unexplored": the writer, a professor of geology, had been over all the summits years before—carrying a fifteen-pound hammer, what's more. He too stayed at Alltbeithe, now the youth hostel.

Munro thought that in Affric as "nowhere else are rock and heather, lochs and islands, natural forests and falls blended in such beauty". He also gives a description of traversing the area with "sentries" popping up every few miles to query his being there. "Of course I was on a right-of-way, and need not have answered, but had I not a passport?" He diverted to take in Mam Sodhail and the Falls of Glomach and ended at Loch Duich—some walk. He nearly wept on arrival to find that the inn was out of beer. (The next day he traversed Sgurr Fhuaran, the next traversed Sgriol via the Mam Ratagan, and then went south by the *Clansman* to Glasgow, to dine the next night in London. Try that today!)

Bill and I sat before the peat fire recalling these giants of yesteryears. We had steaming mugs of tea in the gloaming, for it hardly became dark at nights now, then went out to brush our teeth at the burn, once we had shoved a lurking cow out of the way. The only books were several Bibles which allowed an hour of reading (I carried only a tiny New Testament). I found a suitable text, which has since been pinned up in my Dormobile, a sort of glorified mobile bothy: "Stand ye in the ways and see, and ask for the old paths, where is the good way, and walk therein, and ye shall find rest for your souls."

I

Saturday 29 June   CONBHAIREAN CIRCLE

I was up at seven, and not long after that the warden from Cannich
Y.H. arrived, having *run* up with mail for Bill. Runners have my
admiration if not emulation. I sometimes think that I walk only because
it is too wet, or cold, or hot, or midgy to lie around doing nothing—
which is what would have been nice today. It began with a throw of
mixed colours, the sun dappling the long east ridge of Attow, but it
ended "gey dreich" when a book by the peat fire would have been
saner pleasure.

The Mulloch was never climbed by procrastination. Its vast slopes I
put out of mind by reading my way upwards. I walked into a sheep at
one stage—I don't know who received the greater surprise. The deer
stood and let me pass very close. It was sweltery hot for such a brutal
hill, one with no easy line up, unless it be the link to A'Chralaig, but
that was my way off. Slowly I pushed the cluster of buildings into dinky
proportions, then lost them as I rimmed round the corrie that gives the
hill its name of Mulloch Fraoch-choire, the *top of the heathery corrie*. A
party of four ravens was flying along noisily: father with his deep
croak, the rest with adolescent voices cracking, all the while wheeling
and diving and performing marvellous tricks.

There was a nasty opaque quality to the light as I left the Mulloch.
The crest is broken into pinnacles but in summer a path now wends
through these. In winter it can be quite a place. We were once turned
back in May by double cornices. The grand highway led on to the
south, to A'Chralaig, another massive brute of unrelenting approaches.
A south wind was again proving piercingly cold so I scuttled on round
and down to the Bealach Coir'a Chait to rest there. The day was
rapidly closing in.

> "Shaken mists a space unsettle, then
> Round the half-glimpsèd turrets slowly wash again."

A'Chralaig had been the last Munro of the third time round the
Munros, a winter day with Bob Aitken, Alan Moreland and Andy
Patterson.

I outflanked Conbhairean to reach the outlier of Carn Ghluasaid, a
plateau-like summit which may have a path all the way up from Lundie
on Loch Cluanie, yet still entail a search if it is misty. This group is
worth two visits: perhaps a summer day for the eastern Ceannacroc

Forest circle of hills and a winter day for the big two. The Prince Charlie's Cave marked on the map does exist.

Lorna Marsh, John Lawton, Mike Keates and Peter Miller (all at odd times involved in the Walk) formed our gang which once had a bivy at the cave. The Prince hid there for nearly a week, perhaps using two separate howffs. He had just managed to escape the cordon of Redcoats and probably arrived over Conbhairean, so was no doubt thankful to rest a bit, being well guarded by the Seven Men of Glenmoriston. From here he went down into Affric and Cannich, originally planning to go well north, to take ship at Poolewe, but hearing the ship had gone, he turned south by Glenmoriston and Tomdoun to Locheil country at Loch Arkaig. After two weeks he went to Ben Alder and finally west again to ultimate escape. He must have been a hardy hillman by the end.

I crossed Sgurr nan Conbnaireah, 3,634 feet, the *peak of the dog men*, quickly for there was that sniff-at-the-heels awareness of electricity in the air. My cagoule went on for warmth. The ridge is a far and desolate one, with a long valley on one side and the bites of corries on the other: the first with a Cairngorm-like Lochan Uaine, the second with the Shelter Stone the Prince used, then lesser hollows leading round east—a fine circle to complete. On the col to Tigh Mor na Seilge, *big house of the hunting*, there is a strange slot and the second summit (3,276 feet) is a wilderness of quartz veins. Little Loch a' Choinich had dried out into a black smudge.

Not having been struck by lightning I went on to bag a wanted Corbett, Carn a' Choire Ghairb, which presumably must be a good viewpoint down wooded Glen Affric. I struggled up to the big cairn on the lip of its plateau in driving rain, then dashed over to the real summit and on, following down the westward lie of the land. The glen below was all planted so, after taking a soft, green gully down, I had to deal with fences and furrows to gain a road, by which time I was thoroughly saturated by rain from above and wet from below. Movement produced heat enough and it was enjoyable. I saw an eagle. On top a ptarmigan had attacked my legs, on the Corbett I saw the first grouse for a long time. Alpine bistort flowered both on the Mulloch and in the wood here, and there were lots of orchids and cow wheat. There is *always* something. . . .

The forestry road leads down to Athnamulloch where there was a skirmish in 1721 when the government rent-collectors of forfeited estates were opposed by the locals. I cut the corner, so to speak, and got away with it as all the black bogs lay dry and cracked. Even the River Affric was just a few splashy steps.

I hit the great east–west track just as the rain came on again, and this time it really meant business. The hills remained clear, and there were some odd effects as the sun just failed to shatter the glassy world of wetness during my hour's tramp "home" to the hostel.

Dozens of despondent young soldiers were going the other way. They seemed to have a knack of stepping on the hems of their voluminous capes and sprawling in the mud. "Transport and hot char at the public road," seemed to be the sole vital thought; that they assumed this lay at the Lodge was something I had not the heart to correct—the public road lies an hour to the east. My cheery "Hi!" received looks which clearly said, "Bloody nut case! What's he got to be so cheerful about?" It was all very character-building no doubt. Thirty-seven unhappy figures on I reached the hostel, and char, and a fire—that's what I had to be cheerful about.

A lad from Kent and three of a family made the place seem positively crowded. I hung my clothes, and my map, to dry; then got down to some serious cooking. We thought of the poor lads tramping east, for the wind had gone and the big battalions had arrived: the midges. In the warmth of "the room" I nearly fell asleep writing up the log. Today had been about eighteen miles and 6,000 feet. I was finishing a fifth log-book and guessed I would need one more; so six logs of 40 pages of 220 words made up 53,000 words—so much for "not having written anything"!

Conversation was good. It touched on the reasons for doing this sort of hill game, all very high and lofty were the motivations mentioned; but after a pause we came down to earth. Why do you climb? One of the company answered: "I take to the hills to escape a wife who plays bridge, a son who plays the bagpipes and three daughters fighting over one telephone."

Sunday 30 June CEATHREAMHNAN
Queen Victoria said of the Gaelic, "It is a very difficult language, for it is pronounced in a totally different way from that in which it is written." Either way hardly helps with the above indiscriminate abuse of the alphabet—or what of Mam Sodhail, Carn Eige or Beinn Fhionnlaidh?

These Affric hills are massive rather than beautiful, grand and wild in a Waverley Novels sort of way. Ceathreamhnan is an exception: a tent-ridge summit set above great sweeping flanks and long ridges. It looks fine from all *quarters* and it is good on the ground.

There were logistical problems. The main ridge has some outlying Munros to the north, then Loch Mullardoch blocks off the Lapaichs which would therefore have to be traversed with full pack, especially as the parcel at the other end could well have been consumed by mice, though the keeper at Affric Lodge also had a parcel. The longer I stayed at the hostel the less food I would have to carry—but the more miles to walk. Some compromise was needed and I worked out a tactical plan accordingly; all part of the fun of a trip like this. After so many visits to Morocco I was quick to add *Insh' Allah* (which translates as God, weather and midges permitting)!

The English lad was packing *tins* to carry out, which presumably he had carried in. The Aberdeen trio were away for the same hills and I followed them on the Allt na Faing path, which runs up by a ravine where a hoodie nests blatantly in a tree. The cows had drifted up to over 2,000 feet and speckled the slopes. Given a dog or two it would have been tempting to take them over the pass just to imagine the consternation there would be on finding Glen Affric empty!

The path actually peters out before the col. I left the sack there to add An Socath, a poor wee nameless Munro on the O.S. map. Having swallowed Sgurr nan Ceathreamhnan and others, the O.S. seems to have stuck at Gaelic names too, so just stops naming things hereabouts —though missing the two An Socath Munros seems rather personal. It is interesting that the Munro Tables have been available for all these years, but neither their information, nor other research, has appeared on the new O.S. maps. This area is as blank as ever—at twice the price.

The Aberdonians were coming down as I went up. The pools had evaporated, and skirting Coire nan Dearcag I found the lochan much overgrown with reeds. A golden plover was nesting. I almost stood on the eggs. I had cut the corner again to reach the col north of the big hill. There I hid in a known slot in the rock while big dollops of rain came in. Without the sack Ceathreamhnan gave a happy ascent. It is pronounced something like "Kerranan". It has a double top, linked by a curving ridge which can be good in winter, when I have seen fine cornices on it. The other party had also cut across but gone for far away Aird first so as to home back to the hostel over the big one. I was not coming back, so after a look round I set off after them.

I had a bite at the sack first. Deer below were puzzled. One beast gave a great bellow. The Sithidh river ran like a silver thread in the shadowed tweed of the glen. It looked a long valley—and it was matched by the long ridge above that led to Creag a' Choir'Aird. It looks merely undulating but the reality is all rough and broken, with endless bumps, which the map cannot show. It is as well to keep to the crest. There is a definite col before the Munro, which is bitten into on the east by a corrie of little lochans; then grassy slopes lead to the summit.

I crossed paths with the others; their position had shown up in tiny dots of colour. As this hill is about as "far ben" as you can find anywhere, it was unusual to have people on it. Ken Andrew, writing in the *Scots Magazine*, suggested, "When I die I think I'll give my friends some exercise and ask them to scatter my ashes over the end of Creag a' Choir'Aird."

I left the Munro to bale off down the east corrie, a very steep slope. The flanks lower down were alive with deer: hinds "talking", calves yelping, the odd roar. There were a hundred more across the burn. Gleann a' Choilich, to which I had descended, has the remnants of a path but with the damming of Loch Mullardoch making a great barrier there is little south–north movement apart from walkers. Bogwood fills big peat patches. I followed the path down towards the loch, then cut up when it went down, to find a breezy knoll on which to pitch the tent. I could see a boat on the loch but had to retreat into the tent as the wind dropped.

The tent seemed to attract scores of spidery insects, which covered it, fortunately on the outside. Just a few determined beetles came in, to go scratch-scratching over the nylon. I lay day-dreaming, out of books, out of company. I filled in my log with mixed feelings: "Leave here: tent, stove, pots, sleeping bag, etc. Quite a bit of tea, milk, oatcakes, soup, cheese, etc., so even if Farrar cache eaten, should make Gerry's. The last 30 after that—and with support. Just get this bit over. 'Push!' and 'Tomorrow may be worse' still the goads."

Monday 1 July NEAR PANIC
Gerard Manley Hopkins pleaded, "And I have asked to be Where no storms come". Obviously he was not a climber. You cannot argue with

the wind. If "push" you need, then "push" you must, and if "tomorrow may be worse", then it need not surprise when it is. But it does!

The rain came on at midnight and battered away hard. I kept "giving it an hour" but eventually I set off into it, perhaps more angry than despairing. It was a real soaker, the cloud right down, an atmosphere as stuffy as a hospital. Wild beauty, like a green apple, can have a bitter bite to it.

Aird, for awkwardness, is matched by Beinn Fhionnlaidh up which I climbed straight from the tent. Benula Lodge and the easy approaches are all under water now, so it is a long way from anywhere—another arm jutting out with a Munroists' Munro. I was only sorry to miss the view down Loch Mullardoch, a long reach of water, seen at its best from here. Tom Weir had stayed at Benula Lodge years ago. My favourite book of his is the early, autobiographical *Highland Days*. It has the freshness of youth, and it is quite a shock to see how much things have altered since he wrote it. Many of the families he stayed with have gone now; Hydro schemes, new roads, plantings, pylons, have all changed the landscape.

The story I always recall, though, is one in an old Cairngorm Club Journal. The Rev. D. C. Mackay recounts a winter cycle journey from Loch Duich to Cannich via Benula in 1910. "I came face to face with a pedestrian . . . his astonishment seemed to be greater than mine when he beheld the apparition of a cyclist calmly emerging, as it must have appeared, from the depths of a lonely mountain loch in the midst of a winter storm. In order to reassure him, I remarked it was a fine day, but instead of an answer in the affirmative, or even in the negative, he merely stood and gazed after me. I reflected that probably the poor man was a bit eccentric."

I left a note in the cairn of Fhionnlaidh. It has never come back. Perhaps no one has been there since.

It was compass work again, down and over a bump, and then flanking along under Carn Eige, *cairn of the notch*, which was taking on a certain wildness. This flank once produced life-saving water on a scorching summer trip. Today it was all water—and so was I. It ran down my face, driven by the wind. The effect was mesmeric and I was very glad to come on the ruin of the old deer-watchers' bothy. I had overshot Mam Sodhail, *the barn*. The couple of hundred yards back and up to the top were "more boisterous than pleasant". I "cooried doon" in the hollow cairn and watched the storm fly past above me. It was like being on the *Captain Scott* in a gale in the Minch! The water seemed to be hitting the cairn like breaking waves, quite impressive. Reaching the shelter had left me gasping.

Pierre Mazeaud, in his chatty autobiography, tells of storm "reducing complexities to simplicity", but here it was doing the opposite. True, I was rather finding myself "restored to the stone age" (and I liked my broch), "up against the facts of nature . . ." but I was faced with a situation any general would dread: my lines fully extended and under heavy attack. By Loch Mullardoch, to the north, I had a tent (I hoped); at Affric Lodge, miles to the east, I had an essential food parcel; while at the hostel, to the south, lay the rest of my gear. All I now needed was to break a leg!

I climbed out like some poor Jock ordered "over the top" and set off for Carn Eige, the twin of Mam Sodhail, as Ben More is of Stobinian. At least I could try for it before having to flee downwards. My hand holding the compass froze (and gave agony warming up later) while it was virtually impossible to see ahead. I stumbled down to the col which was like a wind tunnel. Crossing it I was knocked down a couple of times. I battled up to the trig point, at 3,880 feet the highest thing between Ben Nevis and the North Pole. I put my back to the trig point and pondered.

Descent to the tent would be direct into the storm and so was out. Back over Mam Sodhail for the hostel would be easier, but a cheerless prospect of a roof with little food. East it would have to be, and a walk up the glen, then an additional day for the two Munros still further east on this ridge. Of course, going down to the Lodge, the weather *might* clear and I would then be in a position to nip up for the two tops.

I set off, grimly counting steps to be really accurate. I knew the ridge was by no means straightforward: a mile of this easy ground led to a corner bump, Creag na h-Eige, then swung round Coire Domhain in a series of pinnacles. I fought to the corner top. As I paused on it, willing back a picture of the ridge seen years before, the inner picture changed to reality—just like that. It cleared, as quickly as I can say so: one moment a blind, rushing world of wetness, the next, the clouds tore to shreds and before me the rock teeth were against blue sky. Gerard Manley Hopkins had a phrase for that too. I looked down one jewelled corrie after another to Loch Mullardoch and yelled, "Glory be to God for dappled things!"

The transformation was fantastic. I went rushing off in case it changed its mind. As the wind was still yowling on the ragged ridge I traversed upper Coire Domhain. Its lochan lay without a wind ruffle, yet I could hear the blow just a few hundred feet higher on the ridge. I tracked the snow patches of this beautiful bowl, feet saturated, the wet no longer mattering, and regained the ridge for the prow of point 3,705, which I am sure has a name, if only the O.S. would care to tell us. In places the now decaying stalkers' path is actually built as a stair as it comes up the prow. It is not shown on the map.

I kept in the lee for much of the way and reached the combed dome of Tom a' Choinich at 2 p.m. Definitely time to eat. Not long after, two muffled figures arrived from the east. The voices sounded familiar but it took a while to place each other. They were the Crams from Edinburgh. They were Top-bagging for the missus, he having done the Munros in 1939, the eighth and oldest-surviving Munroist. He had retired recently from being a Judge in Africa. There can be few Rolls-Royces to which climbing teams return to dig out the primus for a brew. At present, though, they were roughing it in a caravan. We had a gossip about Africa and Scotland. I had encouraged them to visit Morocco where they ran into the worst weather for forty years—I was surprised they even talked to me. I was given a tomato to eat and had a job convincing them I was not really starving or in need. Not now.

We went our opposite ways. I know the meeting cheered me up. I ran down the east ridge with its criss-crossing path and over the wide reaches to Toll Creagach, where, last year, I had found a cuckoo sitting on the cairn. The views were sharp as they can be after rain, the vivid blue and white of the sky had the brightness of a newly-cleaned painting. I kept chortling away in contentment. I had the two after all, and there lay the Lapaichs, there lay the Farrar Four. "Going to climb you! Going to climb you!" I sang, echoing an old Paul Robeson record. The other way, Conbhairean was at its best, I could see the Cuillin, and Ben Nevis even. And they had all been done! It was to the north I looked again.

I trotted down to join the Toll-Tom path for Gleann nam Fiadh, which was a different world: in the sun and out the wind. I eased off boots to bathe my feet if nothing else. When I took one boot off I found the gooey mess of a squashed black slug between my toes. Obviously I would never make a real explorer. Fancy forgetting to knock out one's boots in the morning! The glen was full of song, but a shorter route direct to the Lodge took me over a ridge instead of down the valley and round. On the moor the baby plovers went scuttling about my feet and dunlin slipped off among the peat hags.

The setting of Affric Lodge is superb: white, well-proportioned house, almost moated by reflecting waters, giving a crazy bonus of pines and birches, while the vivid greens of the lawns and early bracken contrasted to the moors and stony hills. I was there at the back of five but could find nobody about, so sat down to wait, quite content just to look at the magical view—or the busy tits, redpoll and twite. The locked-up dogs gave tongue, hearing the vehicles before I did, and soon the place was a milling confusion of men and dogs back from a day with the sheep.

The Head Keeper produced my parcel. He also had some words to say about a well-known gear-seller whose "advertisoment" he had read and from whom he had bought a jacket which had not been over waterproof. "They do not know what rain is down there." I was inclined to agree.

Sadly I refused Duncan MacLennan's hospitality and set off for the two-hour hike back to the hostel at Alltbeithe. Almost where it had started to rain two days before it did so again—hard. I thought of our Cyprus aunt who was due home soon, for the "summer". Her comments on the weather were usually brief. Of winter she declared once: "The weather's just the same, but in winter they may give you a fire." Bill had a fire on when I got in, first of July though it was.

The tatty Bibles again produced a suitable text, rightly in Job: ". . . No covering in the cold. They are wet with the showers of the mountains and embrace the rock for want of shelter." Even as I copied it out by candle-light a big brown drip fell on to the page from my stockings, hanging before the bogwood fire.

Tuesday 2 July THE LONGEST DAY

Many memories of this day were washed away in its ending, but its many little delights made it a "great day". I was away before seven. A cloudy sky refused to divulge its plans, but I took the cows being lower as a bad sign. I went up the path again and right down Gleann a' Choilich to be at the tent by ten. It was repitched that night at 9.30 after 7,000 feet of rucksack carrying, quite the longest day in hours out.

The Cluanie Curtain seemed drawn across the south and the Lapaichs received a deluge while I was brewing. It was nice not to be singled out for treatment for once. Everything in the tent was dry. I had a plate of porridge while packing up. The tent flaps had been well weighted with stones. These I carefully removed from the grass—there is no sadder sight than a once bright patch of grass given a smallpox rash by campers leaving stones on it. There was another tent where the river ran into the loch: an obtrusive orange one, a cheery sight, but on the whole I prefer tents to be unseen . . .

Past the eroded peat laid bare at the head of the loch I paddled over to the lower slopes of An Socath. There were quite a few ruins, and an old path heads west down to Iron Lodge: wild country all, but with several bothies and long through routes. This west end of water was once Loch Lungard; today it looked as if it were two lochs still for the narrows a few miles to the east were narrower than usual with the low water level. I took myself well up the hillside, on to Meall Shuas, before sitting to look at it. With the sun shining now, and big cumulus cloud-shadows bowling along the bulky hills, it was a scene both cheery yet empty. Larks were singing in breathless flight overhead.

Beyond the rim of Coire Lungard and before the pull up An Socath's cone, I found a bubbly spring of water. Icy refreshment. The view was better than from the summit a thousand feet higher. Bidean–Lurg Mhor formed its centre: two splendid peaks, claimants for the "remotest" title. Maol-bhuidhe Bothy below them is one we have first-footed on several trips, a bothy defended from most directions by deep rivers. If you visit it in winter, be prepared to join the brass monkey club.

Patt Lodge, five miles along the watery glen from the bothy, sits a few feet above the raised level of Loch Monar, which drowned Strathmore Lodge on the other side. It is still lived in, and must be about the remotest habitation in the country. It is served by boat up the loch, but even the loch is reached up one of the longest and emptiest glens in Scotland. Its nearest town, I suppose, is Beauly.

There is a story of the gaugers arriving from Beauly one day at the end of last century and spending a hot and fruitless day searching the glen. Ready to leave finally, they begged a glass of milk at a croft house. This was given—but laced with some of the local distillation. The officer commented it was "the finest milk I ever tasted" and tactfully withdrew. Another local had told the minister that he would always speak the truth regardless, and this was soon put to the test by the excise arriving to search houses. He was a bit nonplussed but then stammered out, "Awa' in, man. You'll find a barrel o' the best under the bed." With a withering comment, the gaugers passed on elsewhere.

An old crone always used the ruse of feigning idiocy whenever a search was on: sticking her tongue out, rolling her eyes and making awful noises—all the time sitting perched on what they were after.

A. E. Robertson, a great collector of local lore, tells of one Jamie MacRae who was such a notorious smuggler that the landowner could no longer ignore his doings and fixed a pact that ended his trade. He dismantled everything and buried his still. Later at Beauly Market he contacted the excisemen and let it be known that he might be able to help them discover a still, if the stated £5 reward was forthcoming. He then led the party back to Patt and discovered his own still for which he was duly rewarded. A. E. Robertson actually knew Jamie, so the event took place not so long ago. It has always struck me as an iniquity and an infringement of personal liberty that one is not free to distil, as one may brew, one's own stuff. However, if it staves off national insolvency, I suppose we have to put up with it.

I had my drink of cold water and wended on upwards. The Cuillins took their place along the skyline. Sgriol was a big feature as well. Since adding the tent to my load, my shoulder, till then crying out with rheumatism, had been all right again. There is a narrower summit crest to An Socath than you would gather from the map, which is true of all these ridges, which are often craggy too. Names are hardly given to peaks or rivers or anything. The white trig point was oddly balanced on the next bump east by a white sheep. As it was recently shorn it must have made a fast ascent. Filthy Munro-bagger! I saw campion and cyphel in flower on the crest before the steep drop down to the col.

An Riabhachan is also steep from the col, the ridge is well-defined, rooftop narrow in one place and full of the ups and downs of crazy strata; the craggy flanks offer no short cuts. It is a strange hill with a summit ridge running for about two miles at over 3,500 feet. With the distinctive paps of An Socath and Lapaich at either end, it is instantly recognisable from a long way off.

It seemed a long ridge today. From the summit I began to contour down and round but the map's slight portrayal of corries proved to be steep-edged, "scrag" (that unhappy cross between crag and scree) and hard old snow. By the time I was down to the next col I was quite weary. My boots, which I had wired together at Morvich, were now splitting up the back as the stitching went.

I stopped at the burn beyond to brew and paddle, which was refreshing, and I went fast up to the col from Lapaich to Sgurr nan

Clachan Geala, a fine top to its south. This *peak of the white stones* is well named, there is a big white scar on its south flank.

The combing effect was awkward going up Lapaich: it was like marching up irregular stairs. I saw a figure descending to the col, an Edinburgh lad, I later discovered, who was wandering through to Affric—one of the very few real gangrels seen on the trip. At the summit, 3,773 feet, Sgurr na Lapaich, *peak of the miry moss*, is seen for the

fine hill it is, the spike having a quite misleading name, being the culmination of big ridges and deep, loch-hiding corries. It shows well from the east, where it is used to give the local weather forecast.

I went down the south-east ridge which is very steep and broken, all boulders and slab and steep gullies sloping off, great stuff in winter and a welcome spur today. I overhauled two figures and hurried on to leave the sack at the col and collect Carn nan Gobhar, for the west had turned a black shade of grey that boded ill. Carn nan Gobhar has two cairns to confuse people: one large and old and wrong; the other, smaller, newer, and 200 yards to the north-west is correct—about forty feet higher though it does not always look it. The two figures caught up:

Suilven Strachan and Marion Niven of the L.S.C.C. Their "Dougie" made me long for my "Kitchy". They were camped down below. I wonder how often Sgurr na Lapaich has three parties visiting its cairn?

Most people do these hills from the Loch Mullardoch dam (the water is taken by tunnel to Loch Benevian). Glen Cannich was once Clan Chisholme country. Chisholme's Stone just along from the dam is mute testimony to the Clearances. It is extraordinary that in 1832 evicted clansmen living in Canada sent their chief an address of loyalty—just after they had all been kicked out of their homes in Strathglass.

Garbh-choire should always be treated as a warning, for frequently it means its name, *rough corrie*. This one proved mild, the long gentle slopes just what the weary lad, running before the storm, needed. I was soon down to the forest level, fine old remnants of Scots pine, but awkward ground and desperately hot and muggy. I forded the Uisge Misgeach, to the delight of the midges, then found a bridge not far below the spot. I scrambled up to the Hydro road and then took the old track to Inchvuilt. The race, though, was suddenly lost. Desperately I fought into waterproofs as the heavens opened. I might as well have been in an automatic car-wash.

Boots and all, I splashed through the River Farrar near where the Uisge Misgeach joins it, then bullied myself up to where my cache lay buried. There was a flat spot for the tent, I knew, and it was soon up. I dug up the parcel. The mice had been at it.

I took it down to the river and cleaned up the mess. It was only then I found that just one of four inner parcels had been destroyed but it had to be the one with the loose things like oatmeal, milk powder, sugar and so on. There were lots of tins, to eat here, and enough light stuff to see me through to Gerry's hostel at Achnashellach. Somehow I found myself with seven Gaz refills again.

I stuffed everything into the tent, did a quick peel-off and followed suit. Apart from my feet I was dry enough. The girls would be having a right time on the hill, though. I drank six cups of tea in a row and felt much better. By eleven I had eaten to a disgusting state and lay back with a last coffee listening to the drum of rain just six inches above my ears. A herd of noisy kylos came and stood looking at the tent, mooing mightily. Even a cuckoo added its monotonous call—the last I was to hear for the summer, though I did not know it then of course. There is a certain romance to rain when one is safely out of it.

The Ripleys probably thought otherwise while here. Their tent-pole snapped in a storm during breakfast and they had to seek shelter at Broulin Lodge. Two days later, at Loch Mullardoch, they were flooded out. Who says history does not repeat itself?

It was too dark to write up the log. It had been a close-run day, all the way from Glen Affric with the Lapaichs thrown in. But I was through, well-stocked, and surely could make Gerry's now. I drifted off to sleep to the swish and roar and patter of water. Chesterton once wrote, "The roaring of the rains of God none but the lonely love." I would not have swopped my little tent in the rain for a palace in the sun.

Wednesday 3 July THE FARRAR FOUR

Over breakfast I wrote up yesterday's log, and there was quite a bit of tidying up, so it was nearly nine before I set off into a world glistening, but dry. Shiel, Affric, Lapaichs, Farrar had given transverse ridges after ridges which I had been stitching together steadily. The Farrar Four were the last of these before the crossing of Strathcarron, a glen which was coming to have the lure that the Great Glen once had had, weeks ago.

A path led up, from near the tent to the west end of the ridge, by the splashy, noisy stream of Loch Toll a' Mhuic, a corrie lochan set round with crags. It then became vague and ended with a rising line under Fearstaig to gain the main ridge. Fearstaig, a Top, means *sea pink* or *thrift* but there was none in evidence. I was soon blown up Sgurr Fhuar-thuill, *cold hole*, the first of the Munros. These four are an easy group, as if nature had expended all her efforts on Shiel, Affric and Lapaich. I like them. There is a grand highway feeling and they are not cluttered round with other hills. North lay the Strath Conon hills, no Munros, so seldom visited—great hills, often admired from Achnasheen over Strath Bran, but seldom climbed. I had been exploring Telford churches when they first showed themselves. The view south and west is of the big ranges. Lapaich is at its best. It is told that one of the Frasers of Strathfarrar, who was to fall with Wolfe at Quebec, slipped out of his barracks at Inverness the night before they were to embark and took his homesick way to the glen just to look west to Sgurr na Lapaich once more.

I could see clearly as far as the Loch Treig hills to the south. North I could see Klibreck, the penultimate peak, in Sutherland. Quite encouraging. Another Top was skipped to gain Sgurr a' Choire Ghlais, the dominant Munro of the four (3,354 feet). You can take your pick of two cairns and a trig point in between. The descent beyond was slippery as the mossy surface was apt to slide off. Number three was another Carn nan Gobhar. In the lee of the cairn I piled on my Damart clothing. The sky was turning grey again—a repeat of yesterday?

I left a note in the cairn and wondered if Suilven and Marion would find it, but they came down by the tent in the evening and said they had not observed it. The paper had been picked up about half an hour after I had hidden it. Harrold Thomson from Glasgow answered the question, "Are you a Munro-bagger? (be honest)" with "Of course!" With 210 clocked up he could hardly be anything else. It was interesting to see how these remoter, beyond the Great Glen ones, were being done by people with big tallies—the Lord High Executioners of the game. I was to meet Harrold in the autumn when showing slides to the Glasgow Glenmore Club. I wonder if he has managed to finish his round yet? The nearer the end, the harder they become.

A quartzy crest drops for the pull to Sgurr na Ruaidhe. The rain came on and it poured all the way up and much of the way down till I was nearly out of the Allt a' Mhuillin glen. I came on a Stevenson Frame with rain gauge and anemometer and recalled once catching my lads "birling" the latter round, quite innocent of what they might be doing to the weather records.

Strathfarrar is a sad, cleared glen, with many ruins pointing to a considerable population once. A mention in 1848 tells of burning twelve miles of pine, oak and birch to "improve" the sheep pasture. Now there are cows back—but not people. Young birds seemed to be everywhere too. I saw young wheatear, stonechat and cuckoo.

Remembering to wind my watch was always an effort. It had stopped again today but the girls were able to tell me the hour. I am sure life was not intended to be lived by the clock anyway. Cycling up here just after the war I once asked a local the time and was told it was "near enough Thursday". In a Bed and Breakfast I asked the date, being confused in my log, and the man of the house searched for a newspaper, then declared, "She is saying the twentieth of July, whenever that was."

I had started steaming a Christmas pudding as soon as I reached the tent so, not for the first time, had my meal in reverse: the pudding with cream; chicken fillets with carrots and cabbage; leek soup. I stayed in the tent for warmth; though dry it was piercingly cold, no doubt snowing on the Lapaich. The landscape had a bruised yellow and black look to it.

The Farrar Four are usually done from the south like this. The glen is barred by a locked gate but a key can be obtained at Struy for day visitors—or you can cycle, an example set by Munro himself, who took a day off stalking in Glen Cannich to bag these hills. He mentions that there was a crofter's cottage where the Allt a' Mhuillin comes down to the Strath. It has now gone. The locals pronounced it Moily, though it is on the map as Mulie, and the Bartholomew map gives Millie. It could simply derive from Mhuillin which is a *mill*. Complications with the transliteration of Gaelic names are not new. It was to an island on Loch a' Mhuilinn that Lovat fled after the 1745 while Cannich was the Prince's furthest north.

I could hear a hunting kestrel from the tent. Wildlife was a vital part of the Walk's enjoyment but being on the side of the birds, I have only made casual mention of commoner things: the haunts of snow bunting, dotterel, greenshank, osprey, divers for instance I would not mention. Gone are the days, I hope, of "There was an osprey nesting in Glen Letmeslay, and I've got the eggs to prove it." Another great pleasure was seeing the grand sweep of seasons: I had gone from purple saxifrage to purple Carlin heather on the botanical scale, from the north-flying geese to the falling-silent of the cuckoo on the ornithological calendar; winter, spring, summer had come with a sweep that was Wagnerian instead of the normal weekend *Eine Kleine Nachtmusik*. There was wonder in it all; on the grand scale and on the small.

The mouse came into the tent with its nose quivering. Did it already know of human goodies, I wondered, one of the despoilers of my parcel? Or was it just hiding from the wind-hovering kestrel? Like as not it happened to live here and I had come along and pitched on top of its High Street. Years ago I recall sitting in a wood when a squirrel came racing along, to trip, head over heels, across my legs—obviously an unexpected blockage on its street. Anyway, the mouse soon began to rummage about. I was lying on my tummy with a bit of Vita Wheat in my hand and it tickled its way across my knuckles and happily started eating it. A piece broke off, so it picked this up and sat back, on my hand still, and nibbled away at it, shoving it in with both hands. At home or in a hut I would no doubt have had another reaction to such daylight robbery; but as we were both living close to the soil, what was a bit of cardboard between friends? Why it should have been so unconcerned I do not know. Perhaps I had been out so long now, that I just smelt part of the landscape.

Thursday 4 July   TRIPLE PEAKS TO TRIPLE COL

Four Gaz cartridges, a jar of honey, a midge spray and some tins were reburied; weeks later Mike Keates collected them when in the glen. It was grey and cloudy when I set off up to the dam. Noisy gulls were calling on the islands with their drowned skeletons of trees. Monar Lodge was noisy with dogs of all kinds. One terrier was all for joining me and several miles on had to be driven off by mock severity and pretended stone-throwing. When Lapaich cleared I heaved a sigh of relief. The day would be all right.

The Lodge slipway only just reached the water, it was so low. Boats lay like stranded fish. Later a buzzing from the west materialised as the shepherd from Patt making a trip out, no doubt glad of a dry day. New stalking paths run along the shore with well-made bridges—a nice change from the usual ill-made Land-Rover tracks gouged out by bulldozers. Being careful I omitted a wanted Corbett, An Sithean, the *fairy hill*, and later in the year received a real drubbing on it for my canniness now. Various routes were possible but I took the most direct approach to today's peak—if peak can be used of such a hill, the flattest of bulks. It is generally known as Maoile Lunndaidh though the Tables gave Creag Toll a' Choin as the highest summit—the new Tables and maps have now reversed this just as they have swopped Creise and Clachlet above Rannoch Moor.

New paths seemed to be everywhere, I followed several in turn, from burn to burn, gaining height almost effortlessly to the lip of the Toll a' Choin, *dog's corrie*, the rim of which I climbed up to the cairn. I went out to the other one and back to make sure of the Munro! Willie Milne of Forfar found the questionnaire I left—several weeks later. To my "Are you a Munro-bagger (be honest)?" he replied, "At times". Humph! With 230 and on that remote spot. He did add, "Today, yes", to hedge his bet.

My log waxed quite ecstatic over the view—which I placed with Dorain and Sgriol as supreme this trip. It ended: "But it was the opening of the north that made the day. Apart from some Deargs, Assynt and Sutherland, all the hills to go were suddenly in view: this whole area, the Coire Lair hills, the Torridon giants, Slioch, the Whitbread Wilderness, the Fannichs, Wyvis . . . Wow!"

Spurred on by this revelation of an ending I wended round the rim of strange Fuar Tholl Mor, crossed the plateau and dropped to the col. The sole was coming off my left boot, now, but I hoped it would last up to Loch Gaineamhach where I wanted to picnic. Just two strides off the loch it flapped off completely. I sat and brewed by the outflow, fixed the sole and then went on round the corrie rim for Sgurr a' Chaorachain of the ringing name. Bidean an Eoin Deirg is just a Top, but a bold, fine peak too: the whole flank above the loch is good in winter as is the traverse from Chaorachain to its twin Munro, Sgurr Choinnich, a peak the O.S. seemed to have given up, for it is no plateau as they suggest, but sometimes knife-edged and builds up big cornices. There is a toplet where the Conbhaire ridge joins, then the summit cairn perched on the precipice, then a lumpy, airy ridge to a grassy bump and the descent to the triple col of Bhearnais.

The view west from this ridge set me into glee again—the dazzle of sea and sun with Rhum, Skye, Sgriol, Knoydart all there. I could even see a tiny Ben Nevis, while the near hills were great, and north lay An Teallach and Coigach—vanishing into a haze of apple redness. Even Moruisg, across the Pollan Buidhe, sprawled like a contented lion, soaking up the sun. "It should purr," I wrote. It is as well we cannot see the future. Moruisg was to growl. This was the last day of fine weather I was to have.

I pitched the tent on the triple col, its door to Lurg Mhor, its back to Feartaig. I sprawled on the dry turf very happily doing nothing, except when frogs would insist on trying to burrow under me. The solitary life was no hardship. I was never lonely. At a lecture after the trip I was taken to task by one gentleman who said in forty years on the hill he had never yet gone alone. I felt sorry for him. Did not Munro, in the very first volume of the S.M.C. Journal, write of the joys of being alone, especially when it was hard. Until one can relish going alone experience is incomplete, or at least, less complete. Solitude, tonight, was like a benediction.

Friday 5 July DIRTY TRICKS

Between the Bealach Bhearnais camp and the Bidean–Lurg Mhor Munros is another Beinn Tharsuinn. I have tried every way to sneak past it and warn the reader, the easiest is just to go over it. It is a good hill which drops steeply to the Bealach an Sgoltaidh beyond which lies the intimidating "end" of Bidean a' Choire Sheasgaich, a cliff deserving some attention from climbers. Walkers go round. If you enjoy a bit of scrambling, a steep gully breaks upwards through the black cliffs to end just beside a tiny pool.

From there, several rock steps lead on along the shoulder. There is another loch, shown on the map, which is deep enough to give a swim. Not today though, the rain had started and it was in a gloomy mist I teetered along to the summit of Bidean a' Choire Sheasgaich. Thanks to Philip Tranter there is now a peak in the Hindu Kush called Koh-i-Sisgeikh. (There is also a Koh-i-Morusg.) *Small peak of the reedy corrie* is the translation of Sheasgaich; Lurg Mhor, its brother, is just *long shank*, which is what it is.

I reached it after a dedicated plod through the rain and left a note there, which was to have quite an eventful life. With the Bernais bothy being worked on by the Mountain Bothies Association at that time, I did not expect it to last long on such a handy Munro. Nor did it. It was found two days later by Bob Aitken, an old Alpine partner and companion on scores of Munros. He and Penny were not at the bothy either, but they wrote to me. Oddly, I had not long ago written to them.

Aberdeen 9th July

Dear Hamish,

I was intrigued to have your letter. I'd begun to suspect something was afoot when I tried to imagine what "big trek" could interest you! Speculation was cut short on Sunday when Penny and I were your "first comers" on Lurg Mhor, two days after you had been.

We went over to the West thinking about Skye but we caught the heavy showers and blasts of gale at Achnashellach so drove over the Bealach na Ba (spectacular in that weather) and—tell it not in Gath—took Bed and Breakfast in Applecross. It was grim, with waves breaking over the road, so we don't envy you your day on Lurg Mhor!

On Saturday we trekked up to the Bealach Bhearnais, camped there, and went up Feartaig to watch a watery sunset. On Sunday we did Sheasgaich–Lurg Mhor. I certainly had not thought to tread so close on your heels. Like Dow or whoever it was said about the four beards over every top before him. . . . Anyway since it was us, we left the questionnaire for the next comers—might be interesting to see how long it is. The M.B.A. however seem out in force. We could see their tents at Bernais from afar. I hope the weather cheers up for you and the midges are not too bad. A night in Glen Etive last weekend warned us.

Look forward to hearing more. Yours,

Bob.

The questionnaire did not turn up. However, in October at Carlisle, at the M.B.A.'s A.G.M. the bothy, ben and bike tandem of Bernard and Betty Heath confessed to having found it. At a ceilidh at Bernais it was filled in so facetiously that they decided it could not be sent! This couple, now living in Thurso, are probably the most famous of all bothy folk. They became engaged while working at one; the only surprise is that they wed in a church. Just think what they missed: an archway of saws and trowels, spotted dick (a sort of Polyfilla) instead of wedding cake, bare boards to sleep on. . . . Bernais was being done up as a memorial to Eric Beard, a friend of mine, a friend of all, who had been killed on the M6. "Beardie" and his honey butties will long be remembered, like Ian Clough, Tom Patey and Jim MacArtney, not just for his feats, but for the marvellous person he was. Those four dying within a year gave Scottish climbing a set-back it took time to get over. Beardie was most famous for his record runs, some never equalled yet: things like the Cuillin Ridge in four hours, or the Cairngorms big four from Glenmore in the same time. He had *run* Nevis—Scafell Pike—Snowdon.

At Gerry's the next day I read about Beardie in *Mountain*, and also of John Merrill setting off on a 1,300-mile walk along the Irish west coast; "the longest ever in the U.K." (I hoped the Republic liked being called U.K.) He expected to carry 40 pounds and wear out a pair of boots. After today I stood at 1,367 miles—and hardly coastal walking. I trembled a bit at the thought that even then someone might just be completing a walk over all the Munros. Though any idea of a race is one I would hate, I did not fool myself about the priority: I wanted to be first.

Anyway, Lurg Mhor was far from anywhere; all would be revealed in a few weeks more. Lurg Mhor was a sentimental journey in that it was Braehead School's last Munro. Coming off it Alan Moreland was adopted by a two-day-old deer calf to his embarrassment. We had done the round from Gerry's. Gerry had been worried that an old couple, the Bells, had set off for these hills and not come back, but I told him Jimmy and Pat Bell were no doubt snug somewhere. They were too.

At over seventy he had found it tough going, so they found a howff for the night. "Och, I had a bar of chocolate to eat and my wife to keep me warm." David McNab, one of the lads, who had climbed on the Ben (and since in the Alps and Norway), was amazed to meet this figure from the past. "He's really *the* J. H. B. Bell who did routes in 1929? But Hamish, he's history!"

I had a brew back on the Bealach Bhearnais while the tent rattled in the rising storm, then followed the flooding path down to the valley, There is a bridge over the Pollan Buidhe down a bit, but with soaked feet I just walked through the river. It was tempting to abort for the day and do Moruisg tomorrow from Gerry's but that would add quite a bit of walking, so being lazy, I did it today—or it did me rather. The eternal optimist I put the tent up "to dry off". In the teeming rain I walked up the road to Glenuaig Lodge. In this game you have to take the bad with the good. "If ye flee wi' the craws ye mun hoot wi' the owls." Moruisg deserves better than it receives from most visitors. Most Munro-baggers nip up and down it from a high spot on the Glen Carron road and get poor reward. Both north and south of Moruisg and on Sgurr nan Ceannaichean in particular are fine corries and winter routes on faces and gullies. The summit is a succession of slight swellings, each cairned, so being sure in mist is problematical unless you have seen it clear previously. I went up by an old stalkers' path behind the Lodge. This led to rainswept bogs. My poor compass hand froze again. I intended to traverse along to Ceannaichean and down to the tent from a path off it, but on reaching its slopes the fight directly into the horizontal rain had become dangerously prolonged and I cut down. Several times I would start to step forward—and end several steps backwards. It was a fight to make any progress *downhill*. Munro, under such conditions, occupied his mind debating whether such activity was classified as "a hobby or a crime". I was concerned for my tent, left lightly pegged in a glen which had become a wild wind tunnel.

The tent still stood. I had left some food soaking, so cooked and ate it and had a brew. Periodically big gusts set everything racketing wildly. One blow was unlike anything I have ever known: for five minutes it just poured through, then casually switched off. I had been hugging the poles. It was high time to remove. About two years later the Corbett Sgurr nan Ceannaichean was promoted to a new Munro. This I think was a mean trick!

I went quickly down the road to Gerry's, for the time was already after seven. There were deer as usual on the strath before the drop into the big forest of Strathcarron. The river was running dirty and high. The hostel was very welcome: known faces, hot bath, a drying room, music. I intended making the most of it.

The iron door to the North was now open at last. I had had eight days in a row since Morvich and they gave high averages of 17 miles and 5,600 feet per day. Mike Keates arrived having come round via Morvich to pick up the bike and parcels—and he brought spare boots.

Saturday 6 July GERRY'S

Mike went off for An Ruadh Stac, one of the area's best hills, though not a Munro. I had a "rest day", which meant telephone calls, clothes' washing, log writing, rubberising the tent seams, dealing with mail, cooking and entertaining visitors.

Bob Wilson and family looked in from a holiday up north in the morning and in the evening Ann Winning and Pam Cain called, *en route* for Bernais bothy. Richard Longford, the resident geologist, gave a lecture on the planets, Liz was typing away in her caravan, Andy Cronshaw was playing his flute upstairs all day. Gerry alone seemed to be taking his ease, enjoying his recent retirement from the railway.

"Hostel" perhaps brings to mind the wrong image; Gerry's, like Nancy Smith's at Fersit, is the very antithesis of the usual youth hostel. One is assumed to be reasonably sane, sanitary and sober for a start. Rules and hours there are none. Those mountain types who have discovered its comforts (beds, baths, drying room, store, music . . .) are in the habit of returning. I am sure I had seen everyone there before. Gerry converted a row of railway cottages into this haven.

Trains pass close to the front fence—the scenic and fascinating Kyle line which probably survives only as a commercial sacrifice to the Mammon of Kishorn. The original line went to Strome (1870), the Kyle addition coming in 1897. Now Strome is the loading place for the platform site. The railway was foretold in the early seventeenth century by the Brahan Seer, who lived near Dingwall. He had prophesied, "Every stream will have its bridge, balls of fire will pass rapidly up and down Strath Peffer and carriages without horses shall leave Dingwall to cross the country from sea to sea."

Achnashellach is a quiet spot where the glen levels out into strath, rather deep-set among the forested hills, rather wet, and very much a haven. It has been the place for several years now to which I have come with Christmas "courses". Christmas dinner there has become a tradition. Gerry makes a fine stuffing to go with the duck—plus all the usual trimmings. It is a crazy contrast to come trekking through the winter hills and then sit down to such *haute cuisine*. One Christmas Day it was so wet the hills were just not possible, so we went down to the Carron for some river-crossing practice, an aspect of training which is apt to be skipped, but several present on that occasion were glad of the knowledge when it had to be applied in reality in arctic Norway. The Carron, 100 feet wide and waist deep, was an impressive sight. In it, my new waterproof trousers filled with water—and then "exploded", the pressure splitting all the seams wide open.

Achnashellach Hostel is sited in a glen without other accommodation and is a key link in through routes: from the east as I'd come, or west to Torridon (Youth Hostel or Ling Hut). The whole area has fine rights-of-way—such as the Coulin Pass just above the hostel, the Torridon end of which A. E. Robertson regarded as one of the most beautiful spots in Scotland. Achnashellach is the *field of the willows*.

James Hogg, the Ettrick Shepherd, explored here in 1803 and letters of his tour, written to Sir Walter Scott, were later published. He walked to Strathcarron from Lochaber. At Craig, Achnashellach, he had hoped for a bed but could only find whisky and Gaelic-speakers so was forced over the pass to Kinlochewe, where he arrived "somewhat fatigued". I knew just the feeling—but I also knew of Gerry's.

Sunday 7 July THE BEGINNING OF THE END

I had originally planned to do a series of regular articles during the walk, but decided this would be a form of slavery and rather impractical as well. Also, I would hate to be beaten and the whole world know it. Now, however, I felt I could let the cat leak out of the bag! It would be an added incentive. So I sent off an article to Lesley Munn at the *Glasgow Herald*, with pictures which had been taken earlier on the trip.

Mike went off to swim up Fuar Tholl. The rain swept along the tops of the forest. I would begin tomorrow with the crossing to Torridon, and beyond lay just on thirty Munros, often in good groupings of five or six a day. I could therefore look on this happy respite as the beginning of the end.

XIII

TORRIDONS

"An explorer says, I am not going to let life trample upon me. I am going to trample on myself. What is more, I am going to do it for fun."

FREYA STARK

Monday 8 July   THE REDS AND THE GREY

The forecast was unhappily correct and I finally left the lost world of Achnashellach Station at 8.30, fully waterproofed for the silvery heather path and the wetness of the forest.

The Station is a lonely spot. In 1892 the engine of the Dingwall–Kyle train was detached in the glen here to do some shunting and the brake van failed to do its job. The engine-less train bore the passengers off down the incline until a rise brought it to a halt. It then began to run back the way it had come. In true Hoffnung fashion it met the engine coming to look for it. Achnashellach was originally a "private" station for Viscount Hill's country residence, but the glory has long since departed.

I splashed away up the path through the great pines. Fuar Tholl, that dominating, heartless bulk of mountain, was hidden in mist. Coire Lair, while as fine as any, was a mess of dirty cloud. I wandered along in a dream, familiar landmarks passing as blindly as features on a foggy trip from office to suburbia, and had to shake myself consciously back to the task in hand. The red Torridonian sandstone then gave good scrambling; up on to the grey Cambrian quartzite, rough and slippery; up to the muffled summit of Beinn Liath Mhor, which was very much a *big grey hill*.

It is the only Munro which needed a third attempt to climb it at all. On the first Joe Matyssek, Mike Smith and I had turned from the Coulin Pass to add it. It chased us off with a wicked summer hailstorm. We ran down the vile flanking screes like mad things just to warm up again. The old hostel at Achnashellach was very welcome that night. The hill also gave a Christmas camp recently when a big dry wind rattled the tents all night. We had no flysheets—optimistically being above freezing level—so it was as well it stayed dry. Candles were blown out *through* the canvas walls. Wild dawn had us looking across to the mighty miles of Liathach: shattered walls leering out of prehistory—a startling reminder of our brief snowy span of years. Red and black and white were the colours of reveille that Christmas day.

Alas, no view today to the Torridon array. It was just, out with the compass, turn about and bundle down to the track, then follow it up

XIII   STRATHCARRON TO TORRIDON

into the throat of the pass. A circle of stones by the shivering lochan gave scant shelter for a snack and once again previous knowledge came in handy—I skirted crags happily through the mist to gain the ridge up Sgorr Ruadh, *red peak*, the highest of these hills twixt Carron and Torridon. I retraced my steps to the pass without a pause.

Coire Lair is lined on one side by the two-mile flank of Beinn Liath Mhor, on the other by Sgorr Ruadh and Fuar Tholl; this latter is the better side, having some savage rock climbing (and good winter climbing) which has attracted climbers such as Patey, Marshall, MacInnes, Boysen—which should be hint enough.

The pass could never be dull, and under the beating of storm gained stature today. Once through it, the path swings west for the Bealach Ban and the Coulags Glen which runs down to Strath Carron again. (All the paths on the map are fine stalkers' paths.) Half way up the Coulags Glen is Clach nan Con Fionn, the *stone of Fionn's hounds*, yet another where this legendary hero is supposed to have tethered his hunting dogs.

The mist cleared on the Bealach Ban, so I had some sardine sandwiches and studied the third peak of the day across the Glen: Maol Chean-dearg, the *bald red hill*. My path cut across the head of the Glen to the Bealach na Lice (pronounced: leek), the *pass of the slabs*, which then descended to Loch Torridon—my obvious way out. Above lay a bald, red buttress, so after a bit of heather bashing I was soon on sound rock again. The best of the buttress proved too wet, so had to be skirted but there was scrambling enough.

I was soon on top—and soon off! Some winters ago we had come up a good winter gully on the north cliff, so curiosity led down it today. It proved a disintegrating rubbish chute in "summer" conditions. Below it lay tiers of lochans, about which deer were milling, having been put up by five walkers. The deer were a strange mixture of pale and rufous colours. The walkers only realised they were being followed later. On one loch a whooper swan was calling and later passed overhead flying down to Loch Torridon with a regular swish of great cloud wings. The path, following the tilted strata of the sandstone, curved round and down to Annat; sea-level again, the last time being way back at Morvich.

One of the oddities of this trip was how seldom the sea-line was followed; a pity as so much of the charm of our hills lies in their balanced relation to the sea, too often it was

> A far-off fringe of sea,
> Half-glimpsed, like eternity.

I wandered along to the cafe at the Beinn Damph Hotel and buntered down a large afternoon tea. Mike had planned to leave the cycle here to cut the road plod up to Glen Cottage, but there was no sign of it, so I set off to walk, speculating imaginatively. . . .

At the Fasag junction someone had daintily painted over a "sheep" road sign to turn it into one showing a mammoth. It rapidly had become a minor tourist attraction, the N.T.S. Tourist Office not infrequently receiving quite serious queries as to where the elephants could be seen. Alas, bureaucracy being what it is, the appropriate road works department was not amused. In the autumn I noticed it was back to a sheep again.

Mike, mercifully, had not gone astray, but had left the bike at another path we had been discussing. As I had the cycle padlock by mistake he had used his, a combination one, to chain it to a fence. A note cryptically told me the combination: "Your house number + $78 \times 100 + 2$." Who but a mathematics lecturer could have dreamt that up? He was soon dishing out game soup, cod and white sauce with delicious fresh vegetables; fruit and cream.

Glen Cottage remains, for many of us, filled with memories of Dave and Liz Goulder who had run it as another independent hostel. Because of their musical talents it came to stand for something as sweet as the song of the pines that gave it shelter. It did not quite suit the tweedy N.T.S. image however; so Dave and Liz went out, and on their separate ways—only Liathach of the red tiers of rock and the grey tears of tumbling waters, only Liathach remained, inscrutable as the Sphinx.

> Stronger than all who sang or wrote,
> Mountain of seasons; it never spoke.

Now the cottage was a temporary Youth Hostel, run by Irene Reilley, while husband Neil was one of the squad working on the palatial new hostel down at Fasag. The Reilleys are kindly folk and the evening passed quickly with chat and song. Neil got out a Jew's harp. An Edinburgh school party made it homely.

The S.M.C. have a hut just up the road by Lochan an Iasgaich—so even when the Glen Cottage closes there is still cheaper, non-institutional accommodation available for climbers.

It had turned stormy again by the time we lay in the bunk house. The pines strummed and danced before the black, blank skerry wall of Liathach. I slept poorly. Too well fed? Or the powerful cups of coffee? Or the cows bellowing the night long?

Tuesday 9 July TRIPTYCH: ALLIGIN

Alligin, gashed and gabled like some semi-ruined fortress, is the furthest west of the great three. Worth a good day for its view of sea and peaks, for us it was still dreich and any idea of all three big Torridon peaks in the day rather went the way of the sun. Mike and I set off up Coire Mhic Nobuil at 9.30, dedicated rather than delighted.

At the first wee fall we crossed the bridge and angled up into Coire a' Mhadaidh. There I enjoyed crossing the huge boulderfield, scrambling in and out of subterranean regions in search of odd plants and just oddities in general. Mike had differing thoughts of what was enjoyable, but having been beguiled into the middle of this geological maelstrom going on was the quickest way out. The Great Cleft of Alligin was the source of this massive stonefall. It must have been impressive to see a few million tons of rock trundle at once!

The boulders wasted a happy hour but the procrastination failed to improve the weather. As we bore up right the falls coming down the cliff were simply being blasted back up again. We zig-zagged up the slopes of Toll a' Mhadaidh Beag to land right by the cairn. It gave a wild picnic spot. The "Horns", the bumpy pinnacles of the eastern arm, briefly showed, with a cloud-churning Liathach beyond. It was as well we had not chosen the full round of Alligin. The going was a bit better away from the cone of Sgurr Mhor, as the highest point is called. Beinn Alligin is the *jewelled mountain.*

Under the cone of the Sgurr, the Great Cleft was "woofing" as the gale drove up its narrow throat. You could step in and out of the flow of wind. The rim round to Tom na Gruagaich gave no real difficulties, but from its top we took a bearing to ensure we descended Coire nan Laoigh. Being the normal ascent route its worn track soon made the compass superfluous.

We met a dog dashing about and lower down the owner peching up, an older lad. I'd taken a photograph of the corrie depths, with Loch Torridon white-lined below. It was raining hard for the heathery, myrtle slopes above the road. Bog asphodel was in flower, no doubt it relished the conditions.

From the cross-roads, we drove on an off-route visit to the Beinn Damph for tea. There deluge followed deluge. Back at the cross-roads I reverted to self-propulsion. I stopped to photograph the road sign of the mammoth. I could not find my precious Rollei camera. Somewhere descending it must have fallen out—it was a very despondent gangrel who returned to the Glen Cottage. I phoned the N.T.S. centre, I left a message for Donny at the shop, I tried to telephone the local police at Loch Carron, but it was his night off. I sulked off to bed to dream of mammoths and prehistoric things trampling cameras on Alligin.

Wednesday 10 July   TRIPTYCH: LIATHACH

> Too much wind is wearing
> But too much rain is sad;
> Better Ardnamurchan
> Than Torridonian slab.

An early start paid off. Forecast and estimations pointed to a reasonable morning before the return of the monsoon. Liathach dry would be a treat.

Mike and I went straight up from behind the cottage: a brutal ascent but Liathach hardly gives any gentle approach. We scrambled up the rocks of the burn itself to avoid the deep heather. It was an impatient stream, babbling a childish persuasion and hurrying off down to the wood, and the meandering Torridon River. From above the view is strangely like a contour relief model, for the rock strata runs horizontally in regular steps. It's a landscape where the hard bones of creation lie just below the surface.

In a *Climber & Rambler* survey I once did, Liathach and An Teallach were chosen way ahead of all else as the two most magnificent peaks in Scotland. Liathach is the more demanding. You could climb An Teallach with your hands in your pockets—but not Liathach. Its long length gives no gentle route; few places outside Skye give situations all day where a slip holds the possibility of testing immortality.

The Torridon hills are N.T.S. property and the Trust, sadly, have signposted paths and encouraged visitors. Bodies, I suppose, always feel they must justify themselves and be seen to be actively developing—but surely that is the last thing good for mountain regions. Any parks system for Scotland has in it these destructive seeds. Kurt Diemberger writes: "It is not only the beautiful which we seek; the tremendous draws us irresistibly." He could have had this barrier of spears in mind.

We climbed our happiness hour by hour up to the crest and perched on the quartzite cone like the lords of creation. Description would be prosaic.

From below the way often looks barred by sandstone steps but these above the cottage can be turned easily enough. (On descent only the heathery ledges are visible and the drops are hidden.) Above half height the last steps are passed and only long grassy slopes remain up to the ridge. From there you look dizzily down to the north corrie lochan—Loch Coire na Caime—and realise just what a crest it is.

Westward lies the Am Fasarinen pinnacles, once dutifully climbed, now, like the Cuillin ridge, often scored with easier by-passing paths. Even the contouring paths are spectacular, however. Originally they were deer or sheep tracks which wended in and out of improbable gullies and crags on the glen side. The cliffs are sheer to the north. Ringing Coire na Caime to the west are the famous Northern Pinnacles. Mullach an Rathain is the fine west-end big peak beyond which lie reasonable routes up or down. Eastward lies the quartz cream-topping to the sandstone cake: Spidean a' Choire Liath, the *peak of the grey corrie*, the highest of all Liathach's spires, once the memory-aiding height of 3,456 feet, now merely 1,054 metres.

It is quite a situation, but all too often it is shrouded in mist and drizzle, if nothing worse; after a score of ascents I cannot recall having had much weather-luck on it. Reputedly you can see from Ben Nevis to Ben Hope; but on a clear night you can see the moon! The "tourist route" is now a worn groove up Coire Liath, a classic example of concentrated use encouraged by cairning. It swings right at the top to gain the crest a long way from the summit. The high slopes of bare grass can be very slippery—both in snow or when really dry. It is a fine ridge-walk once up.

Today, as on most visits, Mike and I descended what I regard as "my" route—which is all I am going to say about it. It takes you down sneakily yet directly. The deep heather just before the road was active with thousands of mottled butterflies. The coos were causing havoc to the tourist traffic by wandering up the tarmac—and not using passing places to allow overtaking. I came on someone I knew, John Cheesmond, who was about to set off up Liathach, so enjoyed a bit of a gossip. Many hours later he came in to the cottage for a brew—very wet and bedraggled. Liathach was back to normal.

As Mike and I were down by 1.30 we went off in his car, first to the Beinn Damph for tea and pancakes then, in the returning deluge, to search the slopes of Alligin for my Rollei. This being the smallest of cameras able to take slides it was precious. We did not find it. I telephoned the police, left word at the N.T.S. centre and with the Reilleys. We continued our trippery doings by running up to Kinlochewe to collect a parcel from the MacBriartys at the hotel.

By the time we were back at Glen Cottage the weather was atrocious.

It blew in mobs of stray French and German lads who stood dripping in the crowded kitchen. Talk of innocents abroad! Names on maps had been taken for villages (back in France) and they had the scantiest of gear to face a Torridon storm. We found one huddle of youngsters under a small canvas square tied between some trees, desperately trying to light a bonfire. The village hall I think took them after desperate phonings by Mrs Reilley, and Jim Hall ferrying them in the Liberton bus. Like fieldfare, the last stragglers seemed to take days to clear the area. We later heard tales all down this coast of their wanderings . . .

The weather was very similar to yesterday's—both as to type and to timings—as if even it could not think up anything original for once. We sat in the noisy, steamed-up common room: walkers and hillmen all. One of the Edinburgh gang was a good guitar player and they all were quietly efficient. It reminded me very much of Braehead. We had a wild dash through the gale to the bunk house, crazy house-lights flooding out among the dancing trees and the rods of rain glittering as they fell on the scurrying figures.

The Torridons were certainly playing it rough. The Ripleys had done all three in the one day—a contrast to this desperate hen-pecking of mine. A Cairngorm Club Journal of 1908 had a nice description of Liathach, now both gladly and sadly done.

> "Liagush, rising sheer
>   From river-bed up to the sky,
>   Grey courses of masonry, tier on tier,
>   And pinnacles splintered on high.
>
> "Splintered, contorted, and riven
>   As though from the topmost crown
>   Some giant plougher his share had driven
>   In a hundred furrows sheer down."

Thursday 11 July TRIPTYCH: EIGHE
"A wicked day: six lashings while out over five and a half hours. Still it was the 250-up and into the twenties to go.

"We used the Coire Dubh path a bit and then crossed the river to plod up to the ridge, keeping to vegetation east of the scree flanks. One pause. Steep but easy going though it landed us on the stony, cloudy ridge further along than expected and there seemed dozens of ups and

Sgurr nan Ceathreamhnan from Beinn Fhionnlaidh

Sgurr na Lapaich group seen from the Strathfarrar hills

Braehead School's last Munro—on Lurg Mhor, east of Achnashellach

Added since this walk as a Munro, Moruisg's neighbour Sgurr nan Ceannaichean

The peaks of Coire Lair above Achnashellach: Fuar Tholl, Sgorr Ruadh
and Beinn Liath Mhor with Liathach to the far right

Maol Chean-dearg from Beinn Damh. Sgorr Ruadh and far Bidean a'
Choire Sheasgaich to left

a Ben Alligin,
  Torridon

b Slioch from Grudie
  Bridge

b

From Shenavall Bothy looking to Beinn Dearg Beag

The heart of the Whitbread Wilderness—a view to A' Mhaighdean, left
and Ben Lair, right

Looking down into Loch Toll an Lochain of An Teallach

Seana Bhraigh—one of the really remote Munros in the north

a A waterfall
spraying up
straight into the
air—not an
uncommon sight to
Scottish hillgoers

b The end—Ben
Hope summit after
112 days

downs before Coinneach Mhor. Occasionally the mist tore apart to give grim views of Coire Ruadh-Staca. The stream falling from the lochan in its black heart waved about at the wind's will. We hurried out to the Munro." Such was the brief log account of a hard-enough ascent, albeit the easiest way to the Munro, Ruadh-stac Mor.

Beinn Eighe (pronounced "A" as in "aid") could roughly be compared to a curvaceous letter F lying on its back so that in the west there is a deeply enclosed north corrie with a long leg running east. The highest point, the vital Munro, of course, is out at the end of one side of the corrie, so it poses problems. My own favourite "bagging" day would be to sweep round the Coire Dubh path to enjoy that walk between Liathach and Eighe, then round to gain Coire Mhic Fhearchair (a claimant for the title of the most dramatic in all Scotland). From there scrambling can lead one to the top of Sail Mhor, the "top" on the western prong of the F. There is a rock step before you can swing east on to the long main ridge. This can cause fun or despair depending on visibility and capability. Once past it you may spot the odd piece of aircraft wreckage. Some of it is strewn right down the cliffs. You can actually belay to wedged wreckage climbing on the routes—some of the finest in the land. I have seen deer chewing away at it.

At Coinneach Mhor, if you want the Munro, you drop down to a col (where we cringed to eat) and out along that prong of the F. You then retrace back to Coinneach and end along the main ridge: peak after peak built into a grey wall between Glen Torridon on the right and a prehistoric landscape to the left—an area of bare rock, bogs and a thousand lochans, bleak in the extreme. This way of doing all the minutiae of Bheinn Eighe ensures the thirsty traveller ends at the Kinlochewe end, where there is an hotel.

Today we were denied any view of the great corrie, its dramatic tiers of crags (routes of classic vintage, routes of frightening severity and routes as yet only dotted lines to the eyes of faith or fancy), its deep-set loch, its view out into that spacious, silver-stippled wilderness with a windy Hebridean sky rimming the furthest beyond. Our heads were bowed as dedicatedly as any mendicant—or bingo-playing housewife. Every now and then the rain squalls knocked us about. We thankfully scrabbled up the final off-white cone of scree, then did a smart about-turn.

From the "picnic" col we traversed fairly easily to the main ridge and baled off down the flank—a midden of scree and scrag but fast.

K

We scattered deer: one fine royal and a switch among them. We chuntered down the Coire Dubh path to the road. Across the lochan we could see the S.M.C. Ling Hut, below its banks of moraine paps. Behind it is Sgurr Dubh, the peak dominating the Glen—one with a host of peculiar lochans on its flanks. Being only a Corbett, it is seldom "done", though a fine wee hill. It was plodding over to the Ling for one Christmas that a plaintive voice commented, as we topped the brae, "Well, at least the path flows downhill now".

Torrents and the Torridons are commonly connected, alas. The Ling Hut had entries enough on this theme. I liked one cynical note:

1.1.62   Beinn Eighe, thawing.

2.1.62   Still raining.

3.1.62   Still raining.

4.1.62   Still raining.

5.1.62   Still raining—probably—went home yesterday.

Ling regards the climber from a picture on the hut wall. He and Glover stand there, two old cronies, figures from forgotten times. Ling was born in 1873 and inherited something of Raeburn's position—they were a formidable partnership—Norway, Alps, Caucasus; but it is perhaps appropriate his hut is here in the North West for he was the great explorer of the remote faces: Fionn Loch, An Teallach, Torridon, Suilven, Sutherland all saw first ascents in the early decades of the century. He died only in 1953—on the way to a climbing meet.

We were into Glen Cottage at the back of one. Mrs Reilley was there alone so we luxuriated in front of the fire, chatting over mugs of tea. Mike made supper while I teased away at the logistical skein. Days went so quickly!

I packed in hope for the next day. The dream of the triptych had somehow fizzled out like a camp fire in the rain. I took a book to bed and read while the wind swayed the Doire Vulich trees in swishing rhythms. The cows bellowed their misery. The sunset was as sad as a withering flower.

XIV

FADA—FANNICH

What are two drops of turbid rain?

LONGFELLOW

Friday 12 July BY SLIOCH TO SHENAVALL

It was not raining in the morning. A peculiar and puzzling "glow" filled the sky to the east. We said farewell to the Reilleys and Glen Cottage. I reached Loch Clair before Mike passed in the car. I was sad to be leaving Glen Torridon, even though it had detained us day by day, Munro by Munro; but, "Ane by ane maks ane an' a'" as George Macdonald wrote.

Torridon is a glen of brutal beauty: Liathach like some giant's castle to which one had to keep turning eyes—in case it planned some mischief to the poor cyclist, then the flanking miles of Beinn Eighe with its consciousness of strength, straddling the landscape like a colossus and secretly, greedily clasping Coire Mhic Fhearchair to its hidden heart. These are peaks such as men dream about and children paint.

A pair of peregrine exploding from the heather verge gave an exciting moment just after Mike passed. He was at Kinlochewe waiting. I phoned Marina, David and Kenneth to say cheerio as they were setting off that evening for Brittany. I had walked right through Dollar's summer term. The walk owed a great deal to their patient management at base.

Brian Ripley, talking to Tom Waghorn, recalled the Kinlochewe midges "in their teeming millions forming something that appeared like a thick fog in Manchester". They were absent today, thank goodness, and not because it was too vile and windy. It was a day with a sun to draw peace from the soul like water from a moss. Bliss! Midges do not like bright sun, nor wind. (The latter ensuring I had them as a fairly infrequent pest this trip!)

Mike and I separated by the end of Loch Maree: he went on to Dundonnell and lugged in a hefty pack to Shenavall, while I was going there via Slioch: the fourth day of but a single Munro, but a glorious change from the last three. The end of Loch Maree may be a short-cut but it entails the crossing of several rivers and lagoons. At the first main river I managed to soak my undies and the next drove me well upstream and demanded a real crossing, waist-deep, with a stick for support and boots on. Struggling in this spate I just about fell over when a jet zoomed across at low altitude.

Loch Maree, with its remnants of old Scots pines, and the background of Slioch, is a loch of outstanding beauty. It is only thirty feet above sea level and the river between loch and sea (Loch Ewe) is less than two miles long. "Kinlochewe" is thus rather misplaced. It is a loch full of legend and equally unlikely history. The Loch Maree Hotel, a famous fishing establishment, had a six-day visit from Queen Victoria in 1877. Her authority was put to the test when the local postie refused to carry her mail *on the Sabbath*: a refusal she both understood and accepted. She visited Isle Maree that day and dutifully read a sermon to the accompanying ghillies. She then added her coins to the lucky wishing-tree!

This island is named after St Maelrubha who came from Ireland in 671 to Applecross where he founded a monastery which became a famous sanctuary. St Maelrubha is second only to St Columba among early Scottish saints. At least four places claim he is buried there. Isle Maree had a curative well, and cures for insanity were long sought here. It dried up after a shepherd tried to heal his dog in it. The island had Druidical connections and a bull was sacrificed as late as the seventeenth century. Strongholds and refuges abounded among the twenty-seven islands and the wild shores. It has known warring Viking galleys and the chugging Victorian steamer "Mabel"—all equally gone. The road has been rebuilt alongside the south-western shore, replacing the original "destitution" road, and ensuring motorists can pass at twice the speed of seeing anything. The Nature Conservancy Council have a visitor centre, forest trail and picnic spots. They own extensive tracts of precious old landscape. In the lay-bys you might even be lucky and see a pine martin or two coming to rummage among the litter bins.

It is only remnants we see of the old forest of Caledon which extended from here right to the Lowlands. Letterewe, along the north-east shore, at one time had ironworks. Ore came by sea and loch from Cumberland and the local oaks were felled for the charcoal. One furnace consumed 120 acres of wood per year. There were seven furnaces at one stage. Many of the workers were Fifers. There is a story told of the first minister to try and convert the folk at Letterewe who so incensed them that they stripped him naked and tied him to a tree to be eaten by the midges. An old crone released him eventually. He was half crazy, as can be imagined. He cursed the place so that no godly people would ever inhabit Letterewe.

An old right-of-way runs down the loch to Poolewe on this north side. Mail was carried originally by runners along it. The road is only nineteenth century. Communications were much more dependent on the western seaboard before that.

I followed the path along to where Gleann Bianasdail comes down from under Slioch and turned up that dramatic gash which separates the peak from a plateau land of tiny lochans. The right-of-way goes round by the Heights of Kinlochewe up to Lochan Fada. This was more direct for Slioch.

A couple were camped in the glen and jumped when I greeted them as they had not heard my approach. There is a fine path and the scenery is spectacular: the deep-set gorge with its inky pools and brown falls, a glimpse of blue Maree and the hulk of Eighe beyond, dazzling in the early sun. They had chosen a delectable site.

I took the path up to its highest point and had a brew before following off up the raking sandstone strata. This led to the east corrie of Sgurr an Tuill Bhain, which is well-defined, a green spot among black and russet crags. I met the campers again, who had come straight up. The mist effects and vivid colouring made it a trigger-happy camera hill. (I was using a spare camera now: an older, heavier one than the Rollei.) We followed the narrow crest round the hollow heart of Slioch to its twin summits. The southern has a trig point from which Loch Maree and the west lies spread like a map; the northern, of almost identical height, looks north from its eyrie situation into the heart of our largest and best tract of unspoilt landscape, to A'Mhaighdean (the remotest Munro) and the sweep of Mulloch Coire Mhic Fhearchair.

I left a note on top of the trig point where it would be obvious. It was noticed two days later by an S.M.C. member, Leslie Kaczynski from Glasgow who, with a tally of 200 Munros, had the neck to say "No" to the question, "Are you a collector of Munros?" Quite possibly he is not, of course. Basically I'm not—and consciously becoming less so. There are too many playing that game now, and certainly at weekends the solitude is often missing.

On the way down I spent some time stalking goats which are often seen along Slioch's flanks. Slioch is *spear head* and presents its western cliffs to the traveller across Loch Maree in what must be one of the finest of hill portraits. The easy approaches are all from the Bianasdail side. Back at the rucksack I brewed again and followed the path down to its end where the river leaves remote Lochan Fada. The view up the loch is one of strange loneliness. Along it a heavy black squall was racing, and it was skins on, up the boggy brae beyond to the Bealach na Croise. Careful navigation was needed as the actual gap on this old drovers' route was hidden by nearer bumps.

Through the pass I found an old distintegrated path which led down to near Loch an Nid. The south-east ridge of the Mulloch above looked like a displaced part of the Cuillin ridge: ragged and flanked by a gleaming wet slab. Along above Loch an Nid great acres of turf have peeled off like a carpet to lay bare the grey quartzite flanks of Sgurr Ban. Above Loch Nid I found the tiny stone shelter where we had brewed a year before—so naturally used it again. I do not regret one moment of the many brew spots on this trip. There was a blessing in lying back with a brew in such scenery. It still, equally, gave its benefit when cowering in lee of a boulder in the storm.

The bealach had been the watershed, and from *loch of the nest* it was just a case of a five-mile tramp down the river Nid to Shenavall bothy— racing the rain and, for once, just winning. At the corner, where the glen swings west to become Strath na Sealga, the Dundonnell track came in. Pennant in 1772 traversed from Dundonnell to Kinlochewe by this route. Back, I could spy the Eas Ban, a favourite waterfall on Creag Rainich, ahead lay the glitter of Loch na Sealga, the *loch of the hunts*, and the red slopes of An Teallach. Deer went prancing across the river, dancing through the silver spray they splashed up.

Mike was already at the bothy so we were soon eating: dehydrated foods, yet willingly so, happy to be on the road again, no longer a "centrist" (even in Torridon).

The Torridon cows were here replaced by noisy sheep. I spread my sleeping bag on a scented bed of rushes. Deer browsed the grass outside the door. It was very much "home".

We sat by the fire, Mike and I, with a couple who had just had a week on Rhum. It was difficult writing up the log. We gossiped. Or read through the bothy book. One entry was apposite: "If you light a fire please put it under the chimney so the smoke will go away."

Another by David Doff, perhaps, should have been a warning: "It

XIV FADA – FANNICH
XV AND THE DEARGS

rained and it rained and the streams rose higher and higher; then the rain ceased and the streams became smaller, the sun appeared and at night we looked at the stars."

Saturday 13 July   THE WHITBREAD WILDERNESS

I had gone out once in the night, setting off the startled deer from the sheep-cropped grass round the bothy. A greenshank cried down by the loch. A rusty moon was half covered with the damp rays of cloud. Not promising. Dawn came very much as if afraid to face the day, like a schoolboy sniffing outside the Head Master's study.

We were not keen to go. I'd shifted my bed as the roof began to leak, the drops tinkling merrily into assorted pots and pans. Willy-nilly, we set off into the saturated world at the back of eight.

The course of the river from Loch an Nid, as it swings round to Strath na Sealga, forms a moat for Beinn a' Chlaidheimh, the *hill of the sword*, which rises opposite the bothy. On the map its top appears as a plateau, under 3,000 feet, its flanks steep but not craggy. In fact the summit ridge is narrow as a roof top, over 3,000 feet, and its flanks are craggy and broken. Not long before the Walk, Jim Donaldson of Braemar had dropped me a note telling that the O.S. had produced two new Munros and other changes. Beinn a' Chlaidheimh was one of the two additions, Ruadh Stac Mor the other. The historic 277 had become 279. (It is now 280.)

About three miles on from this peak lies Beinn Tarsuinn which Sir Hugh missed (like Chlaidheimh) because the O.S. showed it below 3,000 feet. It, earlier on, was added to the Tables as number 277 and given a height of 3,080 feet. Tarsuinn was accepted in 1927, but Chlaidheimh and Ruadh Stac Mor were not, though it was mooted then that they broke above the magic altitude.

Fortunately they both lay on the sweep of this already planned day, so, for the Walk, made no real difference. New Munros—what a nasty moral obligation to face in one's happy retirement!

It was a pity that this foray into the Whitbread Wilderness was having to be made with the weather "contrarious". It is perhaps the finest area of unspoilt landscape in Britain and owes this largely to the redoubtable Colonel Whitbread who does his best to discourage visitors on his land, yet at the same time has fought off Hydro and mineral developments and has not ruined it with Land-Rover tracks. My fear is that when he dies all this will be changed. His may be the name the proletarian gangrels love to hate; but, as with many matters, there are two sides to the question.

South of Shenavall, to the shores of Loch Maree, and west to the coast, lies a landscape which could well be the wildest we have. Areas of it contained more water than land, the land is often bog, yet rising out of this are some of the most magnificent cliffs in the country, plus a whole muddle of Munros, which even the O.S. failed to delineate until 1974. The compass is not always reliable and the map not always accurate. Elitist that I am, I do not intend to describe it further. Today I was just thankful I already knew it well and could steer blind through all the many "interesting parts". Mike, I don't think, had done six Munros in a go before, nor had such a determined mentor. He certainly found it an experience. I hope he has gone back to *see it* since!

We wended up the glen a bit before crossing the river. Taking boots off was wasted effort as the deep, wet heather soon had us soaking from the thighs down. By the end of the day my feet had taken on a horrible purple hue from dye and glue. I'd plastered for possible tendon bruising, but had no trouble beyond one tiny blister on a toe.

Beinn a' Chlaidheimh 3,000 + (pronounced Ben-A-Clay) presents a rugged bluff to Shenavall and wending up this without diversions was one reward of a good memory. You felt and sensed crags and slopes rather than saw them. The smir of rain never eased. The south ridge took us down to cliff-rimmed Loch a' Bhrisidh. We brewed there, and froze waiting for the tea. Never mind, the best view of the day was the billy actually boiling. It was only the driving force of something like the Walk made a continuation at all rational.

We swung round to the grassy flank of otherwise stony Sgurr Ban: a great mound of greasy quartzite. It stayed wet for the pull up Mulloch Coire Mhic Fhearchair, the highest point of the day. The summit was merely wetter and bleaker. Fhearchair is *Farquhar*, another man's name.

We romped down the south ridge and then cut the corner bump to the watery col east of Beinn Tarsuinn, the old number 277. It is a worthy Munro, though today the bars of red sandstone were running with water for the pull up to the main top. Beyond this, after a dip, is "the Table", a flat hunk, then a pinnacled ridge with some wee scrambles offered, including one Adam and Eve step. The drop to the north is sheer and dramatic.

The col west of Tarsuinn is about 1,700 feet and riven by black peat bogs. They never seemed to come into view as we sloshed down wetly through the cloud. We kept south a bit to miss the worst of the bogs, and set a herd of deer careering off. A watery glimpse of Lochan Fada reminded us of the other world below the clouds. We found the burn which ensured we were on the right peak, but in the swirling world of cloud with every stream burbling and rushing, we were glad enough of a glimpse of the deep-set Gorm Loch Mor, as an additional feature. Endless green slopes led to the top of A' Mhaighdean, *the maiden*, (pronounced: Vyejun) perhaps my favourite viewpoint of all Munros. Today the view extended no further than a hundred yards.

The delineation of this peak on the map is as casual as others hereabout and it is one where the compass may be unreliable (something still to verify, as we only realised it might be erratic on this visit, and a clear day is wanted). The peak had great cliffs on its south-west flank and also on its north-east flank, the ridge between, running north-west, being narrow and barred with sandstone walls and stacks. This ridge can be reached from Fuar Loch Mor easily enough. The eastern slopes alone are easy.

The view, normally, is extensive: An Teallach and Beinn Dearg Mhor array finely to the north (with a glimpse of the far north beyond), westward is the splatter of lochans and the glitter of sea, Cuillins and Hebrides, a landscape of water essentially, while south, the miles of Beinn Lair's cliffs are spread like some battlement with armed Slioch and the Torridons peering over.

A' Mhaighdean is probably the least easily reached Munro: defended by long, hard miles, lack of accommodation, and weather of an unpredictable nature; so to sit on its crest and watch a summer sunset is apt to stay a dream for most. Its approach in winter, when the hours of darkness exceed those of sad daylight, is even more chancy; yet I have been blessed by both. The latter was an unusual occasion in that it was made possible by Lochan Fada being frozen into a grand highway, easy going, instead of a snow flounder along its shores of dessicated bog. I had a lift to the Heights of Kinlochewe but walked out to the Ling Hut: a long day, ending under an icy extravagance of stars. Ah, those were the years—when we had genuine winters in Scotland!

Sir Hugh Munro visited it in 1900 along with Ling and Lawson on a day like ours—"the worst of a very wet week". All three carried aneroids and verified the peak was indeed above the magic plimsoll line.

We felt our way down to the col and then zoomed up Ruadh Stac

Mor the other *new* Munro. It presents a dripping, disintegrating face to the col, but it is easy enough to wriggle up and then skirt the worst of the sandstone screes above. The summit has a new trig point, built neatly of the local stone instead of concrete.

We unwound down to the col again and in a mini Shelter Stone had a last brew-up and the only real rest of the day. It was the first dry spot we'd had. I've slept there overnight while a great snowfall blanketed the hills—and slept on to wake, dry and cosy still, to this magical metamorphosis. This whole area is uninhabited. Kinlochewe on Loch Maree to the south, and Dundonnell to the north, are the nearest habitations, besides the western seaboard strip.

Tom Weir, in *Highland Days*, recalls visiting Carnmore by the Fionn Loch (west of A' Mhaighdean) when it was still occupied. He had had his tent and belongings blown away and found a haven indeed with the MacRaes. They rowed in their food supplies twice a year. It must have been one of the remotest family homes in Britain, yet Tom wrote of their content. "Laughter was never very far from them." Shenavall too used to be lived in. A sixteen-year-old teacher travelled round these remote dwellings in turn. It was not uncommon to be cut off from Christmas to Easter.

We picked up the path from the col and skirted down past a bleak Fuar Loch Mor. An eagle soared through the mist and deer danced off out of sight, phantom shapes in the murk. We joined the "main road", the fine right-of-way that comes from Poolewe to Dundonnell over this pass, and set off for the five-mile tramp home. The path does a corkscrew down into Gleann na Muice Beag. The waterslide was thundering in spate after our day of rain. A group of red deer calves stood on a knoll as we passed. Our only pause was to look up Gleann na Muice itself, but instead of its ring of big summits we looked into a swirling wall of cloud.

Larachantivore is maintained and used in the autumn by the estate. Again, whatever people feel, it has no Land-Rover track blasting through to it. The Colonel walks. (The "Whitbread" and malt goes in by pony no doubt.) The wire bridge, with wooden slats, across the river here is periodically damaged by spates and so is dismantled each winter. Cutting the corner today presented no problems: as our boots were full to overflowing we just sploshed through the soupy moss. The Sealga can be a problem.

Many a debate has taken place over its fording. In very dry periods you can leap one spot and boulder hop another, but normally it holds a paddle at the least for those who would head into the wilderness. Long may it stay that way.

We simply splashed through and up to Shenavall. Welcome haven. We had been away over twelve hours with hardly a pause as it was very seldom not raining. There was a smug satisfaction as we sipped our brew by the bothy fire. Every stitch of clothing hung before its smoky bogwood blaze. We agreed it had even been an enjoyable day. I produce a suitable text from the Song of Solomon:

> "Many waters cannot quench love,
> neither can the floods drown it."

Lively conversation round the fire passed the evening hours quickly enough. A lot of it centred on the stalking season, and various problems arising from that. The hills are a fine common denominator and I count many keepers, shepherds and landowners amongst my friends. We all love the same things after all.

It need not be irksome to keep off stalking ground. The largest areas of popular rock-climbing are not stalked over and the largest untouched areas of rock, the sea cliffs, are free of nesting birds then. Even the Munro-bagger can plan his wanderings to utilise N.T.S. and other areas: Glencoe, Glen Shiel and Glen Torridon are three such bases for a start and there are others where stalking does not occur or the weekends are left free. Almost *anywhere* could be visited if diplomatic enquiries are made locally. The great passes and other rights-of-way are expeditions for this season: the big passes in the Cairngorms, the Gaick, Corrieyairack and scores of others. Or perhaps this is the time to visit "Furth of Scotland", for its comparable delights.

On a recent visit to Dundonnell I heard from two English couples of walking through these hills and four times being accosted (in manners ranging from polite to extremely rude) by parties. One redoubtable owner explained that their scent could shift deer. On it being suggested that his no doubt was doing the same he replied the deer were his to do as he liked with. As they were on a right-of-way that argument cuts both ways.

The surest way to trouble is to apply different standards to suit one's own selfish convenience. If it came to the crunch the landowners can only lose. The soft answer still is the easiest way of avoiding wrath.

Deer are as much a "crop" as wheat or cows, so why should walkers

stravaig to the detriment of one more than the others? Jobs are hard
enough to come by in the Highlands; keepers and the like are the salt
of the earth—whatever some may think of those who inherit and trade
the land once filched from the people.

Mountaineering and deerstalking are both important recreational
activities, and also an important part of the Highland economy. They
need not clash as long as each gives the other consideration and
courtesy. Stalking is not just an extravagant sport. Deer numbers,
carefully worked out, have to be culled each year to maintain a healthy
stock and to prevent beasts starving or raiding agricultural land. (They
were originally forest animals and their present way of life is one of
forced artificiality; for better or worse, man has to look after the deer.)
The stags are at their best from mid-August to mid-October, so stalking
takes place then.

Outwith that period few restrictions are imposed by estates on hill
walkers and other visitors—who after all are only too glad to use paths,
bridges and other facilities made available to stalking interests and
money. It is usually not too difficult to find out what is going on—from
the nearest pub, youth hostel, hotel or the estate keeper, factor or
shepherd—and then fix up a mutually beneficial day for the morrow.

The sort of discourtesy shown to the English couples mentioned above
can only cause resentment. They knew nothing at all about stalking,
had they done so they might well have kept away, even though there was
a right-of-way through the glen. Notices, or confrontation designed to
intimidate, can only lead to quick loss of goodwill. Information should
be more obviously available. (A note pinned to a tree five miles up a
side road is *not* helpful.) Quite apart from economics, social ideas, or
politics—with which we may disagree—we should have the respect of
one sport for another, especially as we have to share the same "pitch"—
along with skiers, botanists, geologists, rock-climbers, photographers,
canoeists, bird-watchers, fishermen and others.

Shooting and hunting deer must be as old as man: a flint arrowhead
has been discovered by remote Loch Etchachan in the Cairngorms.
Anyone with an interest in deer should obtain the books of Lea
McNally. He was a keeper and marvellous observer and photographer
of red deer. He now works in Torridon for the N.T.S.

I almost regretted not walking on until the autumn, for what regular
hillman does not thrill at the first sound of the rutting season? To lie in

a lonely tent and hear the first roar fill a frost-misted glen is exciting, an annual shock. The sound has unutterable wildness in it, a deep calling to deep, stirring the ancient depths of urban man who has forgotten the smell of the earth. At the sound of this challenge we all become cave men once more; yet it is also a sad sound, marking a definite season, another year slipping towards its end. The sound reminds of swift-passing time—and shouts out to us to use what is left. Our life's walk is so short.

Sunday 14 July "YOU CANNA' FORGE YON"
An early sortie showed "No a starn in a' the carry" as Tannahill described one murky night. I went back to bed with poor hopes for An Teallach.

We woke at seven and as it looked as bad as ever we went back to sleep again. An hour later Mike got up and began "hyraxing"; rummaging and rustling among our gear like those beasts do. I received breakfast in bed and sat reading the bothy book. We were procrastinating.

The book was full of well-known friends' names and was as chatty as most. The weather was theme number one. "Whoever left Tolkein's *Lord of the Rings* is my hero. Dark days' reading."

"I left a candle in the window to guide the wanderers home."

"A thirty-one hour rain shower recorded."

"Pinned down here by storm, midges and inertia."

Dutch visitors were astounded at the isolation and scenery. Drinking water from streams was to them a sure route to the undertaker. A Danish lad quaintly wrote: "Here is all that which are micing in the Danks natur; it make me happy to see it. I wished I can right better Inglish so I can experes what I want to say." The wooden spoon goes to the Munro-bagger who recorded "breasting The Maiden."

It was heading for noon before we set off in a smir of rain and the tops buried in cloud as ever. We wended up the Shenavall burn and across the spongey moor towards the Dundonnell track. Mike, rather thankfully I suspect, left me to the mercies of An Teallach and headed for his car.

I cut through by the lochan (where sandstone and quartz fuse) to reach Toll an Lochain, one of the top two or three corries in the land. Well is it "toll", or *hole* for the small hollow is completely filled with the loch and girded round by mighty slopes and cliffs which at the far end drop sheer into the water. The skyline, when there is one, is of jagged peaks and pinnacles—an array unequalled outside Skye.

From the end of the loch I just wended back and forth up to the arm of ridge enclosing the loch on that side. I managed to keep on grass all the way till on the ridge which was followed over various sandstone towers to the summit, Bidean a' Ghlas Thuill, the *little peak of the grey hollow*, an odd name for splendid Munro 69, which is girded with red sandstone. I could just see the next peak along, Sgurr Fiona; beyond it lies the leaning summit of Lord Berkeley's Seat, Corrag Bhuidhe, and Sail Liath—all jagged peaks giving the finest of sweeping traverses. From the summit they curve away like a petrified breaker as it topples on some god-forsaken strand.

MacCulloch in his *Highlands and Western Isles* must have recorded one of the first traverses: "I continued along the giddy ridge, in the hope of seeing its termination; but all continued vacant, desolate, silent, dazzling and boundless . . . its apparent altitude greater than of any single mountain in Scotland, excepting perhaps Ben Nevis."

Contrast that to Pennant in his "tour" of 1772: "West, a view where the awful, or rather the horrible, predominates—peaks with sides dark, deep and precipitous; with snowy glaciers lodged in the shaded apertures . . . here Aeolus may be said to make his residence—fabricating blasts, squalls, and hurricanes."

Actually his description is not so inapt. We once battled our way over the mountain, roughly on today's line, with a Braehead party. Ann Winning had to take the lighter girls down; the heavier boys were roped for the towers as the gusts between threatened to blow them away. We *crawled* up the final slope. We all gathered again in the Dundonnell Hotel—of which more anon.

Today lacked the ferocity but gave no better visibility. It was too chilly to linger. No sweeping view of the Lewis coast or the Summer Isles, no distant Macdhui. Again it was navigation from memory; down and along the various pebbly domes to pick up the path which twists its way down to Dundonnell. It comes out just by the Smiddy, a hut belonging to the Edinburgh J.M.C.S. and converted tastefully as a memorial to Jim Clarkson who was killed near the C.I.C. Hut. It looked busy this summer weekend.

I reached the hotel reasonably dry. (The showers had dampened and the wind had dried in balanced combination.) A vast quantity of tea was consumed and the comforts of the hotel enjoyed. It has a snack-bar and various other facilities to pamper the inner man. It also provided a dinner which was one of the two best of the trip: leek soup; silverside; fresh strawberries and cream; Chianti and excellent coffee. It is always a treat, after a self-catering stay at the Smiddy, to dine there. After our wet bothy days it was even more of a treat and we ended the day with a midgey camp at Camusnagaul.

To revert to our Braehead battering on An Teallach. We reached the hotel soaked to the skin and while the girls ordered a spread of tea we, one by one, changed in the toilet. We had a small, cosy, inner room. On the table was placed tea and a great stand of sandwiches, scones and cakes—the sort of thing one sees all too rarely now.

I reached out to pour the tea and my wrist touched the hot water jug. I jerked back, giving the tray a good jolt, Tom grabbed to save the cake stand but instead simply knocked it straight into Kay's lap. She leapt up. The tray toppled. A cat had been hiding in a corner as Kitchy, our dog, was in with us. It bolted. The dog chased. Ann fell over the dog.

All this and more happened simultaneously; within seconds we had reduced the room to a shambles and ourselves to a state reminiscent of a custard fight from the days of silent films. We had a hectic clearing up, and a rather puzzled waitress brought a replacement. "You do have healthy appetites" was how she politely put it. We were nibbling our sandwiches, still in a state of shock, when the door opened and a dainty old lady looked in. She spoke to someone behind her. "I think we should come in here, dear, it's very cosy and peaceful."

An Teallach is perhaps the finest of all British peaks. Tom, after our disastrous Dundonnell tea, had been told that An Teallach (pronounced An Cheallach) meant *the forge*. His reply was, "You canna forge yon. That's the real thing."

Monday 15 July   TO THE NEST OF FANNICH

Across from the camp-site rose Beinn Ghobhlach which though a mere 2,082 feet is a splendid viewpoint, commanding a wide seascape as well as the hills.

Like so many hills here it is built of tiered sandstone. The North West, of course, sets the geologist going with some of the oldest rocks in the world, yet the sandstone (said to be 800 million years old) is only half as old as the gneiss which runs up the coast and gives Sutherland in particular such a scoured, barren and lifeless air—and its peculiar spaciousness and clean brightness, the wide sweeping beauty of "desert". Further in, the hills become more rounded, their contours gentle, their cols fiendishly boggy. These are good old schisty hills, which have edged up westwards over the sandstone and gneiss in "the Moine thrust", the edge of which runs conspicuously to the north of Ullapool.

Mike was going home for a couple of days while I headed off for the Fannichs. Having the bike, it was pressed into service. The run through Dundonnell was pleasant but the brae beyond goes up to 1,100 feet— and, for the first time in weeks, there was an east wind, a perversity well known to cyclists.

This sweep of road up the Dundonnell River, first a gorge full of waterfalls, and then a sweep of yellow moors, is known as Destitution Road, so named because it was constructed as a charity project during the 1851 potato famine by Mackenzie of Gairloch. Many people are surprised how recent such roads are—some of the roads in the west were not surfaced until after the war. We used to go off touring, the whole family on cycles, in the mid forties, when rationing entailed posting parcels ahead. "B and B" signs had not been invented. Ben Nevis, Ben Lomond and other of my earliest Munros were done then. Spare spokes and tyres were never forgotten. As the tourist industry has flourished so the cycling fraternity has dwindled, the remnant being found in the most unlikely spots. It's no surprise that many of the Rough-Stuff gang are also bothy fanatics.

It was tough enough peching across the moor. I paused at Fain, once the boozer for the road builders, and now rapidly falling down. A photograph of it, with An Teallach beyond, showed three ruins in all. Sunny though it was, the scene was truly one of desolation. I pushed on with the Fannichs arrayed ahead. Where the road sweeps down and round for the view of Loch Broom and the deep cleft of the dramatic Corrieshalloch Gorge, a track wends off down to Loch a' Bhraoin, a curl of water overlooked by the spurs of the day's hills.

Cairns by the loch here mark the burial place of raiding Lochaber caterans: far from base, for it was not diplomatic to beggar your neighbour. Raids were sometimes made with dates of cattle marts in mind to save even the bother of driving the beasts home!

Loch a' Bhraoin means *loch of the showers*. Today it was happily failing to live up to its name. Shenavall's rainfall is about 100 inches, Ullapool's less than half of that. A tip for tourists based in the West when the weather forecast becomes "showers of a continuous nature" is to head *even further west*, out on the peninsulas if possible, where you can often enjoy sun and dryness while the backcloth of hills is curtained off, wet and grey.

There is a footbridge at the outflow from Loch a' Bhraoin leading to the Cuileig Glen and once into that quiet glen I brewed, as it looked as if the weather was deteriorating. I kept on the west side of the glen, slowly gaining height, breaking through crags with an enjoyable burn scramble. This landed me in a wide corrie full of deer. I saw another eagle too.

Druim Reidh rises to a bump, unnamed (Toman Coinich) shown as *c.* 2,750 feet but almost certainly over 3,000 feet; a missing Top. I left my sack under an overhang where I sheltered from a brief shower and then wandered up Sgurr Breac. It has a cairn on its grassy dome but a rib of rock to the east seems fractionally higher. Traversing over Toman Coinich I ran into Bill Myles from Edinburgh, along with his dog "Mungie". He was staying at the Smiddy. We chatted for a while but it was a snell spot. Later I received an eight-page letter continuing the conversation. We were talking of access, and of the growing pressures about which we have had so little to worry in the past. They come upon us now, though.

Bill went off for Breac and was coming back for A' Chailleach but I did not see him again. He was not wearing polluting orange after all. Bill saw the questionnaire on Breac and left it; it was found five days later by an "unashamed" collector of Munros from Cumbria, Martin Hudson, who added to his total the ones he "hoped to do" the rest of that week. This was surely chancing fate! (He wrote later to say it rained every day they were in Scotland.)

A' Chailleach *the old woman* is an odd peak of hollows and levels, carpeted in cyphel, and due to its situation a fine viewpoint, even today when the clouds had lopped the summits off the bigger hills. A fence runs from col to summit and I back-tracked to retrieve my rucksack left hanging on a post before "baling-off" down into the Nest of Fannich: a green bowl of glen, teeming with deer. From every rise I looked down on sprawling herds. There were many calves about and they were surprisingly vocal: the young almost mewing and the parents giving gruff barks once they spotted the intruder.

The walk down to Loch Fannich and the Nest bothy was pleasant. Deer gave way to a group of nosey white garrons and then beefy cows. The end of the loch was laid bare in acres of bright sand and contrasting bands of peat where the stream flowed in. It was blowing wickedly cold from the east, waving the trees by the door. After the inevitable brew I simply sat by the window—in a bit of dwam—and soaked in the atmosphere. I wrote:

"This bothy [now not often available] is one of the most peaceful places I know. It weaves a magic that leaves one under a spell. It is hard to describe; it is not outstandingly remote or scenically splendid, but it combines such a galaxy of the almost-best that the result is a delicately-balanced beauty.

"Outside the window shimmering willows dance in the breeze. A redstart rasps away and a baby wagtail noisily pursues its mother, begging for food. Curlews are calling as they arc down to the edge of the loch. A pair of divers go splashing into its glitter. Their call, all wild-ness and freedom, takes me dashing out, to squint into the sun to follow their flight.

"Through the gap, beyond where old Cozae Lodge used to be, beyond the big boulder with its grass tammy, is the unlikely shape of Slioch, blue with distance. Straggling up behind the bothy are scattered groups of trees. They remind me of people stravaiging home after church: friendly and unhurried, free from the pressures of life. Bog cotton nods on the vivid green banks and along the path is a mini garden; tormentil, milkwort, lousewort, bedstraw, eyebright and hawkbits—again, nothing rare, but adding their collective charm."

Martins were playing tig round the chimney pots and peewit, redshank, and summer piper had all added their cacophony of sound as I'd wandered along path and shore collecting the white ribs of bogwood for a scented fire. Being alone was an added pleasure though I could not shake off a feeling of expectancy. Someone was going to arrive I was sure.

> I waited in this lonely place
> For a step upon the yard,
> But no man came to break the peace—
> Nor was the waiting hard.

I thought of the first time walking into the Nest. A twist of the path suddenly revealed the house: gables and windows painted blue, stonework clean and pointed, the slate roof surmounted by a variety of tall chimney pieces, a green corrugated porch added to the entrance. There were even blue and white checked curtains at the windows.

Surely it was occupied; and I had no tent. Perhaps the occupier would allow me to use one of the out-houses. . . .

On the door was the familiar M.B.A. plaque. The porch was stacked with bog wood and resinous pinewood. It was a bothy all right. I settled into the room on the right.

As my days of this long wandering were now consciously ending I felt an almost selfish possessiveness for this marvellous country. I knew it well but the journey had still been a revelation, a renewal of faith.

Tuesday 16 July   PIPELINES AND PIPEDREAMS

I set off at 9.30 in full waterproofing convinced I was going to have another drubbing. The night had been all storm with just one pause as the wind changed from east to west.

Fionn Bheinn is a solitary bump above Achnasheen, miles from any other group of Munros. It had been quite a logistical game to decide just how to fit it in. As I had normally used it on courses as a training peak, or ski school, or even climbed it between trains, always from the south, doing it from Loch Fannich, the north, was the most pleasing possibility.

With the burns in spate and the ground waterlogged it was necessary to go well up the Nest of Fannich to cross its river. Rarely can you usefully cut corners: one of the spectator sports at this bothy is watching new arrivals rounding the end of the loch and running into dead-ends. There is no bridge at the Cabuie Lodge site and the Chadh Bhuidhe river can be a formidable proposition. Iron girders in it told of a past bridge. The Lodge is a heap of brick and mortar, destroyed no doubt by the raised water level. It took me an hour from bothy to south shore of Loch Fannich—about half a mile as the fly crows.

The low level of the loch made it possible to walk along on the exposed gravels, an easier proposition than the cut-up, boggy hillside. Bridges and traces of drowned track were exposed. Two miles along the loch there is the end of a pipeline (and Hydro track) which wends off at a gentle angle along the northern flanks of Fionn Bheinn, capturing much of the water which would have flowed out west.

One Hogmanay the snow was so deep that in the end we found it simplest just to walk along the top of the pipe itself. Tiptoe-ing round the open intakes gave moments of caution. Kitchy was with us on this winter escapade. It was to be his last Munro, for he died a few weeks later.

Today I wended along to intake number 35A, then took to the hill, crossing the burns which drain Toll Mor, the fine northern corrie. I skirted the rim of this on the west, watching stabs of sun darting from the clouds to light up the grey world now and then. The summit trig point (no cairn) was cold and exposed. I continued round the corrie rim and back to the pipeline. The end of the loch gave much less trouble thanks to the six-hour difference in water level: last night's rain had by now drained into the loch. Later a fishing boat drifted up. Three children and several dogs were put ashore to romp on the sands and wander upstream.

I was in at four so was quite pleased with the day. Simple values and simple desires make for content. The challenge of wild nature merely excites: worries are mainly concerned with the things of civilisation, so called. Surely the quality of life is what counts? Living is more precious than longevity.

Picture the Nest at Hogmanay. Five of us went there to be away from it all, but I think there were thirty-seven residents as the Old Year gave way to the New. Many of them were members of the old Corriemulzie Club, rising phoenix-like, at the place of its founding. It was not surprising a memory was drunk to Philip Tranter, for few people crowded their lives with good hill days as he did. Huge in frame and temperament, his enthusiasm led to many adventures in the remotest corners. I remember once sitting next to him at a club dinner and we played a game of just mentioning Scottish place names in turn; each name followed by a minute's silence. We made each other sick with the cup of remembering. One name he mentioned was "Nest of Fannich".

The bogwood fire flickered and smoked, helping the odd candles stuck in empty whisky bottles round the room to give a weird half-light. In the centre of the room an eightsome reel was being danced. Two pipers in the old pantry took turns with providing the music. The rest of us crammed round the walls, three deep, glasses in hand, bottles circulating. Outside, the snow fell steadily, adding to the foot of powder already piled over the landscape. We bedded in the wee sma' 'oors and we rose before daybreak to first foot the white hills of the Fannichs.

I had actually enjoyed a brief pipe-dream out in the sun when, at seven o'clock, Lorna Marsh arrived with some friends—over my hills of yesterday. A real surprise—but she had met Bill Myles at the Smiddy so knew I would be there still. Another odd coincidence was seeing the name Dave Norgate in the bothy book. He shared a flat with Mike who was now helping me over these last days. The book has several entries from cyclists: one who gave the date as the 30th of February. Ann and an L.S.C.C. gang had been there a year previously. The R.A.F. 1970 North-South Traverse team had used the Nest. The Ripleys too had been there, enjoying sizzling hot days in the Fannichs and having their first clash with stalkers. One August entry read: "Sorry to contravene 'close' season—plain lack of knowledge on my English part." There was even an entry from a honeymoon couple!

Wednesday 17 July ROLLING UP THE FANNICHS

The mice were rummaging about in the fireplace all night, making an incredible amount of noise. I left the Nest at 7.10, with no sign of life from the others, and wandered up the path to the col between the western pair and the rest of the Fannichs: which I then began to collar in steady succession. The sharp edges of the ridges were shown up by cloud welling up against their crags. It was clear for Sgurr nan Each with the Choire Mhoir glen below a glitter of silver, but Sgurr nan Clach Geala, one of the two giants of Fannich, stayed cloudy. A dozen piles of orange peel indicated some recent litter-louts. The eastern cliffs make navigation easy. This was a typical Tranter crag: ignored by the O.S., it yielded a 700-foot grade V ice climb ("Gamma Gully", done with Ian Rowe in 1965).

The col beyond has a part time loch on it and a bit to the west lies a large split boulder—both good aids to memory navigation. The dip to Meall a' Chrasgaidh is one of the wettest cols in Scotland. I have never known it dry. Beyond Chrasgaidh are paths which give splendid approaches to the Fannichs. It is a range with more paths than the map indicates. This west end has an openness to it which delights. The Fannichs rather fall over each other, but here the Deargs and An Teallach are seen across miles of clear air.

I splashed back from this outlier, and regained the main ridge for Sgurr Mor, 3,637 feet, a cone of greasy rubble which is unmistakable when seen from distange ranges. I admired the Geala cliffs before climbing up into cloud again. Both these hills had lingering snow patches. Just beyond I once innocently caught a leveret which then proceeded to scream like mad, to my consternation. I also have a picture of Kitchy sitting, like a professor of botany, gazing raptly at a patch of white moss campion on this highest summit of the Fannichs.

Sgurr Mor has cliffs running out to a northern spur with a Munro on it: Beinn Liath Mhor Fannich. A tiny shelter en route allowed me to leave the rucksack. I raced out and back just in time to use the shelter and sit out a nasty sleet and hail shower. I'd brought water up from the col returning (a permanent source) and made quite a good meal. The roof leaked and the sheep had got in to soil the floor, but it was out of the lash of the wind.

The easting after that became pleasant. A back wind for once. The sun shone again. "Truly the light is sweet and a pleasant thing it is for the eyes to behold the sun" (Ecclesiastes 11:7). Meall Gorm was next and just beyond its stone howff I ran into Lorna and company, who were after the lot, east to west, a day comparable to the Mamores. I wished them luck as it was already 2.30. They had come up from the lodge on Loch Fannich to An Coileachan, *the cockerel*.

The rucker was left on the last col and An Coileachan done speedily to race another blatter. It whipped past trailing white curtains of hail. I left a questionnaire. The note lay for about ten days and knowing the finders its return backs the assumption that only Munro-baggers seek the most eastern Fannichs. It came in months afterwards from that inveterate gangrel, Nancy Smith of Fersit, along with her gannet mark II, son, Ewan (14). He did his first Munro at 4 because "he had no other alternative". But ten years later he has—and still goes. They were based on the Nest and apart from the *Captain Scott* watch, the only people returning questionnaires who were not car-based.

I had arranged a meeting with Mike on the Dirrie More for 5 p.m. so had a spur to drive me down the long five miles north to the road. Across my map I had already written "Bog, Bog, Bog" down the route of the River Li. It was a steep drop initially to Loch Gorm. The slopes were covered with athletic frogs which bounced and crashed down the brae. It was quite an enjoyable bog trot, making the meeting spot with two minutes in hand.

After some tea I was busy messing about in the stream like a child, when Mike arrived. He had been held up at Aultguish Inn while they searched for my parcel.

The Dirrie More is the highest reach of this great through route from coast to coast. An Teallach and Wyvis guard its opposing ends. It is seldom without some breeze, so a good spot to camp in midgey summer. The good road was built in the 1800's by the Fishery Society when Ullapool was a busy fishing port. Tom Patey had been Ullapool's doctor. Not far off lived another Doctor Tom—Longstaff, the great Himalayan pioneer.

Mike produced supper while I sat and dealt with a stack of mail, prepared for Wyvis, and studied the days to go. From one of the many boxes in the car I pulled out the twenty-second—and last—map of the Walk. The 1,500 miles had been clocked up today.

A rainbow arched over the view eastwards to Wyvis, north, the Deargs were *liath*; portents had I known it. We would end with a bang not a Whymper, as I think Dougal Haston put it.

Thursday 18 July   THE SCENT OF HONEY

At 3.30 there were midges just to disprove the efficacy of the site, but the west wind was soon blowing again. Mike went off determinedly for An Faochagach and I cycled off for Wyvis. Mike thinks of himself as a gentle soul but I maintained anyone who has collected Munros with half his dedication has quite a share of aggression. He finished his round not long after this trip.

It was good to cycle both with the wind and slightly downhill— though the return journey would have both in opposition. The Glascarnoch Reservoir was grey and choppy. Hidden under the dam at its eastern end is Aultguish Inn, a hospitable place with an air of loneliness akin to the Kingshouse on Rannoch Moor. Its walls are decorated with pictures taken during a period of deep snow when it resembled the Arctic. The half-engulfed vehicles date the scene. Munro had been based there venturing forth on to Fannichs and Deargs, using a cycle —or pony trap.

At Black Bridge Strath Vaich joins the main valley, a favourite glen of mine; at Inchbae, Strath Rannoch joins in, while north and east of it lies some of the most desolate of all moors, leading eventually to Glencalvie and Strathcarron, names sinister in the annals of the Clearances. At Croick Church you can still see names and pathetic messages scratched on the glass, the abiding witness of the evicted crofters who sheltered in the churchyard there in 1845.

Ben Wyvis now has its western aspect planted, a verdant waistcoat, which is not altogether welcomed by walkers. Setting off from Garbat, where I chained my bike to the wreck of a car, I made large alterations to my map. Probably the easiest approach is up to the Bealach Mor and over An Cabar, returning off Carn Gorm to a track west of Meallan Donn. This gives a fine, high, traverse, and Wyvis has a fine view being solitary, all as it should be for the *big, noble mountain*.

My own route used roads and firebreaks to reach the main river which

I then followed up. It grew steadily colder as the wind strengthened. The spongy nature of the ridge's mossy covering made it hard to hurry. One walker-cum-golfer celebrated his Munro completion by saving Wyvis for the last and "playing himself in" along what could well be a golf course. The last hole is Glas Leathad Mor.

I swung up on the lee side: the scalloped eastern corries there being so different from the even western flank, and donned skins simply to combat the piercing wind. Over the summit and from the first dip beyond I trotted down at once. A high square of trees, burnt by the searing winds, gave shelter for a bite, then it was back to the game of linking rakes and tracks down to Garbat.

It had taken forty minutes cycling east; returning took more than twice as long. Mike was back just before me. After supper we went along to the Inn for a drink.

The Ripleys had Wyvis early on their route, of course. After it they had a rest day at Killin Farm near Garve. Their log had a familiar ring to it, apart from the medical statistics: "Festered, picked wild raspberries, sunbathed, ate great amounts of rich food, and pampered feet. Sores and blisters: Brian, 17: Alan, 3; David, 3."

There were 10 Munros ahead for me now; in a rash moment we ordered a half bottle of champagne to be used on Ben Hope.

The day's best memory, though, was nearing Inchbae Lodge and suddenly having a strong scent of honey blow from a field of clover. It had been a long time since I had seen a clover field and the clean, sharpened senses revelled in its richness.

Friday 19 July DIRRIE MORE

Today would have given a repeat of the wet day from Shenavall so we stayed where we were, snug as walnuts in their shells. The long sleep was welcome and I had old Braehead logs for reading. These produced quite a crop of howlers, some of which I noted down:

"We climbed Devil's Point and Cairn Towel . . . walked round the Bend to the C.I.C. Hut . . . shining formica in the rock . . . an eigg for our tea . . . two dukes flying across the water . . . we rumped down the snowslope . . . an insect-invested glen . . . golden plumbers were calling on the moor. . . ."

The tent tended to collect earwigs (golachs or gallachers in the older tongue) so in the afternoon we flitted to Aultguish again. "The muddle of mountains" to the north was still black with cloud. Aultguish is *burn of the pine*, though a singularly treeless spot. Over tea I wrote a review of Desmond Nethersole-Thomson and Adam Watson's *The Cairngorms*, which had been delightful reading for several days.

We collected our small bottle of champagne. I'm not very enthusiastic about it as a drink, but out of respect for Sir Hugh, what else would do? Nor obviously am I very superstitious, buying it in advance. Perhaps I should have been!

We returned to the tents to eat. The weather would have to be very, very bad to deter us on the morrow.

XV

THE DEARGS AND THE NORTH

"Will there be a few folk left in the world when Progress is choked at last by its own too much? Yes there will be, a few folk will return by stealth to the wind and the mist and the silences. . . ."

GEORGE MACKAY BROWN: *Hawkfall*

Saturday 20 July THE EMPTY QUARTER

The overnight "Hunting Winds" had moved on as I set off into the last fighting group, then caught me on Dearg, a hill I have always distrusted. The Dirrie More bogs led to Loch a' Gharbhrain, the largest of five lochs that are strung like irregular beads on the thread of the Allt Lair which runs right up into the heart of the group. Skirting round to the west I came on old ruins and bright green grass, the abiding testimony to past habitation.

It became a great bird hour: a snipe went ricocheting off from the moss, an eagle swung lazily over the line of lochans, up in the corrie the mountain blackbirds were chacking busily among the berries and on the long, bare shoulders of Am Faochagach golden plovers were telling the world of their woe. They certainly eased bog-hopping, river-teetering, and brae-bashing. Am Faochagach is a bit of a mouthful— and one which seems to have been spat out by the rest of the group. It lies in Coventry to the east, the culmination of successive adjectival bumps. The questionnaire left here was not found till August 9; a long wait. It's obviously not an appealing summit! Arnold Hardman, who found it, introduced Munros to his two sons that day—a long way from home in Hampshire.

This hill once gave a gang of us a midsummer bivouac when we simply spread sleeping bags and slept under a glowing sky. Today the call was to hurry. Beinn Dearg had been smoking like a volcano and the "smoke" was streaming eastwards. So I trundled off over Meallan Ban, which has a bigger cairn than the summit, and began to skirt down too soon. Like much "rough pasture" on the maps of the North West this was crags and gullies, so I had to scramble up again before finally descending to the fourth loch: Loch Prille.

Loch Prille ends on the lip of a 500-foot slide of water. Today the slide, working in partnership with the wind, was doing its best to fly back up into the loch again so that the odd stepping stones on the lip were constantly swept by flying sheets of water. You chose a lull—and ran. Yet fifty yards beyond was a nook so calm that I settled for a brew. A circle drawn with this spot as centre and with a radius of two miles, takes in some truly dramatic country—which is enough said. This enormous area north of the Dirrie More, right up to Oykell Bridge, is a great "Empty Quarter". It has some superb through routes, there are a few lonely bothies, the atmosphere is closer to the ice age than the twentieth century, but woe-betide the incompetent or unfit who strays into its fastness. I set off up the *enchanted hill*.

Loch Prille to the top of Cona Mheall was ribbed with rock and steep and clean enough to give scrambling. The wind added an element of the unexpected. Near the top the ridge became a jumble of blocks. The summit was reached in an hour. Yelling Dvořàk themes I followed a drunken course over the boulders. An orange dot in the lee of the wall leading to Beinn Dearg became two figures. Luckily for them the wind was blowing my song in the other direction. Nevertheless they set off up ahead of me. I hid the rucksack under a nook of rock and had a piece. The rain came on. I scuttled up in the lee of the wall, passing the English couple, and then duly received the brunt of the wicked storm on the last exposed slopes. Last time it was an electrical storm. Verily Dearg is an evil mountain. I kicked the cairn and ran.

Beinn Dearg can be a fine summit when clear. It looks to Loch Broom, Coigach, Am Teallach and the Fannichs. Great country, Beinn Eniglair (2,915 feet), two miles over, is the best viewpoint of all and worth including in the group. There are fine paths up from Inverlael. You need them—the going is rough everywhere.

I procrastinated through another snack, but it seemed set foul for the duration. Mike was motoring round to Oykell Bridge and up Corriemulzie to the bothy in Coire Mor—many miles to the north as the crow might just manage to fly. He had all the food and gear. There was nothing left at the Dirrie More. I would have to try to go on. Like the ant called Pythagoras I'd have a few unhappy compass bearings to battle along before writing Q.E.D. to the day.

So I crossed the wall and struggled through the murk to the lochans. The other two appeared briefly and I wondered what they thought of things. The gusts tore great curtains of water off the lochans and smashed them over the boulderfields—once or twice they made attempts at blowing me into the water. I staggered round into the lee and squelched up the sodden slopes of Meall nan Ceapraichean.

The next Munro lay across one of the three east–west through-routes that radiate out from the head of Gleann Beag. My descent followed a threefold pattern, first down sandstone boulders, then wee quartzy crags, then a conveniently angled rake of exposed strata. At stage two the clouds tore apart, the rain stopped, and Dvořák started again.

The stalkers' path at the col is clear but it comes up only as far as the watershed. The descent to Gleann Beag is a do-it-yourself job. From the col it is a mere 500-foot scramble up to the top of Eididh nan Clach Geala where you can amuse yourself trying to decide which of the cairns, 100 yards apart, is the real summit. All I could see in the wild scene was Stac Polly, small enough to cringe below the heavy roof of cloud. I could hardly stand on top of the *summit of white stone*.

After crossing the right-of-way from Gleann Beag to Inverlael the ground becomes even more broken: the contour lines on the map are no indication; it is a relief always to find the rim of the glen of the wending Douchary River, as it is demarcated by crags. On this day the rim was white-lacy with all the water flying up and back in the gale. Verily, it could have been after wandering in the Deargs that the Psalmist penned:

"I sink in deep mire, where there is no foothold;
I have come into deep waters and the flood sweeps over me."

When sure of the col I had a brew—before running the aquatic gauntlet of the flying spray. It was five o'clock by the time I reached Seana Bhraigh, the *old high slopes*, at last. Despair on Dearg, delight on Seana Braigh. Below lay the night's haven. The reefs could be shaken out, an evening spinnaker set.

The Ripleys on Seana Bhraigh recorded: "best day yet—could actually see something!" The Luchd Choire below fell away steeply in big crags: a winter playground first opened up by the Corriemulzie Club, but even in summer presenting ribs and prows and shadowy depths, a landscape on which ancient cartographers could well have scripted "Here be dragons".

I skirted down round the west rim, pausing at a wee lochan embedded in the navel of a gap and then stopping short just beyond when half a dozen deer came careering along straight at me. A branched forest of antlers charging down at one is a bit unnerving but their intent proved non-aggressive. Twenty yards short they suddenly caught sight of me and came to a hilarious motorway pile-up halt before untangling and dashing off down the slope on the port beam. Not far on, a hare almost repeated the performance. Several wheatears flitted up the slope.

Only man could account for such universal panic and sure enough I soon came on Mike contouring up to the ridge.

The west end of Loch a' Choire Mhor was shallow enough simply to paddle across dryshod—a nice change. I collected wood along the shore until the bothy was reached. It was a small bothy rescued from a long line of empty ruins. Dave Simpson and I were back there for the next freezing, moon-blowing Hogmanay. Only three or four parties had visited in between. Mr Stevenson the shepherd from Corriemulzie knew many of the old bothy lads. Only the real gangrel penetrates this remote corrie with its shivering waters and black Sgurr. John Hinde's name was in the book, recording their Hope to Lomond trek. (Ben Lomond was his Munro 277.)

Sandy Cousins on his Walk "enjoyed the evening sitting at the door of the bothy sipping Drambuie, listening to an opera and watching the deer playing like children in the shallow lochan. My pipe smoke drifted out on the calm air . . . I turned in on a warm straw bed." No doubt the same straw that we enjoyed now, three years later.

The Ripleys had not been so lucky. On Ben More Assynt they wrote, "Feet sore and very tired on the path. Very heavy rain. All rivers flooded." Next day they were thrown out of a howff at Oykell Bridge: a "depressing day". On the next they nearly set fire to the bothy here and, leaving it, fell into a river.

The year after the Walk, Hogmanay at Coire Mor was to be the quietest possible. Dave and I both fell asleep early. I actually woke at eleven but the fire had gone out, so I snuggled down in the sleeping bag once more, listened briefly to the call of a wild whooper and the judder of the wind in the roof, and slept the year out.

Now, Mike had bought a newspaper. It told of Makarios being chased from Cyprus, Franco handing over in Spain. There must have been many gaps in my knowledge of current affairs. The paper kindled the fire nicely. Widow night swept the daylight wetly away and, once our candles burnt out, raged wildly all through the empty hours of blackness. Never did bothy feel cosier.

Sunday 21 July AIRBORNE IN ASSYNT

We went out down Strath Mulzie, a lonely glen leading up into the Deargs from the north. There seemed to be a large collection of mechanical debris: old cars and tractors—a hard landscape for steel never mind tender tendons.

Just before the lodge Mike had left the bike after motoring up the lower glen to an impasse. To speed things up we took turns on it and then he went off for his car. The track, as climber Raeburn once put it, "was laid, corduroy fashion". We regrouped at the Oykell Bridge Hotel, quite a contrast, sitting in a carpeted lounge drinking coffee out of Persian Flower china cups along with the tourists and fishermen.

Lord Louden and President Forbes fled this way to Ullapool and Skye in 1746 after the Rout of Moy. Little did they know Culloden would follow so soon after. They could almost have met the Pretender fleeing as well: that would have been an odd quirk of history!

Montrose escaped this way, too, after his last bid for the exiled Charles II. He had his horse shot under him at a skirmish by Loch Shin. Injured and starving he sought shelter at Ardvreck Castle on Loch Assynt only to be betrayed and "sold" by MacLeod of Assynt. Montrose was led, bound, to Edinburgh and execution. MacLeod received £20,000 and a quantity of stale oatmeal from the government. MacKenzie of Seaforth, whose lack of commitment directly led to Montrose's defeat in the north, devastated Assynt. Ardvreck Castle stands a black ruin against the silver loch to this day, not far beyond Inchnadamph Hotel.

The wind was still blowing strongly, shaking the trees by the hotel. It was a dry gale so we decided to push on. With hindsight, we should have known better: every great blow of wind I can remember eventually broke into a wild deluge. However, the mottos also banged away: "Push! Push!" and "Tomorrow may be worse". It had been ten miles from the bothy, now followed ten more, cycling uphill into the wind, a push to sort out the calf muscles.

There was a great deal of new tree planting, which will alter the landscape considerably. Beyond Loch Craggie, nearing the watershed, I became aware of something away ahead. It could only be Suilven. Even as I pushed on to the top, the familiar pap-shape finally cleared of cloud. I had it in me to be jealous, for Suilven is no Munro; nor is Cul Mor nor Stac Polly, nor any of the jumble of improbable Coigach peaks.

Altitude in the North West means little. The peaks rise in startling shapes from watery moors of scarred sandstone in Coigach; and even bleaker gneiss in Sutherland—Quinag, Foinaven, Arkle . . .

Only Ben More and Conival top the magic line and, fine as they are, they do not rouse the connoisseur as some of the lesser heights: single malts, all of them!

In midwinter I remember gazing at them in wonder across the Minch from the *Captain Scott* as she sped, all sails set, in rosy dawn from Stornoway. We anchored that night in the lee of Isle Martin under the flushed sunset walls of Ben More Coigach. Between, all day long, we could look at jagged, arctic summits, seemingly rearing from the sea. Standing aloft among the billowing canvas, it was a scene as romantic as Conrad or Jack London could have pictured. There is nothing in Britain to better the North West.

Sutherland is just *south land*, the South Land of the Vikings, won by them before William the Conqueror landed in England and only lost by them to William the Lion, King of Scots, in 1196. Assynt is probably a Norse name as "Ass" means *rocky* in that tongue. The landscape would fit quite unobtrusively into their homeland.

Limestone in unusual quantity gives a green lushness to vegetation and is responsible for the vanishing rivers, caves and potholes on the western flanks of Ben More near Inchnadamph. The O.S. are not responsible for map rivers vanishing—they do it in reality. Peach and Horne excavated a cave in 1917 and found bones of lynx, arctic fox, bear, reindeer—and man (*c*. 6000 B.C.).

I'd had enough of pedalling by the time I caught up on Mike. He had a brew ready at the Ben More Lodge road end. Unfortunately he used potato powder instead of milk powder in it. It was 2 p.m. before we set off for another good day's hill-bashing; no reason why not with long evening light. Mike planned to circle back over the Assynt pair while I would push on and we'd meet at the north end of Loch Shin. The theory was sound. Had not such an old hand as W. W. Naismith set off at 5 p.m. without map, compass or even decent boots?

These two Munros are most often climbed from Inchnadamph to the west. I recommend adding the sweep of Breabag: as sterile and crazy a hill as you will ever find. Weird formations and utter loneliness mark all this region.

About a dozen years ago a young shepherd from near Inchnadamph was found drowned in a pool near the foot of Ben More. The strange thing was that a few nights previously he had been sitting morosely in the hotel kitchen. When teased by one of the maids he told of a nightmare in which he saw his bones lying out on the flank of Ben More. The area is full of lore and legend, frightening to some people.

The population from the Assynt hills was cleared off in 1812. The landscape is therefore empty. However, a Land-Rover track led off up the Oykell, and was followed by a stalkers' path which vanished for a mile or two for no obvious reason. It was good going: shirts off, company for once, a view of sun and shadowed ridges, and Conival and Ben More Assynt bold at the glen head. Conival has a black pinnacled ridge which faced us and promised fun, while the summits are linked by a ragged sweep of ridge.

We pulled up the path to the Dubh Loch Mor and had a picnic—no brew, though, the wind was too bothersome. We lingered only for a chilly ten minutes and put on more clothing. It took just that much time for the sky to become overcast. A blatter was obviously coming (small streams were already blowing back on themselves) but, we thought, it would be brief, a passing shower. I suppose it did pass, too, but not before toying with us as casually as a boy kicking a ball about a back yard.

The lower slopes of the dark ridge were already sufficiently exposed for the wind to knock us about. We eventually crabbed into the lee. Mike decided to go down, and set off muttering about climbing for pleasure and needing to take out further insurance before joining any more mad Broon escapades.

I could not retreat. I was on par, so to speak, for the estimated finish: just these two Munros and two others away; three days all going well.

Men are sometimes given to dream of white ships sailing everlasting oceans so that an ending is inconceivable: there can be no final port, nor destroying storm, just a dancing bowsprit above the far-eyed figure on the bows, a wild perpetual motion. Now, thinking was put by, not out of fear but because I was sailing out of sight of reason, crashing into the violence of nature with great joy. This element of testing is an inescapable facet of mountain adventuring. Without it the hills would be as antiseptic and puerile as a modern swimming pool.

So I cringed on the lee slope watching Mike stagger off like Charlie Chaplin. He soon vanished into the cloud and horizontal rain. I filled pockets with sweets and chocolate, zipped up completely and crawled back into the fight. It was interesting. The Garbh Choire, on the right,

L

was wonderfully *rough* with the wind roaring as I don't think I have ever heard it before, and the waterfalls smashed and sprayed upwards in utter confusion. I thought of Naismith who had lost himself on this hill. And of Hillaby who had done likewise.

The crest of the ridge became the route, of necessity, for the lee side was craggy, and scrambling on it too dangerous in the gusts, while on the other side, receiving the full blast of the wind, any movement was impossible. It was quite amusing to find the easiest of climbing reduced to such a pantomime. In one rock chimney I suddenly found I was completely airborne above the holds I'd had—static in a bridging position momentarily, but for long enough to realise the sensation, and savour it.

There were indeed times when progress was impossible, when it was a case of holding on, averting face from the wind, and waiting for a lull. The rain beat like rods on the bare bones of the landscape; a magnificent malignancy. I found a pathetic frightened sheep hiding in a niche. A ptarmigan's nest lay deserted, the eggs cold.

The last part of the ridge was easier. Conival's trig point was not exactly cosy. I shoved soggy chocolate into my mouth and groped off by compass for the sweep of ridge to Ben More, invisible in the shredded sky. The world was reduced to elemental noise and motion, intimidating but unavoidable. In glee I yelled Joshua's cry of "give me this mountain!"

Speed was now essential yet caution imperative. There was a long way to go and a rising river to cross. If it became impossible to wade, then I was up the spout—and adventure could topple into disaster all too easily.

It was great, just great! A sheer parody of a progression: wind-dictated quadrilles and waltzes with every now and then a change of channel to a boxing bout with myself on the losing side. I remember at one knock-down just lying there giggling at the situation. How could you explain this madness to the layman?

The slippery ridge eventually rose to a selection of summits for Ben More (Britain's highest *gneiss*) and after dashing from one to another, like a dog in a park, I set off again by compass for the north-east ridge.

The way down felt interminable but was reasonably defined; the compass was not needed. Saturation was complete, the rain sloshing in on the flank. A shivering skin of water covered the grey stones but eventually the rocks gave way to spongy moss and grass equally water-laden and slippery. Steeper slopes led down to rough bog and moor, alive with surprised-looking deer, and the Allt an Aonghais led on to the main Cassley River. It was quite tiring having to hurry, and hurry so carefully.

The Cassley had already risen, and my first effort at crossing, watched by sardonic stags, ended up to my waist in a hole. A second attempt found the river too deep and swift; the third was successful—just. It was not at all cold, fortunately, but the antics of dressing again in the rain were a bit damping.

Difficulties over, the tension of the traverse eased and I splashed happily down the path to some Hydro works where I discovered the remainder of my way out to Loch Shin was tarred road. Anti-climax. I ate most of my remaining food. The exit up over Maovally was effortless with the funnelled force of the wind behind at last. Pipits, rising from the verges, went slicing off—backwards!

It was a trundle down to Loch Shin, cutting corners and skiting on the slimy surface when off the road. A great spout at the end of a pipeline was spraying into the loch. I had a fit, briefly, for there is another loch beyond Loch Shin and I could not see the split and imagined all the extra miles that would be needed. The Hydro had the last laugh for the raised level ran away back into a side valley making a great detour. Here, at Corriekinloch, the full funnelled blast met me again.

So did Mike, and we shot off for friendly Overscaig Hotel, arriving three hours after I'd left the top of Ben More, on which I had, unbeknown, completed my fourth round of the Munros.

Being 9.30, meal time was passed, but, ensconced in our room, we were brought a vast pot of tea, and my sodden garments were carried off to the kitchen for drying. Surreptitiously, out of the wardrobe, we produced and consumed a succession of tinned goodies, not in any standard order, but immensely welcome nevertheless.

Clean sheets, a bath—things which had not even been imagined earlier—made a good end to the miles and feet.

The rain still battered at the window as I tumbled into bed. Like Naismith I would not have missed the day's experience.

Monday 22 July ON AT ANY PRICE

Yesterday's crossing was typical of Assynt's empty landscape; even though the Hydro road and structures protruded a human element seldom found among the bens and glens here. Prebble writing of Sutherland well pictured it: "Lonely, brooding mountains that seemed to be awaiting the resumption of creation." The Clearances have a great deal to answer for; but not quite so much as many people today seem to think. The changes had already started. The end result is Sutherland's present population of only 7 persons per square mile.

The weather was still vile; dry clothes were donned with a certain despair. I had originally planned to walk across to Crask, but with the continuing deluge there could well have been problems with rivers and also with new plantings. I opted to cycle round. Loch Shin gave midgey stillness, but the rain came down hard for the ten-mile drag beyond to Crask. We met there for a good bar-lunch, then abandoned "Long Walk" activities for the day.

We went down to Altnaharra, another fishing hotel, and read the day away. The car-park was lined with Rovers and Volvos—and Mike's wee Simca. One plush shooting brake had, on its bonnet, a model of a dog holding a pheasant. The company at dinner was decidedly "tweedy" too and the talk all boasting or excusing the result of the day's fishing. From the windows we could see the rain-stippled reaches of Loch Naver, reminding again of the Clearances.

I was amazed once when English friends, one a history teacher, declared they had never heard of the Clearances. *The Highland Clearances* by John Prebble tells the story and is now readily available in paperback.

Basically, sheep were found to be more profitable than people—so the people were removed—evicted and scattered to the corners of the earth, beaten by laws they did not understand often delivered in a language they did not speak; they were coerced by a ministry (arrayed on the side of the owners) who told them it was God's will they move; they were betrayed by centuries of faith in their chiefs and leaders, who now were either absent or the instigators of their betrayal; they were, if need be, physically compelled: their houses burnt over their heads, their goods destroyed, their persons beaten and abused.

It is not a pretty story, though it is an enigmatic one. As one writer points out, by 1837 Skye had produced 21 Lt. and Maj. Generals, 48 Lt. Colonels, 600 other officers, 120 pipers and 10,000 N.C.O.s and men. Napoleon discovered their martial prowess to his cost. Sutherland soldiers had followed Gustavus Adolphus and gained a European reputation. The Highlanders had been used again and again as soon as the 1745 furore had passed away. Culloden itself was no Anglo-Scottish battle. The Clearances, likewise, cannot be simply put down to Gael-Sassenach antipathy.

On the whole, the work of Clearances went smoothly. Between 1831 and 1832, 120,000 people left the Highlands, with no major rising or resistance. The old system that finally collapsed after 1745 had been very much a military world: the chief needed his people. After 1745 he was more likely to need a lawyer and a factor. The army gave work for his surplus clansmen. But older even than Culloden, was the growth of population: Thomas Pennant had reported large-scale food shortages in the north; there was appalling poverty; potato blight periodically caused famine. Often the men went off to the army to avoid starving.

Strathnaver, which runs down from Loch Naver, opposite Altnaharra, was part of the Sutherland domain. In 1812 there were 2,000 people living in the glen. They were driven to the coast and told to become fishermen. At Rossall, Patrick Sellar evicted 88 people with great brutality. For fifty years a native of Strathnaver, Donald MacLeod, who settled in Canada, waged a war of words against the Sutherland atrocities. His "Gloomy Memories" are included in Alexander Mackenzie's *Highland Clearances*, probably the most important old book on the subject. At Kildonan only three families (out of a population of 2,000) were not burnt out of their homes. The emigration ships were often little better than slavers; the cholera and misery were indescribable.

The outcome is the deserted Highlands of today, brought home to me again and again when enjoying the hills of Ireland. You can stand on top of Galtee More and both see, and smell, the turf (peat) reek. The hills rise from a patchwork quilt of fields and cottages. It is a living landscape. The view down Strathnaver was no doubt similar once.

"A great shining thing is gone forever from the glens," was how George Mackay Brown put it. *Cha till, cha till, cha till mi tuilleadh.* I will return no more.

Tuesday 23 July PENULTIMATE
If everything begins it must likewise come to an end. I was certainly not keen to take up civilisation again, "a round of demands, provocations and doubts", as Bonatti pictured it. I had rediscovered the provocative call to the next horizon. It had been salutary. Depressions, whether meteorological or personal, eventually fill. Life is usually sunny periods,

with showers. For long periods of rain one simply dons oilskins and wellies—and plods on. To full measure I had enjoyed Clemenceau's definition of liberty: "the right to discipline ourselves in order not to be disciplined by others".

I had no complaints. I have always believed that good adventures are given to those who are already walking in the right direction. People have since said to me about the Walk, again and again, "Oh, I'd love to do something like that, but . . ." This walk was essentially a rebellion against the *but*.

Breakfast was rather dull and I was glad to be whisked up Strath Vagastie and back to Crask to resume business. The greens and yellows of the strath were lit by sunshine, while from Crask the view westwards over the moors was to rainbow-split blackness.

A fine path led east up Strath a' Chraisg. I picked up dozens of big hairy caterpillars, which eventually uncoiled and began crawling. Hands and arms were covered in them eventually but the game palled when one adventured down my neck.

I turned off up the Allt Domhain which soon became a nice secretive stream. Up one deep slot which I was following I had a unique ornithological experience: a dipper had been flitting ahead and on this occasion splashed just out of sight into a pool on a bend; *instantly* it came shooting back past me, only reduced to diminutive size. My initial wonder turned to laughter—the dipper had landed beside, and frightened off, a wren, and their identical shapes did the rest.

I reached the ridge near Carn an Fheidh, when a look at the stormy west set me scurrying along the miles of Ben Klibreck, the *mountain of the fish*. I was rather peeved to see no real problems between Loch Shin and Crask; yesterday I'd missed a good walk for a hard cycle. By Loch Bad an Loch, a tent gave the only vivid colour. The final cone, Meall nan Con, was trailing clouds, and snug inside the circle round the trig point I ate and waited for Mike. An orchestration of wind was playing through the stones. I recalled a previous visit when we'd arrived to find the summit shattered, the boulders scarred and scattered. A lightning hit we presumed.

The Vagastie slopes have some crags. Rock-climbing up one buttress we once scrambled into an eagle's eyrie. It had incorporated a number of fence posts with which the ridge is littered. But those cliffs will forever be associated in my mind with a winter escapade which could have been a serious affair.

Lack of snow low down lured us upwards without ice-axes, and the gully began as an easy route—simple step kicking. It steepened. We continued. It became harder. Eventually we stood on disintegrating ice masking the vertical fall which threatened to topple everything down. With a considerable drop we had little inclination to climb and even less to descend. Luckily in David McNab I had a companion who was steady, even if still at school. After a spell of cutting ice with a penknife, it was obvious any traverse out was hopeless. We must go up. A bulge of ice blocked the view. We had the dog, Kitchy, and he was "sacrificed" to the reconnaissance. I heaved him over the bulge. A few minutes later his "come on" bark came from some distance away, so on his advice we forced the pitch and escaped. A silly escapade, but the person without any such tales is the loser. I don't try to justify climbing, or danger; but I defend the right of man to choose to look higher, to try harder. Life should be like a kaleidoscope; no matter what turns it takes, it falls into a many-coloured pattern. Contrast is one of the great pleasures of the mountains: dry must follow wet, laughter must know tears, ease come of toil, joy after fear, mountain and valley, rock and ice, bird and flower, land and sea, man and God, life and death.

George Meredith rather overstates it: "every step is a debate between what you are and what you might become." My own personal fear is one summed up by Chris Bonington: "The real danger to a climber isn't on things like the Eiger in winter but just in doing a lot of climbing over a long period". And during the last few months alone I had enjoyed a lifetime of mountains. I live on borrowed time!

I had nearly fallen asleep when Mike arrived to rouse me. He had returned the car to Altnaharra, and come up from the north-west. We went off along the ridge and were rewarded with a clearance. Loch Choire below was an area of bog and lochan and great loneliness. Morven was the only big hill beyond. Northwards our eyes were irresistibly drawn to Ben Hope and Ben Loyal, those Tolkein twins at the end of the walkers' world. Assynt remained wrapped in its black habit.

We strode along with the wind and then off the col to hit the Klibreck Burn for its last mile to Loch Naver. The strath seemed luxurious after the windy tops. The farm had crow-stepped gables and harling to remind me of Fife.

An hour in the Altnaharra Hotel with tea and scones prepared for the

last pull. I would use the bike and we could camp below Ben Hope;
then climb it tomorrow.

The River Mudale was being fished by one of the serious gents from
the hotel. His wife gave me a queenly wave from their Rover as I
pedalled past. There was a very heavy shower on the Meadie brae but I
dried out again quickly. All the way from Altnaharra to Loch Meadie
has been forested. West lay Ben Hee, dramatic in the storm clouds of
the next attack. The poor lilies in Loch Meadie were in flower, but
underwater as the level of the loch had risen above their elastic stalks.
A dead adder lay by the roadside, a victim of a passing car.

I raced down Strathmore as hard as I could, but the shower caught
me a quarter of a mile short of the camp Mike had set up. I dived into
the car and we sat for ten minutes while the rain hammered noisily.

Just up the road was Dun Dornadilla, a fairly-well preserved
Pictish broch. Ling, the explorer of so many hills in the north, thought
it "a suitable name for a fly". The last brochs I'd seen had been in
Glen Beag before Glenelg: aeons of experience ago.

While Mike produced supper I (not presumptuously I hoped)
worked out the final figures. Tomorrow would be a busy enough day,
all going well. Before turning in I also finished the Gospel of John: saved
as the titbit for my traverse of the New Testament during the Walk.

It was nice to end from a camp even if the rain, midges and wind
took turns at pestering. It is when two of those three combine that life
becomes unbearable.

I had no feeling of being poised on the brink of a "success"; the last
night in the tent was, as so many others, self-contained and contended
despite the fact that tomorrow I would return to the traffic of life—and
you know, perhaps, what Monsieur Hulot makes of that.

My thoughts were mainly forward. Music-starved for many months
I could have a glut of all the favourites. I actually wrote down my
thoughts there and then: Beethoven's Ninth first, then the March
from Aida (these were utterly linked to the hills back in Braehead
days), then Fauré's Requiem, Greig's Piano Concerto, *Butterfly*, the
wide spaces of Sibelius and the shock of the Russians, Andes folk music,
some of our own songs from Liz and Dave, James Fisher and The
Corries, *The New World* . . . I forced myself away from the game. It
was too much to contemplate.

Financially I decided I could not manage the Alps and they somehow
seemed too cosmopolitan and brash after these solitary weeks. Skye

first then, for the B.F.M.C. Meet and to help Mike along some of the bits that rather discourage walkers. Then home, above all else; to sink down into that bliss. The future could wait, though I realised it could never be the same after these months of freedom.

It had been a disciplined, slow progression—which was very good for me no doubt being of somewhat choleric disposition. Its solitary nature had rather worried me in prospect. I was introverted enough! But the result had been all good, I had become a calmer individual and learnt more of content and peace. Few are lucky enough to escape the ties of life and ascend their happiness; and, having done so, I found a veritable ladder leading up to Heaven. It was also a very humbling experience.

There have often been periods when I have known the hills alone. Many of my early doings were solitary simply because I never knew others with like interests. Eventually one made one's own converts, a small gang who roamed the Ochils locally. Over the previous score of years I'd climbed over 1,500 Munros (even the poor dog had done 700). Yet of the 279 only about 60 had ever been done alone. I'd now rectified that with a vengeance. By the end of 1974, with two more visits to Skye, all the Munros had been covered, solo. With so much of the time during the hill years synonymous with responsibility, being alone had been a tonic.

One of the delights had been the length of it. The idea of stopping just seemed unbelievable, and unwelcome. There was a marvellous rhythm in this simple life. One of its joys had been to see, from within, as it were, the sweep of the seasons: frost and snow to summer monsoon; bird migrants arriving, eggs, young and fledglings—first cuckoo heard, last cuckoo heard; deer endlessly (speckled fawns through to stags in velvet), divers and eagles (120 birds listed), foxes, otters. . . .

So now it's all but over.

More than ever I love my own land—its sweeping and often bewildering changes and challenges, its joys and delights, its incomparable peace and beauty.

Wednesday 24 July TO LIVE IN HOPE

We moved about in bare feet over the soft, wet-clean turf. Breakfast did not take long. The midges saw to that.

We donned boots and waterproofs, then just plodded off at 8.30, up the saturated grass, and broke through the scarps on to the upper slopes. I suppose there was reasonable motivation for being out on such

M

a dreich day. The hill simply looked like a dead sheep: bare ribs sticking out through a tatty fleece of cloud.

We played about on little rock problems. A raven croaked in the mist but the weather steadily became wetter and piercing cold. After eighteen days of varying degrees of wet and cold it was only moderately unpleasant.

The scruffy cairn and trig point came at last. I patted the cairn with a heartfelt "Thanks be to God", then we scuttled like crabs into its lee for shelter, had a snack, and opened the hoarded bottle of champagne with numb fingers; very unobstreperous rejoicing. Was champagne ever drunk in such miserable setting? Our argument whether it was supposed to be served chilled or at room temperature was resolved; here they were the same thing.

Ben Hope, 3,040 feet (Norse word *hob* meaning a bay), deserves a bit of praise—it is a great wee hill. Had we not kept it for last after all? It lies east of and above the loch of the same name in a great tiered cliff, riven with gullies and ribs, explored by J. H. B. Bell to be sure. David McNab and I spent part of one Christmas poking around on the cliffs in gales and horrible snow before going off for our daft day on Klibreck. The eastern side is gentler but gives long approaches. Most people simply ascend from the sheep buildings a mile down from the broch of Dun Dornadilla—as we were forced to do on this unsmiling day.

I deposited my very battered woodpecker feathers on the cairn. This was a bird extinct in Scotland after about 1850 but recently it has been steadily moving north. Ben Lomond to Ben Hope is a big jump however . . . We chuntered down in an hour deciding champagne had much to recommend it after all. It was a warmer, cheerier descent though the weather had not altered.

The last two verses of "Jude", a great doxology and a ringing tune, kept repeating themselves in my head. How often they had rung out after fine hill days—what more appropriate here? God, it was good.

Wet layers were soon peeled off and then we both jumped into Mike's car and drove off. I think that brought it home. It was over, dared and done: the 1,639 miles of padding and pedalling, the 112 days, the 449,000 feet of ascent. I picked up my Dormobile from Bonar Bridge where it had been left by David at a garage. Mike and I met again for dinner in the Station Hotel at Inverness. Posh clothes again. And a bed eventually. And a bath. And for the first time, simply no necessary compulsion for the morrow. No set course. We could go out all night. Celebrate.

In fact it was merely sad, as are so many endings. The success was, ultimately, unimportant—the quality of the living alone really mattered.

> "Yet the mountaineer who sidles on
> And on to the very bending,
> Discovers, if heart and brain be proof,
> No necessity ending."
>
> BROWNING

Tomorrow we would head for Skye and Cuillin verticality—a nice holiday for "Hamish the Hill". We would join a club Meet there and that for certain would bring back joyful normality. It had been a good trip but it would be good to be home.

Oddly, the first thing I found once home was something I scribbled many, many years ago. I was looking for another reference at the time but nothing could be more appropriate than the "Ten Commandments of Mountaineering".

I hope I have kept the faith.

1. Thou shalt prepare thoroughly before starting.
2. Thou shalt set out early.
3. Thou shalt set out properly equipped.
4. Thou shalt choose thy company with care.
5. Thou shalt not destroy anything that is thy neighbour's.
6. Thou shalt often keep silence to hear the mountain speak.
7. Thou shalt leave no sign of thy passing.
8. Thou shalt remember others in their strength or weakness.
9. Thou shalt bend to the weather and be strong.
10. Thou shalt be humble—and praise God.

AFTERMATH—OR REASONS WHY

As soon as the Walk was over Mike and I rushed off to Skye where we had a highly successful week's climbing. Had I in fact been mentally or physically run down; or stressed or suffering deficiencies (all gloomily forecast), a week such as we had would have been impossible. I have never felt so relaxed as I did towards the end of the Walk, I was fit and co-ordinated, and crafty enough to reap Skye where other Braes o' Fife members were cursing the place and fleeing its brand of weather-made frustration. I returned home for my fortieth birthday.

I'm not so naïve as to underestimate the strength of my assault. I loaded the dice as far as I could but, looking back, I also had my ration of luck. If April and July weather had been reversed there could well have been no story to tell. But if you plan with the worst in mind the outcome must seem not so bad after all: the optimist is often a fool heading for disappointment whereas the pessimist finds life full of pleasant surprises. Besides, I trusted in God—and kept my porridge dry.

Reasons for mountaineering are as varied as the participants and largely subjective. Analysis is of doubtful validity, I fear. Basically we do it for fun, or no doubt a Frenchman would express it better: it's a passion, a love-affair—and who would ask to justify love? To the unhooked it is just damn silly—but so is stamp collecting, sailing, or any activity done for pleasure. But the layman wants some understanding of what he regards as a dangerous activity, though I doubt if he can find it, any more than he can understand why a runner strains to achieve a four-minute mile.

There is a whole mixture of coloured pills: the lure of challenge and testing, the delight of achievement, the contact with our ancestral simplicity, the escape from a normal petty existence, the finding of values, of beauty, of vision. These are worth living for—and possibly dying for.

Walter Bonatti in the preface to his autobiography said the following which gave my teenage situation exactly: "As a child I always found it much easier to deal with nature than with men. I have always found in her a sort of loyalty which made possible a silent and affectionate communion, whereas I found myself floundering, bewildered and unprepared amid the often underhand methods used by man. This contrast between the world of nature and the social world was in my eyes the essential contrast between happiness and unhappiness. So I fled to the mountains with a feverish eagerness."

As a child, chased about the East by war, as a refugee in racial South Africa, as an omnivorous reader . . . I was all too aware of the "greatness and misery of man". If man could be so beastly, how could there be God?

Yet living in the country, with hills ranged around (whether Valley of the Thousand Hills in Natal or couthy Ochils at Dollar), I was also intensely aware of the marvellous and beautiful in nature. When things were intolerable (and I also, no doubt, intolerable) I used to flee quite consciously to the hills for balm. The dichotomy between man, sin, evil and creation, harmony, beauty was a despair. There had to be God? But how reconcile the opposites?

The answer came in the Mull of Kintyre at a "Highlands and Border Camp" where among regular Bible readings I attended, I heard a marvellous exposition of Paul's letter to the Romans, which gave me an experience of God's grace that lifted the clouds, so to speak.

During the Walk I read right through the New Testament again; if not quite in one go, in fairly large hunks—a delight. Such treats, too, are crowded out so easily in the rat-race of so-called civilisation. Life's pressures are very seldom a problem except at home—and are often the result of an inability to solve basic problems.

My Walk represented a long pilgrimage, a time of quiet renewal. God is best found among the hills—there are few pagan shepherds. But the hills are no idyll: the countryman knows most of birth and death, dawn and dusk, sun and star sweep—and finds God real. God is sure and steadfast; it is man who breaks himself against life. At the deepest level I suspect this is why I climb.

I suspect, also, that in some circles despair rather than hope is the driving force: climb the great peak or route and at least there will be some earthly immortality! Is this too cynical? With today's lack of reverence for life I don't think so. For some "at the top" it is a very important element. Some struggle to remain there, others having made their rude gesture climb no more. A psychiatrist would enjoy the company of those Tom Patey called "Apes and Ballerinas".

The silent majority, the millions who may climb for a lifetime and never write a word or do anything to catch the eye of fellow mountaineers or the wider public, have, I suspect, the steadfast rewards. Truth is seldom found in extremes. The average all too often keeps silent. This Walk in some ways was also a gesture—the average stepping out of line and singing his song of faith in a world which has lost faith, of finding hope, at the last—and a certain, secret, vindictive delight. This is mine and nothing can undo it, no legislation cancel out a mile of it, no man tax it, or destroy it. In some ways it's a gesture bordering on the blasphemous, only my heart-cry on coming to that misty trig point was, in all humility, "Thanks be to God".

For so many things. Above all else for the fun and enjoyment—which has never been put better than in the good book itself: "For ye shall go out with joy, and be led forth with peace: the mountains and the hills shall break forth before you into singing, and all the trees of the field shall clap their hands." ISAIAH 55: 12.

APPENDICES

BIBLIOGRAPHY

INDEX

EQUIPMENT

This appendix will no doubt come in for its share of criticism as well as providing hopeful ideas—after all, magazine articles, price lists (inflation has done away with catalogues it seems), manuals and whole books are given to discussing gear *minutiae*. I have no magic formula.

My gear was good. Some of it was new for this trip and chosen from years of bitter testing in the Highlands and Islands but I'll wager the old ex-W.D. gear with which I began, so archaically regarded by today's youngsters, was little worse or heavier. The substitution of man-made materials for natural has been no improvement. The efficiency of gear seems to be related in inverse ratio to its price.

Some items were chosen simply because of availability: I could not afford to renew with possibly better, lighter items. Being diverse, even perverse creatures, no two of us would pack the same gear, choose the same route, wear the same clothes, eat the same food. . . . *Chacun à son goût*—which a pupil of mine once suggested meant "chuck in what's good".

I don't cut the handle off my toothbrush. These little objects, even in total, are not where weight accumulates. The biggest weight accumulators are things like waterproof trousers and jacket, bivy bag, tent, rucksack, stove and sleeping bag.

Kugy, in his great book *Alpine Pilgrimage*, was a bivy adept in the rugged Julians. "We travelled light. . . . And strange to say all went much more easily than today, when heavy rucksacks convey for me all the marvels of the modern age of climbing." Cynicism is not new it appears!

But to take the items one by one.

Tent: I had one of Dave Challis' *Tulloch Mountaincraft* tents. It weighed a bit over 3 lb. The groundsheet was tray-shaped (to float above all wetness) but instead of being sewn-in, which ensures that condensation drains inboard, it was held in place by elastic tabs to the tent proper, which was simple single skin nylon one, high at the front and streamlined to the feet end. Condensation thus ran into the ground harmlessly. No inner needed. Door extensions were made of cotton and zipped in various ways. It had valances. In a hurry 8 pegs saw it erected.

Stove and Cooking Items: Most of the time I used a 120 *Camping Gaz* stove, a compromise choice, preferring its clean, non-spill, easy-to-work running to the more efficient *Primus*, which gave difficulties for carrying and storing paraffin safely. In early days and for the Lochaber trip I used a *Meta* stove, ultra-light but fiddly to work. The new-type stand is ludicrously fragile for hill use.

For cooking I had the smallest (2 pint) dixi from a set: the pot did for cooking, the lid for brews and an extra wafer-thin disc of aluminium served as an extra lid so what was on the stove could always be covered, thereby saving time and fuel. A squashy 1 gallon watercarrier proved excellent—when folded my nylon mesh string-bag of food fitted into its odd shape well. (String-bag is strong and contents are visible.) A quarter of a *Golden Fleece* scourer likewise was worth its ounce of weight. My spoon was edged sharp enough to cut so I had no knife/fork or other bits and pieces. Three plastic or aluminium containers of differing sizes served (1) as milk-maker/container at camp and waterbottle on hill, (2) for holding jam/honey etc., (3) for salt. All other foods went into poly bags—as many as necessary for safety.

Sleeping Bag: A Black's *Norseland* (4 lb) gave reasonable weight/quality ratio. It was my heaviest single item. A light sheet liner was always used.

Bivy Bag: Usual bright orange thing.

Rucksack: Packframes I dislike on the hill and after many years of using a "Tiso Special" in many lands, that was my choice. It has an armpit-length pull out so could serve as extra bedding, either under me or with me inside it. No exterior pockets either. Simplicity often equals efficiency.

No insulation, padding, matting or what have you was used. Except on snow these are just bulky extras. The rucksack, tent-bag, waterproofs and any spare clothes did just as well.

Clothing: I wore a long-sleeved *Damart* vest which doubled as pullover, plus a good shirt with sleeves long enough to cover hands in place of gloves. If still cold, the cagoule jacket went on. Non-nylon underpants and ordinary flannels did the nether regions (breeches are a big con for hill walking). When hot the trousers rolled up, otherwise they tucked into good, soft wool stockings. The Damart vest also proved better than a shirt in the heat. Spare clothes were a Shetland pullover; a sun/rain hat; long-johns to start, then nylon swimming shorts; and a pair of thin nylon socks—the last purely for decency in hotels when stockings were probably hanging out the window drying!

Boots: In the year of preparation I bought three pairs of *Sportiva* boots which were cheap enough, light, fairly soft, and also fitted my wide flipper-feet. A large plaster sometimes seen on my left heel was to stop bruising the tendon. (One foot is half a size different.) I take sizes 9½ (left) and 10 (right) so anyone with the same problem, but in reverse, please get in contact! Three pairs allowed reserves and they were all broken in thoroughly in advance. Blisters were never a problem. Anklets kept dirt out.

The price of the boots went up a considerable percentage in the year of planning—so even as an investment this did no harm. Three pairs were used, but because one right and one left disintegrated, in reality, I only irrevocably lost one pair—which I think good going.

Waterproofs: I started with my ordinary set till I realised how heavy they were, so soon swopped to lightweight ones. The jacket was replaced by a *Tulloch* one and it did till the end.

A sponge-cloth, rolled up, fitted my back to mop up sweat and keep the rucker off a bit.

Camera: I carried a tiny Rollei 35S which took many hundreds of transparencies (Kodachrome 25) until I lost it on Alligin. For black and white a Yashica sometimes came up at weekends.

Odd Box: A waterproof plastic box contained the following:

Toilet paper	Youth Hostel membership card
Jiffy tin opener	Emergency Procedure Form
Compass (*Silva*)	Money and cheques
Whistle	Odd change—for phoning
Matches	Thread, wool and 2 needles
Spare film(s)	Repair strip (for cloth, nylon or canoe)
Comb	Lens cloth and brush for camera
Mini-scissors	Vitamin pills (never used)
Stamps, stationery	Two wound dressings
Savlon ($\frac{1}{2}$ tube)	Elastic bandage
Safety pins, 2	Some swabs
Cycle chain link	Dressing strip and various plasters
Piece of scourer	a few Panadol tablets
Biro, pencil stub	Toothbrush (no paste)

Soap and soap powder were in cache boxes now and then. A piece of candle was carried at the start and later midge cream and a gut fishing line were added. A watch and a hanky lived in a pocket, odd bits of string usually ended there too.

Tools, spare tube, etc., for the cycle lived with the brute so were not carried.

At any time I usually had a paperback to read, one of the six log-books I filled, one of the 22 maps required, the small loose-leaf Route book (brother had the duplicate)—and a slim 2 oz. New Testament.

It seems a fantastic amount when written down but it was all used, or might in certain emergencies, and it is a slimmer list than most would produce. The test was in the carrying. As Tilman says: "It is rather a problem deciding what you must take and what you can leave behind, but it is amazingly simplified when you know that you have to carry it all yourself."

The rucksack weighed about 23 lb and only twice ever exceeded 30 lb.

Accumulating and sorting went on for a year in advance; spares had to be in appropriate caches or in the Dormobile. No lack ever continued beyond the next weekender's visit.

FOOD

"A well-balanced diet costs little more than an ill-balanced diet, and
it is only a question of care."

ERIC SHIPTON

Many years ago I went through the phase of learning all about vitamins and
calories and so on, but being fond of my food I soon came to the conclusion
that eating reasonably gave all the calorific intake required for my modest
mountaineering.

Walking off into the blue struck me as being a poor reason to forgo the
pleasures of eating ("God hath given us all things richly to enjoy") so I ate
well; which was, besides, much easier than trying to relearn all that alpha-
betical mathematics concerning food.

Food I divide into three kinds, in descending order of preference—and
probably nutritious value—fresh, then tinned, then dehydrated.

Fresh: This was fixed through my family in Dollar who had a weekly standing
order: (1) for mail and newspapers, film, toilet paper, and requests given by
phone; (2) for food: 4 slices bacon, 6 eggs (boxed), fresh meat and vegetables for 2 meals, 3 bits of fresh fruit, 2 tomatoes, ½ lb. cheese, poke salt,
smallest brown loaf, odd home baking, 2 pints milk, ½ lb. butter, spices.

This was brought up by the weekend support teams and ensured I ate
very well for at least two days a week. Only between Glen Shiel and Strathcarron did I have a weekend without it. I was too difficult to find at that
stage.

Tinned: Every cache contained at least one meal of tinned items: meats,
vegetables, fruit and so on (see list below) which were a great morale booster.
(The strawberries and cream after the Knoydart depression will never be
forgotten!) Their food value was obviously good.

Dehydrated: The rest of my weekly cycle. Improvements in variety and
flavour have been made recently by manufacturers, and I usually mixed
fresh or tinned food with it. Vegetables I tended to soak at the mid-day
brew so they reconstituted as I walked.

The following were always regular items: tea bags, Tetley coffee bags, sugar,
milk powder (Millac), bread-substitute (Vita Wheat, Macvita, Tuc, Water
or Cracker biscuits), oatmeal, muesli (Alpen), biscuits, sweets, packet soups
(quick-cooking ones, but not "instant" horrors), Knorr cubes, one of
potato powder/rice/spaghetti/macaroni, one of jam/honey/syrup/marmalade,
K.P. peanuts, raisins, chocolate, cheese and West's sardines.

I normally kept to tinned meat as much as possible even if this gave some extra weight. (I'd challenge that the weight of fuel to reconstitute non-tinned meat is probably as great!) These were bought in bulk, established favourites that never palled, even once a week for months on end: Shippam's Chicken Supreme, Chesswood's Curry with Beef and Mushrooms, Plumrose's Bacon Grill and Beef Olives, Grant's Haggis. I also enjoyed Scotbeef Mince, Goblin Hamburgers, Heinz Beefburgers, Fray Bentos Steak and Kidney Pudding, Meat Balls, and various curries and cold meats, ham, tongue, chicken, etc.

Tinned mixed vegetables (Smedley's) and Indian corn (Green Giant) were regulars, spinach a treat (Lin-can).

Heinz Steam Puddings, Christmas puddings, Bird's Instant Whips and Angel Delights, tins of all kinds of fruit, Ambrosia Creamed Rice and Semolina, Nestlé's Cream, condensed milk, these rang the changes for a sweet—along with the basic Bachelor's or Swell dried apple flakes.

Bachelors have long been my regular provider of dehydrated vegetables: peas, beans, carrots, cabbage and onions being the choice.

At times I had Drinking Chocolate, Ovaltine and Horlicks to drink (the last dangerously like potato powder in texture and colour).

Biscuits were a personal choice: various Simmers' ones, gingernuts, wheaten, oat crunchie and Jacob's Club. As ever I consumed many Lees Macaroon and other bars, Bournville, Duncan's Wholenut, Red Bounty, were the regular chocolate choices. (The R.A.F. lads, going N–S, once rose to an input of 12 bars a day—each.) I managed 2 at the most but relished sweet treats now and then like Fry's Turkish Delight, condensed milk or tins of fruit. Robertson's bramble, Nelson's marmalade and various Scott jams went on pieces. Sometimes I had peanut butter. Sardines and Kraft Cheese Slices were regular lunch fillings. Crawford's shortbread became a great favourite.

I liked my regular items and never knew what a cache would contain so I was never disappointed, and often cheered, by dealings with food.

THE QUESTIONNAIRES

I intended covering many more of the remoter summits with my question-naire but became very lax about this. All too often I left them in the tent or rucksack only to remember on the summit. However, some patterns did emerge.

I left 29 and 23 came back. 2 were found the same day as left, 3 the next day and only 6 lay for more than 10 days. (18, 19, 15, 19, 15 and 20 days—generally on dull and remote tops.)

During April and on to mid-June 75 per cent were picked up by week-enders, from mid-June to the end of July 100 per cent were picked up by those on holiday—BUT, these were by then beyond the Great Glen where this would be a natural tendency. The weekenders were still no doubt busy further south. Six of the returns were from residents south of the border.

Ages: 2 in teens, 11 in 20's, 4 in 30's, 6 in 40's and 1 in 60's. (You have your fling, tail off, and come back it seems.) The younger tended to be weekenders, the older used holidays—but again the survey shifted north into the holiday period. Ages at which they began "collecting": 1 at 4, 8 in teens, 11 in 20's, 2 in 30's, 1 in 40's.

The lowest "bag" was 20, 9 were in the 100's and 7 over 200 (including one who said he did not collect Munros).

Of the 23 only 3 were with the dreaded official parties (of 14, 8 and 13 people).

Nineteen of the replies admitted using private transport (cars) whether at weekends or during holidays, 1 pair was hitching (aged 49 and 14), 1 party was camping in the Cairngorms but did not say how they reached them and 1 gang arrived by sailing ship (the *Captain Scott*).

The pressures on other land users is very slight on the whole. Apart from mid-June onwards they hardly exist: keepers, shepherds are tending to have weekends off, these days—and that's the only time the hills are busy. Later, the holidays start and people will be encountered every day doubtless; but the lambing is past, the birds are hatched and the stalking is to come. There can hardly be complaint at usage at this period. I should imagine a clash of interest only comes from mid-August into September (a period I make sure of being abroad!) and then it is clearly up to climbers to co-operate their pleasure into other's profit.

Generally the remoter landscape has not suffered from wear-and-tear or litter. The areas of pressure are blatant: places like Glencoe, Cairngorms, Torridons. These are dramatic and romantic and the tourist bodies, N.T.S., etc. all cry "Come!" Thank goodness it's a far cry to Seana Bhraigh.

STATISTICS

This is the only time I have ever worked out careful statistics. One interesting figure which comes out is that, on average, you take 1,500 feet and four miles per Munro. All the long trips (Ripley, Hinde, Cousins) give the same result—so you can work out your life tally. It is not advisable to try and work out the average cost per Munro. Inflation makes this difficult as well as discouraging. Make what you can then of the following facts and figures from the Long Walk.

Mileage: 1,639 (estimate was 1,254)
Footage: 449,000 (estimate was 360,000)
Time: 112 days (estimate was 112 days)
Daily average: 4,000 feet + and 14½ miles.

There were 279 Munros at the time (now there are 280) and 5 were climbed a second time. Five Corbetts were also done, so 289 peaks of note were involved. Tops and other bumps were not particularly noted; they are on the whole artificial and less interesting.

Of these summits 213 were clear on top, 76 obscured. People were encountered on 44 peaks. Six friend(s) accompanied me on 12 hill days over 29 summits (12 in Skye). I was alone for 100 days over 260 summits. April had a run of 23 dry days; July had 2. Snow fell on 10, rain on 69.

Accommodation. Nights were spent: 62 camping in 47 sites, 19 in 10 different Youth Hostels, 7 in 4 huts, 10 in 8 hotels, homes, a private hostel and 13 nights in 10 different bothies.

14 days gave no Munros, 12 being compulsory "rest days" and 2 storm-bound at the C.I.C. Hut. On 10 I travelled but collected no summits. 19 days gave 1 Munro, 17 gave 2, 15 gave 3, 17 gave 4, 7 gave 5, 8 gave 6, 2 gave 7, 2 gave 8, 1 gave 10.

April, 27 days, gave 58 Munros, 1 repeated, 3 Corbetts = 62 peaks.
May, 31 days, gave 100 Munros, 4 repeated, 1 Corbett = 105 peaks.
June, 30 days, gave 66 Munros, 0 repeats, 1 Corbett = 67 peaks.
July, 24 days, gave 55 Munros, 0 repeats, 0 Corbetts = 55 peaks.

1974 gave a tally altogether of 344 Munros while only 9 times have I ever struggled to an annual haul of 100 plus.

21 days gave less than 1,000 feet of ascent.
3 days gave 1,000 feet + of ascent.
3 ,, ,, 2,000 ,, ,, ,,
9 ,, ,, 3,000 ,, ,, ,,
8 ,, ,, 3,500 ,, ,, ,,

19 days gave 4,000 feet + of ascent.
10 ,,   ,,   4,500 ,,   ,,   ,,
10 ,,   ,,   5,000 ,,   ,,   ,,
 7 ,,   ,,   5,500 ,,   ,,   ,,
 7 ,,   ,,   6,000 ,,   ,,   ,,
 6 ,,   ,,   6,500 ,,   ,,   ,,
 5 ,,   ,,   7,000 ,,   ,,   ,,
 3 ,,   ,,   7,500 ,,   ,,   ,,
 1 day   ,,   10,000 ,,   ,,   ,,

12 camps were over   500 feet.
20   ,,   ,,   ,,   1,000 ,,
 3   ,,   ,,   ,,   1,500 ,,
 4   ,,   ,,   ,,   2,000 ,,
 3   ,,   ,,   ,,   2,500 ,,
 1 camp was over 3,000 feet.

MOUNTAINEERING GAELIC

This is not the list of a Gaelic expert; it is largely gleaned from my own experience of mountain names and therefore is likely to be of use to others who have faced similar confusions. Maps and guide books will often give different spellings, many corrupt, never mind the shades of meaning that allows the *white hill* for instance to be spelt six different ways.

The very word HILL has a multitude of descriptive variations. A *ben, beinn* or *bheinn* may be any shape but *stob* implies pointedness and a *sgor* or *sgurr* will be dramatically so; pinnacle is often *stac*. A *stuc* will be big and rough while a *meall, mheall* will be a dull lump and a *druim* a long back or ridge. Bold peaks may also be *bidean, bidein, binnean. Carn* or *cairn* may imply a stony, rounded summit as well as the pile of stones. *Cruach* will be a bold hill shape, *maol* a bare top, *mam* used for a gentle-sloped hill and *monadh* often covers a plateau of old pasture or gentle summits. *Aonach* sometimes means a ridge and a *sron* or *sroine* is one running down into the valley, *druim*, ditto, or merely a spur. A hillock can be variously *tulaich, torr, tom, cnap, cnoc* or *sithean* (pro: shee-an, often a fairy hill). *Ord* is a solitary out-lier. *Creag* or *craig* is a crag or craggy summit. *Fiacaill* is a toothed ridge.

Corrie (the Welsh *cwm*) can be spelt *coire, choire, coir'*, etc. *Beag, beg* (small) and *mor, mhor* (big) are very common adjectives. Many of these names are a reflection on the importance of cattle in the highland way of life at one time. A hill stream is usually *allt*, sometimes *easan* or *eas* (also means straight waterfall) or *uisge* (i.e. water). Burn is a lowland Scots word. *Glen, gleann, ghlinne* is a narrow valley and a *strath* a large, open one. A pass in the sense of a col is usually *bealach* (pronounced: balloch), *lairig* is a through valley, and *mam* may be used of one with gentle sloping approaches. Lake is *loch*; *lochan, lochain* the diminutive—and you might even meet wee lochans! *Abhainn (avon)* is river.

Pronunciations; some basic sounds: *Bh* or *Mh* at the start of a word is aspirated "V" (e.g. Meall a' Bhuiridh = Mell a' Vooree). This shows what happens with final *idh* too. An initial *Fh* is silent, *Ph* sounds f, *Sh* or *Th* sounds h. *Ch* is always pronounced guttural and *g* hard.

Many names are corrupted, which adds difficulties. Achintee, for instance, should be Ach'an t-Suidhe, meaning Field of the Seat. For fuller lists of mountain names consult the lists in W. H. Murray's *The Scottish Highlands* or the other district guides of the S.M.C. The following list is kept brief, mainly using commoner descriptive words which will help to piece names together. Names can help in many ways—see my June 16 day for one such use.

a'/an	the (definite article)	achadh	field, plain
		airgiod	silver
aber/abhair	confluence	airidh, airigh	shieling

ard/aird	promontory, height	cul	back
ath	ford	cumhann	narrow, strait
auch/ach	field	dal/dail	field, flood plain
bad	clump of trees	damh/diamh	stag
ban/bhan	white, fair, pale	darach	oak (wood)
beith	birch	dearcag	berry
b(h)eoil/beul	mouth	dearg/dheirg	red (pro: jerrag)
bo/ba	cow/cattle	deas	south
brae/braigh	upper part, height	diollaid	saddle
		diridh	divide, watershed
breabag	little upland	doire	small wood, thicket
breac	speckled		
brochan	porridge	domhain	deep
bruach	bank, steep place	donich/donn	brown
buachaille	shepherd	drochaid	bridge
buidhe	yellow (pro: boo-ee)	dubh/duibhe/ dubha	black/dark
cabar	antler	dun/dhuin	castle, fort
cadha	narrow pass, ravine	each/eich	horse
		eadar	between
cailleach/ chailleach	old woman	eag/eagach	rocky gap, notch
caisteal	castle	ear	east
camas	bay, bend	eas(a)	waterfall
caochan	small stream	eighe	file
caora (ch)	sheep	eilean	island
caol, chaolais	kyle, strait, thin	elrig	deer pass or trap
cam	crooked	etchachan	juniper
cas	steep	eun/eoin	bird(s)
cat/chait	cat	fada/fhada	long (pro: Attow)
cean/ceann/ken/ kin	head (pro: ken)		
		fearn	alder
chaorachain	torrent	feithe	bog (pro: fey)
chaoruinn	rowan	fiadh/fheidh	deer
choinneach	boggy or mossy place	fionn	white, light-coloured
cioch/ciche	pap	fraoch	heather
ciste	chest, coffin	fuar	cold
clach	stone, stony	fuaran/fhuarain	well, spring, sward
clunie/cluanie	meadow place		
coille	wood (pro: coo-lee)	gabhar/gobhar, etc.	goat
con/choin	dog	gall	lowlander/ stranger
creachan	rock		
cuaich/quoich	deep hollow, cup	gaoth/gaoith	wind(s)

garbh/ghairbh/ garve	rough or thick	oidhche	night (pro: Oech-a)
geal(a)	white, bright	or	gold
gearr	short	poite	pot
giubhas	fir(s)	poll/phuill	pool/mud
glac	narrow valley, defile	raineach/rainich reidh(e)	fern/bracken smooth, plain
glas/ghlais	grey/green	riabhach	brindled/greyish
glomach	chasm	riach	speckled/greyish
ghobhlach	forked		buff
gorm	blue/green	righ(e)	king (ban-righ =
iar	west		queen)
inbhir/inver	river mouth	ruadh	red (bright)
inch/innis	island, river meadow	rubha/rhu ruigh/ruidhe	point/cape shieling/cattle
iolaire	eagle		run
iubhair	yew	sabhail (toul)	barn
ladhar	hoof/fork	sagairt	priest
lag/laggan	hollow/small hollow	saighdeir sail	soldier heel
lair(e)	mare	sean(a)/sin	old
laoigh	calf	seilge/sealg	hunt(ing)
larach	site of ruin	seileach/seilich	willow
leac/lice	slab, stony slope	sgairaich	screes
leacach	stony place	sgiath	wing
leathad	slope	slochd/sloc	deep, hollow
leitir/leitreach	hillside, slope	sluggan	gorge, gullet
leum	leap	sneachd(a)	snow
liath/leith	grey	socath/succoth	snout/between
linn(e)	pool (below falls often)	spidal/spittal/	streams hospice
luib/lub	bend	spideal	
mairg	rusty-coloured	spreidh(e)	cattle
mara/mhara	sea	sput(an)	(small) fall,
meirleach	thieves, robbers		spout
mhaim	breast/pass	subh	berry
mhadaidh	foxes	suidhe	seat
mheadhoin	middle (pro: vey'n)	tarbh/tarf tarmachan	bull ptarmigan
mhaighdean	maiden	tarbet/tairbeart, etc.	isthmus
mhuilinn	mill	tarsuinn/	across, trans-
min/mine	smooth	tharsuinn	verse
moin(e)	peat bog/moss	teallach	forge, hearth
nid/nead	nest	teanga	tongue
odhar	browny-coloured pro: ower)	tigh(e)	house

tionail	gathering, assembly	tullach/tulaich/ tulloch	knoll/hillocks
tobar/tiobair	well	uaine	green (pro: oo-an)
toll/tuill/thuill	hole, deep corrie		
torc/tuirc	boar	uamh (a)	cave (pro: oo-a)
traigh	beach (pro: try)	uisg(e)	water
tuath	north	ulaidh	treasure

ADDITIONAL WORDS AND EXPLANATIONS

baile/bal	township	eilde	hind(s)
bar	top/point	fas	level place
bodach	old man	frith(e)	deer forest
bran	raven (Fingal's dog)	ghluasaid	moving
		glais	burn
braon/braoin	shower(s)	glomach	cleft/chasm
caim	twist	greigh	cheek
caora(ich)	sheep	labhar	loud/resounding
capull	horse	leis	lee(ward)
chroin	cloven	muc/muic	pig
chrois	cross	ob	bay (dim: Oban)
cill/kil	cell/church	puist	post
cir/chir	comb	socath	snout
clachan	hamlet	steall	waterfall
croit	croft	uig	bay
dris/driesh	bramble spot		

This is only a brief list. You *could* find 50 words for HILL alone, so I have not tried to be systematic. The *reds* and *blacks* and *whites* are too easy, yet so many names are now so corrupted or puzzling as to be meaningless: Aosda, Claurigh, Chrasgaidh, Creise, Faochagach, Fhuaran, Ghaordie, Heasgarnich, Keen, Mayar, Mharconaich, Narnain, Sgriol—for a start. Others like Bynack or Macdhui or Nevis have several conflicting derivations suggested. This is why you will certainly find differences between the old and the new O.S. maps, my text, Jim's maps in this book, and Munro's Tables. There is no hill with the Gaelic for *sheep*, for they came later—when Gaelic itself was being evicted. The innumerable *goats* might just have a bearing on our recreational activity!

A SHORT BIBLIOGRAPHY
AND USEFUL ADDRESSES

These are just a few of the books which have influenced or delighted me. Fiction is included. Public libraries will often obtain books no longer in print.

Baker, E. A.: *The Highlands with Rope and Rucksack* (1923 and reprinted recently)

Barnett, Ratcliffe: *The Road to Rannoch and the Summer Isles*. 1946, and other titles

Bell, J. H. B.: *A Progress in Mountaineering*. Oliver and Boyd 1950. (A classic work)

Borthwick, A.: *Always a Little Further* Jn. Smith or Faber. (Highly amusing)

Broster, D. K.: *The Flight of the Heron*; *The Dark Mile*; *The Gleam in the North*. (Jacobite romantic fiction, in paperback)

Brown, P. and Waterson, G.: *The Return of the Osprey*. 1962

Buchan, John: *John Macnab* (poachers' tale); *Montrose* (historical)

Campbell, M.: *Argyll, The Enduring Heartland*. Turnstone 1977

Clark R. W. and Pyatt, E. C.: *Mountaineering in Britain*. Phoenix 1957. (History)

Climber and Rambler. Monthly magazine; some Scottish articles. News

Darling, F. F. and Boyd, J. M.: *The Highlands and Islands*. Collins/Fontana paperback. (Classic work on ecology)

Firsoff, V. A.: *In the Hills of Breadalbane*. Hale 1954

Fraser, D.: *Highland Perthshire*. Standard Press, Montrose 1971

Frere, R. B.: *Thoughts of a Mountaineer*. Oliver and Boyd 1952

Gordon, Seton: Any books of his are worth finding. Start with: *Highways and Byeways in the West Highlands* (1935), and *Central Highlands* (194.), both Macmillan, and *The Cairngorm Hills of Scotland*. Cassell 1925

Gilbert R.: *Memorable Munros* (Advertisers Office, Easingwold, York), 1976 (one man's round of the Munros. Details about Munro)

Grant, I. F.: *Highland Folkways*. Routledge 1961 (now paperback)

Haldane, A. R. B.: *The Drove Roads of Scotland*; *New Ways Through the Glens*. Both Nelson. (Authoritative and readable)

Heinzel, Fitter, Parslow: *The Birds of Britain and Europe*. Collins. (A fine handbook)

Holden, A. E.: *Plant Life in the Scottish Highlands*. Oliver and Boyd 1952

Holmes, W. K.: *Tramping Scottish Hills*. E. Mackay 1946. Oliver and Boyd reprinted as *On Scottish Hills*

Humble, B. H.: *The Cuillin of Skye*. Hale 1952. *On Scottish Hills*. Chapman and Hall 1946

Johnson, Samuel: *Journey to the Western Isles of Scotland*. 1775. (O.U.P paperback)

Lindsay, M.: *The Discovery of Scotland*; *The Eye is Delighted*. Hale (Accounts of the early travellers)

Linklater, E.: *The Prince in the Heather*. Hodder 1966

Macrow, B.: *Torridon Highlands*. Hale 1969

MacCulloch, D. B.: *Romantic Lochaber, Arisaig and Moroar*. Chambers 1971

MacInnes, H.: *Call Out*. Hodder 1973. (Mountain rescue tales)

Mackenzie, Osgood: *A Hundred Years in the Highlands*. Bles 1949. (A classic)

MacLeann, C. I.: *The Highlands*. Batsford 1959. Paperback 1975.

MacNally, L.: *Highland Year*; *Highland Deer Forest*; *Wild Highlands*; *Year of the Red Deer* (all Dent). (Expert naturalist/photographer)

Matthews, H.: *British Mammals*. Collins N. N. 1952

Moir, D. G.: *Scottish Hill Tracks*. Bartholomew 1975 (2 vols.)

Munro, Neil: *The New Road*; *John Splendid*, etc. Blackwood. (Novels)

Murray, W. H.: *The Scottish Highlands*. S.M.T. 1977. (Wide in scope, a must). *Mountaineering in Scotland*; *Undiscovered Scotland*. Dent. 1947, 1951; the former in paperback. (Most famous of Scottish climbing books). *The West Highlands of Scotland*. Collins Companion Guide 1968. (Thorough)

Nethersole-Thompson, D.: *Highland Birds*. H.I.D.B. 1971

Nethersole-Thompson, D. and Watson, A.: *The Cairngorms: Their Natural History and Scenery*. Collins 1974. (Superb)

Nicolaisen, W. F. H.: *Scottish Place Names*. Batsford 1976

O'Dell, A. C. and Walton, K.: *The Highlands and Islands of Scotland*. Nelson 1962. (Geography)

Patey, Tom: *One Man's Mountains*. Gollancz 1971. (Collected writings, songs)

Plumb, C.: *Walking in the Grampians*. Maclehose 1935

Poucher, W. A.: *The Magic of Skye*. Chapman and Hall 1949. (Lavish picture book)

Prebble, J.: *The Massacre of Glencoe*; *The Highland Clearances*. Secker and Warburg; also in Penguin paperback

Price, R. J.: *Highland Landforms*. H.I.D.B.

Raven, J. and Walter, M.: *Mountain Flowers*. Collins N.N. 1956

Scott, Walter: *Rob Roy*; *Waverley*. (For starters)

Scottish Mountaineering Club Journal. Published each June, the authoritative journal on all things Scottish. Older copies are fascinating

Scottish Mountaineering Trust. The S.M.C. publications have no rivals. The large District Guides, useful for Munroists, cover: Southern Highlands, Western Highlands, Northern Highlands, Central Highlands, Island of Skye, The Cairngorms. They are reprinted, revised or rewritten at intervals. Older ones are worth seeing for the photographs and additional lore. Munro's Tables are worth having in the 1974 edition for the useful maps, etc. S.M.T. also publish many rock-climbing guides. (But see also the selective ones of MacInnes, Constable, and those of the Cicerone Press)

Simpson, W. D.: *Portrait of the Highlands*; *Scottish Castles*. Hale

Sissons, J. B.: *The Evolution of Scotland's Scenery*. Oliver and Boyd 1967
Slesser, C. G. M.: *Scottish Mountains on Ski*. 1970
Smith, Janet Adam: *Mountain Holidays*. Dent 1948
Stephen, D.: *Highland Animals*. H.I.D.B. 1974
Steven, Campbell: *The Story of Scotland's Hills*. Hale 1975. *Glens and Straths of Scotland*. Hale 1970
Stevenson, R. L.: *Kidnapped*; *Catriona*, etc.
Stewart, Mary: *Wildfire at Midnight*. Hodder, paperback. (Murder set on Blaven)
Taylor, W.: *The Military Roads in Scotland*. David & Charles 1976
Tranter, Nigel: prolific novelist, try his trilogy on Robert the Bruce, in paperback
Wainwright, A.: Scottish Mountain Drawings. *Westmorland Gazette*. Pleasant sketches for a change. In course of publication; six volumes
Walsh, M.: *The Key Above the Door*. (A romance)
Weir, Tom: *Highland Days*. Cassell 1949. (Youthful wanderings). *The Western Highlands*. Batsford 1973. *The Scottish Lochs*, 2 vols. Constable
Wood, Wendy: *Moidart and Morar*. Moray Press 1950

Some useful addresses:

Courses, etc., are run by Hamish Brown, Mountain Holidays, 21 Carlin Craig, Kinghorn, Fife, KY3 9RX; Highland Guides, Aviemore, Inverness-shire; Dave Challis, Fersit, Roy Bridge, Inverness-shire; Glencoe Mountaineering School. Glencoe, Argyll; Glenmore Lodge, see Scottish Sports Council. Most advertise in the *Climber and Rambler*, monthly magazine.
Mountain Bothies Association. Secretary: 81 Dundas Street, Edinburgh 3.
Mountaineering Council of Scotland. Secretary: 11 Kirklee Quadrant, Glasgow G12 oTS (the national body).
National Trust for Scotland. 5 Charlotte Square, Edinburgh, EH2 4DU.
Scottish Ornithologists' Club, 21 Regent Terrace, Edinburgh EH7 5BT
Scottish Rights of Way Society. 28 Rutherland Square, Edinburgh, EH1 2BW.
Scottish Sports Council/Glenmore Lodge. 1 St Colme Street, Edinburgh, EH3 6AA.
Scottish Wildlife Trust, 8 Dublin Street, Edinburgh, EH1 3PP.
Scottish Youth Hostels Association, 7 Glebe Crescent, Stirling, FK8 2JA. (Useful publications. Various activity courses.)
The Highlands and Islands Development Board, Bridge House, Bank Street, Inverness, IV1 1QR, produce an invaluable comprehensive transport timetable each year: *Getting Around the Highlands & Islands.*

INDEX OF THE MUNROS
AND OTHER PHYSICAL FEATURES
(For A', Beinn, Meall, Stob Coire, etc., see the next word)

Achaladair, Beinn, 48, 63–66
Achnacarry, 193, 199
Achnashellach, 252, 279–281
Aden Ben, 203, 206, 215
Affric, Gates of, 253, 254
Affric, Glen, 256–261
Aide, Sgurr na h-, 201
Aighenan, Beinn nan, 42, 43
Aird, Creag a' Choir, 262
'Airde, Mam na Cloich, 201, 205
Alasdair, Sgurr, 234, 235
Albannaich, Stob Coir' an, 43
Alder, Ben, 160–162
Alligin, Beinn, 284, 285, 287
Altnaharra, 324, 325, 327, 328
Aonach Air Chrith, 249
Aonach Beag (Alder), 176
Aonach Beag (Nevis), 157, 170, 171
Aonach Eagach, 22, 55, 63, 171
Aonach Meadhoin, 251
Aonach Mor, 157, 170
Aosda, Carn, 122
Ardair, Stob Poite Coire, 185
Ardrain, Cruach, 94
Arkaig, Loch, 193–197, 200, 201
Arnisdale, 209, 210, 223, 224
Artney, Glen, 100
Attow, Ben, see Fhada
Aultguish Inn, 311–313
Avon, Ben, 134, 137
Avon, Loch/River, 130, 134, 137–139
Awe, Loch, 38, 39

Ballach, Carn, 179
Balquidder, 95
Ban, Carn, 179
Ban Mor, Carn, 147
Ban, Sgurr, 294, 297
Ban, Stob (Grey Corries), 166
Ban, Stob (Mamores), 172
Banachdich, Sgurr na, 238
Banchor, Glen, 179, 180
Bannoch, Cairn, 130
Barrisdale, Mam, 212, 214
Beag, Sgurr, 218
Bhac, Carn, 119, 120
Bhasteir, Am, 241
Bhasteir Tooth, 240

Bhealaich Dheirg, Sgurr a', 251
Bhearnais, Bealach, 275, 276, 278
Bheithir, Beinn a', 50, 51
Bheoil, Beinn, 160, 161
Bhlair, Mullach Clach a', 146
Bhreac, Beinn, 136
Bhrotain, Beinn, 145, 146
Bhuidheanach Bheag, A, 157
Bhuird, Beinn a', 39, 40, 134, 135
Bhuiridh, Beinn a', 39
Bhuiridh Meall a', 58
Bian, Bidean nam, 46, 47
Binnein Beag, 164
Binnein Mor, 164
Blackrock, 56–58
Blair Atholl, 111, 118
Blaven, 231, 232
Bodach, Am (Mamores), 164, 166
Bodach, Am (Aonach Eagach), 56
Braemar, 131–133
Braeriach, 143, 149
Braigh Coire Chruinnbhalgain, 114
Breabag, 320
Breac, Lochan nam, 214, 215
Breac, Sgurr, 306
Broad Cairn, 130
Broadford, 227, 228, 243
Bruach na Frithe, 240, 242
Buachaille Etive Beag, 45, 46, 63
Buachaille Etive Mor, 45, 46, 63
Buidhe, Beinn (Knoydart), 207
Buidhe, Beinn (Loch Fyne), 80, 82, 86
Buidhe, Meall (Chreachain), 207
Buidhe, Meall (Knoydart), 207
Buidhe, Meall (Lyon), 67, 68
Bynack More, 135, 139

Cac Carn Beag/Mor, 130
Cairn, Carn na, 158
Cairn Gorm, 139
Cairn Toul, 134, 143
Cairnwell, 48, 122
Caisteal, An, 93
Callater, Glen/Loch, 130
Camusrory, 205, 206
Capel Mounth, 126
Carnach River, 205, 206
Carron, Glen/Strath, 278–280

Ceannaichean, Sgurr nan, 278
Ceapraichean, Meall nan, 317
Ceathreamhnan, Sgurr nan, 255, 261
Chabhair, Beinn, 92, 93
Chailleach, A' (Fannichs), 306
Chailleach, A' (Monadh Liath), 179
Chairn, Stob Coire a', 164
Chaluim, Beinn, 69, 73, 76
Chaorachain, Sgurr a', 275
Chaorruinn, Beinn a' (Cairngorms), 136
Chaoruinn, Beinn a' (Laggan), 183, 184
Chlachair, Beinn a', 169, 182
Chlaidheimh, Beinn a', 296, 297
Chlamain, Carn a', 118, 119
Chleibh, Beinn a', 80
Chno Dearg, 174, 175
Chochuill, Beinn a', 40
Choin, Creag Toll a', 274
Choinneach, A', 138, 139
Choinnich, Sgurr, 275
Choinnich Mor, Sgurr, 172
Choinich, Tom a', 265
Choir' Aird, Creag a', 262
Choire Ghlais, Sgurr a', 271
Choire Liath, Spidean a', 287
Chonzie, Ben, 101
Chosaidh, Druim a', 215
Chralaig, A', 250, 258
Chrasgaidh, Meall a', 310
Chreachain, Beinn a', 63, 65, 66
Chroin, Beinn a', 93
Chroin, Stuc a', 99
Chuaich, Meall, 158
C.I.C. Hut, 167-169
Ciche, Sgurr na, 201-204, 207
Ciste Dhubh, 250, 251
Ciste Duibhe, Sgurr na, 251
Clach Geala, Eididh nan, 317
Clach Geala, Sgurr nan, 310
Clach Glas, 231
Clach Leathad (Clachlet), 58, 274
Claise, Cairn of, 124
Claurigh, Stob Choire, 172
Cloich-mhuillin, Carn, 21, 145
Cluanie, 249, 250, 256
Cluanie Ridge, 216, 247-250
Cobbler, The, 84-86, 89
Coileachan, An, 311
Coinneach Mhor, A', 289
Coireachan, Sgurr nan (Glen Dessary), 203, 204
Coireachan, Sgurr nan (Glen Pean), 197
Coirean, Mullach nan, 166
Coire Ardair, Stob Poite, 185
Comrie, 100
Conachraig, 129

Cona' Mheall (Deargs), 316
Conbhairean, Sgurr nan, 247, 258, 259
Conival (Cona-mheall) (Assynt), 320-322
Corranaich, Meall, 105
Corrour Bothy, 142, 144, 145
Coruisk, 230, 234
Coulin Pass, 280, 281
Creagach, Toll, 265
Creise, 58, 274
Crianlarich, 76-79
Cruach Ardrain, 94
Cruachan, Ben, 39, 40, 42
Cuillin Hills, 230-242
Culra, 159, 176, 182

Dalwhinnie, 154, 158, 169, 176
Damh, Creag nan, 248
Dearg, Beinn (Atholl), 118, 119
Dearg, Beinn (Loch Broom), 310, 315 316, 317
Dearg Mhor, Bheinn, 298, 302
Dearg, Carn (Alder), 176
Dearg, Carn (Loch Ossian), 162
Dearg, Carn (Monadh Liath), 179, 180
Dearg, Carn Mor, 170
Dearg, Chno, 174, 175
Dearg, Meall (Aonach Eagach), 55
Dearg, Sgorr (Ballachulish), 51
Dearg, Sgurr (Cuillins), 236, 237
Dee, River, 133, 142-145
Deirg, Bidean an Eoin, 275
Derry Cairngorm, 138
Devil's Elbow, 123
Devil's Point, 143, 144, 146
Dhearg, Creag, 207
Dhearg, Sgorr, 51
Dhonuill, Sgorr, 51
Diamh, Stob, 39, 40
Dirrie More, 311-316
Dochart, Glen/Loch, 33, 76, 79
Dorain, Beinn, 26, 60, 63
Dothaidh, Beinn, 63
Driesh, 125
Druim Shionnach, 249
Drumochter Pass, 154
Dubhag, Meall, 147
Dubh, Bealach, 160, 176, 182
Dubhchraig, Beinn, 79, 80
Dubh Lochain (Knoydart), 208, 213, 214
Dubh, Sgurr, 290
Dubh Mor, Sgurr, 233, 234
Dubh na Da Bheinn, Sgurr, 233-235
Dundonnell, 303-305

Each, Sgurr nan, 310

Eag, Sgurr nan, 234
Ealar, Carn, 117, 118
Easain, Stob Coire, 172, 173
Easain, Stob Coire an, 172
Eibhinn, Beinn, 176
Eige, Carn, 263, 264
Eighe, Beinn, 288–293
Eilde Mor, Sgurr, 163, 164
Eniglair, Beinn, 316
Etchachan Coire/Loch, 137, 138, 301
Etive, Glen/Loch, 43, 46–48
Eun, Meall nan, 44
Eunaich, Beinn, 40

Falloch, River, 91
Fannich, Loch/hills, 306, 308–311
Faochag, 246
Faochagach, Am, 312, 315
Farrar Four, 265, 271–273
Fersit, 174, 175
Feshie, Glen, 144, 146–149
Fhada, Beinn, 253–255
Fhidleir, Carn an, see Carn Ealar
Fhionnlaidh, Beinn (Glen Coe), 48
Fhionnlaidh, Beinn (Loch Mullardoch), 263
Fhuaran, Sgurr, 251, 257
Fhuarain, Sgurr an, 219
Fhuar-thuill, Sgurr, 271
Fiannaidh, Sgor nam, 55
Fionn Bheinn, 308, 309
Five Sisters of Kintail, 250–252, 255
Fort William, 160, 168, 189,
Fraoch-choire, Mullach, 256, 258
Fuar Tholl, 244, 280, 281, 282
Fyne, Glen/Loch, 82, 83

Gaibhre, Sgor, 162
Gaick Pass, 157, 158
Gairich, 219, 220
Gaoith, Sgor, 148
Gaor Bheinn (Gulvain), 195
Garbhanach, An, 164
Garbh Chioch Mhor, 203, 204
Garbh, Meall (Lawers), 107
Garbh, Mheall (Rannoch), 108
Geal Charn (Alder), 176
Geal Charn (Feshie), 149
Geal Charn (Laggan), 182
Geal Charn (Loch Ericht), 155
Geal Charn (Monadh Liath), 178, 179
Gearanach, An, 164
Ghabhar, Carn nan, 114
Ghabhar, Stob, 59
Ghairb, Carn a' Choire, 259

Ghairbh, Sron a' Choire, 191, 192
Ghaordie, Meall, 71, 72
Gheoidh, Carn a', 120, 121
Ghlas, Beinn, 106
Ghlas-bheinn, A', 253–255
Ghlo, Beinn a', 113, 114
Ghobhlach, Beinn, 304
Ghluasaid, Carn, 258, 259
Ghreadaidh, Sgurr a', 238
Ghru, Lairig, 115, 142, 143
Gillian, Sgurr nan, 234, 240, 241
Glas Bheinn Mhor, 43
Glas Maol, 123
Glas, Meall, 73, 74
Glen Brittle, 236, 239
Glencoe, 46, 47, 52–56
Glen, Cottage, 283–291
Glen Dessary, 197, 203, 205
Glenelg, 222, 226, 227
Glenmuick, Spittal of, 129
Gleouraich, 215, 221
Glomach, Falls of, 255–257
Gobhar, Carn nan (Farrar), 272
Gobhar, Carn nan (Lapaichs), 269
Gorm, Carn, 108
Gorm, Meall, 311
Great Glen, 186–190, 225
Greigh, Meall, 107
Grey Corries, 171–172
Gruagaichean, Na, 164
Gulvain, 195

Heasgarnich, Beinn, 71, 72
Hone, Ben-y-, 101
Hope, Ben, 327–330
Hourn, Loch, 209, 210, 214, 221–225

Ime, Beinn, 84–86
Inaccessible Pinnacle, 21, 237
Inchnadamph, 319, 320
Inverie, 211
Inverlair, 172–174, 188
Inverlochy, 178, 189
Inversnaid, 91
Inveruglas, 86, 87
Iubhair, Mullach Coire an, 182
Iubhair, Sgor an, 164
Iutharn Mhor, Beinn, 119, 120, 134

Jock's Road, 125

Keen, Mount, 126–128
Killiecrankie, Pass of, 111
Killin, 102–105
Kincraig, 152

Kingie, Glen, 195, 218, 219
Kinglass, Glen, 42
Kinlochewe, 291
Kinlochewe, Heights of, 293, 298
Klibreck, Ben, 271, 326, 327
Knoydart, 198, 202–215
Kyle of Lochalsh, 243, 279
Kylerhea, 227

Ladhar Bheinn, 208–210, 214, 226
Laggan Bridge, 178, 179, 181
Laggan, Loch, 181, 185, 187
Laoigh, Beinn (Lui), 79, 80
Laoigh, Lairig an, 134, 137, 138, 144
Laoigh, Stob Coire an, 172
Lap, Beinn na, 162, 175
Lapaich, Sgurr na, 268–271, 274
Lawers, Ben, 101, 102, 105, 106
Leacach, Creag, 123
Leachach, Lairig, 172
Leathain, Sgurr an Doire, 248
Lednock, Glen, 100
Leith, Meall a' Choire, 105
Liath, Carn (Ghlo), 113
Liath, Carn (Meagaidh), 185
Liath, Meall (Rannoch), 108
Liathach, 284, 286–289
Liath Mhor, Beinn, 281, 282
Liath Mhor Fannich, Beinn, 310, 311
Lochain, Beinn an, 84
Lochain, Sgurr an, 248
Lochain, Stuchd an, 69
Lochay, Glen, 69, 71, 73
Lochnagar, 110, 129, 130, 133
Lochy, Loch, 188, 190–193
Lomond, Ben, 89, 90, 330
Lomond, Loch, 86, 87–91
Lui, see Laoigh
Luinne Bheinn, 207, 214, 215
Lunndidh, Maoile, 274
Lurg Mhor, 275–277
Lyon, Glen, 65, 68, 69, 71, 104, 105, 107, 109

Macdhui, Ben, 140, 141, 144, 303
Mairg, Carn, 108
Mamores, The, 163–166
Mam Sodhail, 257
Maol Chean-dearg (Loch Torridon), 283
Maol Chinn-dearg (Cluanie Ridge), 249
Maree, Loch, 291–294
Mark, Glen/Water of, 127, 128
Mayar, 125
Meadail, Mam, 207
Meadhoin, Aonach, 251
Meagaidh, Creag, 183–185, 224

Meran, Gleann, 66, 67
Mhadaidh, Sgurr a', 238, 239, 240
Mhaighdean, A', 293, 298, 299
Mhaim, Bealach a', 239
Mhaim, Carn a', 141, 144
Mhaim, Creag a', 249
Mhaim, Sgurr a', 164
Mhanach, Beinn, 65
Mhaoraich, Sgurr a', 221
Mharconaich, A', 155
Mheadhoin, Beinn, 135, 137
Mheadhoin, Stob a' choire, 172, 173
Mhic Choinnich, Sgurr, 235, 236
Mhic Fhearchair, Mullach Coire, 293, 294, 297
Mhic Nobuil, Coire, 285
Mhuilinn, Carn Cloich-, 145
Mhor, Creag (Glen Lyon), 109
Mhor, Creag (Mamlorn), 72
Mhor, Sgurr (Alligin), 285
Milehouse, 150–152
Moine Bheadlaidh, 135
Moine Mhor, 146
Monadh Mor, 146
Monaidh Liath Hills, 154, 177–180
Monar, Loch, 267, 274
Mor, Carn (Glen Pean), 197, 201
Mor, Carn Ban, 147
Mor, Sgoran Dubh, 148
Mor, Sgurr (Fannichs), 310
Mor, Sgurr (Loch Quoich), 217–219
Morar, Loch, 199
More, Ben (Crianlarich), 77, 94, 95
More, Ben (Mull), 35
More Assynt, Ben, 320–322
Moruisg, 275, 278
Morvich, 244, 252–254
Moy Reservoir, 181–186
Mullardoch, Loch, 261–264, 270

Narnain, Beinn, 84, 85
Naver, Loch/Strath, 324, 325, 327
Nest of Fannich, 306–311
Nevis, Ben, 83, 167–170
Nevis, Glen, 164, 190
Nevis, Loch, 203, 205, 225
Newtonmore, 179, 180

Oban, 33, 37
Oban (Loch Morar), 200, 202
Odhair, Stob a' Choire, 59
Orchy, Bridge of, 62, 63
Oss, Beinn, 80
Ossian, Loch, 160, 162, 175, 176
Overskaig Inn, 323
Oykell Bridge, 316, 318, 319

Pattack, Loch, 159, 160, 182
Pean, Glen, 196–198, 200
Pitridh, Creag, 182, 183

Quoich, Loch, 215, 216, 219–222

Rannoch Moor, 57, 58, 65–68
Rathain, Mullach an, 287
Rest and Be Thankful, 83, 84
Riabhachan, An, 268
Righ, Carn an, 120
Rinnes, Ben, 134, 149
Ruadh, Sgorr, 282
Ruadh-stac, An, 279
Ruadh stac Mor, 296, 298, 299
Ruadh-stac Mor (Eighe), 289
Ruaidhe, Sgurr na, 272

Saddle, The (bealach), 138, 139
Saddle, The, 214, 245–247
Sagairt Mor, Carn an t-, 130
Saileag, 251
Schiehallion, 109–111, 149
Seana Braigh, 317
Sgairneach Mhor, 155
Sgarsoch, An, 117, 118
Sgiath Chuil, 73, 74
Sgine, Sgurr na, 214, 246, 247
Sgriodain, Stob Coire, 174, 175
Sgriol, Ben (Sgritheall), 223–225
Sgulain, Carn, 179
Sgulaird, Beinn, 48, 49
Sheasgaich, Bidean a' Choire, 224, 267, 275, 276
Shee, Spittal of Glen, 123
Shenavall bothy, 294, 299–302, 305
Shiel, Glen, 245–253
Shin, Loch, 320, 323–326
Sligachan, 228, 230, 231, 239, 242
Slioch, 291–294
Sloy, Loch, 86
Slugain, Glen, 134
Socath, An (Affric), 261
Socath, An (Cairnwell), 120, 121
Socath, An (Lapaichs), 267, 268
Sodhail, Mam, 263, 264

Spainteach, Sgurr nan, 251
Spidean Mialach, 221
Staoineag, 163
Starav, Ben, 42, 43
Stobinian, 77, 94, 95
Strathyre, 95–98
Streaps, The, 195, 196, 203
Stuc, An, 106, 107
Stuchd an Lochain, 69
Subh, Meall nan, 71

Tarbet (Loch Lomond), 88
Tarff, Falls of, 115
Tarmachan, Meall nan, 102, 105, 106
Tarsuinn, Beinn, 296, 297
Tay, Loch, 101, 102, 150
Teallach, An, 302–304
Teanga, Meall na, 191
Tharsuinn, Beinn (Bearnais), 275
Thuill, Bidean a' Ghlas, 303
Thuilm, Sgurr (Cuillins), 238, 239
Thuilm, Sgurr (Glen Pean), 195–198
Tigh Mor na Seilge, 259
Tionail, Meall, see Mullach Clach a' Bhlair
Tilt, Glen/River, 114–119
Tolmount, 124, 125
Tom Buidhe, 124, 125
Tomphuibil, 110
Tuirc, Carn an, 124
Tulaichean, Beinn, 94
Tulaichean, Glas, 120
Tulla, Loch, 57
Tulloch, 171, 174

Uamha, Sgurr na h-, 240, 242
Udlamain, Beinn, 155
Ulaidh, Sgor na h-, 48

Vane, Ben, 86
Vorlich, Ben (Loch Earn), 48, 86, 99
Vorlich, Ben (Loch Lomond), 48, 86, 92

White Mounth, 130
Wyvis, Ben, 274, 311–313

THE WALK